DATE DUE			
~~May 13'74~~			
Aug9 '77 D			

The Structure of Language

THE STRUCTURE OF LANGUAGE
A New Approach

By
Petr Beckmann
Electrical Engineering Department
University of Colorado

THE GOLEM PRESS
Boulder, Colorado
1972

410
B38s
88451
april 1974

International Standard Book Number: 0-911762-13-2
Library of Congress Catalog Card Number: 72-77116

THE GOLEM PRESS
Box 1342, Boulder, Colorado 80302

Preface

The reason why the approach to the structure of Language presented in this book is considered new is twofold. First, it introduces a coding or information theory which appears better suited to investigating natural languages than Shannon's original information theory. Second, it regards Language as an error-correcting code, a proposition which is experimentally demonstrated by basing a computer program to construct grammatical sentences on the corresponding generative grammar, and one which, I believe, gives new insights into the structure of natural languages.

Neither the use of information theory, nor the computerized synthesis of grammatical sentences is, of course, new in itself. The advent of information theory in 1946 gave rise to a large number of works applying it to linguistics. But by and large, the results were not extraordinarily conspicuous; certainly not as conspicuous as in communication engineering. The reason appears to be that communication engineering is only interested in the formal, small-scale structure of the messages transmitted through a channel of communication, not in their functional structure as determined, for example, by the grammar and syntax of a natural language. Shannon's information theory is an unusually powerful tool for investigating the former aspect of messages, but it is not well suited for the latter purpose. To give an analogy, chemistry regards a railroad truck as an inhomogeneous mixture of chemical compounds; but such a description, whilst no doubt true, does not tell us what its wheels and springs are for. The theory sketched in the first part of the book attempts to deal with the functional, as well as the formal structure of messages; it ties them in with the events that gave rise to them. It is not very interested in the fine acoustic structure of a spoken message, but rather in the function of its macroscopic blocks; it can, for example, describe the interaction of formal and semantic decoding of a message transmitted in a code such as a natural language.

The treatment of Language as an error-correcting code, in which the optional alternates with the required (required by the grammar of the code), can provide new insights into the structure of natural lan-

guages. It can provide answers, or partial answers, to some puzzling
questions. Why, for example, does English use *her* in *She shrugged
her shoulders* (when she could not possibly have shrugged anybody
else's shoulders), whereas French, German or Russian do without the
possessive adjective in this sentence? Why does English forbid the
word order *I was yesterday in Denver*, whereas German or Russian
would allow it? Why can the relative pronoun in *the house that I saw*
be omitted in English, but not in Latin, French, German or Russian?
Why does Bulgarian have articles, which are not found in any other
Slavic language? Why does English allow structures such as *the poor,
the French, the downtrodden, the humiliated,* but not *the Boston, the
epileptic, the liberal, the transient,* whereas Latin or Russian can use
such nominalized adjectives without restriction? What makes English
shorter than Russian? What makes Russian less prone to ambiguity
than English? The approach regarding Language as an error-correcting
code may provide some of the answers.

However, it is only fair to the reader to supplement these claims by
some limitations. First, this book is neither a textbook, nor an exhaustive monograph. If you insist on giving it a label, call it a *causerie*. The
version of an information theory presented in Chapters 2 and 3 is a mere
sketch; it is based on Shannon's fundamental ideas, but it does not
attempt to parallel the rigor of Shannon's theory. In part, this is due to
my desire to keep the mathematics simple, for the book is addressed
primarily to linguists; the mathematician will have no difficulty in with-
drawing some of the simplifying assumptions at the price of more sophisticated mathematics.

Second, when someone thinks he has found a new approach to a problem, he all too often believes it to be exhaustive and omnipotent. I hope
to have made it abundantly clear throughout the book that I have no such
illusions. I have found the error-correcting-code approach fertile for
many applications, but I do not believe it to be the only one. For some
applications, such as detecting the structural difference in Chomsky's
sentences *Johnny is easy to please* and *Johnny is eager to please,* it
cannot compete with transformational grammars. On the other hand, it
will detect the ambiguity in Chomsky's sentence *Flying planes can be
dangerous* in a way which, in my opinion, is simpler and provides more
insight. But the generative grammar used for programming a computer
(Chapter 6) does not seek to compete with grammars of Chomsky's type,
let alone improve or replace them; it simply hopes to be useful for certain applications and to provide an additional tool for obtaining insight
into the structure of language.

Whilst I hope to persuade the reader that the approach does accomplish these aims, I have little doubt that many places in the book are
marked by linguistic amateurishness, and perhaps I owe the reader an
explanation why, as an electrical engineer whose primary interest is
electromagnetic wave propagation and probability theory, I am tress-
passing into the field of linguistics. In part, of course, this is because

modern electrical engineering is not as far removed from linguistics as it used to be: Information theory, coding theory and computer programming are now a permanent part of the electrical engineering curriculum, and artificial intelligence, including its linguistic aspects, is beginning to make frequent appearances in it. But apart from that, I have always been fascinated with words, grammar, and the many other aspects of Language. My knowledge of languages is neither due to particular talent nor particular diligence; my life simply brought me into close contact with them. I was brought up bilingually (Czech and German), and took French and Latin at school. My knowledge of English and Russian is ultimately due to men like Adolf Hitler and Joseph Stalin, whose contribution to this book is hereby acknowledged, though without a trace of gratitude. I also tried to learn Danish and Hungarian, but did not get very far, and though I can understand spoken Yiddish fairly well, I cannot read it, for lack of practice. I worked my way through college as a teacher of English (in Prague), which gave me an excellent opportunity to study English grammar in detail; later I was also employed as a consecutive and simultaneous interpreter (from Czech, German and Russian into English), and I have also had occasion to translate several scientific books (from Russian into Czech, from French into English, and from Russian into English). I have been engaged in these activities as a side line of my main profession, and though this was sometimes profitable financially, quite often I undertook a translation for the sheer joy of it: Whatever uses Language may have for the professional, I regard it as the greatest toy ever devised.

I have, throughout the book, frequently quoted from Earle Tempel's collection *Humor in the Headlines* (Pocket Books, New York, 1969), a collection of ambiguous and otherwise funny nespaper headlines that have appeared in print. The author presumably did not realize that what he was collecting, as often as not, were English sentences with some of their check morphemes omitted, and I have used this property to point out the function of check morphemes in English. Though this was not the original purpose of Mr. Tempel's collection, I gratefully acknowledge his contribution in providing a fertile source of excellent examples.

I am also indebted to the Electrical Engineering Department of the University of Colorado, and its chairman, Dr. Frank Barnes, for the use of the Librascope computer to run my programs of English sentence synthesis; and to the staff of Golem Press for the enthusiasm with which they have produced this book.

P.B.

Boulder, Colorado
Spring 1972

Contents

1

Introduction

CONSIDER a traffic light at a street intersection. Red means "Stop" and green means "Go." (The amber signal is not important to the point we wish to make.) The traffic light uses a code; it codes the facts, or supposed facts, that the intersection is open or closed to the pertinent direction. It is too early to give exact definitions in this introduction, but we shall call such facts, or supposed facts, "events." This is a term borrowed from probability theory, where "event" corresponds not only to such occurrences as "My aunt died last week," but also to such facts, or supposed facts, as correspond to "n is an even number," or "cats like milk," or "I order the engine stopped." A code is used to transmit the information originated by these events; it codes them. The set of events that a code is capable of coding will be called the semantic base of the code. Thus, for a traffic light, the semantic base consists of the events "go" and "stop," and its code alphabet consists of the two code words "red" and "green."

The code of a traffic light is a very primitive one. The most sophisticated group of codes, no doubt, are natural languages. The code of a traffic light cannot be used to express anger, to state a mathematical theorem, or to formulate a contract; yet all codes have certain properties in common, and all codes must obey certain laws which are not immediately obvious. Let us look at a few examples of what a traffic light code and Language have in common.

First, we note that the colors selected for a traffic light are red and green; not, for example, a lighter and darker shade of pink. This is obviously done to lower the risk of ambiguity. Similarly, Language uses very differently sounding words for meanings that must be well protected from ambiguity. The words *yes* and *no*, or *left* and *right*, exhibit a high contrast in sound in all languages, or as the coding theorist says, they are separated by a large distance in signal space, thus lowering the risk of ambiguity. Ambiguity is the uncertainty in deciding what event of the semantic base a coded message corresponds to. The risk associated with an event E can be measured numerically: It increases with the probability of the event E, and with the penalty paid if the event E occurs.

Second, the code of a traffic light is redundant, that is, it gives the receiver more information than is absolutely necessary for decoding the message (for deciding which event was coded). A color-blind person, for example, can decode the messages of a traffic light, because the red is always on top, and the green is always the lowest light. Natural languages are redundant, too. The event coded in English by the grammatical sentence *John Fitzgerald Kennedy, President of the United States, was assassinated* contains a number of redundant elements, which are omitted in the newspaper headline JFK ASSASSINATED. The redundancy, in both cases, is not something incidental, but it serves a useful purpose: It protects, once more, the coded message from ambiguity; it makes it more "noise resistant." Noise, as understood by communication engineers, is anything that degrades the signal in the transmission channel. Color blindness, for example, is "noise," for if we regard the driver's eyes as part of the channel (his brain or consciousness as the receiver), then color blindness is a defect known to the communication engineer as "loss of bandwidth;" the channel will transmit only a limited part of the visible light frequency range. There are, of course many other types of noise that can degrade the signals transmitted by a traffic light: fog, the failure of a light bulb, dirt on the lens, mechanical or electrical failure, interference (the red light of a nearby advertisement), and many others. These can be combated by introducing more redundancy. For example, doubling or trebling the number of traffic lights in parallel, as is often done at large or heavily used intersections, represents such a redundancy. However, from the point of view of coding theory, repetition is a very inefficient way of introducing redundancy, and Language uses it only rarely (*Calling Mr. J.E. Smith, calling Mr. J.E. Smith, will Mr. Smith please report to the TWA desk, I repeat: Will Mr. Smith please...*).

Third, as we increase the redundancy of the code, we must pay a price in the time (or space) used in transmitting the coded message. The "efficiency" of the code decreases as its noise resistance increases. This, as we shall see, is a law that applies to all codes. A traffic light without redundancy, and therefore 100% efficient, could be designed as follows: Light on (say, red) means "Stop;" light off means "Go." Such a code would, among other things, use only half the power of the usual code, half the light bulbs, half the space, etc. But it would be extremely prone to noise: If the bulb burnt out, it would give the wrong signal; it would also, on "go," give no indication that there was a traffic light there in the first place. Different codes strike different compromises between redundancy and noise resistance. For example, some railroads use a single light and move a red filter in front of it for "stop" and a green one for "go." This eliminates the "above-below" redundancy, but does not go as far as the "on-off" efficiency; it is more efficient, but also less noise resistant than the traffic lights used in road traffic. Similarly, the coding efficiencies of different natural languages show significant variations. The coding efficiency of Russian is smaller than that of English. Yet its noise resistance is not higher by the same fraction, which brings us to the following point.

Fourth, whilst it is certainly true that to combat noise we *must* introduce redundancy, the converse does not necessarily follow; that is, it is possible to make the code more redundant (ineptly) without raising its noise resistance. Suppose, for example, that for "stop" we used two lights, one red, the other infrared. Obviously, the infrared is redundant without increasing the noise resistance – except against dirt on the lens, and only for a driver equiped with an infrared detector. The example may seem far fetched, yet many languages have redundancies that protect them against quite improbable types of noise. For example, there is no probable noise that will change the word order in a language, and many languages, particularly English, use word order to distinguish meanings (*Cain killed Abel, Abel killed Cain*). On the other hand, heavily inflecting languages, such as Latin or Russian, have a very flexible word order, which amounts to a high redundancy, but it protects them from a practically non-existent type of noise. This is one of the reasons why Russian has a smaller efficiency than English without achieving a proportionate increase in noise resistance.

Fifth, we note that a red light is not only used in a traffic light, where it means "Stop." It is also used in hundreds of other codes, the context (surroundings) indicating not only the code, but also the meaning of the code word. If a red light could act as only one code word in only one code, we would soon run out of code words. The analogy in natural languages is provided by homonyms. If this concerned only words like *calf* in English or *Tor* in German, this point would indeed be trivial. However, the economy attained by using *systematic* homonymity for coding is fundamental to the structure of some languages. In particular, English uses systematic homonymity to such an extent (e.g., verb +*-ing* may act as present participle, adjective, gerund or nominalized verb) that its efficiency often reaches, and sometimes transcends, the border line of ambiguity.

The sixth example is different from the preceding five. So far, we have considered some properties of the *formal* structure of the code. The above five examples would remain essentially unchanged if the red and green traffic lights did not code the events "stop" and "go," but, say, "speed limit 20 mph" and "speed limit 40 mph." Yet the semantic base of the code can affect its structure considerably. The risk of ambiguity is not the same for "stop" or "go" on one hand, and "Scenic area ahead" or "Historic marker" on the other (because the penalties differ in the two cases). Not all coded messages are equally important, they do not carry the same amount of information, nor the same penalty if misunderstood. Some artificial codes (such as minimum-risk codes) protect some of their messages more against noise than others. Natural languages usually do, too. Life forces natural languages to adapt themselves to this requirement (for example, the British R.A.F. abolished the word *airscrew* after a number of unpleasant confusions with *aircrew* had occurred in telephone, radio and teleprinter channels). The concept of information to be used in this book differs somewhat from the usual concept as introduced by Shannon in that it is determined by the semantic base, and not by the formal structure of the signal. Disregarding aspects of credibility of the source and interest of the receiver, we may for the time being say that the information content of a message increases with the unexpectedness of the event which it codes, and decreases with its predictability. The message *JFK assassinated* has zero information content for most people, because they already know; but thinking back to that November day in 1963, we may remember how that enormous amount of information startled us. If you live in a town with more than about 30,000 inhabitants, it may perhaps surprise you that there must be at least two citizens who have exactly the same number of hairs on their heads; this message therefore contains non-zero information. A little thought (plus the knowledge that there are up to about 30,000 hairs on a human head) will show that the message is entirely true, and if somebody else tells us the same thing again, the same message has zero information content, because we have already assigned a probability of one to it; it is entirely predictable. If we find a way in which to measure the information contained in the messages of a code, such as the sentences of a natural language, we shall have found a way for the quantitative comparison of languages and for the quantitative comparison of different sentences of the same language. We can, for example, measure the difference in information contained in the sentences 1) *my mother's sister died today,* 2) *my aunt died today*, and 3) *meine Tante ist heute gestorben.* (The first carries more information than the second, and the second carries more information per syllable than the third.)

The fact that the same message may have a different information
content for different receivers is true for all codes, even for the code
of a traffic light. As I drive to work in the morning, I have to pass five
traffic lights. Of these only the first transmits its message to me with
a high information content (the semantic base contains two equiprobable
events, and the coded message therefore carries one bit of information).
But the other four traffic lights transmit much less information, because
their messages are highly (though not entirely) predictable. The reason
is that traffic lights, like electric clocks, are activated by synchronous
motors, whose speed is strictly tied to the frequency of the power mains.
The relative timing of the traffic lights in the same city is, therefore,
fixed (until the police or the maintenance people tamper with one of
them). If you drive through the same traffic lights every day, you need
not know about synchronous motors to notice that, say, the third lights
always go red just before you reach them. The information content of
their messages is therefore as low as that of the statement *Nobody tam-
pered with the lights since you last looked at them*, which is very low,
because that event is highly probable. However, for a person who drives
through these traffic lights for the first time (or who is very unobservant),
the information content is much higher; it is, in fact, one bit of information for every one of the considered traffic lights.

Loss of information through predetermination, in particular, through
interdependence, is very common in Language. The three dots in the following phrases replace an omitted word which is, with high probability,
predetermined and therefore carries little or no information: *lock, stock
and...* ; *could not be had for love or for ...* ;   *the United States of ...*;
etc.

The concept of loss of information through predetermination is a
very important one for the structure of Language. A grammatically prescribed "sequence of tenses" predetermines, in some cases uniquely,
the tense of the subordinate clause through the tense in the main clause.
The subordinate tense will therefore carry little or no information (we
shall find this confirmed presently). Yet the sequence of tenses, in the
languages that prescribe one, has not died out like many other grammatical rules that served no useful purpose. From this we conclude that
a sequence of tenses, even though it usually results in little or no transmission of information, has some other useful purpose.

To see what that purpose is, consider some more obvious examples
of redundancies in natural languages. What, for example is the purpose
of the word *her* in the sentence *Jean shrugged her shoulders* ? The purpose is obviously not to indicate whose shoulders Jean shrugged, since
she could not have shrugged anybody else's shoulders but her own.
Other languages would not attribute the shoulders to anybody: In French

and German, Jean would shrug "the" shoulders, and in the Slavic languages she would simply "shrug shoulders." But in English, Jean shrugs *her* shoulders; English requires all parts of the body to be attributed to their owners whenever they are known. But the rule, like most grammatical rules, is purely phenomenological: It tells us *that* a possessive adjective is required, but not *why* it is required. The plural ending -*s* in *shoulders* is equally redundant; it is not likely that Jean shrugged only one shoulder (and it is impossible for her to wring only one of her hands). In Hungarian, double parts of the body (shoulders, ears, eyes, arms, legs) are singular; what to an Englishman is a one-eyed man is a "half-eyed" man to a Hungarian, again showing that the plural in this sentence is an unnecessary feature. But English grammar, and that of most other languages, insists on plural endings if the number of objects is greater than one (why not greater than seven?), even if this information is superfluous, obvious, or uninteresting. Grammar is, of course, not legally binding, and if a foreigner, talking broken English, says *Jean shrugged shoulder*, it is not particularly difficult to understand what he means. The evolution of English shows that grammar was quick to discard many redundant rules (especially after the Norman Conquest, when radical changes were not obstructed by the standardizing influence of education and literature), yet English grammar insists that *Jean shrugged shoulder*, though not difficult to understand, is ungrammatical. Why?

Let us look to some artificial codes for an answer. There are artificial codes, too, where the optional items, that is, the informational items selected by the transmitter, alternate with redundant items which must be inserted because the rules of the code require it. Digital error-detecting codes are structured in this way. A message (or perhaps a string of messages) coded in a binary parity code looks like this:

100100101011101000001101101111101110000010100... etc.
    *   *   *   *   *   *   *   *   *

(The asterisks have been included here only for explanatory purposes.) The digits marked by asterisks above are redundant; the message is contained in the other digits, in the groups of four *information* digits each. Each group is followed by a *check* digit, which is inserted according to the following rule: If the sum of the preceding information digits is even, insert a 0; if it is odd, insert a 1. The code could also be designed in many different ways: The check digits could be inserted in accordance with some other property of the preceding group of information digits; they could also be inserted *before* the information digits, or sometimes before, and sometimes after them, provided only that the receiver is aware of the rules of the code. In such a code, the transmitter is free to choose the information digits as he pleases, that is, he is free to say whatever he wants to; but having once made his decision, the rules of the code, i.e., the grammar of the code, then strictly prescribes the manner in which he must insert the check digits.

It is one of the basic propositions of this book that the structure of Language is essentially that of an error-detecting (or error-correcting) code. Evidence for this contention is given in some of the subsequent chapters, and the viability of such a model is demonstrated experimentally by a computer program which constructs grammatical (English) sentences on the same principle as that used for the insertion of check digits in digital error-correcting codes.

The purpose of error-detecting and error-correcting codes is, of course, to detect or correct errors that have occurred in the transmission of the message. If the check digit does not match its group of information digits, this indicates that one of the digits in the group is in error. An error-correcting code is a more sophisticated type of error-detecting code, which can not only detect, but also pin-point the error, so that it can be corrected.

The *her* in *Jean shrugged her shoulders* has much the same function as a check digit in an error-detecting code. This may seem a somewhat wild statement at present, but more evidence will be offered in later chapters. At present, we may note that the missing word in the distorted message *Jean shrugged XXX shoulders* can easily be restored; so can the missing word in the distorted message *Jean shrugged her XXXXXX*. In many cases, the English possessive adjective is a check morpheme (analogous to a check digit) which resolves a syntactic ambiguity; the designation of ownership is usually quite uninteresting in such cases. The *her* performs this function in the sentences

> *Jean refuses to give up her biting dog*
> *Jean refuses to give up biting her dog*

or

> *John stopped shaving his head*
> *John stopped his shaving head*

and prevents the ambiguity that would result from *Jean refuses to give up biting dog* or *John stopped shaving head*. Different languages have different check systems, though the principle is the same. French, German, Czech, Russian or Latin do not have to say to whom the dog belongs, because the ambiguity is prevented by other check morphemes; English relies on its check features (including word order) to resolve such ambiguities as result from the same morphological form for present participle, adjective, gerund, and nominalized verb (*shaving, biting*). The indication of ownership, which English always favors, and sometimes demands, is such a check feature; it is not needed in other languages, because they have other check features not needed in English.

INFORMATION

2.1. The Probabilistic Approach

A quantitative measure of information was evidently first introduced in 1928 by Hartley, who realized that such a measure must be logarithmic.[1] However, not until after World War II did Shannon publish a theory of information which went far beyond definitions and established a number of fundamental theorems without which modern communication engineering would today be unthinkable.[2] Yet its impact on linguistics was slight. The reason is not hard to find, but before we come to this point, it will be well to review the broader approach of 20th century science, of which information theory is but a typical child.

In the 19th century, science searched for so-called exact solutions. Today, these solutions are not called exact, but *deterministic*, a word which is being more and more associated with "idealized, unrealistic, specialized," and above all, "shorn of information." For today we know that these so-called exact solutions merely take out a single statistic (the mean) from a much broader context, and in so doing they lose most of the available information. To obtain these deterministic solutions, 19th century scientists clang to idealized models. The model typifying the wave equation, for example, was the vibrating string; a string that was infinitely thin, perfectly elastic, and had no inertia (no mass). Not

---

[1] R.V.L. Hartley, *Transmission of Information,* Bell System Technical Journal, vol. 31, pp. 751-763 (1928).
[2] C.E. Shannon, *A mathematical theory of communication,* Bell Syst. Tech. J., vol. 27, pp. 379-423, 623-656 (1948).

only did the scientists of the 19th century (with a few very notable exceptions) fail to realize that the probabilistic approach and the use of random variables yields a more general picture, from which the deterministic solutions can easily be extracted as special cases, but they smugly looked down on probability theory and statistics as a second-rate substitute for "exact" methods. The brilliant successes of statistical thermodynamics did little to change this prejudice; even Albert Einstein, who is generally considered the founder of modern physics, still harbored the classical mistrust of the probabilistic approach in much of his thinking, and from this point of view he might more justly be regarded as the last of the old scientists rather than the first of the new. These new scientists (Planck, Bohr, Dirac, de Broglie and the other pioneers of quantum mechanics) had a totally new way of looking at things. They no longer regarded an electron as a small, well-defined sphere located at a certain co-ordinate at a given time and traveling along well defined orbits.[1] An electron became a collection of statistical properties, with a probability function defining where it was to be found. It did not run into Chinese-wall barriers that began exactly here and ended exactly there, but into barriers that could be traversed with a certain probability depending on the electron's energy, which was itself a random variable subject to certain probabilistic laws.

Gradually this attitude permeated most of physics, and it is penetrating the engineering and other sciences ever more deeply. There are thousands of examples showing that the probabilistic approach gives deeper insight and that the old, deterministic way of looking at things is simply a special case which can easily be extracted from the more general probabilistic description. However, there are still scientists in the exact sciences who are not conscious of the power of the new approach, and who have managed to steer clear of the impact of quantum mechanics, cybernetics, information theory, operations research, and other disciplines to which the probabilistic approach is essential. It is therefore not surprising to find it used even less in the humanities, for example, in linguistics. (Statistical linguistics is, on the whole, no exception, if it simply measures the frequency of certain phenomena without analyzing the deeper implications of the empirically obtained statistical distributions.)

A question that is typical of the 19th century approach in linguistics is the question of whether the length of a sentence can amount to infinitely many words. The answer is trivial: Of course it can; if for no other reason, because every element in the infinite set of positive

---

[1] Actually, they did, at first, as is evident from Bohr's original "permitted" and "forbidden" orbits. However, in a brief background survey, there is no need for these details. I am referring to the attitude that developed later, and which is firmly entrenched today.

integers has a name, and these names can be substituted in the sentence *The number of molecules in a body is one, or two, or three, or...* But what is more interesting than the answer is the very fact that such a question should be asked. The much more searching question asks not for what is conceivably possible, but what is probable; in this case it would ask for the probability that the length of a sentence exceeds a given number of words. The probability distribution of the number of words in an English sentence (and apparently in many other languages) is lognormal; from this (and the first two moments of the distribution) it follows that the probability of the length of a sentence picked at random from the volumes of the Library of Congress exceeds, say, 500 words is given by a number so small that for all practical purposes it is indistinguishable from zero. Thus, the probabilist is not interested in what is academically possible, but what is realistic, and what is actually going on. To give an analogy from physics, we recall that the atoms of matter are so small and so distant from each other that most of the volume of a body is empty space. It is theoretically possible to throw a brick through a glass window without a single molecule of the brick colliding with a single molecule of the glass, so that the brick flies through the glass window without breaking it; however, *possible* merely means that the probability of this happening is not exactly zero. This probability can actually be calculated; but it is so absurdly small that for all practical purposes such an event will never happen.

By the middle of the 20th century, the probabilistic approach had become firmly entrenched not only in physics, but in many allied branches of science. It is not surprising that one of its important achievements, information theory, arose from the needs of communication engineering, for messages and signals are in their very essence random. Indeed, if we could accurately predict what a signal about to be received is going to be, there would be no need to transmit it.

It would be hard to imagine contemporary communication engineering, computer science or coding theory without the benefits of information theory. Yet its impact on linguistics was, in comparison, very slight. True, many attempts were made to apply information theory in Shannon's form to natural languages, and the results ranged from investigations of the entropy of Welsh words to simulations of a language by higher-order Markov chains (resulting in such "English" words as *whissitably*, "German" words such as *die Laufurcht*, and "French" words such as *le mouplas*). But the impact on linguistics was nowhere near as strong as, say, Chomsky's introduction of a transformational grammar.

The reason is that information theory, in Shannon's version, deals with the formal structure of the signal, not with its meaning (a point that has been missed by many, even though Shannon himself was careful to stress it). To give an example, the meaningless sequence of phonemes heard on pronouncing the syllables *shchoo-sa-zoom-chee-chee* carries much more information, by the criterions of Shannon's theory, than the meaningful sentence *My aunt died today*, for the simple reason that the former contains sybillants which need a wider bandwidth for transmission through, say, a telephone channel. And this is as it should be, at least from the communication engineer's point of view. It is his job to get the signal from the speaker's mouth to the receiver's ear with as little distortion as possible. If the speaker chooses to waste his money by using the channel for transmitting meaningless strings of phonemes, that is "not the telephone company's business."

But that is not the way linguists — at least those concerned with semantics, syntax and the general structure of natural languages — look at the problem. They will feel that it is "wrong" to regard *shchoo-sa-zoom-che-chee* as carrying more information than *My aunt died today.* However, let us not talk of "right" and "wrong." Let us talk of "suited" or "unsuited" instead, or, if you like, of "expedient, convenient, applicable."

A close analogy will make this clear. From the point of view of chemistry, *a railroad truck is an inhomogeneous mixture of chemical compounds.* This statement is obviously true; it is also obviously trivial and fails to give insight into the nature of a railroad truck. Chemistry deals with the fine structure of matter, and it is not concerned with bearings, wheels, windows or springs. It may give insights into the nature of the elasticity of a material used for springs, but it is not very interested in the *function* of a spring in a railroad truck. It deals with the microstructure of matter, not with the purpose of macrostructures. That does not mean that chemistry is "wrong;" it is simply the wrong science to use instead of railroad engineering.

Quite similarly, information theory (in Shannon's version) deals with the microstructure of a signal; it is not usually interested in the *function* or *meaning* of the signal as a "macrostructure." That is why it assigns a higher information value to *shchoo-sa-zoom-chee-chee*, and that is why it is as poorly suited for handling language structure a chemistry is for handling railroad trucks.

Yet Shannon's ideas can be adapted to develop a theory suitable for not merely the formal structure of signals, but for their relation to the world which generated them and to which they refer. An attempt to develop such a theory was made by the author some years ago.[1] A somewhat improved version of its basics will be given below. It is modeled

---

[1] P. Beckmann, *Versuch einer semantischen Informationstheorie mit Anwendungen auf gesprochene Sprachen,* Zeitschr. d. Hochsch. f. Elektrotechnik Ilmenau, vol. 4, pp. 275-297 (1958).

on Shannon's principles, but it works with bigger blocks of the message and it incorporates the meaning of the message, not merely its formal structure. It therefore seems appropriate to call it a semantic information theory.

2.2. A Few Items from Probability Theory

The next logical step would be to describe the general transmission system, but this already needs a few results from elementary probability theory, and since it is expected that most readers of this book are linguists with little training in probability theory, some terms and results will be briefly explained at this point. The reader familiar with distribution functions, conditional probability and other basics of probability can omit this section and proceed to Sec. 2.3. The reader unfamiliar with probability theory can read through this section casually, and return to individual items whenever they are referred to in later sections.

The probability that an event E will occur (or has occurred) under certain conditions is denoted by $P(E)$. It is a dimensionless number lying between 0 and 1. An impossible event has probability zero, and a certain event has probability one; but the converse is not necessarily true, i.e., an event with zero probability need not be impossible, and an event with probability one is not necessarily certain. For example, the probability that your telephone will start ringing in exactly 27 minutes, 5 seconds and 14.5 billionths of a second, being one of infinitely many possibilities, is zero; yet it is not impossible, since it will start ringing at *some* moment, and that moment, had it been prespecified, would also have had a probability of zero. Similarly, the probability that it will *not* start ringing at the exact point in time when you switch on the coffee pot is one, yet such an event is obviously not impossible.

The probability $P(E)$ is determined as the ratio of favorable to total possibilities, provided that the total possibilities are exhaustive, mutually exclusive, and equally likely. Alternatively, it is measured by recording how often the event E took place under identical conditions; $P(E)$ is then defined as the ratio of favorable to total trials when the number of trials is very large. (The conditions are, of course, only seemingly identical; if they were truly identical to the last detail, the event would have to be certain or impossible, at least to those of us believing in the consistency of nature.) Thus, by looking up the birth statistics and regarding each birth as a trial, we find that if E denotes the event of a boy being born, $P(E)$ is close to 51%.

The probability of an event E is conditional if the event is to take place (has taken place, is assumed to take place, etc.) jointly with an event B. This is written $P(E \mid B)$ (read "probability of E, given B");

the event E is random and may or may not occur, whereas the event to the right of the vertical stroke is a given condition which is certain.

Let K be the event that a randomly selected American will die of cancer; let S be the event that this American is a heavy cigarette smoker; let D be the event that he is an alcoholic and reckless driver; and let C be the event that he is a coin collector. Then, obviously,

$$P(K \mid S) > P(K) \tag{1}$$
$$P(K \mid D) < P(K) \tag{2}$$
$$P(K \mid C) = P(K) \tag{3}$$

That is, a cigarette smoker is more likely to die of cancer than an unspecified American (who might be a non-smoker); a reckless drunk driver is less likely to die of cancer (because he is more likely to be killed in an automobile accident); whether or not somebody collects coins makes no difference to his chances of dying of cancer.

Relation (3) says that coin collecting has no effect on the chances of contracting cancer, i.e., that the two events are independent. Quite generally, two events A and B are called (statistically) independent if

$$P(A \mid B) - P(A) \tag{4}$$

It can be shown[1] that the probability of either A or B (or both) taking place is

$$P(A \text{ or } B) = P(A) + P(B) - P(A, B) \tag{5}$$

where $P(A, B)$ denotes the joint ocurrence of A and B.

In particular, if the events A and B are mutually exclusive or incompatible, then $P(A, B) = 0$, and (5) simplifies to

$$P(A \text{ or } B) = P(A) + P(B) \tag{6}$$

or more generally, for n mutually exclusive events A_j we have

$$P(A_1 \text{ or } A_2 \text{ or } \dots \text{ or } A_n) = \sum_{j=1}^{n} A_j \tag{7}$$

which is known as the *addition theorem*.

The probability of the joint occurrence of two events A and B is given by the *theorem of joint probability*

$$P(A, B) = P(A \mid B) P(B) = P(B \mid A) P(A) \tag{8}$$

In particular, if A and B are independent, we have from (4) and (8)

$$P(A, B) = P(A) P(B) \tag{9}$$

which is known as the *multiplication theorem*.

---

[1] P. Beckmann, *Elements of applied probability theory,* Harcourt, Brace & World, New York, 1968.

Suppose an event B can take place under n mutually exclusive conditions A_1, A_2, ... A_j . If we know the conditional probabilities $P(B \mid A_j)$ for all n conditions, then we can find the unconditional probability of B by using the *theorem of total probability*

$$P(B) = \sum_{j=1}^{n} P(B \mid A_j) \, P(A_j) \tag{10}$$

Suppose we know the conditional probability $P(B \mid A_j)$ (e.g., the probability that a person will die at a certain age, given that he is a heavy smoker), and that we wish to find the probability $P(A_j \mid B)$ (the probability that someone was a heavy smoker, given that he died at a certain age). Then it is easily shown from (8) to (10) that

$$P(A_j \mid B) = \frac{P(B \mid A_j) \, P(A_j)}{\Sigma_j P(B \mid A_j) \, P(A_j)} \tag{11}$$

where, as before, the conditions A_j are mutually exclusive. Relation (11) is known as *Bayes' Theorem.*

A variable that assumes one of many possible values at random is called a *random variable.* If the possible values are discrete (most often, integers), it is called a *discrete random variable.* For example, the number K of girls in a four-child family is a discrete random variable, the possible values it can assume being 0, 1, 2, 3 or 4. Since it must assume one of these mutually exclusive values, the probabilities $P(K)$, that is, $P(0)$, $P(1)$, $P(2)$, $P(3)$, $P(4)$, must add up to one. The way in which this total probability of one is distributed over the various possibilities is called a *probability distribution.* Figs. 2.1 to 2.4 show a few typical discrete probability distributions. How these distributions were derived mathematically need not concern us here; the reader can find this in any textbook of elementary probability theory.

More often, a random variable is not limited to certain discrete values, but it can assume any value out of a continuous interval. Thus, whilst it is not possible to have 3.78 daughters, it is perfectly possible for some time interval to last 3.78 seconds. A time interval is a *continuous random variable* ; so is weight, height, velocity, temperature, voltage, age, and thousands of other variables. The probability that a continuous random variable X assumes a specified value x (exactly) is, for the reasons discussed on p. 22, zero, and the probability distribution of a continuous random variable is therefore described by a *probability density function p(x).* The probability that the random variable X assumes a value lying in the infinitesimal interval dx and including all values between x and $x + dx$ is

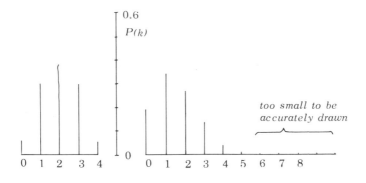

Fig. 2.1. Probability distribution of k, the number of girls in a four-child family (binomial distribution).

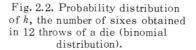

Fig. 2.2. Probability distribution of k, the number of sixes obtained in 12 throws of a die (binomial distribution).

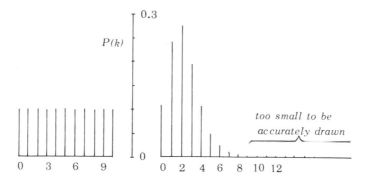

Fig. 2.2. Probability distribution of k, the number denoted by the last digit of a telephone number (uniform distribution).

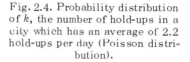

Fig. 2.4. Probability distribution of k, the number of hold-ups in a city which has an average of 2.2 hold-ups per day (Poisson distribution).

$$P(x < X \leq x + dx) = p(x)\,dx$$

that is, by the area of the infinitesimal strip $p(x)\,dx$ shown shaded in Fig. 2.5. The probability that X assumes a value in the finite interval (a, b) is therefore given by

$$P(a \leqq X \leqq b) = \int_a^b p(x)\,dx \qquad (12)$$

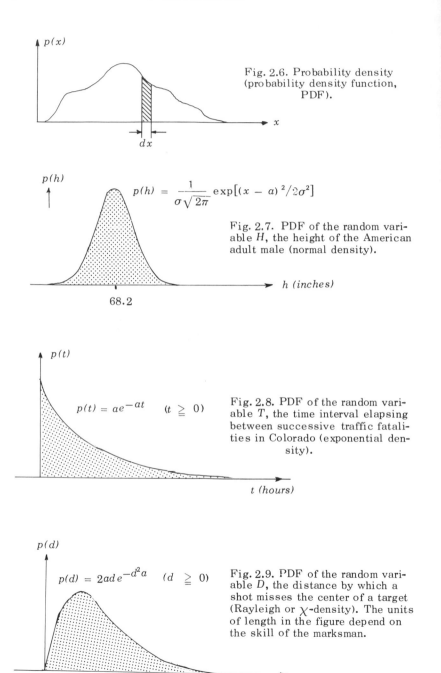

Fig. 2.6. Probability density (probability density function, PDF).

$$p(h) = \frac{1}{\sigma\sqrt{2\pi}}\exp[(x-a)^2/2\sigma^2]$$

Fig. 2.7. PDF of the random variable H, the height of the American adult male (normal density).

$$p(t) = ae^{-at} \qquad (t \geqq 0)$$

Fig. 2.8. PDF of the random variable T, the time interval elapsing between successive traffic fatalities in Colorado (exponential density).

$$p(d) = 2ade^{-d^2a} \qquad (d \geqq 0)$$

Fig. 2.9. PDF of the random variable D, the distance by which a shot misses the center of a target (Rayleigh or χ-density). The units of length in the figure depend on the skill of the marksman.

Since "smaller than a" means "between $-\infty$ and a," and "greater than a" means "between a and ∞," it follows from (12) that

$$P(X \leq a) = \int_{-\infty}^{a} p(x)\, dx$$

$$P(X > a) = \int_{a}^{\infty} p(x)\, dx \tag{13}$$

and since a random variable must assume *some* value, we have

$$\int_{-\infty}^{\infty} p(x)\, dx = 1 \tag{14}$$

Figs. 2.7 to 2.9 show some typical probability density functions (PDF's). The reader is again referred to a textbook of probability (e.g., footnote 1, p. 23), to see how they were derived.

The information contained in the curves of Figs. 2.6. to 2.9 cannot be reduced to that given by a single number. However, in some cases it is convenient to describe certain characteristics of the distribution by characteristic values, i.e., by individual statistics. The two most important statistics are the mean and the variance of a random variable. The mean (or expected value or average) is the arithmetic mean of all values assumed by a random variable; it gives us a rough idea of the order of values assumed by the random variable. For a discrete random variable, the mean is

$$<X> = \sum_{j=1}^{n} X_j\, P(X_j) \tag{15}$$

and for a continuous random variable, similarly,

$$<X> = \int_{-\infty}^{\infty} x\, p(x)\, dx \tag{16}$$

and the mean of a function $f(X)$ of a random variable X is

$$<f(X)> = \int_{-\infty}^{\infty} f(x)\, p(x)\, dx \tag{18}$$

The variance of a random variable is the mean square deviation of a random variable from its mean; it indicates how widely the values assumed by the random variable are scattered about its mean. It is given by

$$D(X) = \int_{-\infty}^{\infty} (x - <X>)^2 p(x)\, dx = <X^2> - <X>^2 \tag{18}$$

The dimension of the variance is the square of the dimension of the random variable; to revert to the original dimension, we need only take the square root of the variance, obtaining the

$$\text{standard deviation of } X = \sqrt{D(X)} \tag{19}$$

The occurrence of a random event often involves the payment of a penalty (an example will be given below). The *risk* associated with a random variable (or several random variables) is the mean penalty; if C_j are the penalties for individual values of the random variable, the risk is therefore

$$R = \Sigma_j C_j P(X_j) \tag{20}$$

for a discrete random variable, or

$$R = \int_{-\infty}^{\infty} C(x)\, p(x)\, dx \tag{21}$$

for a continuous random variable.

For example, the windspeed W in a certain area is a random variable; let its probability density be $p(w)$. Suppose an insurance company in the area writes the following policy: All damage caused by winds up to 100 mph will be paid les $100 deductible; damages caused by hurricanes (defined as winds with speeds of more than 100 mph) are considered Acts of God with no liability on the part of the insurance company; if no wind damage is claimed in one year, the premium for the next year is reduced by $10.

Let the penalty associated with the random event E_1 (wind damage) be $C_1(w)$ (this is at most $100); the penalty associated with E_2 (hurricane) is the entire insured value C_2; the penalty for no damage is $-$10 (since a reward is simply a negative penalty).

Assuming that windspeeds up to 10 mph cause no damage, the risk taken by a man insured under the above policy is

$$R - C_1 E_1 + C_2 E_2 - 10 E_3$$
$$= C_1 P(10 < W < 100) + C_2 P(W > 100) - 10 P(W < 10)$$
$$= \int_{10}^{100} C_1(w)\, p(w)\, dw + C_2 \int_{100}^{\infty} p(w)\, dw - 10 \int_{0}^{10} p(w)\, dw \qquad (21)$$

The risk is measured in the same units as the penalties. In this case, they were expressed in dollars. In other cases, they may be expressed in other units, including human lives.

The risk taken in transmitting messages is the mean penalty paid for messages that cannot be decoded or that are decoded incorrectly; the penalty is generally higher for the latter.

2.3. Knowledge and Learning

Whether we know probability theory or not, the knowledge stored in our brains consists to a large extent of probability distributions. If we are told that somebody is 5 feet 8 inches tall, we think it not very interesting, because that is highly probable. If we are told that he is 6 feet 8 inches tall, we find it astonishing, because we know that this is not very probable. If we are told that he is 12 feet tall, we refuse to believe it, because we know that such a height is too improbable to be true.

If we are told that grass is green, we find the message trivial. If we are told it is brown, we infer that it is dead, for under this condition it is very probably brown. If we are told by a reliable source, such as our own eyesight, that grass is orange and blue, we infer that it is artificial (plastic) grass. In these examples, we estimate the probability of a condition on the basis of a conditional probability. Mathematically, this is done by Bayes' Theorem [(11), p. 24], but the example shows that we are doing this mentally all the time. We do not, of course, perform numerical calculations, and the mental process of such inferences may be far removed from the workings of Bayes' Theorem; but the result is the same as if we had used it. To give an analogy, a driver who brakes on seeing an obstacle is changing the kinetic energy of his car into heat in the brake linings; even if he is totally unaware of it, this is what he is doing.

If information is received and *believed*, it often alters the corresponding probability distribution stored in our brains. We know that a tankful of gas costs around $3 to $4; if the attendant says it costs $3.45, he has altered the probability distribution that we unconsciously carry in

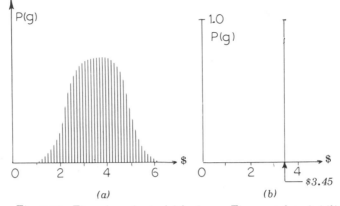

Fig. 2.10. The price of a tankful of gas. The mental probability distribution (a) before, (b) after, the filling station attendant has told us the price.

our heads (and which is shown in Fig. 2.10 without claiming that this is really what it looks like in our brains). If he charged $20, or nothing, we would find this so improbable that we would ask further questions to test the reliability of the message.

The process of learning consists in establishing new probability distributions in one's mind, and changing already established ones. On learning the price to be paid at the gas station, the distribution changes as in Fig. 2.10, but this will hardly affect many other distributions. On the other hand, learning (in 1971) that President Nixon decided to visit Red China was something that did not merely change the distribution for the places where President Nixon might go; it changed many other distributions as well (at least, for people interested in foreign affairs).

Some of our knowledge, or conviction, is fundamental; a lot of other distributions depend on it. We assign a probability of one to the case we "believe in," and a probability of zero for all alternatives. These convictions include such fundamental things as a belief in God or, alternatively, the rejection of anything supernatural; trust in loved persons, etc. We do not like to tamper with these fundaments: A religious person is rarely (and never quickly) persuaded of the nonexistence of a God, and an atheist is not easily persuaded of His existence. However, when such a fundamental zero–one distribution is upset by overwhelming and reliable information, the result is shock, or perhaps even permanent mental damage, such as experienced by the "true believer" on discovering that his fundamental beliefs were based on a fraud.

A message can also be received without altering the current mental probability distribution. One reason is that the message may only confirm it, so that it carries no information (e.g., the message A *local call from a pay-phone costs a dime).* There are three other reasons: The receiver does not understand the message, does not believe it, or is not interested in it. For example, the message *The impedance of free space is 500 ohms* is one to which the typical English speaking person cannot assign any meaning, that is, he or she has no probability distribution stored in his brain that he could alter, or he does not know which one is to be altered; he does not know what event is coded by this message. On the other hand, an engineer or physicist knows the event which is coded by this message, but he will refuse to alter the corresponding probability distribution (refuse to believe it), because the original distribution was set up on receiving the information from sources deemed more reliable (the impedance of free space is, in fact, approximately 377 ohms). Finally, the receiver may know the meaning of the impedance of free space, but he could not care less whether it is 3 or 3 million ohms. We shall investigate the degree of disinterestedness in more detail later; for the present, we will only note that this case corresponds to a limiting state of disinterestedness in which the receiver obtains no information because he assigns a probability of one to the event coded by the message *The impedance of free space has a value between minus and plus infinity.*

Although most of the above examples contain numerical statements (which makes the explanation easier), it should be noted that this is by no means a condition. Events coded by messages such as *grass is green, Mr. Nixon went to Peking, Jim loves Jill, better to have a smart enemy than to have a stupid friend* are also capable of having probabilities assigned, and will therefore do just as well to illustrate the point.

2.4. The Transmission System

In Shannon's information theory, the origin of the message containing information to be transmitted is the "source," which is formed, for example, by the Roman letters to be transmitted, say, by teleprinter. The meaning of the message is irrelevant; indeed, it does not matter if the message to be transmitted is meaningless.

In the present attempt to develop a semantic theory of information, the origin of a message is in the actual event described by the message. The message *My aunt arrived this morning* has its origins in the very fact that the speaker's aunt arrived (or is believed to have arrived) this morning, and this origin of the message is quite independent of its form: It makes no difference whether this event is coded by the code words *my aunt arrived this morning* or *ma tante est arrivée ce matin* or *meine Tante ist heute vormittag angekommen* or even by a purple flare that has previously been agreed to code the occurrence of this event.

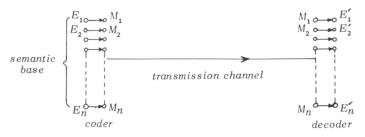

Fig. 2.11. Ideal transmission system.

In order to explain the general transmission system, we use the idealized model shown in Fig. 2.11; we shall successively make it more realistic by taking into consideration noise, unreliability, ambiguity of coding and other factors, which at first would only complicate the essential features. At this point we will only recall that "occurrence of an event" is used in the sense of probability theory, where it includes concepts that would normally be more clearly expressed as "existence of a state."

The semantic base consists of the set of possible events whose occurrence (states whose existence) is to be coded for transmission. This conversion into coded messages is accomplished by a transmitter or coder, which may be a natural process, an artificial device, or a human being. This is probably best explained by some examples. What they have in common is the fact that the coder provides a coded output for each element (event) of the semantic base.

Example 1. The semantic base consists of two events (states): A person is dead; a person is alive. Coder: the human heart (not the only coder, of course). Code: the acoustic signals transmitted by the heart beat; their presence signals the message that the person is alive, their absence signals that he or she is dead. In this example, the coder is a natural device, namely the human heart. It is not the only coder; there are the pupils, respiration, body warmth and other indicators. Nor is the coding unique (mutually single-valued); the mere cessation of acoustic signals emitted by the heart beat is not, by itself, considered sufficient evidence to pronounce a person dead. Nor are the acoustic signals the only code transmitted by the human heart; it also transmits electric signals in the form of a fluctuating voltage which can be detected by a cardiograph, etc.

Example 2. The semantic base consists of two events: A light ray is or is not interrupted by an opaque object. Coder: A photoelectric burglar alarm, which codes these two events into two messages, the ringing or silence (respectively) of an alarm bell. Assuming that the equipment is reliable (does not malfunction), the coding is unique: There is one, and only one, message for each event.

Example 3. The semantic base consists of the set of events observable at a street intersection. The coder is a human being who has observed a traffic accident and codes this event into a natural language for transmission (say, by telephone) to the nearest police station. He might code the message as follows: *There has been a bad accident at the intersection of 17th Street and 4th Avenue. Two people are badly injured.* Or he might code it like this: *Ein schwerer Verkehrsunfall hat auf der Kreuzung von der 17. Straße und der 4. Avenue stattgefunden. Zwei Personen sind schwer verletzt.* The coding is certainly not unique, since the message can be formulated in very many different ways, even in the same language.

The three examples above correspond to a natural coder, an artificial coder, and a human being acting as a coder, respectively. It is hoped that they are sufficient to consider some general principles involved.

First, we note that there is a certain arbitrariness in the definitions of the semantic base, the coder, and the code. We could have defined each of them in many different ways. For instance, in the second example, we could have defined the semantic base as consisting of the two events that there is, or is not, a burglar in the house. We could have defined the coder not as the entire alarm system, but only as the photoelectric cell that ceases to provide a voltage when it receives no light. We could have taken the presence or the absence of that voltage as the transmitted messages. And these are just some of many other possibilities. How are we to decide what exactly constitutes the semantic base, the coder, and the code?

The answer is that the choice is dictated only by convenience, for a measure of information can be so defined that it is independent of that choice. For example, the probability that there is a burglar in the house is much smaller than the probability that the light ray has been interrupted; however, the credibility of the message, when interpreted in the former way, is also smaller by a corresponding amount, and as we shall see in Sec. 2.6, these two factors counteract each other in such a way as to leave the information of the message (ringing of the alarm bell) constant.

As for the choice of coder, it should be pointed out that the transmission of the message through the channel may, and usually does, involve several *re-coders* which translate one code to another. For example, the man who is calling the police in Example 2 is using a microphone which changes speech into an electric current; this code is con-

verted back to speech by another recoder in the form of the telephone
receiver membrane; perhaps the message is received by a dispatcher
who writes the message on a slip of paper to be forwarded to the officer
in charge, in which case the dispatcher acts as a re-coder; etc. Since
we are going to characterize the entire channel on the basis of its
input-output characteristics, the properties of the re-coders contained
in the channel are already included in the channel characteristics, and
do not have to be specially considered. It is therefore not very important
whether we regard, for example, only the photoelectric cell, or the entire
burglar alarm as a coder; in the former case, the remaining parts of the
alarm system simply become a part of the channel.

The above examples have been chosen for their simplicity. But we
are mainly interested in the structure of natural languges as codes for
the transmission of information, and a language is obviously much more
complicated than the simple code of a burglar alarm. The above examples
might give the impression that the theory to be developed is going to be
a very mechanistic one, which will treat Language only insofar as it
serves to signal simple happenings. To dispel this suspicion, let us
consider the following sentences, or code words of English, which have
been selected as being very far removed from the message of an alarm
bell.

(a) *Cap'n, art thou down below?*
(b) *The reasonable man adapts himself to the world; the unreason-*
     able one persists in trying to adapt the world to himself. There-
     fore all progress depends on the unreasonable.
(c) *I had as lief not be as live to be in awe of such a thing as I my-*
     self.
(d) *Salem softness brings freshness to your taste.*

Example (a) is a question; like all questions, its primary purpose
is not to transmit information, but to signal a request for information
to be transmitted. Yet it fits our model of transmission, for it codes the
event that the speaker is sending such a request. Neither this event itself, nor its timing, is generally known with certainty (not to speak of
the identity and mood coded by the voice of the speaker); the question
therefore codes an event of some semantic base, and requires the receiver to take a decision whether and how to react to it. The same applies to orders.

Example (b) is a statement by George Bernard Shaw (*Maxims for
Revolutionaries*). It has the form of reasoning, that is, from statements
whose truth is accepted by everyone, and by rules that are acceptable
to most people, it arrives at a conclusion which, by itself, is surprising.
The first sentence merely draws the attention of the receiver to events
which he presumably has already accepted as true, in order to show what

the conclusion is based on. The conclusion is the important part of this message; it is so surprising, and the reasoning so loose, that many people regard it simply as an amusing witticism (but I, for one, am convinced of its truth). Incidentally, mathematical derivations (except for special methods such as *reductiones ad absurdum* or proof by induction) are based on the same principle of referring the receiver (student, reader) to facts that have already been accepted as true, and using methods that have already been accepted as valid, to derive a new result, although the process is, of course, carried out with much greater rigor. In mathematics, too, the result is regarded as "interesting" when it is surprising. The theorem that the mean value of a constant is that constant, though quite difficult to prove rigorously, is not at all surprising; but the fact that a finite surface can encompass an infinite volume, or that a rubber ball bounced off the ceiling comes down with a smaller velocity than if the ceiling had not intervened in the upward journey of the ball, are not at all obvious; they are "interesting" results of the corresponding derivations. To return to Shaw's statement, it is a message that does not report, but one which reasons. The event that is being coded is the event that all progress is due to unreasonable men; the preceding sentence (coding an event known to most people) is intended to render the message more credible. A statement of this type, which is surely more "profound" than, say, *my mother does not take sugar in her coffee*, evidently fits the proposed model of transmitting messages quite as well as the messages that merely report a simple happening or state.

Example (c) is a quotation from Shakespeare's *Julius Caesar*. We will suppose that it is being transmitted in the context of the play, by the actor playing the part of Cassius. The semantic base in this case is fictitious; the receiver (spectator) is being asked to cooperate in imagining that it is actually true, i.e., that the events described in the play are actually taking place. Beyond that, there is no difference as compared with a "true" semantic base, and there appears to be no reason to regard this as a particular important special case of the transmission of messages by a code. The event being coded by this sentence is a conviction of Cassius, or at least his professed conviction, with which he seeks to impress Brutus. In being informed of these events, the probability distributions at the backs of our minds change when we see or read the play for the first time: It is certain that Cassius is dissatisfied; it is highly probable that he is jealous of Caesar; it is probable that he intends to conspire against Caesar and that he is seeking fellow conspirators; perhaps (at that point it is not at all clear yet) he even intends to kill him. Other such statements change these probabilities nearer to certainty or impossibility, even if they are not matter-of-fact announcements or reports; for example, the probability that he is jealous of Ceasar is increased by his statement *He doth bestride the narrow world like a colossus.* The fact that the semantic base is fictitious, and that Caesar has been dead for some 2,000 years, has very little bearing on the point that is being made, namely, that these messages code events of a semantic base, whether true or fictitious.

The last example (*Salem softness brings freshness to your taste*) is, in my opinion, different from the others. One could, perhaps, stretch this case to come under the title of a message coding an event, and conceivably the man in Madison Avenue who agglomerated these words saw a meaning in them. I fail to see it, however; I see no more meaning in it than in the sequence *eeny, meeny, miny, mo.* This does not mean that this sentence serves no purpose; obviously, it not only has a purpose, but it achieves this purpose, or Salem Cigarettes would not spend vast amounts of money to disseminate it. However, this is one of several cases when Language is not used to transmit information, but to evoke an emotion. Here it seeks to create a pleasant impression and to associate it with Salem cigarettes. Salem's slogan conveys no information (other than secondary information of the type "Salem is advertising"), and therefore it can be investigated from the point of view of its formal structure, but not from the point of view of the meaning that it codes; for if we understand "meaning" as correspondence to an event of a semantic base, Salem's message has no meaning (for receivers unable to identify such an event). Thus, whilst the first three examples fit our model even though they code events that are far removed from simple occurrences or states, the fourth example does not code an event in any sense of the word, whatever other purpose it may fulfil. There are other uses of Language and formally grammatical utterances that do not immediately serve the purpose of conveying information, but are intended only to evoke emotions. They include pure lyrics, religous rites, talking to oneself, speaking in a soothing voice to a baby or an animal, and the like. The only events coded by such uses of Language are secondary: the mood and identity of the speaker, the fact that he is making such utterances, and the time at which he makes them.

Although we shall have occasion to examine the formal structure of Language in Chapters 4 to 7, we shall disregard such uses of Language in developing a semantic information theory.

The final stage of the transmission system (of which we have so far considered semantic base, coder and transmission channel) is the receiver. In general, this is a device capable of decoding the message, that is, capable of associating it with the event of the semantic base to which it corresponds, and to react to it, if it decides to do so. Decision processes can today be carried out by mechanical devices, in particular, computers; however, although the theory does not in any way exclude such mechanical decision makers as receivers, in the following we will primarily be interested in human beings, and by "receiver" we shall usually understand the human brain. The receiver decides to what extent the transmitted information is to be accepted (believed), that is, to what extent the currently stored probability distributions are to be altered; it also decides whether and how to react to a received message and to the information contained in it, for example, if the received message is a question, a threat, or a message that requires an action other than a reply in Language.

We can make our model of an ideal transmission system identical with that used in Shannon's information theory by defining the semantic base as equal to Shannon's source. If, for example, the source consists of the string of letters QXZYU MPOLJ NUHGT ..., then we can simply define the semantic base as the Roman alphabet; the events that are being coded are "the first letter is a Q," "the second letter is an X" etc. A transmission system of this type then becomes a special case of the one to be used in the present approach.

To make our system realistic, we have to consider the ambiguity that necessarily arises in coding, and the noise entering the channel which mutilates the coded messages. Before we do this, we will consider a measure of information.

2.5. Information

In defining a measure of the information contained in a message, we shall endeavor to meet the following requirements:

A. It must correspond to what people generally understand by "information;" for example, our measure of information should assume a higher value for messages like *JFK assassinated* or *It's a boy; mother and child doing fine* than for messages like *I cleaned my teeth this morning* or *Honesty is the best policy.*

B. The measure must have the property of additivity; that is, if the messages coding two independent events have information contents I_1 and I_2, then we require that the total information content of the two messages is

$$I = I_1 + I_2 \tag{1}$$

C. Our measure of information must be subjective (receiver dependent), since the same message does not contain the same information for two different receivers; for example, it contains no information for the receiver who has already been informed of its contents previously, no matter how much information it may contain for the receiver who has not heard the news before.

D. The above three items are the principal requirements; we shall find it a relatively easy matter to refine the measure of information to take account of such factors as the credibility of the transmitter and the interest of the receiver.

We start with requirement A. What makes an item of news startling, sensational, interesting, what causes it "to make the headlines" is always its unexpectedness. The messages *JFK Assassinated, Russia Invades Czechoslovakia, Los Angeles Hit by Major Earthquake* made the front page headlines; the messages *Grass is green, Mrs. Smith cleaned her teeth this morning, one dollar has 100 cents* will not even get into a newspaper. There was a time when the message *Airliner hijacked to Cuba* made the front page headlines; but as hijackings continued (at one time) with an average frequency of about two per week, and thus became highly predictable, the corresponding items appeared under small headlines buried deep inside the newspapers. The first Apollo landing on the moon held the entire world spellbound; the second aroused little interest; the third (which failed and the astronauts only just manages to return) made people realize that an enterprise of this kind did not have as high a probability of success as they may have thought; the fourth manned mission to the moon was therefore again followed with great interest.

From these and many other examples we conclude that the measure of information contained in a message must be related to the probability of the event which it codes; the information should increase with decreasing probability. It is evidently the probability of the event itself that is important, not the way in which it is coded. Surely, the information conveyed by the message *JFK assassinated* is the same as in the messages *JFK assassine* or *JFK ermordet.*

As a first try, we might therefore define the information contained in a message coding the event E as

$$I(E) = 1/P(E)$$

where $P(E)$ is the probability of the event E. Such a definition would be consistent with requirement A in that messages coding very improbable events would have a very high information content; however, this definition would violate the requirement of additivity B, for the informamation contained in a message coding two independent events would now be

$$I(E_1, E_2) = 1/P(E_1, E_2) = 1/P(E_1) \times 1/P(E_2)$$

where we have used (9), p. 23; on the other hand, requirement B would require

$$I(E_1, E_2) = I(E_1) + I(E_2) = 1/P(E_1) + 1/P(E_2)$$

and the discrepancy of the last two results shows that our first try has
to be discarded as unsuccessful. However, the only thing wrong with it
is that the information amounts multiply, whereas we want them to add;
therefore all we need to correct our definition is to use a function that
will convert multiplication to addition. The function which accomplishes
this is, of course, the logarithmic function; the definition of information
that satisfies both requirements A and B is thus

$$I(E) = \log 1/P(E) = -\log P(E) \tag{1}$$

and this is the definition we shall adopt (except for a few ramifications
that will follow shortly). It is now easily verified that (q) satisfies not
only requirement A in that the information content of the message increases from its minimum value zero for $P(E) = 1$ to higher values for
decreasing $P(E)$, but it also satisfies the requirement B of additivity,
since we now have

$$I(E_1, E_2) = -\log P(E_1, E_2) = -\log P(E_1) - \log P(E_2)$$
$$= I(E_1) + I(E_2) \tag{2}$$

The base of the logarithms has not yet been defined; however, since
a change from one base to another amounts only to multiplication by a
constant factor, the choice of base will only determine the units in which
the information is measured; it will not change the basic properties of
the concept. Shannon, who arrived at the expression (1) by somewhat
different reasoning, chose logarithms to the base 2, and the resulting
unit is called a *bit* (a contraction of *binary unit*); if natural logarithms
are used the resulting unit is a *nat* (natural unit); for decadic logarithms
(base 10), the resulting unit is called a *hartley* (see footnote 1, p. 18).

It should be noted that the definition (1) is formally the same as
that used in Shannon's information theory; however, conceptually it is
different, for in Shannon's theory $P(E)$ stands for the probability of the
state of the source, such as a symbol (letter) of the message to be transmitted, whereas here $P(E)$ is the probability of an actual event E, regardless of how this event is coded for transmission. In other words,
E in Shannon's theory is a formal element of the message; here, E is
an event which is a member of the semantic base.

Since the choice of the logarithmic base is not important, we choose
decadic logarithms for the sake of convenience (they require a minimum
of arithmetic); however, we shall call the resulting units *semantic units*
(SU) rather than hartleys, in order to emphasize that the corresponding
information concerns the semantics of the message, not its formal structure. The numerical equivalents are then

$$1 \text{ SU} = 1 \text{ hartley} \approx 2.3 \text{ nats} \approx 3.3 \text{ bits} \tag{3}$$

As a simple example of (1), consider the message *It's a girl!* given to the father of a child that has just been born. The probability of this event is close to ½ (actually a little less if we consider the possibility of twins or triplets, and if we recall that girls have a slightly lower birth rate), so that the information content of this message is

$$I(E) = -\log_{10} \tfrac{1}{2} = +\log_{10} 2 = 0.303 \text{ SU}$$

We assume that the father has no reason to doubt the nurse's word and believes her; this means that he changes the probability distribution in his mind from $P(\text{girl}) = \tfrac{1}{2}$, $P(\text{boy}) = \tfrac{1}{2}$ to the distribution $P(\text{girl}) = 1$, $P(\text{boy}) = 0$. Suppose now that by some circumstance a second nurse tells him *It's a girl!*, then the information the second nurse has given the father is $I = \log 1 = 0$, i.e., no information at all, and this is as it should be.

There are, however, four unusual circumstances in this rather artificial example. First, the event is one to which a numerical probability can easily be assigned. Second, the father was interested in the information, in fact, he was probably interested in the subject to the exclusion of everything else. Third, he knew what the subject would be as soon as the nurse addressed him; this is, however, untypical, since often we receive information "out of the blue" without prior warning or expectations as to what the subject of the information, let alone the information itself, is going to be. Fourth, he had no reason to doubt the nurse's word, and this is not the general case, for in our daily lives we are constantly being assaulted by messages that are in error (*it will be ready by the end of the week*) or are small lies (*so glad to have met you*) or big lies (*This does not represent an escalation of the war*) or not to be taken seriously (*You're in the Pepsi generation*) or utterly void of any meaning (*Hills Brothers coffee is 10% richer now*), so that only rarely do we change a probability in our minds to zero or to one; more often we change it only slightly, or we do not change it at all on receiving a message.

Before we refine our measure of information to take account of these points, we must turn to a point of central importance, namely, how the probability $P(E)$ involved in (1) is to be defined. In applied probability theory, one uses either the classical definition (ratio of favorable to possible elements of a set of equiprobable, incompatible and exhaustive events) or the statistical definition (ratio of favorable to total, very large number of trials); in rigorous probability theory, one uses a definition based on Kolmogorov axiomatics (for which we have no use here). When all three definitions are applicable, they yield the same result. The object of these definitions is to provide an "objective" measure of probability, one that will give the same result under the same circumstances;

and this is precisely why they are not usable for the present theory, for (semantic) information must, by its very essence, be subjective, i.e., receiver-dependent. It may surprise you, for example, that the number of murders in New York City in 1970 was greater than the combined total for Britain, the Netherlands, Ireland, Switzerland, Spain, Sweden, Denmark, and Norway. A criminologist will be less surprised, even if he has never heard the statement before; he assigns a higher probability to this event on the basis of the facts that he has studied, and therefore this statement brings him less information. If you are a linguist, it will not seem particularly strange to you that most Slavic languages have three words for *to marry*, depending on whether a man or a woman marries, or whether they marry each other, even if you have never studied a Slavic language; but persons who have never taken an interest in linguistics often consider this very funny, because they would have thought this very improbable. Thousands of other examples might be quoted to show that the same statement, that is, a message coding the same event of a semantic base, carries very different amounts of information to different receivers.

It is therefore evident that the probability $P(E)$ is not the objective probability of the event E as determined by measurement or calculation, but the *probability that the receiver assigns to this event* on the basis of his previous knowledge, even though this probability may be (and quite often is) wrong in the sense that it does not agree with the objective probability that would, for example, result from the calculation by a statistician who is in possession of the pertinent facts. Since different receivers will assign different probabilities to the same event, the resulting information becomes receiver dependent, as it should. We therefore modify the definition of the information content (1) as follows:

$$I(E) = -\log P(E \mid K) \tag{4}$$

where K stands for the total knowledge of the receiver, that is, all the probability distributions already stored in the receiver's memory (all the probabilities previously assigned to events of which the receiver is conscious). The probability $P(E \mid K)$ in (4) is the conditional probability that the receiver assigns to the event E, given all other relevant data known to the receiver. [The total knowledge K of the receiver includes, of course, also irrelevant data, but by definition of independent events, these do not affect the probability assigned to E, and therefore no harm is done in including them in the definition (4)].

Let us illustrate this by a simple example. Consider the message *J.C. Smith was arrested in 1964, at the age of 19, on a county road for driving while intoxicated*, which codes the following events:

E_1 = a certain J.C. Smith was arrested in 1964
E_2 = the arrest took place when he or she was 19 years old
E_3 = the arrest took place on a county road
E_4 = the reason for the arrest was driving while intoxicated

Let the receiver be a person or a computer whose knowledge includes the statistics on arrests issued by the US Department of Justice for 1964. The uncodnditional probability for a randomly selected person (such as J.C. Smith, about whom we know nothing) was $P(E_1)$ = 0.00005 in 1964, yielding an information of roughly 4.3 SU; the fact that Smith was arrested now enters the receiver's knowledge and is used in assigning the probability of the event that Smith's age was 19; that is, we no longer ask for the unconditional probability that Smith was 19 years old, but for the probability that he or she was 19 years old given that he or she was arrested (a conditional probability that can easily be calculated from the available statistics). Similarly, we could find the probability of E_3 given E_2 and E_1, and finally, the probability of E_4 given E_1, E_2, and E_3. Each of these messages updates our knowledge for use in assigning a probability to the event coded by the next message. This is important for interdependent events such as the ones coded in our example: In 1964, the probability of being arrested for driving while intoxicated at the age of 19 was much smaller than at the age of 30; it was also much smaller than the probability of getting arrested for larceny or for disorderly conduct at this age; being arrested for driving while intoxicated on a county road had a small probability (since most arrests for this offence took place in cities and suburban areas); etc.

It would be an easy matter to substitute the numerical values for all of these probabilities; they are either contained in the statistics issued by the Department of Justice for 1964, or they can easily be derived from them. However, we shall not bother to do so, since the importance of the example does not lie in the numerical value of the information content, but rather in the general way in which the information of a message coding interdependent events is evaluated: In general, the information of a message coding n events, some or all of which are interdependent, can be found by repeated application of the theorem of joint probability (8), p. 23. If K_0 represents the knowledge of the receiver before being informed of the n events E_1, E_2, ... E_n, the use of (4) and the theorem of joint probability yields

$$I(E_1, E_2, ..., E_n) = -\sum_{j=1}^{n} \log P(E_j \mid E_1, E_2, ..., E_{j-1}, K_0)$$
(5)

where the first term in the sum is $-\log P(E_1 \mid K_0)$.

If we now define the *current knowledge* K as the set of events of which the receiver is aware before being informed of the jth event, i.e.,

$$\{K\} = \{K_0, E_1, E_2, ..., E_{j-1}\} \tag{6}$$

then (5) yields

$$I(E_1, E_2, ..., E_j) = -\Sigma_j \log P(E_j \,|\, K) = \Sigma_j I(E_j) \tag{7}$$

i.e., our measure of information is additive, whether the message codes independent events or not.

2.5.1. NUMERICAL VALUES OF INFORMATION

In the example of J.C. Smith being arrested, it was possible to assign numerical values to the probabilities involved. Can this be done in the case of a message such as *JFK assassinated* and other events for which few statistics are available? In any case, need this be done?

As for the first question, it is possible to assign probabilities to most events. For example, the probability that a president of the United States will be assassinated during a given interval of his tenure can be calculated on the assumptions that the assassinations are independent and that the average rate of presidential assassinations does not change over long periods.. These two assumptions are sufficient to determine the probability that exactly k presidents will be assassinated within a time span t; it is given by the Poisson distribution

$$P_t(k) = \frac{(nt)^k}{k!} e^{-nt} \tag{8}$$

where n is the average rate of presidential assassinations (now about 1 per 25 years); we can also calculate the probability density of the "remaining time" to the next assassination, etc. For example, by this calculation, the unconditional probability of a president being assassinated within a given span of 24 hours is 0.0001095; the probability that more than 10 years will elapse between now and the next assassination is 0.67; etc. Since only four presidents of the United States have been assassinated, these figures are not very reliable, but it might be pointed out that for other so-called "rare events," such as major fires claiming more than 100 lives, the above line of reasoning is uncannily precise: The calculated probabilities agree with the statistically measured ones to three decimal places.

But all this is not very relevant. The vast majority of people are not trained in probability theory, and the few that are did not, presumably, rush for their tables of the Poisson distribution on being informed that President Kennedy had been assassinated. Thus, our measure of information is based on a probability assigned by the receiver, although the receiver does not, except under very unusual circumstances, assign a numerical probability.

This is a situation met quite often in mathematical modeling. If an artist and a computer are both instructed to draw a cube as seen from above and from the right, they will both produce a similar result. The computer must be given the coordinates of the corners and the exact angle of observation; it will then calculate the coordinates of the imaged corners, decide which edges are visible and which are hidden, and draw the cube. The artist makes no numerical calculations, but the result is the same as that produced by computation.

A second example is probably nearer the mark. Quite often we set up a mathematical model simulating some phenomenon or process taking place in real life. The mathematical model relies on numerical data, whereas the actual process involves no numbers (at least not explicitly). As an example, consider game theory. This is a mathematical discipline which deals with conflict situations – not only with games like poker or blackjack, but with general conflict situations such as war, economics, law enforcement, etc., where all the "players" are bent on achieving some objective, but only some of them can be successful. The theory revolves about a concept called the "pay-off matrix," whose elements indicate what gain or loss awaits a player on a certain combination of his and his opponents' strategies. These elements are numbers; they represent dollars, human lives or other units. For a game like blackjack, it is comparatively easy to assign these numbers. But for a conflict situation such as law enforcement (the game of "cops and robbers"), this is much more difficult. In calculating the optimum dislocations and patrol routes of police officers, some penalties involve loss of property, others injury or even death. What is the value of a human life in dollars? What is the probability that a hold-up man will prefer to shoot it out rather than run when confronted? Here the experts on game theory, resource allocation, and decision theory run into trouble – if they are after hard numerical values.

One way of solving the problem is to assign the required numerical values in a way that we feel comes nearest to the true state of affairs, and possibly correcting these values on the basis of their performance. This is the method used by the practical man, the one who has to feed data to a computer, for computers will not accept theoretical discourses. On the other hand, the theoretician is not very interested in numerical values; on the contrary, since a numerical value necessarily represents a special case, it will, as a rule, prevent the insight that can be gained by processing functions, distributions, laws and tendencies that show the general behavior of a process rather than a particular, limited result.

This is also the attitude we shall adopt in the following. Just as most game theoreticians prefer to think of the pay-off as a matrix element a_{ij} rather than a number in dollars or other units, so we will think of the probability assigned by a receiver as $P(E_j \mid K)$ without assigning a particular numerical value.

Let us give an example of calculating the information contained in a Latin sentence; it involves no numerical values, yet gives a result which is not immediately obvious. Legend relates that Alexander the Great consulted the Oracle of Delphi before setting out on his last great campaign. The oracle, Roman historians reported, said

IBIS REDIBIS NON MORIERIS IN BELLO

but failed to supply the punctuation. If a comma is inserted before *non*, the sentence means *You will go, you will return, you will not die in war*, but if a comma is inserted after *non*, it means *You will go, you will not return, you will die in war*. Even if Alexander regarded the oracle as a reliable source of information, he was evidently no wiser after hearing this ambiguous statement than he was before, and at first sight it would seem that it contained no information. A statement such as *Grass is either green or it is not green* codes two incompatible events, one of which must occur; the probability of either event taking place is one, and hence the information is zero. But Pythia, the priestess who manufactured the ambiguous prophecies in Delphi, goofed. Let us ignore the *ibis*, which is common to both meanings, and which did not give Alexander any new information. Let the coded events be the following:

E_1 = *redibis* $\qquad\qquad$ E_1^* = *non redibis*
E_2 = *morieris in bello* $\qquad$ E_2^* = *non morieris in bello*

Then the information corresponding to one meaning of the message is

$$I(E_1, E_2^*) = -\log P(E_1) - \log[1 - P(E_2)]$$

and the information corresponding to the other meaning is

$$I(E_1^*, E_2) = -\log[1 - P(E_1)] - \log P(E_2)$$

The information contained in a choice between the two meanings is, on applying (6) and (8), p. 23,

$$I(E_1, E_2^* \text{ or } E_2, E_1^*) = -\log [P(E_2^* \mid E_1) P(E_1) + P(E_1^* \mid E_2) P(E_2)]$$
$$= -\log[P(E_1) + P(E_2)] \qquad (9)$$

since both conditional probabilities equal unity. This information is zero only if $P(E_1) + P(E_2) = 1$, which, in turn, is true only if E_1 and E_2 are incompatible and exhaustive events. But they are not exhaustive: By inserting the words *in bello*, and thus qualifying the circumstances of death, Pythia left out one more event that makes the set exhaustive: *You will not return, you will die, but not in war.*

Perhaps the Gods noticed this, for they chose neither to let Alexander return nor to let him die in war, but to let him die far from Greece of natural causes. He died shortly after a banquet in Babylon in 323 B.C.

Thus, Pythia's ambiguity does contain the information (9), corresponding to the prophecy that Alexander will not die abroad of causes other than war. This somewhat surprising result was obtained without use of numerical values; it does not matter how Alexander assigns the probabilities $P(E_1)$ and $P(E_2)$.

2.5.2. ACCESS INFORMATION

The father in the waiting room of a maternity ward already knows the subject of the message that the nurse is going to bring him, even though he does not yet know the content of the message. Alexander knew the subject of the message the oracle would give him, because he asked for a forecast on this subject. This is not so in general. The message *JFK assassinated* came "out of the blue," not in answer to a question. Much other information, especially that coded in a natural language, reaches the receiver without previous solicitation and more or less unexpectedly.

The human brain, like a computer, stores information; but it also provides access to this information. The two activities are distinct, as is obvious from the fact that often we know that we have an item of information stored in our memory, but we are unable to provide access to it, i.e., to remember it. The path of access apparently leads through other items of information ("associations"), and sometimes another received item of information will trigger the right association and open the access path — whereupon we will suddenly remember the item to which we temporarily had no access.

The simplest statement in a computer program consists essentially of two items: the information (number) to be stored, and the place where to store it (the latter is called the "address"). For example, the BASIC statement LET N = 3 or the FORTRAN statement N = 3 gives the computer the following instruction: Store the number 3 at the address N (at the memory element called N). Similarly, before the brain can alter an existing probability distribution, it must find access to the "file" where it is stored. The message *JFK assassinated* first triggers the realization that the message concerns the president of the United States before the information can be processed. The message *Colorado has 300 sunny days a year* triggers the realization that it concerns geography and climate before it can be processed, i.e., before the corresponding probability distribution can be altered. Psychologists or brain physiologists do not know exactly how information is stored in the brain, much less how this information is accessed.* But whatever the system of "filing" used by the brain, it is certain that the different "files" are not accessed with the same frequency (probability), and similar "files" are not accessed with the same frequency by different persons. Most people will rarely access the file "nervous system of spiders," but some biologist might do so many times every day.

Any probability that a receiver may assign to an event coded by a message is a probability assigned after he has accessed the corresponding "file." The instruction telling us which file to access is an important part of the message, which itself carries further information. The value of this access information follows the same rules as the information conveyed by the message itself. There is no need to re-define our measure of information to take account of the access information as a distinct item. It is sufficient to regard the subject of the statement as the first of the coded events. For example, the message *The President of the United States has been assassinated* can be regarded as one which encodes two events: E_1 = the message concerns the President of the United States, E_2 = he has been assassinated. Formula (4) will take care of both. The event E_1, which originates the access information, is, of course, important only in "locating the file," e.g., in reading a newspaper headline. The statements made in the article below the headline concern more or less the same subject; the probabilities of the "file" are now very high, and therefore the access information in the subsequent messages is quite low.

In conversation, the subject matter may range over widely separated fields, but the course is run without startling changes; "one thing leads to another," and the access information is thus kept low. People do not like to access a disconnected file suddenly, without a high access probability. Any doubts on this point can be dispelled by trying to butt into a general conversation with the statement *There are more than 10 countries in the world today in which slavery is still legal*, which is true, interesting, and has a high information content for most receivers. But the startled stares and embarrassed silence that will probably follow will show that people do not like to receive high access information in general conversation.

2.5.3. *INTEREST OF THE RECEIVER*

Consider the following messages transmitted in reply to the question "What is the time?":

---

* The computer age has made *access* a widely used transitive verb, and I am using it as such. I note that the 1950 edition of the Oxford Dictionary of Modern English does not recognize it as a verb of any kind.

1. *When the leading edge of the next pulse starts rising, the time will be 11 hours, 25 minutes, 12.578436 seconds, plus or minus 5 microseconds.*

2. *It is 25 past eleven.*

3. *Don't worry, we still have plenty of time.*

By our definition of information, the first statement has the highest information content, and the third the lowest. Yet the first statement really gives information only to an astronomer or a researcher at a time-frequency laboratory; for the average person it conveys no more information than the second statement.

Consider another example, where numerical values can easily be assigned. Suppose someone wants to know the value of the circle ratio π. Like most people, he knows that it equals approximately 3.14, but he would like to have a more exact value. The decimal digits of π are statistically independent, and for a person who does not know the next digit, this digit can be one of the ten digits (0 to 9) with equal probability. Therefore, as he looks up the value of π, each previously unknown digit provides him with an information of one semantic unit $[-\log 0.1 = +\log 10 = 1]$. The value of π is, at the time of writing, known to 500,000 decimal places, and if the enquirer uses the corresponding report in which they were published, he receives no less than half a million semantic units of information, at least by the definition of information that we have so far been using. But this is patent nonsense, because the enquirer will almost certainly not need the value of π with such precision. For very precise computer programming, no more than 18 digits are needed, and any other practical application needs even less; the remaining decimal digits are superfluous, the user will not even look at them, and they therefore convey no information to him.

This aspect of information, to what degree the receiver is interested in the information conveyed by a message, can be taken care of by a system of sets that mathematicians call a "sigma algebra." We have no need, however, to explain what this is, for the point to be made is quite simple. Every event of the semantic base can be broken down into a number of component events. For example, the message *He is 28 years old* conventionally codes the event "He is more than 28 years old, but has not yet reached his 29th birthday;" the latter event can be broken down into the component events "His age is 28 years and 1 month," "His age is 28 years and 2 months," ..., etc. Conversely, each event is itself a component event of a "coarser" event. For example, the event "He is 28 years old" is a component event of "He is not yet 30," which, in turn, is a component event of "He is an adult," and so on.

Thus, the event coded by our first example, which gave the time of day to the nearest 5 microseconds, is a component event of "It is 25 past eleven," which itself might be a component event of "We still have plenty of time." The event coded by the message $\pi = 3.141592...$ is a component event of the "coarser" event $\pi = 3.14...$, which, in turn, is a component event of the coarser event "π is a positive number."

We can now take care of the limitations imposed on the received information by the receiver. Let us call component events "finer" events, and events made up of component events "coarser" events, so that "He is an adult" is a coarser event than "He is in his late twenties," and "He is 29 years old" is a finer event than "He is not yet 30." Obviously, a message coding a certain event automatically also codes all coarser events associated with it; the message *He is 29 years old* automatically also codes the events "He is not yet 30," "He is an adult," and all other coarser events.

To make the information conveyed by a message dependent on the receiver's interest, we need not change the formal definition (4); we need only interpret E as the *finest of all coarser events in which the receiver is still interested.*

As an example, consider the message

The windspeed in Boulder, Colorado, was 90 mph yesterday, with individual gusts reaching 150 mph.

The events coded by this message are of great interest to Boulderites, who were holding on to their hats yesterday and hoping the roof would not be blown away; they want to know the exact windspeed that was measured. On the other hand, if a New Yorker happens to read this item in the newspaper, his interest may reach only as far as the coarser event coded by the statement

They had pretty high winds in the Rockies.

This event has a much higher probability, and therefore the message carries less information. And if some reader in Zambia happens to read the original message, he may not be interested at all, and the probability may be assigned to the even coarser event coded by the message

The windspeed was high at some place at some time.

The event coded by this message has probability one, and therefore the message itself carries no information; the only information left is the access information, and even that is eliminated in the very coarse event

Something happened somewhere.

Similar examples pertaining to the time of day, the value of π, or other events are, it is hoped, obvious.

The reduction in information due to lack of interest is, of course, caused by the fact that coarser events must necessarily have a higher probability.

2.5.4. SECONDARY INFORMATION

We have so far only been concerned with the information conveyed
by a message by virtue of the events that it codes. We shall call this
the primary information of the message, and in our investigations of the
structure of Language this, as a rule, will be the only information of
interest. However, for the sake of completeness, we should note that a
message also contains secondary information by virtue of the fact *that*
it is transmitted, and *how* it is transmitted. Consider, for example, the
messages transmitted by the two bumper stickers *America — love it or
leave it* and *Viet Nam — love it and leave it*. Neither of these two messages contains much primary information; the main purpose is to transmit secondary information of the type "This is my political philosophy,
I want everybody to know that I stand up for it." It is highly probable
that the two car owners have very different opinions not only on the subject of the message itself, but also on busing, repression, permissiveness, supreme court decisions, long hair, welfare, loyalty oaths, drugs,
and a hundred other subjects not at all contained in the messages of
the bumper stickers. If the information carried by these messages were
to be measured, the probabilities would have to be assigned to the events
"This is my political philosophy" and "I consider it necessary to adver-
tise it." As usual, conditional probabilities are involved. The message
Viet Nam — love it and leave it, for example, is more often seen on Volks-
wagens than on late model Mercuries, and on overtaking a new Cadillac
with the bumper sticker *America — love it or leave it*, it would be quite
a surprise to see it driven by a long-haired, bearded youth wearing blue
sunglasses and several necklaces of love beads.

The secondary information conveyed by the way in which a message
is transmitted, regardless of the primary information contained in it, includes (in the case of transmission by speech) such things as the sex
of the coder, the mood of the speaker, his or her local accent, etc. This
type of information is transmitted, for example, in a telephone conversation, but not in a telegram. In many telephone conversations, this type
of information is quite superfluous, and since it uses up quite a lot of
the capacity of a telephone line (bandwidth), communication engineers
have long been trying to filter it out. One way of doing this is to use an
electronic device which recognizes words and codes them digitally for
transmission; at the receiving end the words are re-coded to sound, but
in a synthetic voice, not the voice of the speaker, so that the primary
information is retained, but the secondary information of mood, sex, etc.,
is lost. More conversations can be transmitted over one line in this way,
because the bandwidth of this type of telephone transmission is smaller.

Written language naturally contains much less secondary information
than spoken language. Even so, it contains an appreciable amount, e.g.,

the personal character of the writer. If a speaker is quoted in written language, the secondary information may include such items as the education, mood, and character of the speaker: The messages *I ain't got no nutt'n* and *I have not got anything* contain the same primary information, but the secondary information is very different. Similarly, *to terminate employment* and *to fire*, *underprivileged* and *poor*, not to mention Latin anatomical expressions and their four-letter equivalents, refer to more or less the same concepts, but carry very different information concerning the speaker or writer.

2.6. Credibility

In the preceding sections we introduced a measure of information that depends on the probability of the coded event as assigned by the receiver, and therefore dependent on the receiver's knowledge, on the access probability, and on the interest of the receiver. However, all of this, and the other characteristics of information discussed above, assumed that the coder is reliable, i.e., that the transmitter will not commit errors in coding an event of the semantic base, or miscode deliberatly (lie). Yet our measure of information would be an unrealistic one if it applied only to trustworthy transmitters. Obviously, it needs further modification to account for the fact that the same message does not carry the same information when coded by a trustworthy coder or by a liar, since in the latter case the probability to be stored after decoding will not reach unity; in fact, in some cases, as we shall see, it may even decrease the stored probability of the coded event rather than increase it.

Since the information contained in a message coding the event E and coded by a trustworthy (or at least trusted) coder is

$$I = -\log P(E) \tag{1}$$

it is natural to define the information coded by *any* coder as

$$I = -C \log P(E) \tag{2}$$

where C is a factor whose value ranges from 0 to 1, and whose nature (and hence method of calculation) is to be determined below.

To make the credibility factor C useful and realistic, we impose three requirements on it.

First, we note that the credibility of a message is not entirely determined by its coder. We tend to believe a message coding an event with high probability even when it comes from a well known liar, and we tend to doubt its reliability when it codes a highly improbable event, even if the message is coded by a usually very reliable coder. Thus, we would not doubt the truth of the message *Grass is green*, even if it were transmitted by such a notorious liar as the Soviet government; on the other hand, we would doubt the truth of the message *The sun will not rise tomorrow*, even if it were transmitted by the most trustworthy professor of astronomy. We therefore require that the credibility factor C be a monotonically increasing function of the probability $P(E)$, where E is the event coded by the message. This condition is expressed mathematically as

$$\partial C / \partial P(E) > 0 \tag{3}$$

Second, if the coder is considered perfectly trustworthy by the receiver, C shall equal its maximum value one. Let M be the message coding the event E. "Believing" a message, as has been discussed before, means assigning a probability one to the event E on receiving the message M coding it, i.e., $P(E\,|\,M) = 1$. Our second requirement can therefore be expressed as

$$C = 1 \quad \text{for} \quad P(E\,|\,M) = 1 \tag{4}$$

The third requirement concerns the circumstances under which C reaches its minimum value zero, and this requires a little thought. At first sight it might appear that the lowest possible credibility should be assigned to the messages coming from a consistently lying transmitter, i.e., a coder who always transmits the message non-M when the event E occurs, and the message M when the event non-E occurs. However, such a consistent liar would, in fact, be just as good as a perfectly trustworthy transmitter once we learn to decode his messages correctly. For his very consistency would convince us of the truth that the opposite of his statements is true. If he said *Jack loves Jill,* his consistency would guarantee the truth of the event that Jack does *not* love Jill. The liar whose messages are totally unreliable is not the one who codes them *contrary* to the facts, but the one who codes them *independently* of the facts.

Thus, if *Pravda* transmits the message that Comrade Ivanov has been relieved of his post at his own request for reasons of health, or that one Vasil Vasilyevich Vasilov has been sentenced to 5 years hard labor for slandering the Soviet people, it does provide us with some information: The chances are high that Ivanov is in perfect health and has been fired, and it is practically certain that Vasilov did not slander the Soviet people, but was overheard disagreeing with the Soviet government. Goebbels was badly mistaken in believing that a lie becomes the truth when it is repeated a million times. It doesn't; it only trains people to decode properly.

On the other hand, the messages transmitted by astrologers and crystal gazers do not necessarily contradict the facts; they simply have nothing to do with them. An astrologer transmits his messages on the basis of the constellation of the planets and other omens which are

demonstrably independent of the events that the messages code.
The message transmitted by an astrologer after consulting the planets,
cards, a crystal ball or tea leaves is totally void of any information, because the chain of the transmission system is severed between the semantic base and the coder; the effect is the same as if it were severed
at some other point, e.g., if the receiver were deaf, or the astrologer
talked into a dead telephone line. No information is transmitted.

It is quite easy to formulate these considerations mathematically.
The probability that the event E is true (has occurred or will occur)
after the message has been received is $P(E \mid M)$; for a consistent liar,
this probability is $P(E \mid M) = 0$, from which it follows that $P(E \mid$ non-$E)$
$= 1$, and the latter relation implies by (4) full credibility, provided M is
decoded properly, i.e., that it is decoded as corresponding to non-E
rather than to E. On the other hand, for the astrologer, we have from (4),
p. 23, $P(E \mid M) = P(E)$. The condition for zero credibility is therefore

$$C = 0 \qquad \text{for} \quad P(E \mid M) = P(E) \tag{5}$$

The conditions (3), (4), and (5) do not determine C uniquely; however, a natural expression for the information contained in the message
M, which is transmitted by any coder and codes the event E, is

$$I = \log P(E \mid M) - \log P(E) \tag{6}$$

which satisfies both (4) and (5); if the value of (6) is negative, this is
an indication that the decoding is to be inverted (the message should
be decoded to non-E rather than to E), and this will make the information content positive in agreement with what has been said above. Comparing (6) and (2), we find the credibility given by

$$C = 1 - \log P(E \mid M) / \log P(E) \tag{7}$$

and by applying Bayes' Theorem to the numerator, it can easily be shown
that condition (3) is satisfied also; as before, a negative value of the
credibility implies that the decoding should be inverted (which will make
the credibility positive).

Expression (6) is the general expression for the information content
of a message; it obviously reduces to the expression used in the preceding sections when the coder is perfectly reliable.

In the above examples, we have chosen the extreme cases of liars
and astrologers to explain the concept of credibility. However, the expression we have derived is particularly useful for the much more frequent cases when the credibility of a message is lowered due to the
meaning with which the *receiver* associates it. The following example
shows that the information received by the receiver remains constant,
regardless of how the receiver interprets a message.

Let us again consider a photo-electric burglar alarm, which surrounds a house with a perimeter of invisible rays and which rings a bell when the perimeter is interrupted by an opaque object. The coder is the alarm installation (which we assume perfectly reliable); the message transmitted by it is the ringing (or silence) of the bell. Suppose the bell is ringing (message M). On receiving this message, a receiver might interpret this message (decode it) in different ways; e.g., he might assign one of the following meanings to it:

E_1 = the ray has been interrupted by an opaque object
E_2 = the ray has been interrupted by a stray dog
E_3 = the ray has been interrupted by a harmless person
E_4 = the ray has been interrupted by a burglar

These events are (presumably) ordered in decreasing probability, so that if the messages coding them were reliable, they would carry increasing information. However, only the first interpretation is, in fact, correct and the message thus interpreted is reliable, i.e., $P(E_1 | M) = 1$. In the remaining cases, $P(E_j | M)$ is less than one, and its value decreases with increasing j. It is easily shown that the credibility of the message decreases to the same extent as the information $-\log P(E_j)$ increases; the two exactly compensate for each other, so that the ringing of the bell always carries the same information, no matter how the receiver interprets (decodes) the message:

$$I = \log \frac{1}{P(E_1)} = \log \frac{P(E_2|M)}{P(E_2)} = \log \frac{P(E_3|M)}{P(E_3)} = \log \frac{P(E_4|M)}{P(E_4)} \quad (8)$$

The proof of (8) follows from the theorem of joint probability

$$P(E_j | M) P(M) = P(M | E_j) P(E_j)$$

so that

$$\frac{P(E_j | M)}{P(E_j)} = \frac{P(M | E_j)}{P(M)}$$

But the probability in the numerator on the right is (due to the reliable operation of the alarm) equal to one. Hence all expressions in (8) equal $-\log P(M)$, and therefore they equal each other; the ringing of the bell always conveys the same information, no matter how its meaning is interpreted.

3

CODING

3.1. Signal Space

Coding theory defines a code as a mapping of the source alphabet into the code alphabet; in our case this would correspond to a mapping of the semantic base into the set of meaningful combinations of the code elements. Rather than explain the exact meaning of "mapping," we start off with an example. Consider a binary code, whose elements are 0 and 1. Let the coder be the autopilot of an aircraft, and let the semantic base consist of four events, which are coded into messages as follows:

Event	Message
aircraft is off proper course to the left	00
aircraft is off proper course to the right	01
aircraft is above proper course	10
aircraft is below proper course	11

To be specific, let us suppose that these messages coded in binary code are transmitted to the servomechanisms correcting the course of the aircraft.

It is useful to plot this code graphically, each message corresponding to a point in space. Each message is a combination of two code elements $(0, 1)$, so we choose two axes, one (say, the horizontal axis) corresponding to the first digit, the other to the second. The message 11 is then plotted as the point with coordinates $(1,1)$ as shown in Fig. 3.1a. Fig. 3.1b shows the eight points obtained in a binary code whose messages combine three digits, and Fig. 3.1c corresponds to the possible

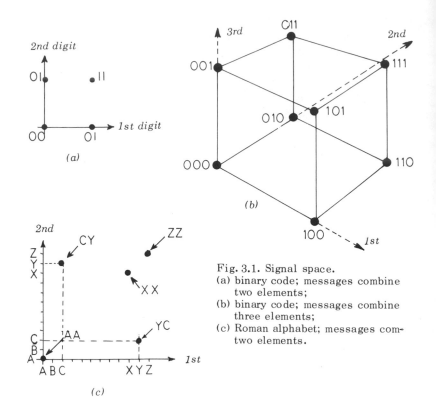

Fig. 3.1. Signal space.
(a) binary code; messages combine two elements;
(b) binary code; messages combine three elements;
(c) Roman alphabet; messages com- two elements.

using the 26 letters of the Roman (English) alphabet and forming the messages by combining them two at a time (only some of the $26^2 = 676$ messages have been labeled so as not to overburden the figure).

The space in which these coordinate points corresponding to the messages lie is called the *signal space*. (The messages are "mapped" in this space.) For example, in Fig. 3.1b, the signal space corresponding to this code is formed by a cube, with the messages mapped at its eight corners.

The representation of the messages of a code in signal space is a very useful aid to our imagination. Consider, for example, the concept of *distance*. Suppose in Fig. 3.1b the message 101 has been transmitted. It is possible that in transmission one of the digits is distorted, resulting in the "false" messages 001 or 111 or 100. It can be seen from the figure that this corresponds to a displacement in signal space from the original corner of the cube 101 to the three nearest corners along the edges of the cube. This is the smallest possible distance for such a displacement reaching another message. Distortion of two digits is less likely and corresponds to a larger displacement: The signal now has to be displaced along the diagonal across one of the three faces intersecting at the original point 101 to reach the points 110 or 000 or 011. Distortion of all three digits is still less likely and corresponds to a still larger distance of the displacement, namely along the diagonal through the cube from the original corner 101 to the opposite corner 010.

Let the original point in signal space be x, and let it have coordinates x_1, x_2, x_3 (corresponding to the distances along the first, second and third coordinate axes, measured from the origin); let the distortion of the signal displace the signal from the original point x to a point y with coordinates y_1, y_2, y_3. Then the geometrical distance through which the signal has been displaced in signal space by distortion is, by Pythagoras' Theorem,

$$d = \sqrt{\sum_{j=1}^{n} (y_j - x_j)^2} \tag{1}$$

where $n = 3$ for a three-dimensional signal space. Most codes, and especially natural languages, combine more than three elements of the code to form a message. In that case the corresponding signal space has more than three coordinate axes; in general, signal space is n-dimensional. People who are not familiar with n-dimensional geometry are often frightened, quite needlessly, of the concept of n-dimensional space; they associate it with science fiction and Einsteinian brilliance which is inaccessible to normal mortals. In fact, however, there is really one significant difference between three-dimensional and n-dimensional spaces: We can easily draw a picture of a geometrical body in three-dimensional space (such as the cube in Fig. 3.1b), but we cannot do so for n-dimensional space with $n > 3$. But this is an obstacle only to those who must think in terms of pictures; it presents no difficulties if we think of distance not as a straight line joining two blobs representing the end points of a segment, but as the expression (1). It is easily verified that (1) gives the distance between two points along the only coordinate axis if $n = 1$, that it gives the distance in a plane if $n = 2$, and that it gives the distance in three-dimensional space if $n = 3$. There is nothing to stop us defining (1) as the distance between two points for any n, i.e., in n-dimensional space. Similarly, the locus of all points equidistant from the origin is formed by two points $-r$ and r on the only coordinate axis for $n = 1$; by a circle for $n = 2$; by the surface of a sphere if $n = 3$; and by the surface of a hypersphere if $n > 3$. All of these are described by the same formula [namely, the square of (1) equals r^2, where r is the radius of the circle, sphere or hypersphere]. The fact that we can draw pictures of the locus for $n = 1,2,3$, but not for $n = 4$ or more, is not at all significant.

In the following, we shall have n-dimensional space in mind when we talk about signal space, but if we want to illustrate a point graphically, we shall choose the special case of a two- or three-dimensional space (i.e., a code that combines two or three elements to form a message) in order to be able to draw a picture. The generalization is then carried out by a formula, such as (1). We can always visualize the point to be made by imagining the example of a three-dimensional space.

Let us do this to illustrate the use of the distance concept. The example we started with (the autopilot) was a rather artificial one, for to assign a meaning to every possible combination of code elements is to invite difficulties. Such a code would work only if we could be absolutely sure that no distortion will ever set in, and this is unrealistic. A well designed code, and certainly all natural languages, uses only some of its possible combinations for messages, leaving the others meaningless. This redundancy protects the messages from noise, for if the receiver receives a combination with no meaning, he can either restore the message by looking for the nearest "occupied" point in signal space, or, if this still leaves an ambiguity, he is at least given a warning that the transmitted message has been distorted; the receiver can thus correct the error, or at least detect it.

Suppose, for example, that we code two events (such as "aircraft off course to the left" and "aircraft off course to the right") by a binary code combining three digits per message. Then, for obvious reasons, we will choose the corresponding points in signal space as far apart as possible, at diagonally opposite points of the cube in Fig. 3.1b. Let us choose 101 and 010. This leaves the other corners of the cube (000, 001, 010, 100, 110, 111) "empty," i.e., with no correspondence to a meaning. However, a glance at the figure shows that three of these "empty" points are nearer to the message 101 than to 010, whereas the remaining three are nearer to 010 than to 101. Thus, if the receiver receives the meaningless combination 111, he will restore the meaningful message 101, which is nearer than the meaningful message 010: The distance is 1 in the former case, but 2 in the latter. (What this represents, of course, is that it is more probable that only one, not two, digits have been distorted.) Naturally, if all three digits have been distorted, so that the signal moves all the way along the diagonal of the cube, the receiver will get the wrong message without warning. There is nothing we can do to avoid this case completely, for it can be proved that it is impossible to design a code that will correct *all* possible errors;* we can, however, make the probability of an error incapable of detection as small as we please by increasing the redundancy of the code. For example, by assigning opposite cor-

---

* P. Beckmann, *Probability in Communication Engineering,* Harcourt, Brace and World, New York, 1967.

ners of a binary cube in n-dimensional space, the probability of an incorrigible error is reduced to p^n, where p is the probability of any one digit being distorted, and where we have assumed that the errors are independent. By using sufficient elements per message (e.g., 00000000 and 11111111, eight elements), we can therefore reduce the probability of an undetectable error to an arbitrarily small value, though, of course, the efficiency of the code will decrease, since we are wasting more and more points in signal space by leaving them empty (for eight elements, we would use only two out of $2^8 = 256$ points).

It should also be pointed out that in general the distance defined by (1) is not exactly proportional to the probability of the corresponding distortion, as can easily be verified by comparing the displacement along an edge to that along a diagonal. It is desirable to make the two proportional to each other, and this can be done by using a definition of distance which differs from the geometrical distance (1); however, since we shall apply this point to natural languages only in a qualitative way, we shall not bother with this modification.

In all of the above examples, the combinations of code elements (whether corresponding to a meaningful message or not) occupied only discrete points in signal space. It is also possible for them to fill a volume in signal space continuously. Suppose, for example, that we have a telemetering device for measuring the temperature and pressure of the atmosphere. Let the coder transmit a radio signal whose frequency is proportional to the temperature, and whose amplitude (strength) is proportional to the pressure. This (hypothetical) code combines two elements, and therefore its signal space is two-dimensional (a plane), which is reminiscent of Fig. 3.1c; however, whilst Fig. 3.1c has only 26^2 discrete points corresponding to possible signals, we now have two coordinate axes (frequency and amplitude) consisting of a continuum of points; the entire area of the resulting rectangle shown in Fig. 3.2 is now filled with possible signals.

If the code uses n variable parameters to code n continuous variables, the corresponding signal space will be formed by a continuous volume in n-dimensional space; the above example is a special case for $n = 2$.

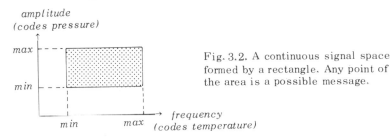

Fig. 3.2. A continuous signal space formed by a rectangle. Any point of the area is a possible message.

A special chapter will be devoted to the investigation of Language as a code, but at this point we will discuss how signal space can be used to map a natural language. We first note that the elements of a code are not uniquely defined by its code words (messages); the decision as to what we regard as the elements of the code is to some degree left to our convenience. For example, we can regard the Morse code as being made up of dots, dashes, short pauses (within a letter) and long pauses (separating letters). But if we find it convenient, we can equally well consider the Morse code as being made up of dots and short pauses only, for we can regard the dash as a succession of three dots (not separated by pauses) and the long pause as a succession of two short pauses. The first approach regards the Morse code as made up of four elements, the second regards it as made up of two elements; we can also regard it as made up of some 50 elements by considering the 26 letters and the space (plus digits, punctuation, and others) as elements *en bloc*. Obviously, the Morse code as such remains unchanged; our decision alters only its representation in signal space.

Messages coded in Language consist, as a rule, of grammatical sentences, but here we have an even wider choice in deciding what to regard as the elements of a language: Phonemes, morphemes, syllables or words are just some of the many possible choices. We also have the choice of considering the spoken or the written language. As a rule, it is the spoken language that is of interest, for writing or printing is merely a way of recording the spoken language, i.e., re-coding it. It is a very cumbersome way of recording it; a tape recorder, for for example, essentially performs the same function more quickly, and with less loss of (secondary) information. Nevertheless, written language is much more easily investigated; for example, it is much more easily represented in signal space, and therefore we shall sometimes treat written language when the point to be made is essentially the same for both, and the additional properties of spoken language would only introduce needless complications.

Suppose we choose phonemes as the elements of spoken language. A phoneme is not a precisely defined element; the phoneme $\int$ (*sh*) is pronounced differently by different people, and (as harmonic analysis shows) not even the same person can duplicate it exactly on two occasions. Therefore a combination of several phonemes is not represented in signal space as a point, but rather as a sphere (or a volume of other shape) about that point. The volume of the sphere contains the infinitely many points of the individual variations, but it does not intersect the sphere centered at the nearest point representing another combination of phonemes. In other words, such a sphere accommodates the infinitely many ways of pronouncing *shot*, and another sphere accommodates the infinitely many ways of pronouncing *shod*; but the two spheres do not normally overlap (a point common to both spheres would represent an ambiguity, i.e., the inability to distinguish the two words). The signal space implied by this representation is the space assigned to combinations of three English phonemes. The coordinate axes of this space correspond to the first, second and third phoneme, and each axis carries phonemes rather than numerical units. The first sphere is centered at the point with coordinates *sh, o, t,* the second at the point with coordinates *sh, o, d.** The coordinates themselves are taken as "mean" or "standard" phonemes.

The very fact that it is possible to draw these spheres (or quasispheres or blobs) without running into other spheres means that a language leaves enough "unused" space between words and other structures to accommodate a wide range of flexibility. The three-phoneme word *shirt* is pronounced *shoit* in Brooklyn, *shairt* in Birmingham, England, *shurrt* (with a rolled *r*) in Scotland; a German will pronounce it as if it were spelled *Schöhrt* in his own language, a Russian will use his own *sh* that has no counterpart in English, and a Frenchman might use his guttural *r.* Yet these very different pronunciations are easily decoded as the same article of clothing; a 100% efficient code would assign a different meaning to each of them, and ambiguity would result very easily.

However, languages do differ in their exploitation of signal space; the more efficient ones (and therefore the ones more prone to ambiguity) crowd more words into the same volume than the inefficient (and noise-resistant) ones. As we shall see later, English has a very crowded signal space; Russian and the other Slavic languages use it very lavishly, leaving much more space "empty."

In the above examples, we used phonemes as elements of a language. The corresponding signal space was based on coordinate axes carrying phonemes as scales. It is possible to choose even finer elements, e.g., Fourier coefficients (which is, very roughly speaking, what orthodox information theory does). However, since we shall be mainly interested in the grammatical and syntactic structure of Language, phonemes are too fine a unit. In investigating words and sentences of a language, we shall use syllables (and later, morphemes) as a convenient unit. For example, the word *sister* would be located in the signal space of two-syllable English words at a point whose coordinate along the first axis is marked *sis,* and whose coordinate along the second axis is marked *ter.* This example, and some of the others above, is intended to show how a word can be mapped in signal space; however, a lone word such as *sister* does not ordinarily code an event.

---

* It is expected that not all readers of this book are familiar with phonetic notation, and unless confusion could easily result, ordinary letters rather than phonetic symbols will be used to denote phonemes.

Whatever we choose as the elements of a language, there is one tacit assumption in all of the above considerations, namely, that these elements can be marked along a coordinate axis in such a way that similar sounding elements are near each other, and very different sounding elements are far apart. If, for example, the elements are English syllables, *dim* and *din* would be near each other on each coordinate axis, and far from *child.* However, to order syllables like *child, dim, sane* and *rot,* a general rule would be needed; more specifically, they could be ordered only if each syllable had a single numerical parameter associated with it, and this parameter would have to be such that the difference in the values for two syllables characterized their dissimilarity. Such a parameter can be found (by use of harmonic analysis and the sampling theorem) if the elements of the code are chosen much finer than phonemes. For phonemes, syllables and words, there is (to the author's knowledge) no such single parameter. But this is not as tragic as might seem at first sight. In specific cases of similar and dissimilar syllables, we shall have no difficulty in estimating distances in signal space; in the general case, we shall simply assume that the syllables are ordered in some way reflecting their similarity or dissimilarity as best possible, though no such method of one-dimensional ordering is going to be perfect. As we shall see, this shortcoming will make very little difference to our considerations involving the mapping of language in signal space.

We have hitherto interpreted "meaning" as the correspondence of an event of the semantic base to the message by which it is coded. For natural languages, this means, in general, that the coded messages are sentences. A single word, such as *shirt*, does not code an event, it only expresses a certain concept. Apart from rather artificial exceptions, the word *shirt* cannot form a message coding an event, and as far as the present theory of transmitting information is concerned, this word, by itself, has no meaning, though it can occur in a meaningful message such as *He wore a blue shirt*, which codes an event of the semantic base.

Nevertheless, for some considerations it is useful to construct a signal space using, say, syllables as elements, and marking points corresponding to words in that space, even though these points do not correspond to messages. For example, in the two-dimensional space (plane) corresponding to all combinations of English syllables, we would mark the word *sister* at the point whose coordinates are *sis* and *ter;* on the other hand, the point with coordinates *ter* and *sis*, which corresponds to the combination *tersis*, is not a point occupied by an English word. (Let us think of printed English for simplicity; spoken English introduces stressed and unstressed syllables and other complications.) Similarly, in three-dimensional signal space with syllables on the coordinate axes, we would mark the words *September* or *condition*, but the combinations *tem-sep-ber, tember-tion, con-tem-ber*, etc. are not English words; the corresponding points are "empty." It is obvious even from these few examples that the vast majority of the points in signal space of a natural language are "empty;" only very few carry words.

In the signal space that we are interested in, namely, the signal space containing messages (sentences) and carrying syllables on its coordinate axes, a point corresponding to a message (a meaningful sentence) is obviously going to be even rarer among the vast quantity of points corresponding to meaningless combinations of syllables, since only some combinations of syllables form words, and only some combinations of words form sentences. Even so, the combination of 10 syllables *The teacher wilted hysterically* forms a sentence that violates no rule of formal grammar, but it does not code any event of a semantic base, and is therefore meaningless; the corresponding point in this 10-dimensional signal space is just as empty as the point mapping the 10-syllable combination *bibibibibibibibibibi*. Natural languages, then, exploit only an extremely small fraction of the available points in signal space to code their messages.

Before we formulate this idea quantitatively, there is one more point to be discussed, which may have disturbed the reader. If we use syllables as elements along the coordinate axes, the point *sister* lies in a plane, the word *condition* in a three-dimensional space, and the combination *The teacher wilted hysterically* is represented by a point in a 10-dimensional space. Is there just one signal space, or are there many spaces, one corresponding to each n, where n is the number of elements to be combined? Personally, I like to visualize signal space as a number of spaces side by side: two-dimensional, three-dimensional, four-dimensional, etc. When a code is designed and the messages fill up the two-dimensional space (or more often, the density of messages reaches a certain value), further messages must be relegated to three-dimensional space (they must be formed by combining three elements), and so on. However, if this is considered crude, one may also visualize a single signal space of n dimensions which also accommodates messages of up to n elements by marking a "zero" syllable on the coordinate axes; this is a syllable of zero duration (and therefore not to be confused with the pause). If we denote this auxiliary syllable by 0, then the monosyllabic word *fish* can be mapped in, say, three-dimensional space as the point with coordinates *fish-0-0*; precautions must be taken, however, to count this word only once by leaving the effectively identical combinations *0-fish-0* and *0-0-fish* "empty."

Let us now introduce a quantitative measure of the degree to which a code exploits the available points in signal space.

Let a code form its messages by combining n code elements (or, using the artifact of a zero element, up to n elements). Let the number of different elements (including the zero element, if necessary) be N. Then the number of possible combinations, not all of which need be exploited as messages, is N^n, and the signal space of this code is formed by an n-dimensional cube consisting of N^n points. For a binary code combining three digits, this cube is three-dimensional; it is shown in Fig. 3.1b, p.56 ($N = 2$, $n = 3$, so that the cube consists of $2^3 = 8$ points). Some or all of these points may correspond to messages. In the example discussed on p. 58 (aircraft off course right or left), only two of the eight points corresponded to messages, all other points were left meaningless in order to facilitate restoration of a distorted message. In general, let there be K such points used as messages, leaving $N^n - K$ points empty. Then we can define the ratio

$$\eta = \frac{K}{N^n} \tag{2}$$

so that (obviously)

$$0 \leq \eta \leq 1 \tag{3}$$

When we mentioned this ratio previously, without having explicitly defined it, we called it the *efficiency* of the code, or the *coding efficiency*, for that is what a conceptually closely related quantity is called in coding theory. However, efficiency is a word that generally denotes a desirable property, and a high coding efficiency is, with rare exceptions, very undesirable, as it lowers the noise resistance of the code. We shall therefore find an alternative name useful, and we shall also call η as given by (2) the *exploitation*, since it is representative of the degree to which the code exploits the available points in signal space for transmitting its messages, leaving the remaining points meaningless, empty, or unexploited.

In many codes, including natural languages, different messages combine a different number N of code elements. In that case K, and hence also η, are functions of N.

The code described at the beginning of this section has an exploitation of 100%, since all four possible combinations are assigned a meaning. The code described on p. 56 uses only 2 of the 8 points of the cube, so that its exploitation is only 25%. A traffic light combines its messages in space rather than in time (top, center, bottom rather than first, second, third). If we disregard the colors, which only identify the position of the element in the group, there are only two code elements (on or off), so that the signal space consists of a three-dimensional cube with 8 points, of which only three (top on, center on, bottom on, the others always off) are used in the U.S., yielding an exploitation of

$\eta = 3/8 = 37.5\%$. In Britain, the amber lights up by itself after green ("leave intersection"), but together with the red before a green ("get ready to go"), yielding an exploitation of 50%. The combinations red-green or red-green-amber are unexploited. On the other hand, if we do not regard the colors as merely an identification of position, but ask what could be done with four elements (red, amber, green, off) in three positions, the signal space would consist of a three-dimensional cube with $4^3 = 64$ points, of which only 3 in the U.S., and 4 in Britain, are exploited, yielding an exploitation of only 4.68% and 6.24%, respectively. This would take into account that such signals as red in the center or green on top (with whatever combinations of the other two lights) are never used.

For natural languages it would be very tedious, though not in principle impossible, to measure the exploitation directly. It is doubtful that such an undertaking would be worth the effort, since the effort would be very great, even if computerized. However, we shall be able to estimate the relative exploitation of different languages indirectly, e.g., by comparing translations, i.e., different languages coding the same events.

3.2. Formal and Semantic Decoding in the Presence of Noise

We have hitherto assumed that the message transmitted by the coder reaches the receiver without distortion in the transmission channel. This is, in fact, rarely the case. Physical deficiencies of the transmission system, unreliable re-coders, and other factors will often change a message to a form which the receiver is unable to decode (i.e., to which the receiver can assign no event of the semantic base or meaning) or worse, to a form corresponding to a different event, so that the receiver misinterprets it (assigns the wrong meaning to it, decodes it incorrectly).

All factors causing the distortion of a message are collectively known as *noise* in information and coding theory. The word comes from the most commonly met cause of distortion in electrical channels, namely random voltages due to the thermal agitation of electric charges in some conductors of the communication equipment (thermal noise), electrical discharges in the atmosphere (atmospheric noise), and thermal noise from space radiated into the beam of the receiving antenna (cosmic noise). When the corresponding voltages and currents are amplified (together with the signal) and converted to sound by an electro-acoustic converter such as a loudspeaker, they are perceived as a background of crackling, hissing and rustling, hence the name "noise." The signal-to-noise ratio in telephones or commercial broadcasting is nowadays so high that the average citizen is not very familiar with this type of noise; however, it cannot be missed in listening to the voice of the dispatcher in the radio of a taxi.

But apart from the historical origin of the word, we need not go into further details of this type of noise. For more generally, *noise* means any type of signals (meaningful or meaningless) which enter the channel in other ways than direct coding and which are prone to distort the original message. Thus, noise is not only the actual noise of a motorcycle passing by and making it difficult or impossible to understand what a speaker using a natural language is saying; a misprint by a typist who is recoding a message is also noise; the lisp or other speech impediment that makes one unsure whether the speaker meant to say *sink* or *think* is noise; fog that makes signs badly legible or illegible at a distance is noise; the text transpiring from the other side of a page printed on insufficiently opaque paper is noise; etc. In short, noise is anything that, when raised to a sufficiently high level, will cause the received messages to be undecodable (meaningless), ambiguous, or misinterpreted.

We shall find it convenient to make four exceptions to this statement, that is, to exclude four types of what would otherwise also be noise from this definition. Two of them we have already met. The unreliability of a coder (not re-coder) is a type of noise, since its messages are ambiguous. This type of ambiguity we have already taken care of by our definition of the credibility of a message (Sec. 2.6). Similarly, at the receiving end, a perfectly undistorted message may be ambiguous or meaningless for the receiver owing to his insufficient knowledge (see p. 31 on the impedance of free space). This is taken care of by the fact that the receiver assigns the probability of the coded event not objectively, but according to his own knowledge.

The third exception is one which we will discuss in more detail later, since it is one that particularly concerns natural languages, namely, the ambiguity of undistorted messages. Ambiguity may be the result of an unreliable coder or to distortion in the channel; but it may also be due to the code itself. A code may be so structured that the same combination of code elements corresponds to two or more events. Examples are to be found in many codes, but they are particularly abundant in natural languages. Any ambiguous sentence (as, for example, shown by two possible phrase marker trees in Chomsky's grammar) is an example. *We were not allowed to criticize his speech, which was unfair* is one of very many such examples. This type of ambiguity is highly interesting for the linguist, and we shall discuss it more fully in Chapters 4 and 5.

The fourth case of noise which we shall find convenient to exempt from the general category of noise is ambiguity due to the transmission rate being too high (or in the case of a code that combines elements in space rather than in time, due to the density of the elements being too high). Even when no other type of noise is present, there comes a point when the receiver can no longer decode the messages of a code, because

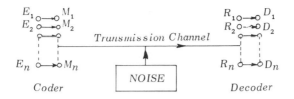

Fig. 3.3. Transmission of information in the
presence of noise

it is being transmitted too fast. Anyone familiar with the Morse code,
for example, can decode it when only one letter per second is being
transmitted; the world record of receiving Morse code is about 500 letters per minute. At some intermediate rate, the receiver will begin to
make mistakes in decoding, so that the message will become ambiguous.
Similarly, for codes combining their elements in space, such as print,
the receiver who would otherwise decode it correctly will begin to obtain ambiguous messages when the density becomes too large (the print too
fine).

   Our model of the transmission system, which was previously given
by Fig. 2.1 for a noiseless system, now includes a source of noise. This
will result in the possibility of the message M_i being distorted into a
received combination of code elements R_j (which may or may not be a
meaningful one). The general model of such a system is shown in Fig.
3.3. As before, the channel may include re-coders (such as microphones,
telephone receivers, typists, interpreters, etc.).

   On receiving a message R_i, the receiver is now left in doubt as to
the event that was (or should have been) originally coded, because the
received message could be due to some other transmitted message having been distorted by the noise in the channel. This doubt is increased
if the transmitter is unreliable and the code ambiguous.

   Let the event E_i be coded by a reliable transmitter as the message
M_i (not M_j), and let this message after being transmitted through a noiseless channel be received as R_i. If the coder is unreliable and the channel noisy, neither of these results is certain; in general, the probability
that a received message R_i implies that the corresponding event E_i
really has occurred is

$$P(E_i \mid R_i) = P(E_i \mid M_i) P(M_i \mid R_i) \tag{1}$$

   The first factor of the product on the right is already known to us; it
is the reliability of the coder. The second factor,

$$P(M_i \mid R_i) \tag{2}$$

might be called the reliability of the channel. However, as we shall see, this probability depends not only on the channel, but also on the type of code, and since we will be more interested in codes (natural languages) than in the channel technology, we shall call this quantity the (formal) noise resistance of the code. The "formal" refers to the ease with which formal, not semantic, decoding of a mutilated message can be performed, a point to which we will return presently.

Relation (1) takes no account of the possibility of mutual compensation between unreliability of the coder and distortion by noise in the channel, such as a witness perjuring himself and the court stenographer recording the truth by mistake. This would be quite easy to incorporate (by changing the subscripts of M on the right to j and summing the entire expression over all j), but the probability of compensation is so small that we shall simply ignore it.

In order to calculate the noise resistance of the code (2), we note that the effect of noise is always to degrade the receiver's ability of distinguishing certain elements of the code, and thereby introducing uncertainty as to what was really transmitted. In the absence f noise, we can distinguish English syllables from each other. A comparatively low noise level, however, suffices to make it impossible to distinguish between *dim* and *din* (transmitted by themselves), even though both can still be distinguished from *child*. As the noise level increases, a point will be reached where not even *child* can be distinguished from *din*, and eventually the noise level can become so high that no syllable can be distinguished from the pause (silence), so that communication is totally interrupted.

We will characterize the noise entering the channel from this point of view. Let the noise be such that the elements of the code merge (become indistinguishable for the receiver) in groups containing (on the average) σ elements. Where the receiver could, without noise, distinguish the distinct points marked along an axis in signal space, he will now be able to distinguish only segments carrying several such points. For example, if the code is (spoken) English, and the noise is actual acoustic noise, the receiver might not be able to distinguish the syllables *dim, din, tim, tin*; they would merge into a single group that could be distinguished from other groups, but resolution inside the group would not be possible. Let us define the *resolution* (definition, resolving power) as

$$D = 1/\sigma \tag{3}$$

If the code is made up of N elements, we obviously have

$$1/N \leq D \leq 1 \tag{4}$$

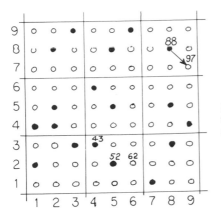

Fig. 3.4. Distortion of messages in transmission. The full circles represent messages, the empty circles meaningless combinations.

A resolving power D thus implies a decrease of the number of distinguishable elements from N (original elements) to DN (groups of elements).

We assume that the elements merge in equally long segments along the coordinate axes in signal space, i.e., that each resolvable group contains the same number of elements. We also assume that the merging is the same along all coordinate axes (i.e., that the noise is constant in time or space). Finally, we assume that the groups of uncertainty have sharp and distinct boundaries in signal space.

None of these assumptions is very realistic, but they can be withdrawn at the price of more sophisticated mathematics in the following. But as we do not want to lose the essentials in a mass of refinements, nor to include long calculations in this sketch, we will accept these assumptions to keep things simple.

Let us illustrate the merging of the elements into groups and the resultant procedure of decoding by the following simple example. Let the number of code elements be $N = 9$, and let each message be made up of $n = 2$ elements, so that the resulting signal space is a square of 81 points as shown in Fig. 3.4. Let us denote the elements by 1 through 9, and let this correspond to their order of similarity (1 and 9 are the most dissimilar elements). The black dots correspond to messages, the empty circles are "empty" points in signal space, i.e., meaningless combinations of code elements. Let the noise be such that the elements merge in groups of three, dividing the signal space of this code into nine domains of uncertainty. Suppose the message 88 has actually been transmitted, and that the channel noise has distorted this into the combination 97 lying in the same domain, and this is what the receiver receives. If the code had an exploitation of 100%, the receiver would get the wrong message. However, in the case shown in Fig. 3.2, the exploitation is less than 100%, and the combination 97 is assigned no meaning, enabling the re-receiver to *detect* that an error has occurred. Moreover, since for the assumed noise level the domain of uncertainty containing the meaningless combination 97 contains only a single meaningful message, namely, 88, the receiver can also *correct* the error, i.e., restore the original message; under the conditions shown in Fig. 3.4, no other message but 88 could have resulted in the meaningless combination 97. Of course, if the noise level is sufficiently high, or the exploitation of the code sufficiently great — either case resulting in several messages being contained in the same domain of uncertainty — the reception of a meaningless combination will only enable the error to be detected, not corrected. Even so, the possibilities of what the originally transmitted message could have been are limited to only a few messages lying within the given domain of uncertainty. For example, in Fig. 3.4, reception of the meaningless combination 62 implies that either 52 or 43 must have been transmitted, for these are the only messages in the same domain. The receiver is not helpless in deciding which of the two messages is more likely the genuine one. He has two very different criterions to go by: *the formal similarity of the messages, and the probabilities of the events that these messages code.* The former concerns the formal structure of the signal (which is the subject of orthodox coding theory); the second concerns the *meaning* of the message. If only the first criterion were important, the receiver would, on receiving 62, decode to 52, which is separated by a shorter distance, and therefore closer in form. From this point of view, on reading the non-existent word *plam* in English text, a reader (receiver) might decode to *plan* rather than to *pine*; however, if *plam* occurred in a list of trees, he might be more inclined to decode to *pine*, using meaning as well as formal similarity to restore the original message.

The above considerations and Fig. 3.4 also make it obvious that the higher the exploitation of a code (the higher the density of black dots in Fig. 3.4), the less noise-resistant a code must be. Conversely, to make a code noise-resistant, it is not sufficient merely to keep the number of messages small compared to the number of meaningless combinations; we must also distribute these messages in signal space as widely separated from each other as possible. As we shall see later, natural languages do this to a remarkable degree.

Let us now formulate the above ideas mathematically.

Let the code elements merge in groups of σ elements; then a code using combinations of n elements as messages will have domains of uncertainty in n-dimensional space, each domain containing σ^n points, of which $\eta\sigma^n$ are messages, and $(1 - \eta)\sigma^n$ are meaningless combinations of code elements, where η is the exploitation of the code.

Let a signal R_j (which might be either a message or a meaningless combination) be received. Let us "test the hypothesis" (find the probability under the given circumstances) that the originally transmitted message was M_i. By Bayes' Theorem, (11), Sec. 2.2, we have

$$P(M_i \mid R_j) = \frac{P(R_j \mid M_i) \, P(M_i)}{\sum_k P(R_j \mid M_k) P(M_k)}$$

$$= \frac{1}{1 + \dfrac{\sum\limits_{k \neq i} P(R_j \mid M_k) \, P(M_k)}{P(R_j \mid M_i) \, P(M_i)}} \tag{5}$$

Now $P(R_j \mid M_k)$ is the probability that R_j is received given that M_k was transmitted. Since by our simplifying assumption all distortions within a domain of uncertainty are equiprobable, we have

$$P(R_j \mid M_k) = 1/\sigma^n \tag{6}$$

where σ^n is the number of points in the domain. Also, the sum in (5) has positive terms only for the k corresponding to points of meaningful messages, since $P(M_k) = 0$ otherwise. The number of such points is $\eta \sigma^n$; and since the sum excludes the point $k = i$, the number of terms in the sum is

$$\eta \sigma^n - 1 \tag{7}$$

Denoting the arithmetic mean by angular brackets averaging over the probabilities of all messages M_k in the domain, and substituting (7) and (6) in (5), we have

$$P(M_i \mid R_j) = \frac{1}{1 + A} \tag{9}$$

where

$$A = A(M_i) = \frac{(\eta \sigma^n - 1) \, <P(M_k)>}{P(M_i)} \tag{10}$$

is the *ambiguity* of the message M_i thus decoded. It is easily shown from (10) that the ambiguity is non-negative.

To gain insight into this quantity, let us temporarily suppose that the transmission of all messages M_k in the domain is equally likely. Then

$$<P(M_k)> = P(M_k) \quad \text{for all } k$$

and (10) yields

$$A(M_i) = \eta \sigma^n - 1 \tag{11}$$

From this it follows that the ambiguity vanishes, and therefore by (9) the noise resistance of the code is 100%, only if

$$\eta \sigma^n = 1 \tag{12}$$

i.e., if there is a single message in each domain of uncertainty. Using (3), we can also write (12) as

$$\eta = D^n \tag{13}$$

from which it follows that a code with 100% exploitation can be 100% noise resistant only if the resolution $D = 1$.

In general, the number of messages in a domain of uncertainty is

$$\eta \sigma^n \geq 1 \tag{14}$$

so that by (11)

$$A(M_i) \geq 0 \tag{15}$$

Numerically, the ambiguity is equal to the number of possibly transmitted messages in excess of one.

The number of neighboring code elements merged by the noise is σ, and unless we can control the noise (which is rarely the case), we can lower the ambiguity, as shown by (10), only by decreasing the exploitation η.

When we design an artificial code, we can, of course, manipulate the exploitation as we please. But do we have any control over η in a natural language? To some extent, we do. For many codes, and certainly for natural languages, η is a function of n; moreover, for natural languages, which allow only some combinations of syllables as words, and only some combinations of words as sentences, $\eta(n)$ is a (rapidly) decreasing function of n:

$$\partial \eta / \partial n < 0 \tag{16}$$

One way of lowering the exploitation is therefore simply to code messages made up of more elements. The words *United States of America* are obviously more noise-resistant than the abbreviation *U.S.A.*, and the 13-letter combination *seven dollars* in written English is surely more noise-resistant than the two-letter combination *$7*. Other implications of exploitation and noise resistance for natural languages will be discussed in the next chapter.

But all of our discussion up to this point involves merely the formal structure of the received message, and the resolution of an ambiguity on that basis. This is the approach of the communication engineer, who usually does not know the meaning of the messages transmitted through the channel for which he is responsible. Yet this formal type of decoding is only the smaller part of the process of decoding a distorted message when that message has been transmitted in a natural language (or, for matter, in any other code, provided the receiver knows what the message is likely to concern). Consider, for example, the distorted printed message *He worked as a uidow cleaner*, which does not occupy a point in the signal space of grammatical English, and therefore indicates that an error (misprint) must have occurred in transmission. The nearest occupied point in signal space is probably the message *He worked as a widow cleaner*, and this is what *formal* decoding would lead us to. Yet few people would actually restore the distorted message in this way, for they know that cleaning *widows* is a very improbable occupation, whereas cleaning *windows* is much more probable; they would therefore restore (decode to) *He worked as a window cleaner*, even though this is not the message nearest to the received signal in signal space (where messages are distributed with respect only to their formal similarity, quite regardless of their meanings). We shall call this type of decoding *semantic* decoding to distinguish it from *formal* decoding. Semantic decoding is the more powerful of the two methods; the message *He worked as a widow cleaner* is a grammatical sentence and therefore occupies a message point in signal space, giving no warning of a misprint by its *formal* structure; yet the event coded by this message is so improbable that most people will recognize (or at least suspect) a misprint.

The resolution of an ambiguity by both formal and semantic decoding can be mathematically described as follows. The expression (11) and the following considerations applied to the case when all messages in the given domain were equiprobable, i.e., these considerations concerned only the noise resistance of the formal structure of the message, not its actual meaning. The additional factor $<P(M_k)>/P(M_i)$ that distinguishes the general expression (11) from its special case (10) is, in fact, what is used for semantic decoding. To see this, let us assume that the coder is perfectly reliable, so that

$$P(M_k) = P(E_k) \qquad \text{for all } k \tag{17}$$

Then the ambiguity of a received message coding the event E_i is by (10)

$$A(M_i) = \frac{(\eta\sigma^n - 1)<P(E_k)>}{P(E_i)} \tag{18}$$

where $<P(E_k)>$ is the mean probability of the events coded by all messages lying in the domain of uncertainty. The probabilities of these events are, of course, assigned by the receiver independently of the noise in the channel, and as before, they are assigned by the receiver on the basis of his knowledge. With sufficient knowledge, the receiver can often reduce the ambiguity of a received signal to zero by decoding it semantically, where formal decoding (to the nearest point in signal space) would leave a positive ambiguity.

This is best explained by another example. Let the code be printed English, the code elements the letters of the English alphabet, and let the noise take the form of misprints. Suppose we receive (read) the following signal: *The XY observatory measures the sun's radiation at a frequency of 1.1 MIGAHERTZ*. This signal is a meaningless combination of code elements, since there is no such word as *migahertz*; the nearest words (in signal space) are either *megahertz* or *gigahertz*, and the signal becomes a meaningful message if either of these is restored.

For simplicity, we will assume that this is the only error (involving one of two letters) that has occurred. This would correspond to a domain of uncertainty of $2^2 = 4$ points given by the combinations containing ... *mega...*, *...giga...*, *...miga...*, *...gega...*, of which only the first two are messages. Let E_1 and E_2 be the events of the observatory measuring the radiation at 1.1 megahertz and 1.1 gigahertz, respectively. With $\eta = 0.5$ and $\sigma = 2$ in the domain of uncertainty, the ambiguity of each of the corresponding messages M_1 and M_2 is from (18)

$$A = (4 \times 0.5 - 1) < P(E_k) > / P(E_i) \qquad (i = 1, 2) \qquad (19)$$

Now if the signal is decoded only with respect to its formal structure, or by a receiver who has no knowledge of the sun's radiation, then

$$P(E_1) = P(E_2) \qquad (20)$$

making the ambiguity of both messages A equal to one, and the channel reliability 50%; that is, either message (about the radiation of 1.1 megahertz or 1.1 gigahertz) is considered equally likely to be the correct one.

However, the receiver familiar with electromagnetic radiation will know that the sun's radiation at 1.1 megahertz is screened off by the earth's ionosphere, so that it cannot reach the earth's surface. His knowledge tells him that $P(E_1) = 0$, which makes $P(E_2) = 1$; under these circumstances, (19) yields an ambiguity of zero for the message $M_2 = $ *The XY Observatory measures the sun's radiation at 1.1 GIGAhertz.*

The receiver, incidentally, need not know so much about the sun's radiation as to realize that $P(E_1) = 0$; it is sufficient if his knowledge tells him that

$$P(E_2) \gg P(E_1)$$

which is sufficient to decode the signal almost unequivocally.

There are thousands of other examples of semantic decoding. A garbled telegram can most easily be decoded by the receiver for whom

it was intended, since he will not decode it only by the probabilities
of formal distortion, but by the probabilities of the possible meanings.
No one could decode the words of a bellowing drill sergeant without
knowing that a drill sergeant is choosing from a limited set of orders;
no one could decode an American auctioneer's machinegun-like rattle
without semantic decoding; and no one would decode the signal *Outside!*
as the message *Hold tight!* without knowing that it was transmitted by
a London bus conductor at a bus stop before signaling the driver to
move on.

The ambiguity as given by (18) is in certain respects analogous to
Shannon's *equivocation*, but it differs from the latter in several respects,
two of which are: 1) The ambiguity is determined by the semantic significance of the message, not only by its formal structure and the corresponding distortion probabilities; 2) it is assigned to each message individually, whereas Shannon's equivocation is determined by the statistical mean of all possible messages.

The concept of ambiguity is easily generalized for the case of an
unreliable coder. However, this would take us too far from our goal of
studying the structure of Language, and we therefore omit this point.

3.3. Information Density and Message Volume

Let a message consist of n elements of a code, and let its information content be I. Then we define

$$H = I/n \tag{1}$$

as the *information density* or the *compactness* of the message. For example, the message *It's a boy!* delivered to the father in a maternity
hospital has an information density or compactness of $(-\log \frac{1}{2})/3 =$
0.1003 semantic units per syllable (assuming the message to be perfectly credible); the same message, if printed or written, would have a
compactness of 0.0274 semantic units per letter (the space is, as usual,
counted as a letter).

Information density is a quantity which is important from at least
three aspects.

First, it is a convenient measure for comparing different codes, in
particular, different natural languages. It is, for example, not easy to
determine the numerical value of the information content of the message
My aunt arrived today, for the reasons discussed in Sec. 2.5.1. It is,
however, very easy to measure the *relative compactness* of two messages
coding the same event in different codes, i.e.,

$$H_{xy} = H_x/H_y \tag{2}$$

where H_x and H_y are the information densities of the messages coding the same event in code X and code Y. In the case of the message *My aunt arrived today*, we can compare it to the German message *Meine Tante ist heute angekommen*; if both information densities are expressed in semantic units per syllable, the relative compactness of the German message (relative to English) is 54.5% (6 English syllables for 11 German syllables). Similarly, the equivalent Russian statement Моя тетка приехала сегодня also has a relative compactness of 54.5% with respect to English; the equivalent Czech statement has a relative compactness of 85.7%, etc. In each case English is used as the standard with a relative compactness of 100%.

The second reason why information density is important is that a receiver can understand a message only up to a certain value of the information density; beyond this value he can no longer decode it. The critical point varies for different messages and different receivers; but such a point can usually be identified for a given message and a given receiver. This can perhaps be seen most easily by noting that the action of *defining* or *explaining* a message (or even a word or phrase) in the vast majority of cases amounts to reducing the information density of the message. The message *White is stalemated* means the same, and therefore has the same information content, as the message *It is the turn of the chessplayer with the white stones to make a move, but he can make no legal move, and his king is not checked, i.e., not under attack.* The second message, which has 37 syllables, is understandable to most English speaking persons, even if they are not chess players; the first, which has only 5 syllables, can probably be decoded only by English speaking chess players. The *explanation* of the message involves a reduction in information density by a factor of more than 7 (if measured in semantic units per syllable). Similarly, the statement *x is a prime* can be decoded by fewer English speaking persons than the equivalent message *x is a positive integer which is divisible without remainder by no other positive integer than itself or unity.* The explanation, or definition, involves a reduction in information density. The message *QDM 210* is decodable only by persons familiar with the Q code (a code used in air traffic); it can be explained to persons familiar with both English and navigation by the less compact message *Your magnetic course is 210 degrees*, and to persons familiar with English, but not with navigation, by the even less compact message *The direction in which you are flying makes an angle of 210°, measured clockwise, with the direction of the needle of an unperturbed compass.* Hundreds of other examples could be given; in fact, "learning," whether from our parents at an early age or in schools later on, consists to a remarkable degree of learning to decode messages (and words) with an increasingly high information density. Psychologists have found that it is possible to explain the concept *horizon* to a ten-year old child on a single trial, whereas it is impossible to explain it to a four year old, because the latter does not know the components of the explanation.*

There are, of course, exceptions. *My father's only child* is quite evidently less simple to decode than the single word *I*; and if it were possible to give a unique definition of *window*, it would probably be less clear what is meant, though certainly the information density would be reduced. Similarly, legalistic and medical obfuscations of perfectly simple matters always have a very low information density. However, these are rather exceptional cases where the reduction in information density is self-serving and carried to extremes; the more usual tendency is the one outlined above, where "explaining" is practically equivalent to reducing the compactness of the message.

Whilst information content can be associated only with a message as a whole, information density is evidently associated with individual words and phrases, for the information density is not uniformly distributed over the message. In the message *It's a boy!* almost all of the information is concentrated in the word *boy*; the message could easily be restored and decoded if the words *It's* were obliterated by noise.

The third reason for introducing the information density concerns the rate of transmission of code elements, i.e., the speed with which messages can be transmitted if the code combines its elements in time (e.g., spoken language), or the density with which the code elements are concentrated in space if it combines the elements in space (e.g., printed language). This rate of transmitting code elements and the information density jointly determine the rate of transmitting information. The rate of transmitting information is a concept of central importance for the communication engineer, who designs and processes the formal structure of the signal in such a way as to maximize it. For the linguist, it might seem, this characteristic is unimportant, for few linguists are interested in the speed with which people talk. However, the rate of transmitting information does not depend merely on the formal frequency of syllables uttered per unit time; it also depends on how much information is contained in the message, i.e., on its meaning. If someone is "beating around the bush," his rate of transmitting information is small, no matter how fast he talks. A Chinese speaker utters fewer syllables per second than his simultaneous English interpreter, who is transmitting information at the same rate. Various languages use various devices to manipulate the rate of transmitting information, and the question of maximum attainable transmission rate therefore throws considerable light on the structure of codes,

---

* J. Kagan and E. Haveman, *Psychology — an introduction*, Harcourt, Brace & World, New York, 1968.

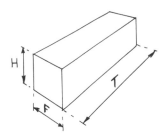

Fig. 3.5. The signal volume.

including natural languages. True, in communication engineering, the results of orthodox information theory can often be used for the actual calculation and prediction of the properties of the optimum signal. On the other hand, the result that we will obtain below will never *teach* people how to write editorials or other communications using Language; but it does provide some insight into what is going on when, say, an advertiser is making maximum use of the space he has bought to convey some information.

Consider a message whose duration in time is T, or if it uses a spatial code, whose code elements occupy a space of T units. Let the message be formed by n code elements; then the rate (or density, for a spatial code) at which these elements are transmitted is

$$F = n/T \tag{3}$$

code elements per unit time (or per unit space, such as cm, cm^2 or cm^3). We now define the *volume* of the message as

$$V = FTH \tag{4}$$

where H is the information density (1). The message or signal volume is actually the same thing as the information content of the message, as follows from the identity

$$I \equiv \frac{n}{T} \times T \times \frac{I}{n} \tag{5}$$

obtained by substituting (1) and (3) in (4). There is, nevertheless, a good resason for writing the information content of the message in this way and giving it the name "volume." Let us represent the volume (4) by the volume of a prism with sides F, T, H (Fig. 3.5).

In our theory, the information content of a message is entirely independent of the code in which it is transmitted. The information contained in the message *Your magnetic course is 210 degrees* remains the same no matter whether it is expressed in English, the Q code, Braille or Cherokee. The volume of this message, that is, the volume of the prism shown in Fig. 3.5, is therefore constant and independent of the code.

However, the shape of the prism, i.e., the length of its edges, is given by the three factors on the right side of (5), and each of these factors depends on the code used to transmit the message. In particular, the compactness of the message changes with the code; the German message *Ihr magnetischer Kurs ist 210 Grad* has a slightly higher information density, and if the frequency of syllables per second is the same, its duration is slightly shorter. If the coder speaks more slowly, in English or German, he is still conveying the same information, but the edge F is shortened at the expense of lengthening the duration T, again leaving the volume constant. In the Q code, the message *QDM 217* (invariably transmitted in Morse) has a very high information density H, but the frequency of Morse code (in letters per second) is rather slow, making the duration T of the signal long, and once more keeping the volume constant. The same message always has the same volume, but the shape of that volume changes for different codes.

We may therefore imagine the signal prism in Fig. 3.5 to be made of some plastic, but incompressible material; we may deform it to another prism of any shape we please (by using different codes and different transmission rates), but we cannot alter the total volume (the information) of a message coding a particular event.

The volume only changes from message to message, since some messages contain much information, others very little. In other words, the volume of the message is determined by *what* a speaker says, that is, by the events he is coding; its shape depends on *how* he says it — in English or Russian, loquatiously or concisely, and talking slowly or quickly. *My father's daughter perspired* has the same volume as *My sister sweated*, but the signal prism is higher and shorter in the latter case.

The signal volume is particularly useful for illustrating the decoding capacity of the receiver, a concept to be discussed in the next section. However, it can also provide us with a little insight for problems like maximizing the information conveyed by a message which is subject to certain constraints. Consider, for example, a message transmitted by an advertisement in print. We are thinking of an old-fashioned advertisement promising certain properties of the advertised product, not the meaningless lyrics of the type "Come alive! You're in the Pepsi generation," which are concerned with image building and associations rather than conveying information about the advertised product. Let the code be a printed natural language, say, English. Two of the three dimensions of the signal prism are more or less predetermined: The space (area) T is determined by how much space the advertiser buys in the medium; the frequency (spatial density) of transmission F is determined by the size of the print, and this is chosen as high as possible (fine print) without dissuading the reader from reading it. (The numerical value of the density F can be found from the line length, type face, point size and leading by simple arithmetic on which we will not waste time. You are now reading 10 point type; the type used in advertisements is rarely less than 7, and never less than 5 points.)

This leaves the copy writer only the information density H to be manipulated. He will (unconsciously, of course) seek to maximize it in order to maximize the signal volume. Since $H = I/n$, this means minimizing the number of code elements and maximizing the transmitted information. The number of code elements n is kept small by using short words instead of long ones whenever there is a choice. No copy writer will use the words *contemplate, procrastinate* or *anticipate* when *think, delay* or *expect* will do just as well. The number of code elements can also be reduced by transmitting incomplete sentences such as *Widely acclaimed as America's best laxative*, leaving the receiver to restore the omitted words *This product is*. Similarly, *Money back if not satisfied* is one of thousands of such ungrammatical statements (messages not admitted by the rules of the code), which the receiver can easily decode by restoring (if he wishes) the missing words.

The other possibility, maximizing the information, can be achieved by maximizing the parameters which increase the information of the message. Apart from the receiver's interest (which is usually captured by the headline and the photograph), this is the improbability of the events that are being coded, and the credibility of the coder (the manufacturer of the product or his advertising agency). Almost any advertisement stresses (in effect) the low probability, or the unusual circumstances, of the bargain being offered; it claims (in effect) that any product having such good properties or low price is an unusual event. It does this by exclamations such as *Now! At last! Special! The bargain of a lifetime!* etc., by adjectives such as *unique, unbelievable, wonderful, sensational,* and by other means. On the other hand, the very fact that advertisements code events with low probabilities leads to a loss of credibility (Sec. 2.6), which the advertiser seeks to restore by testimonials (direct, or indirect such as a US Patent number, statistics of sales, etc.), offering a money-back guarantee, etc.

Of course, the advertisement that contains the most information is not the one that "pulls" most customers; however, a high information content is surely one of the requirements of an effective advertisement. Nor is it claimed, even remotely, that a copy writer consciously seeks to increase the signal volume; but that is what he is doing (to a large extent), though he does so by experience, intuition, and the use of certain professional rules rather than by referring to the model of communication described here.

3.4. Decoding Capacity

The representation of the information contained in a message by a prism made of plastic, but incompressible material is useful for determining the maximum rate (or maximum density in space) at which information can be transmitted to a receiver through a given channel. We will call this maximum rate the decoding capacity of the receiver. In information theory, the analogous quantity is called the channel capacity.

It should be pointed out here that in Shannon's information theory, the concept of channel capacity plays a central role, and Shannon's Channel Capacity Theorem is probably the most brilliant result of his theory. One of its rather surprising consequences is that it is possible to encode information in such a way that the information can be transmitted *reliably* through an *unreliable* channel. For the communication engineer, whose job it is to transmit information with maximum speed, economy, and reliability, Shannon's Channel Capacity Theorem is (by now) something like the law of the conservation of energy for the physicist, or the survival of the fittest for the biologist. However, the communication engineer is not interested in the actual information that is transmitted by the codes and through the channels he has designed – this is, as it were, not under his jurisdiction. There is something pathetic about the way in which the technology of, say, television is engineered to make the transmission of information steadily more reliable and economic, whilst simultaneously the contents of the transmission (the programs) descend ever lower into Madison Avenue's bottomless sewer.

For the linguist, the achievable *rate* of transmitting information is of considerably less interest. Nevertheless, it does have a bearing on the structure of Language (as we shall see in the next chapter), and we shall attempt to derive a relation for the maximum information that can be transmitted through a noisy channel; this relation is in some respects analogous to Shannon's Channel Capacity Theorem, though it differs from it both formally and in significance.

We have already noted that a receiver can decode a message only up to a certain level of the information density; we observed this when we discussed such messages as *White is stalemated*. Similarly, there is a limiting frequency of code elements per second (or per unit space) beyond which a receiver is unable to decode the messages; to follow a speaker who is rattling off his messages at the rate of 10 syllables a second is extremely difficult, and most people cannot (and certainly are unwilling to) read type of less than 5 points. (The point size is, of course, also a measure of the number of characters per inch, though it is not so defined.) This book is printed in 10 point type; 5 point type looks like this:

524 N. Michigan Ave. ● 62 E. Randolph St. ● 16 S. La Salle St.
1723 Sherman Ave., Evanston ● North Mall, Old Orchard
1028 Lake Street, Oak Park ● Oakbrook Center
Evergreen Plaza ● River Oaks

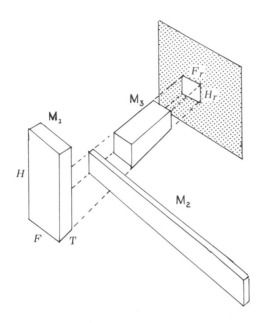

Fig. 3.6. Message volume and decoding screen.

We can represent these two limiting factors by a screen with a rectangular aperture of dimensions H_r and F_r, corresponding, respectively, to the limiting information density and frequency for which the receiver can still decode a message in a certain code. He has to be familiar with the code, of course, so we might label the screen, for example, "French." As depicted in Fig. 3.6, the receiver is able to decode a message only if the signal prism is of a shape that will pass through the aperture in the screen, i.e., the message must be so encoded that its information density H and its frequency in code elements per unit time (or space) F satisfy the relations

$$H \leq H_r \tag{1}$$

$$F \leq F_r \tag{2}$$

It is assumed that the receiver has unlimited time to decode the message, so that no requirement is imposed on its duration.

For a noiseless channel, the receiver can decode the message (assign the corresponding event of the semantic base to it, understand its meaning) if he is familiar with the code, and if conditions (1) and (2) are satisfied. For example, if the message M_1 in Fig. 3.6 is formed by the English words *White is stalemated* (to use the same example again), the average English speaking receiver, who is not a chess player, will fail to decode the message, because the information density is too high; the prism cannot pass through the window in the "English" screen. If now the message M_2 = *It is the turn of the chess player with the white stones to move, but he cannot make a legal move, and his king is not checked, that is, his king is not under attack* is transmitted, the information density H will (usually) be sufficiently reduced for the receiver to understand it, i.e., the vertical dimension of the prism is sufficiently small to pass through the window of the screen. However, if the duration of the message – say, two seconds – is left unchanged, i.e., the message M_2 is rattled off in two seconds, the receiver still would not be able to decode the message, because its frequency F (syllables per second) would be too high to satisfy (2). The way to pass the signal prism through the window, i.e., to enable the receiver to decode the message, is to leave the frequency unchanged (talk sufficiently slowly), and to reduce the information density H at the expense of the duration T of the message. In all three cases the volume of the message prism is the same, since each of the messages codes the same event.

Now consider the more interesting case when the message is transmitted through a noisy channel, that is, a channel that may distort the the original message for any reason, such as acoustical noise, human error, malfunctioning of electrical channels, etc. Let the code be composed of N distinct elements; then the number of combinations of not more than n elements each is

$$W = N + N^2 + N^3 + \dots + N^n = \sum_{i=1}^{n} N^i \tag{3}$$

If the exploitation of the code is less than 100%, not all of these combinations are messages; the number of messages is only

$$U = \eta_1 N + \eta_2 N^2 + \dots + \eta_n N^n = \sum_{i=1}^{n} \eta_i N^i \tag{4}$$

where η_i is the exploitation of the combinations made up of i elements.

We can rid ourselves of the sum by including a null element in the N code elements (see p. 63). The null element is, however, not counted in assessing the frequency F of transmitting code elements. Then instead of (3) we have

$$W = N^n \tag{5}$$

and instead of (4),

$$U = \eta N^n \tag{6}$$

where $\eta = \eta_n$.

In both cases, n is the maximum number of elements that are combined to form a message.

If the code is not ambiguous, the number of messages U given by (6) is also the maximum number of events that can be coded by this code; it is not necessarily equal to the number of events in the semantic base, because many codes (especially languages) can use several different messages to code the same event (I *must go* — I *have to go*). However, for simplicity, we will assume that the U messages in (6) correspond to U different events, all of which are equiprobable, incompatible and exhaustive. Then the probability of each event in this semantic base is

$$P(E_i) = 1/U \tag{7}$$

For a reliable coder, the information density of a message is then

$$H = I/n = (-\log \eta N^n)/n \tag{8}$$

Now let the channel be noisy, so that in accordance with Sec. 3.2 the resolution D, given by (3), p. 68, decreases from 1 to $1/\sigma$, where σ is the average number of code elements that become indistinguishable from each other. As we know from Sec. 3.2, the resulting garbled message (meaningless combination of code elements) can be uniquely decoded if

$$\eta \leqq D^n \tag{9}$$

If (9) is not satisfied, the ambiguity of the received combination can be reduced by semantic decoding as described in Sec. 3.2, provided the probabilities of the coded events are, contrary to our simplifying assumption (7), unequal; however, though semantic decoding will reduce the ambiguity, it will generally not reduce it to zero.

On substituting (9) in (8), it follows that a garbled message can be uniquely decoded if the information density of the original message is

$$H < (-\log D^n N^n)/n = \log DN \tag{10}$$

The actual information transmitted through a noisy channel, i.e., the amount of information received by the receiver, is

$$I^* = nH^* = -n \log DN \qquad \text{(for } \eta > D^n) \tag{11}$$

which is zero only if D assumes its minimum value $1/N$, i.e., when it becomes impossible to distinguish the individual elements of the code from each other. In all other cases it is possible to design a code *using the same N elements* to transmit any number of messages reliably through a noisy channel by choosing n sufficiently large and making the exploitation η sufficiently small.

Mathematically, this result is obvious, for unless D reaches it minimum possible value $1/N$ (making $\log DN = \log 1 = 0$), we can always choose n so large as to attain any required value of I in (10); at the same time, we can make W in (5), representing the number of points in signal space, arbitrarily large by increasing n, so that the number of messages to be transmitted becomes an arbitrarily small fraction η of the total W to be exploited, and condition (9) can therefore always be guaranteed.

Before we give an example, it is well to recall that the pause (or the space, for spatial codes) must be counted as one of the code elements. Unlike the null element, which has zero duration, the pause or the space have positive duration or occupy a positive space. They can make a substantial difference in meaning; for example, in printed English, the combination of characters *for age* and *forage* will result in very different meanings of the message of which it forms a part. The pause or space is therefore simply another code element.

As an example of (10), let us suppose that we are to design a code for signaling between ships, and that the code elements are to consist of a red, a white, and a blue flag; the messages are to be coded by hoisting these flags in different positions and numbers. Then the number of code elements n is not three (red, white, blue), but four, for we must include the space, i.e., no flag at all, as a code element. This is necessary not only to distinguish the combination red-space-blue from the combination red-white-blue, but also for another, more important reason: *A channel becomes totally impermeable to information only when no code element can be distinguished from the pause or the space.* Suppose, for example, that it is dusk, so that the colors of the flags can no longer be distinguished from each other, but it can still be discerned how many flags are up and where the spaces (if any) separating them are. Then (10) promises that we can still signal, with reduced information density, through this noisy channel; and indeed, we can: Using combinations of n flags and spaces, up to 2^n messages can be reliably transmitted (in binary code, e.g., 10011, where 0 stands for a space, and 1 stands for a flag of any color). But when night falls, a flag can no longer be distinguished from a space, and (10) will yield zero information, as it should. The same is true for codes combining their elements in time. For example, a telephone line becomes useless for the transmission of information only when the last difference between a dead and a live line has disappeared, which is long after it fails to transmit speech.

Since neither D nor η can exceed unity, it follows that if (9) is not satisfied, the received information I^* is less than the transmitted information I, for in that case we have

$$I^* = -n \log DN < -\log \eta N^n = I \qquad (\eta > D^n)$$

On the other hand, if (9) holds, the received information is

$$I^* = I = -\log \eta N^n \qquad (12) .$$

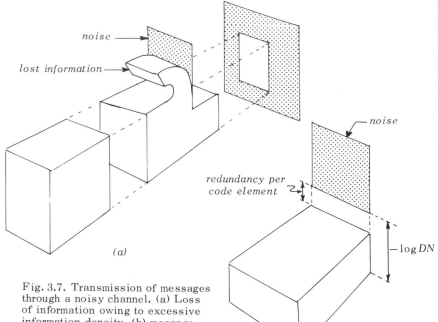

noise

lost information

noise

redundancy per code element

$-\log DN$

(a)

(b)

Fig. 3.7. Transmission of messages through a noisy channel. (a) Loss of information owing to excessive information density, (b) message encoded so as to be unaffected by the noise.

Combining (10) and (12), we have for the received information

$$I^* = \begin{cases} -n\log DN & \text{for } \eta \leqq D^n \\ -\log \eta N^n & \text{for } \eta > D^n \end{cases} \tag{13}$$

or simply

$$I^* = \min(-n\log DN, \ -n\log \eta N) \tag{14}$$

where min (minimum) means "lesser of the two quantities."

This can be illustrated with the aid of the message volume as in Fig. 3.7. The volume (information) of the message is to pass through the opening in the receiver screen as explained before in Fig. 3.6, but this time there is an additional obstacle: a knife, representing the noisy channel. Its edge is at a height

$$H = -\log DN \tag{15}$$

corresponding to the maximum permissible information density given by (8) and (9). If the information density of the message, i.e., the vertical dimension of the message prism, is less than the value (15), the prism will pass below the knife, and the entire information will reach the receiver (if, as we shall assume, it is so coded as to pass through the aperture in the receiver screen), possibly after decoding by restoration. This is the case corresponding to the upper line in (13) and is shown in Fig. 3.7b.

However, if the information density is so great as to violate (9), the knife will shave off part of the information, as shown in Fig. 3.7a. That information is lost to the receiver, not due to the limitations of his decoding ability (represented by the receiver screen aperture), but due to the noise in the channel. The partial information of the message that penetrates the channel is the volume that passes under the knife; its value is given by the second line in (13), corresponding to an information density (15). Some, but not all, of the transmitted information is lost. It is, however, obvious, that such a loss could have been prevented by recoding the message, i.e., by remoulding the message volume (as in Fig. 3.7b) so as to decrease the information density at the expense of a longer message (containing more code elements).

In the example of the flag code (p. 85), Fig. 5.7a would correspond to the case when the colors of the flags are still being used to distinguish different code words, although dusk has made it impossible to discern individual colors. The messages will then become ambiguous, and much, but not all, information is lost: If the receiver sees the signal flag-space-flag, he does not know whether the original message was red-space-blue or blue-space-red (for example); but he does know that it was *not* red-red-blue (for example). How much information this represents will depend on the events that the flag code codes; it could be that the original message was *We sail tomorrow at 7 a.m.*, and that the mutilated signal (flag-space-flag) still manages to convey the information coding the event *We sail tomorrow* or *We sail*, which gives the receiver *some* information (apart from the secondary information that a message is being transmitted at all). But this loss of information could have been avoided by using binary code (space or flag of any color), which will make the code words longer (more flags are needed per coded message), but will reduce the information density, so that the message volumes now creep through under the noise knife in Fig. 5.7b.

It should be noted that due to our numerous simplifying assumptions the above model is strongly idealized. In reality, the knife representing the channel noise will not stand at the exact height (15), but it will have a random height, of which (15) is merely the mean value. Moreover, whenever the noise is not constant in time, the knife will fluctuate in time, attacking some parts of the message more severely than others. The knife will also attack different parts of the message selectively, since some parts of the message may be more prone to distortion than others. (A white flag is, presumably, more easily discerned from a red flag than from a blue one at dusk.) However, we are concerned with basic ideas here, and once again, we do not want to lose the main thread in a mass of details. The above objections to our idealized model are certainly justified; but the corresponding ramifications of the theory are fairly obvious (to the probabilist, anyway) and need not be considered here by the corresponding generalizations of our formulae. It is sufficient to realize that the knife which we take as fixed at the height (15), in reality fluctuates about that height, producing (in Fig. 3.7a) a volume which is not a prism, but a body whose upper surface is randomly corrugated.

Fig. 3.7 shows that unless the knife is at zero height, making the channel totally impermeable for the transmission of information, a fraction of the transmitted information will reach the receiver. More important, it shows that the transmitted information can always be so encoded that all of it reaches the receiver inspite of the channel noise, that is, *a message can always be sent reliably through an unreliable channel.* In the case of the flag code, ambiguities were prevented by the simple expedient of reducing the number of code elements to reduce the information density. Natural languages also protect their messages against ambiguity by a low information density, i.e., by using long combinations of code elements; however, they do so by a system which is far more subtle than merely reducing the number of distinct code elements. This system will be discussed in Chapter 5.

3.5. Concluding Remarks

The reader familiar with Shannon's Information Theory cannot have failed to note both the similarities and the differences between Shannon's theory and the rudiments of a semantic information theory sketched here.

The basic ideas, including the revolutionary idea that it is always possible to send information reliably through unreliable channels, are, of course, Shannon's. The present theory merely adapts these ideas so that they can be more conveniently applied to the *meaning* of the message, and not merely to its formal structure. At the same time, this concern with the meaning rather than formal structure is the main difference between the present theory and Shannon's theory. The roots of this difference lie in the assignment of probabilities: In Shannon's theory, the basic probabilities are those of a certain code element being transmitted, and these probabilities are objective; here, the basic probabilities are those of the actual events that are being coded, and they are assigned subjectively by the receiver.

There are other differences. In particular, Shannon's theory works with concepts (such as entropy or equivocation) which represent an average over all possible messages; here, we can evaluate each message separately. The evaluation depends on the semantic significance of the message, not only on its formal structure.

There are many things that Shannon's theory can do, but the present theory cannot. For example, Shannon's theory can evaluate the information transmitted in several bars of music. The present theory cannot do this (unless the music codes an event of a semantic base, as it might, perhaps, in some espionage code). Conversely, Shannon's theory will assign the same value of information to the combinations of code elements

and
> *The fluid wilts hysterically awash*
> *Mr. Nixon went to Peking this year,*

since both have roughly the same duration (they have the same number of syllables), and both have the same statistical characteristics, namely, those of English.

The question which theory is "better" is meaningless. Let us repeat our analogy: To the chemist, a railroad truck is an inhomogeneous mixture of chemical compounds, whereas to the railroad engineer, it is a vehicle of transportation. That does not make railroad engineering "better" than chemistry; it makes it more convenient for a particular job. Chemistry, like Shannon's theory, is interested in the structure of things from the point of view of their *composition*; railroad engineering, like the present theory, is interested in the structure of things from the point of view of their *function*.

There is a further difference between the two theories which I would not like to pass over. Shannon's theory is, within its scope, exhaustive, with precisely defined concepts, and presented in a number of rigorously proven theorems. The present theory merely sketches rudimentary ideas (which are ultimately borrowed from Shannon's approach), and uses very elementary mathematics applied under simplifying assumptions. It is certainly not intended to compete with Shannon's theory in any way, least of all in quality or rigor. However, the simplifying assumptions can be withdrawn at the cost of more sophisticated mathematics (and it was assumed that the type of reader to whom this book is addressed would not be keen to pay this price), and even in its present state the theory may perhaps be useful for describing the mechanics of communication when the meaning of the messages plays an important role.

4

Language as a General Code

4.1. Is Language a Code?

We have taken it for granted so far that Language is a code for the transmission of information. True, it has been pointed out that not all uses of Language serve this purpose, for it can also be used for evoking moods and emotions, for pastimes, etc.; but in essence, we have assumed that Language is a code comparable with other codes, whether natural or artificial. Is this assumption justified?

According to many eminent linguists, it is not, and many papers have been written seeking to disprove that Language can be regarded as a code. But as in most similar cases, the answer to the question depends entirely on what is understood by "code." Let us consult the experts on coding theory. Abramson,* for example, defines a code as follows:

> Let the set of symbols comprising a given alphabet be called $S = [s_1, s_2, \ldots s_n]$. Then we define a code as a mapping of all possible sequences of symbols of S into sequences of symbols of some other alphabet $X = [x_1, x_2, \ldots x_r]$. We call S the *source alphabet* and X the *code alphabet*.

The reader who is not mathematically inclined may replace "a maping of ... into" by "the establishment of a correspondence of ... with." Note that this correspondence need not be single-valued. Also, the term "alphabet should not necessarily be taken to mean some kind of ABC; the colors of a traffic light, red, amber, green, also form a code

---

*N. Abramson, *Information Theory and Coding*, McGraw-Hill, New York, 1963.

alphabet (or, in some applications, a source alphabet). Beyond that, Abramson's definition seems clear enough.

The above definition is very general, and it appears that few people have this in mind when they discuss the question of whether Language is a code; what they usually have in mind (often without realising it) is a *block code*, which Abramson defines as follows:

> A block code is a code which maps each of the symbols of the source alphabet S into a fixed sequence of the code alphabet X. These fixed sequences of the code alphabet (sequences of x_i) are called *code words*.

For example, the Morse code is a block code. Its alphabet can be considered to consist of the symbols dot, dash, short pause, long pause. It maps the letter (source symbol) A of the source alphabet always into the fixed sequence of code symbols dot—short pause—dash—long pause. The sequences of electrical impulses transmitted by a teleprinter are also code words of a block code: Depressing the same key always activates the same sequence. On the other hand, the secret cyphers used in diplomacy or espionage are never block codes, as a block code is too easy to crack; they use a variety of symbols (or their combinations) of the code alphabet for the same symbol of the source alphabet, varying the correspondence according to some key which, the correspondents hope, is known only to them.

Now when linguists discuss the question of whether Language is a code, they almost always assume, tacitly or explicitly, that the *words of a language* are identical with the *code words* of the supposed code. Many linguists examining this question have therefore concluded that Language cannot be regarded as a code, and considering their tacit assumptions, this conclusion is not surprising. If the code words of the language are regarded as the code words of the code whose existence is under discussion, then it is indeed highly debatable whether such a code exists. My personal opinion is that under these restrictive conditions Language cannot be regarded as a code, for whilst (the candidates for) the code alphabet and the code words are clear enough, it is difficult to imagine a source alphabet that these words should correspond to. What, for example, is mapped by the word *been*? Or by the words *is, him, the, can, other, this, very, not, of, because*?

If, throughout this book, we nevertheless regard Language as a code, then this is so because we do *not* make the assumption that the words of a language are the code words of that code. For our purposes, Abramson's definitions are quite acceptable, at least after a small, "cosmetic" modification, namely, that the word *symbol* is to be omitted or to be replaced by *member of the set*. But this is only because *symbol* is too restrictive; Abramson's definition is then slightly generalized to

Let S be the set of elements E , so that $S = [E_1, E_2, ... E_n]$.
Then we define a code as a mapping of all possible sequences
of the members of the set S into sequences of the members of
some other set $X = [x_1, x_2, ... x_r]$. We call S the source alphabet and X the code alphabet.

Using this definition, I see no reason why Language should not be
a code, especially from the point of view presented in the preceding
chapter: S is the semantic base (which we prefer to its synonym *source
alphabet*), the E_i are the events of which the semantic base is composed, and the code alphabet, in the case of a language, is composed
of graphemes, phonemes, syllables, words, or whatever other elements
we find convenient (as we have seen in the preceding chapter, the code
alphabet, unlike the code words, is largely a matter of convenience).
The code words of the language, i.e., sequences of members of the code
alphabet, are messages which can be assigned to the corresponding
events of the semantic base. But messages coding these events in a natural language are not, in general, made up of single words of that language. They are generally formed by *sentences*. Thus, the *code words*
of the code are *sentences*, whilst the individual words of the language
may be regarded as elements of the code alphabet — if we choose to do
so; we can also regard the code words or sentences as combinations of
elements of some other code alphabet, e.g., an alphabet of phonemes,
or graphemes, or syllables, or morphemes. The sentences, code words,
or messages M_i of a language are the sequences of code alphabet members x_j (a sequence of several x_j's corresponding to a single M_i), and
such a sequence in turn corresponds to some E_i, a member of the source
alphabet, or as we prefer to say, an event of the semantic base. From
the point of view of coding theory, there is nothing unusual about any
of these statements. The code words *John has two daughters* and *John
a deux filles* are code words of two different codes (English and French)
coding the event (fact, member of the semantic base, member of the
source alphabet) that John has two daughters.

The event that the sun will rise tomorrow is coded by the English
code word or sentence *The sun will rise tomorrow*, just as it is coded
by the German code word or sentence *Die Sonne wird morgen aufgehen*.
In both cases the code words consist of several grammatical words, just
as they consist of many phonemes or morphemes or syllables. The event
that the transmitter is urgently requesting help is coded by the English
code word *Help!*, which happens to consist of only a single grammatical
word, but the French code word coding the same event is *Aux secours!*,
which consists of two grammatical words.

Thus, provided we do not assume that the *grammatical* words of a
language are identical with the *code* words of that language, and pro-

vided that we allow probabilistic events to form a source alphabet, there appears to be no reason why natural languages should not be regarded as codes. Our findings do not contradict the conclusion of Mandelbrot, Andreyev and others who claim that natural languages cannot be regarded as codes, because their conclusions are based on different premises. The issue discussed by these investigators is simply evaded by our approach.

4.2. Instantaneous Codes

We have discussed codes in general in Sec. 3.1, and we have given a precise definition in the preceding section; our concept of a code is so wide that it allows even for, say, the color of leaves to code their biological state (if a maple leaf is brown, it codes the event that it is dead). The number of different codes is therefore very large, probably infinite. Yet they not only have certain common characteristics, but also certain characteristics which divide them into large groups.

The most obvious criterion for a subdivision is the type of code alphabet, and the way in which the code alphabet members are combined into code words or messages. They may be combined in time (as in the Morse code) or in space (printing) or both (sign language used by the deaf). The elements themselves may be letters, digits, colors, holes in punched cards, and hundreds of others. A digital code, in turn, may be binary, octal, decimal, etc.

A natural language, in the spoken form, is a code combining its elements in time. The elements are phonemes, syllables, morphemes, words, or other combinations of phonemes that we find convenient in our choice of a code alphabet. In written or printed language, the elements are graphemes (or their combinations such as words), which are combined in space rather than in time.

But apart from these basic criterions, there are many others by which codes may be divided into classes. In coding theory, which deals mainly with artificial codes, codes are divided into nonblock and block codes; the latter may be singular or nonsingular; the latter may or may not be uniquely decodable; in the latter case the code may be instantaneous or not. Most of these definitions will not concern us, and we will therefore discuss only some types of codes, in as far as they may have a bearing on the structure of Language.

An *instantaneous* code is one whose messages (code words) can be decoded without reference to subsequent code words, i.e., a code that can be decoded as it is received, without having to wait for further code words. For example, the events E_1, E_2, E_3 can be encoded in the following instantaneous code:

$$E_1: \quad 10$$
$$E_2: \quad 01 \qquad\qquad\qquad\qquad (1)$$
$$E_3: \quad 201$$

There is no difficulty in decoding the string 1001 as the events E_1, E_2; similarly, the sequence 2011001 codes the events E_3, E_1, E_2. On the other hand, the following code, whilst also uniquely decodable, is not instantaneous:

$$E_1: \quad 1$$
$$E_2: \quad 10 \qquad\qquad\qquad\qquad (2)$$
$$E_3: \quad 100$$

The difference between the two codes is that in the case of code (1), we know that 201 codes the event E_3 as soon as we receive the the combination; we do not have to wait for further digits before we are sure. Not so in the case of code (2): On receiving the digits 10, this might be the end of E_2 or the beginning of E_3; we have to wait for the next digit to see which it is. Thus, E_2 cannot be decoded instantaneously on reception; it can be decoded only after the beginning of the next code word is received. Code (2), therefore, is not an instantaneous code. It can be shown rigorously that, as the reader may already have supposed, a code is instantaneous if and only if no message forms the beginning of another message. Code (2) is not instantaneous, because the message 10 is also the beginning of the message 100 (which does not, however, stop it from being uniquely decodable). One way of designing a code that is assuredly instantaneous is to use a *comma code*, in which the individual messages are separated by "commas." In the Morse code, the long pause acts as a comma; the following is a binary comma code:

$$E_1: \quad 10$$
$$E_2: \quad 110 \qquad\qquad\qquad\qquad (3)$$
$$E_3: \quad 1110$$

Here the three events are essentially coded by 1, 11, 111, and the zero acts as the comma separating the messages from each other when a string of them is transmitted. Since no message can be longer than the string up to the comma, no message can form the beginning of another message, so that the code is instantaneous.

Are natural languages instantaneous codes? The answer is not at all obvious.

Let us assume that all messages are coded as grammatical sentences, and let us consider the simpler case of written or printed language. It would seem that this is a comma code, since the end of every sentence is signaled by a period (or question mark or exclamation mark). Spoken language would therefore also seem to be an instantaneous code, since

since the punctuation is more or less reproduced by intonation and pauses. However, a closer look reveals that not even printed language is an instantaneous code. Often a second message (sentence) can change the meaning of a previously transmitted message, so that we cannot be sure of the exact meaning until we have "heard the whole story." This means that the code is not instantaneous, since a message cannot be uniquely decoded immediately on reception.

However, this situation is comparatively rare; it is, in fact so rare as to be funny by its unexpectedness, and many jokes are based on this scheme: The punch line reveals that a previous message should have been decoded differently than was assumed. There is, for example, the story of the man who played golf for the first time in his life, and then said, "My score was 129" (message M_1). On being complimented that this was not too bad for a beginner, he replied (M_2): "But I hope to do even better on the second hole." In this case, the message M_1 would not usually be decoded correctly until M_2 was received. Thus, language is not an instantaneous code, in spite of the fact that its structure in individual sentences with well recognizable ends makes it reminiscent of a comma code. The reason why this does not contradict the above theorem on instantaneous codes is that language is not even a uniquely decodable code, a point to which we will return in a moment.

There are thousands of other jokes based on the principle of unexpected decoding revealed by a subsequent message. ("You do not have an inferiority complex. You *are* inferior." Or: "Yea, though I walk through the valley of the shadow of death, I shall fear no evil. For I am the meanest son of a bitch in the valley.") But the very fact that it is jokes that are based on this phenomenon shows that it is an unusual one, for we laugh only at the unusual and the unexpected.

At the same time, the above examples show what is surely obvious anyway, namely that language is not a uniquely decodable code, if, as before, decoding means assigning an event to a message. *My score was 129* could mean the score for 18 holes, or for one hole, or for a game other than golf, etc. The statement *You do not have an inferiority complex* denies that the person in question has an *inferiority complex*; it also denies, as the above joke shows, that the person has a *complex*; it also denies that *the person* has an inferiority complex, etc. There are probably very few messages in Language that can be ascribed to a unique event; a few mathematical theorems using specialized language (*in a circle, equal arcs subtend equal chords*) might perhaps be argued to code a unique event, but in general, a statement in natural language codes a wide range of events which is indicated rather hazily. Even a simple sentence like *Grass is green* corresponds to a vast number of events. What, for example, is indicated by the word *green*? A color is, ultimately, given by a spectral curve indicating the relative power with which various wavelengths of light are represented in the observed radiation; but there are infinitely many spectral curves which are all described as "green" by all persons with normal eyesight. This example alone shows how ambiguous a code language is; it is perhaps unnecessary to go into the ambiguities of more complicated statements, such as *Excessive permissiveness is harmful for society*. This ambiguity in assigning messages to events is characteristic of Language. In Chapter 6 we shall see that if a computer is to construct "intelligent" English sentences (rather than reproduce prefabricated sentences stored *en bloc*), then the corresponding program must "coarsen" the events of which the computer has knowledge; it will, for example, code a well defined event stored as numerical knowledge by the rather hazy statement *Your wife is very tall for a woman*.

It is the ambiguity in the correspondence between code words and semantic base that prevents Language, on rare occasions, from being an instantaneous code. A good speaker, writer or teacher will formulate his sentences in such a way as to make them instantly decodable.

When decoding is understood in its formal, not in its semantic, sense, there is little doubt that Language is an instantaneous code. Formal decoding pays no attention to the meaning of the message, i.e., to the event of the semantic base that is being coded; it merely decodes to the extent necessary for re-coding into another code. A secretary taking dictation, for example, can re-code spoken language into shorthand or typewritten copy with only a bare minimum of understanding the meaning of the corresponding messages. She is re-coding, not semantically decoding. Similarly, in reading aloud, or re-coding written to spoken language, there is little need to understand the meaning of the messages, especially in languages that adhere to consistent rules how to pronounce written words, such as Czech or Hungarian. In English there are no such rules (at best only tendencies), and this necessitates knowledge of how each word is pronounced, and in many cases even knowledge which of two or more pronunciations is applicable under given circumstances (*present, present*), but it does not involve semantic decoding in full. In fact, for this type of re-coding (as opposed to semantic decoding), it is possible to define a code whose code words are identical with the grammatical words of the language: The source alphabet consists of written words, and the code alphabet of spoken words, or vice versa. In this restricted version, written language is an instantaneous comma code, with the spaces acting as commas.

Translation from one language to another is an "intermediate" case of re-coding; semantic decoding plays a comparatively minor role. True, a good translator will read the entire book first, in order to preserve the

style and spirit of the book in his translation. However, a consecutive
interpreter (who translates a speaker after each sentence or paragraph)
is proof that for purposes of translation, language is an instantaneous
code if we regard a whole sentence as a code word. A simultaneous or
cabin interpreter, who translates into a microphone as he is listening
to the speaker in his headphones, cannot wait until the speaker has finished a sentence, or even until he has grasped the meaning of what the
speaker is about to say. If he did so, he would not catch up with the
speaker again. Since some languages are, as it were, "more instantaneous" than others, simultaneous translation is easier for some languages than for others. Simultaneous translation from Russian into English is very much easier than from German into English. The reason is
that, by and large, Russian word order is quite similar to English word
order, so that the interpreter can translate phrase by phrase, if not word
by word. On the other hand, in German, the interpreter is warned of big
trouble ahead every time a conjunction requiring inversion in the subordinate clause comes through (*da, obwohl, wogegen*, etc.). All he can do
is sit out the convolutions of German syntax and prey for the verb to
come soon. When deliverance at last arrives, he must rattle off everything he has heard during the time he has been waiting, and do so extremely quickly, for in the meantime the speaker is usually tying himself up in further convolutions. In this sense, German is further from
an instantaneous code than French, English or Russian. In the words
of Mark Twain, "a German sentence is like a man diving into a sea of
words, and emerging with the verb in his mouth." Although German no
longer considers the convoluted structures of a sentence the mark of an
erudite writer (as was the case in the last century), the inversions remain and they make a clause unintelligible until the speaker supplies
the deciphering key in the form of the verb at the end of the clause.
(The last part of the preceding sentence would be rendered in German
as "until the speaker the deciphering key in the form of the verb at the
end of the clause supplies.") Apart from inversions, which are the main
obstacle to instantaneousness, German also allows adjectival clauses
of the type *die in der Küche arbeitende Frau*, "the in-the-kitchen-working
woman," i.e., *the woman who is working in the kitchen*. Russian, no
doubt under German influence, allows this construction also; but German
can even nest these adjectivals within each other, as in *die in der ausser-
halb des Hauses stehenden Küche arbeitende Frau* – the woman who is
working in the kitchen which is detached from the house. (This type of
nesting, incidentally, is strongly reminiscent of the way in which brackets are nested in computer languages.)

The fact that German is a particularly non-instantaneous code is
apparent not only in simultaneous translations. In English or Russian,

a listener can follow the speaker (decode his messages) continuously; in German, his understanding proceeds in the jumps of a step function. Even if the listener can guess the clarifying verb that is imminent, the speaker may often surprise him by inserting *nicht* before it.

It is the inversions, of course, that give German this character. The nested adjectivals have only a secondary effect in this respect, since they are, as a rule, not very long. Besides, not only German has them; English sometimes uses similar constructions, e.g., *I don't like your to-hell-with-the-others-as-long-as-I-am-OK attitude*, where the hyphenated words form an adjectival attributed to *attitude*. However, it is debatable whether such a sentence is grammatical, and in any case, such adjectivals are usually used only one at a time; possibly several of them could be used consecutively, but they cannot be nested within each other as in German.

Lest we loose the main thread of our discussion, let it be repeated that since we regard entire sentences as code words, German is just as instantaneous as English; the contortions and convolutions of phrases within a German sentence make no difference to this conclusion. The above remarks concerned the ease with which a listener can follow the structure of a sentence even before it is finished, which is interesting from the linguistic point of view, but does not strictly come under the definition of an instantaneous code once we have decided to equate entire sentences to code words.

The division of codes into instantaneous and non-instantaneous codes is only one of very many possible divisions into groups and subgroups. (A comma code, for example, is a subgroup of instantaneous codes.) There are very many other criterions which serve as a basis for dividing codes into classes.

An *optimum code* maximizes the rate at which the messages so coded can be transmitted; it is certainly not, however, "optimum" as far as other characteristics (such as noise resistance) are concerned. We shall examine some aspects of Language related to an optimum code in the next section.

Error-detecting and *error-correcting codes* are so designed that errors due to distortion by noise can be detected, and in a more sophisticated version, corrected, at the receiving end of the transmission system. It is one of the basic tenets of this book that natural languages are, in principle, structured very similarly to artificial error detecting codes, and we shall examine this point in more detail in Chapter 5.

A *minimum-risk* code is so designed that the average penalty for a distorted message, that is, the risk, is minimized. It is one of the few types of artificial codes whose design pays attention not only to the formal structure of the code words, but also to their meanings. For example, let a code be used to transmit commands to a rocket engaged in telemetering the atmosphere. Let M_1, M_2, M_3 code the commands "begin measuring the humidity," "begin measuring the pressure," "destroy the rocket by setting off its explosives," respectively. Obviously, the penalty (in dollars or other units) for M_1 being distorted to M_2 is not as great as the penalty for M_1 being distorted to M_3; in the former case the pressure will be measured instead of the humidity, which is an error that can be rectified as soon as it is detected, and which would not entail a large penalty in any case, but in the latter case, the mission of the rocket will turn into a total failure. By various methods, such as padding a large neighborhood of the message M_3 in signal space by empty points (meaningless combinations of code elements), the probability of the latter error can be made very small, and the risk, given by (20), p. 28, can be minimized.

There are very many other ways by which codes can be divided into classes according to their structure, application or other criterions. However, we shall have no need of these in discussing the code of Language.

4.3. Optimum Codes

An optimum code is one which maps the source alphabet into the code words of the code alphabet in such a way that the rate of transmission is maximized. The messages of an optimum code can thus be transmitted faster than those of any other code.

Even without the use of information theory, it is obvious that an optimum code must assign the shortest code words to the most frequent (most probably transmitted) elements of the source alphabet, and the longest code words to the rarest source elements. Certainly this much was clear to Samuel Morse, a century before the advent of information theory, when he assigned the shortest code words to the most frequent English letters E (dot), T (dash) and I (dot-dot), and long code words to the rarest letters X (dash-dot-dot-dash), Z (dash-dash-dot-dot) and J (dot-dash-dash-dash). Incidentally, the Morse code was taken over by all other nations using the Roman alphabet without substantial modifications, regardless of the frequency of the letters in their languages, so that the Morse code is less efficient in other languages, as shown by the following table giving the first three most frequent letters in some languages using the Roman alphabet:**

Croatian	a, u, o	German	e,* n, r
Czech	o, e, n	Hungarian	e, t, a
Dutch	e,* n, a	Italian	e, i, a
English	e, t, i	Spanish	a, e, o
French	e, s, t	Vietnamese	n, h, t

* More frequent than the space. ** Compiled from N.D. Andreyev, *Statistical and Combinatorial Methods in Linguistics* (in Russian), Nauka, Leningr., 1967.

Samuel Morse's intuitive criterion is only qualitative. The quantitative relation between the length of a code word and the frequency (probability) of the corresponding element of the source alphabet has only been derived by the methods of information theory and amounts to the following. Let the code alphabet have r members, and let the length of the code word coding the source alphabet member s_i be L_i, where L_i is measured by the number of code elements (letters, digits, etc.) it combines. Let the frequency of the source element s_i, i.e., the probability of its occurrence in the sequences generated by the source, be $P(s_i)$. This, incidentally, is the probability of the formal occurrence of the element s_i in the sequences generated by the source, for we are now considering a source alphabet composed of, say, individual letters, not a semantic base composed of events in the real world; however, we can also retain the concept of a semantic base by letting s_i represent the event "the source is now generating the letter (or word, or sentence) s_i." The relation between $P(s_i)$ and L_i that must then be satisfied to ensure that the resulting code is an optimum code is*

$$L_i = -\log_r P(s_i) \qquad \text{for all } i \qquad (1)$$

or, by elementary algebra,

$$P(s_i) = r^{-L_i} \qquad \text{for all } i \qquad (2)$$

These relations cannot be satisfied exactly for a general probability distribution $P(s_i)$, since r (the number of elements in the code alphabet) and the L_i (the number of elements in a particular code word) are integers, and one would have to be very lucky to be given the $P(s_i)$ in such a way that they all happen to be reciprocals of the same integer raised to an integral power, for this is what (2) requires. However, though it is not possible to satisfy (1) or (2) exactly, there are procedures of encoding the s_i into code words of an r-letter alphabet in such a way as to come as close as possible to satisfying (1); and if the source is "extended," i.e., if the source elements are not encoded individually, but in sequences of n source elements (nth extension of the source), then it is even possible to come arbitrarily close to the condition (1). Such procedures have been found by Huffman, and by Shannon and Fanno.*

However, we will not pusue these procedures (except, later, for one case corresponding to extending the source), for we are interested only in the question of whether natural languages are optimum codes. We shall find that they are not optimum codes, even approximately, but that they nevertheless use some devices which speed up the transmission of information. Some languages have more such devices than others; in particular, English has many, and very effective, devices of this type.

---

*P. Beckmann, *Probability in Communication Engineering*, Harcourt, Brace & World, New York, 1967.

There are so many ways of demonstrating that natural languages are not optimum codes that we choose only some of them.

First, it can be shown that an optimum code is necessarily also a maximum efficiency code (no matter whether efficiency is defined in Shannon's sense or in the sense of exploitation as on p. 64). An optimum code must not leave any combinations unexploited, but no matter how we choose the code alphabet of a natural language, we will always find an almost unlimited number of combinations to which no meaning is assigned. If we choose words as code elements, we can combine them in any amount of meaningless combinations, e.g., *The killed how*; such combinations combine English words, but they are not code words (meaningful sentences) — they are merely unexploited code words. If we choose finer elements to form a code alphabet, e.g., syllables, morphemes or phonemes, we again find a limitless number of unexploited code words, e.g., *It is unpossible to be inkind* or *joykin must windish* are unexploited combinations of English syllables.

Second, if a natural language were an optimum code, its messages could not, by definition of an optimum code, be shortened without loss of information; it could have no redundant elements such as redundant words. But this is obviously not so. In English, for example, the most frequent word, *the*, is in most cases quite redundant, and it is therefore omitted in telegrams and newspaper headlines. (Redundant does not, however, mean useless, as we shall see in the next chapter.) The slangs, dialects and colloquialisms of all languages often shorten its messages (sentences) without loss of information; the fact that this is often ungrammatical is not relevant to the issue of whether the code is an optimum one. Thus, in English, *going to* is shortened into *gonna*, and *have not* into *ain't*; in French slang, the redundant *ne* is omitted before *pas*, *rien*, *personne*, *que*, etc.; most German dialects contract *haben wir nicht* to *hammer nich'*; similar contractions are used in the slangs of the Slavic languages, and presumably in every other language, since the motivation is the same: to convey information without the effort of adhering to the rules of grammar.

Third, if (1) and (2) held for natural languages, then equally frequent sentences would have the same length, and the more frequent sentences would be the shorter ones. But this is not even approximately so. The code word (sentence) *Partly cloudy skies with scattered showers are forecast for tomorrow* is surely a sentence with relatively high probability, at least in the English sublanguage of broadcasting. Its probability is surely much higher than that of the two-syllable sentences *Ewes slept. Mums wilt. Sue puked. Knaves winked, Birds soared.* This shows that natural languages are not even close to an optimum code: Not only do they come nowhere near the requirement (1) or (2), but they do not even satisfy what we might call the "Morse" criterion of assigning the short-est code words to the most frequent members of the source alphabet, i.e., to the most frequent events of the semantic base.

But then, sentences are formed from words by certain syntactic rules, and it might therefore seem more justified to look for a "Morse" criterion in the lengths and frequencies of individual words. But it does not even apply there. For example, the three-letter word *the* is the most frequent English word; the one-letter words *I* and *O* are less frequent, and many other three-letter words such as *din, don, jig, sag, rim, cue, ant, Hun, dye*, are very much less frequent than *the*; they are even less frequent than the six-letter word *really* or the twelve-letter word *considerably*. The argument holds just as well if we count the word length (more suit-ably) in phonemes: *the* and *lee/lea* both have two phonemes, yet the lat-ter is very much less frequent, even in the English naval, textile or lyric sublanguages, and the two-phoneme word *lee/lea* is much less frequent than the seven-phoneme word *quality*.

There are many more ways to show that natural languages are not optimum codes, or even close to optimum codes, but it is hoped that the above arguments will have made the point. In the next chapter, we will attempt to find the principle on which the structure of Language is based; but for the time being, we can say this: *The structure of Language is not based on the principle of transmitting information at the maximum rate*.

Nevertheless, natural languages do use a number of devices, some of them very ingenious, to increase the rate of transmission of informa-tion. Before we examine this other side of the coin, we note that the reason why the shortest words are not the most frequent is, at least in part, historical. Many short words were frequent words in bygone ages; these words have taken up the "good" positions in signal space (or po-sitions in the signal space of single syllables), and the words that are more frequent now have been relegated to less advantageous positions (or to a multidimensional signal space for words with several syllables), i.e., the more frequent, modern words are longer. Consider some examples in the following two lists:

hunt	*unemployment*
tribe	*disarmament*
speer	*establishment*
club	*environment*
tent	*aggression*
sword	*nationalism*
slave	*education*
serf	*technology*
kill	*accelerate*

Such lists are not limited to English, as shown by the examples in the following table:

(English)	*hunt*	*sword*	*unemployment*	*amplifier*
(French)	*chasse*	*epée*	*chômage*	*amplificateur*
(German)	*Jagd*	*Schwert*	*Arbeitslosigkeit*	*Verstärker*
(Czech)	*hon*	*meč*	*nezaměstnanost*	*zesilovač*
(Russian)	охота	меч	безработница	усилитель

There are, of course, some counterexamples: Many old words have remained frequent words (*day, night, life, death, God, fire, sun, moon,* etc.) and some modern words are short (*coach, jet, ion*), or cut short (*'fridge, amp[ere], gas[olene]*), or shortened into acronyms (*WASP*). A particularly striking example of the last group is the verb *to lase*, which is widely used by scientists in all its morphological forms; it is derived from the noun *laser*, which is itself an acronym (*Light Amplification by Stimulated Emission of Radiation*). But in spite of these counterexamples, the tendency remains for old words to be short and for modern words to be long; besides, there seem to be no conterexamples of old, but long words.

The reason why modern words tend to be longer is evidently that modern concepts are more complicated, and the corresponding words can therefore be built up from simpler words, as in *ac|celer|ator, dis|arm|a-|ment, step|-|down | trans|form|er*, etc. This makes the new words more easily comprehensible, especially in languages which (unlike English) form more complex words from their own simple words.

Yet if a language did develop according to the principles of coding theory (and it is in no way claimed that this is the case), the result would probably be the same, i.e., new words would have to be made longer. True, there are many monosyllabic combinations of English phonemes, involving typically English sequences, which are not exploited as words, e.g., *plam, swilk, swesh, strape, dripe*, etc. So if the development of English could be governed by a panel of efficiency experts, the more shortsighted members of the panel might vote to replace *unemployment* by *plam* or *tranquilizer* by *swilk*. But the more farsighted members of the panel, though driven by the same materialist motives of saving time, ink and paper, would probably vote against such a proposal as being counterproductive. As we have seen in the preceding chapter, a low coding efficiency protects the coded messages from ambiguity. The development of a language automatically strikes a reasonable balance between information density and noise resistance by adopting well padded words (padded by a neighborhood of empty points in signal space) and abandoning words leading to dangerous ambiguities (examples will be given later). English, as we shall see presently, already has an unusually high compactness, which is brought about, in part, by an unusually crowded signal space. No responsible coding expert would attempt to crowd this signal space still further by introducing more monosyllabic words of the above type into it. *Plam* would be dangerously near *plan*, *swilk* would be near *swill*, and *dripe* near *tripe*. Confusing *unemployment* with *plan* or *tranquilizer* with *swill* could have untoward consequences, which would eventually waste more time, paper and ink than was originally planned to save. Thus, even from the very narrow point of view of coding theory the reason for relegating new words to less advantageous positions in signal space is quite natural.

A hypothetical panel of the above type would, of course, prove utterly futile in a democratic society in any case. There are, however, committees attempting to regulate the development of Language in totalitarian states, and it is heartening to note that their effect is very slight, even though they can impose their will on a centralized radio, press, and publishing industry. Nazi Germany had a movement of zealots trying to weed out foreign words to preserve the Ayryan purity of German. Some of their innovations, such as *Lichtbild* for *Photographie* or *Fernsprecher* for *Telephon* have partially survived, but many more were laughed to death. It was proposed to replace *Elektrizität* by *Bern* (because *Bernstein* means *amber*, which the ancient Greeks associated with static electricity). It was also proposed to replace *Lokomotive* by *Zieh* (pull); if it became necessary to distinguish electric railroad engines from steam engines, the former would be called *Bern-Zieh*, and the latter *Zieh-Zieh*, which is as funny in German as, say, *gaga* in English. What apparently killed the proposal was the replacement of *Transformator* by *Treiber* (driver); the logical term for a step-up transformer would then be *Auftreiber,* and for a step-down transformer it would be *Abtreiber*; but the latter already means *abortionist*. The proposal ended in a fiasco, with the Nazi Party issuing a warning not to take the campaign too far.

Something similar is now going on in the USSR. The ideological watchdogs of marxist-leninist purity warn against "bourgeois frivolity" in coining new technical terms, and appeal to scientists to replace foreign words by "fatherlandish" (отечественные) ones. The "frivolity" refers to terms like *flip-flop*. This is an electronic circuit, which on being triggered by an input signal produces a single oscillation (it flips) and then returns to its quiescent state (it flops) until the next trigger signal is received. The noun *flip-flop* is widely used by electronic engineers not only in the English speaking countries, but all over the world, including the USSR. Soviet engineers invariably refer to the circuit as a flip-flop, but in publications they use (or the editor will correct it to) some monstrosity like "monostable multivibrator," which, by the way, may be less "frivolous," but is hardly very "fatherlandish."

Other attempts to interfere with the development of a language by decree have not met with much success. De Gaulle's campaign against *franglais* evidently did not achieve much. Perhaps the sign over a Calais cafe *Le five o'clock tea à toutes les heures* has now gone; but it is very doubtful whether French antenna engineers have stopped using the term *l'overspill*. As for post-war German, if the author of *Zieh-Zieh* survived the war, he must surely have been killed off by current German usage; it abounds with expressions such as *der Killer, der Boss, der Teenager, das Establishment, der Bestseller, das Design, Software und Hardware, der mit dem Computer kompatible Plotter, die Sexwelle...*

What side-tracked us into *die Sexwelle* was the attempt by a hypothetical panel to make Language into an optimum code. Let us now return to some properties of a language that affect its rate of transmission of information. We have already met one device for hastening that transmission: the ungrammatical shortening of words and phrases in dialects, colloquialisms and slang. There are, however, many other, and more effective, devices by which Language speeds the transmission of information. Not all languages use these devices to the same extent, so that some languages are "shorter" than others; their average information density is higher, so that they take less time or space to convey the same messages.

First, we note that the larger the code alphabet, the shorter the code words, and therefore the higher the transmission rate for any code. For an optimum code, this statement immediately follows from (1), since a logarithm is a decreasing function of its base. For a code that is less than optimum, the validity of the assertion can also be demonstrated. The signal space of a code with more elements is an n-dimensional cube with a longer side, and it has therefore more points. A code with fewer elements in its code alphabet will fill the $n$dimensional cube to a permitted density (exploitation) earlier, and will have to use $n + 1$, $n + 2$, $n + 3$, ... element combinations for its code words when, under otherwise equal conditions, the code with more elements is still using combinations of only n elements, because it has a bigger cube in which to place its code words. This is quite easily seen in coding the natural numbers in binary and decimal notation. The former has only two elements $(0,1)$, the latter has 10. The number one thousand nine hundred and fifty-seven is coded in decimal notation as

$$1957 \tag{3}$$

and in binary notation as

$$11110100101 \tag{4}$$

leaving little doubt that decimal notation is shorter (but longer than duodecimal notation, etc.). Both notations have an exploitation of 100% (with the possible exception of combinations starting with one or several zeroes), but if this were not so, the two notations would simply be lengthened. The decimal notation would remain the shorter one, if the two exploitations were kept equal. Thus, the larger the code alphabet, the faster the transmission rate.

Two comments should be added to this statement. First, the relation between the two quantities is not linear, but logarithmic; however, since we shall touch this point only superficially where languages are concerned, the qualitative statement that the transmission rate increases with growing size of the code alphabet will suffice for our purposes. Second, it is *possible* to increase the transmission rate with increasing code alphabet, but this is not guaranteed; a sufficiently inept code designer could succeed in keeping it down.

The principle of shortening the code words by using a larger code alphabet is at work in various forms in Language. We would expect a language with more syllables (which we find convenient as elements of a code alphabet for this purpose) to form shorter words, and hence shorter sentences. Although this is by far not the only factor determining the compactness of a language, the conclusion appears to be supported by the experimental evidence: For example, English appears to have more distinct syllables than German, and German more than Russian, and if a large number of sentences coding the same events in these languages (i.e., translations) is examined, it is found that English has less syllables per sentence than German, and German has less than Russian.

English has evidently more distinct syllables than German or Russian, because it has more phonemes (especially vowels, including diphtongs), but above all because it distinguishes syllables with voiced or unvoiced consonants at the end (*bid, bit*), which neither German nor Russian is able to do. These two features alone must result in a far larger code alphabet in English; they cannot be compensated by the fact that German and Russian use combinations of consonants in the same syllable which English does not use (e.g., *pf* in German or *shch* in Russian).

This code alphabet of "basic" syllables is increased by modifying the syllables in length and stress. If all syllables could occur as either long or short, and either stressed and unstressed syllables, the basic code alphabet would be multiplied by a factor of four in size. Although this cannot be done with all syllables in English and German, it can be done with many, perhaps most, syllables in the language, and the syllable can be modified in length and stress independently. (E.g., the basic syllable *bid* can be short, stressed, or short, unstressed, or long, stressed, or long, unstressed, as in *forbid, rabid, the bead, the love bead,* respectively.) On the other hand, in Russian, a stressed syllable is, with few exceptions, automatically lengthened, so that Russian can only (roughly) double its basic syllables, whereas German can (roughly) quadruple them. We would therefore expect English to be shorter than German, and German to be shorter than Russian. We shall find this expectation confirmed; however, we shall also find that the above is only one of the reasons, and probably not the most important.

Suppose now that a language has a greater number of syllables than English, not necessarily because it has more "basic" syllables, but because it can modify these "basic" syllables by several inflections (of the kind used in Indo-European languages only for expressing moods, questions, orders, etc.). Then such a language would have a far greater number of distinct syllables, i.e., a much larger code alphabet, and therefore we would expect it to be capable of transmitting information at a faster rate than English. Chinese (I am told) is such a language capable of mulyiplying the size of its "basic" code alphabet by different intonations of the same syllable. It is also quite evidently "faster" than English, as I observed on listening to the English simultaneous translation of a Chinese speaker; the speaker spoke at what to me seemed quite a leisurly rate, but the simultaneous interpreter was rattling off the English translation as fast as he could speak.

The second obvious method of increasing the transmission rate of a code is to increase the exploitation of signal space, since this will lead to shorter code words for much the same reasons as in the case of increasing the size of the code alphabet; in particular, a higher exploitation will postpone the point when one runs out of short code words.

To check this for languages, we should compare their code words, i.e., sentences. But, for obvious reasons, it is not easy to measure the exploitation of signal space for sentences directly. This is more easily estimated for grammatical words, which have no well defined significance in the code as we have defined it. Nevertheless, grammatical words represent frequent sequences making up the total sequence of the code word (the sentence). It is therefore in keeping with our general approach, if not with the exact definition, to consider the density of words in a signal space based on phonemes to obtain a rough idea of the various degrees of exploitation of signal space for different languages. Consider, for example, the words that are formed in various languages by three phonemes, the first of which is *b*, the second any vowel of the language, and the third either a *t* or a *d*. (The possible combinations will correspond to points in a space not unlike Fig. 3.1b on p. 56, although there will be many more points, because the alphabet is not binary.) Only some of these combinations are exploited as words of the language. In English, we obtain the following words (recorded orthographically, not phonetically):

bat, bait, bade, bet, bed, bit, bid, but, bud, beat/beet, bead, Bert, bird, boot, bite, bide, boat, bode, beard, bard, bout, bawd,

a total of 22 words, not counting the technical word *baude* (a unit in telegraphy), or the dialect word *baht* (Yorkshire for *without*), or the dialect pronunciations *boid* (Brooklyn for *bird*) and *baird* (Birmingham, England, for *bird*).

But if we try this experiment in German, we obtain a mere three words:

> *bat/Bad, Beet, Boot.*

In Czech, we find only two points exploited as words:

> *bit/byt* and *bít/být.*

One such experiment is, of course, not enough to show that the exploitation of signal space is much higher in English than it is in German or Czech (or Russian). However, the reader may devise other experiments of this type; he will find the experience confirmed in the great majority of cases.

Besides, there are other ways to show that the signal space of English is very crowded (highly exploited). One way, which is more convincing, if less direct, is to examine the noise resistance of English. We know from Chapter 3 that a high exploitation must lead to a low noise resistance; this is so because when noise moves the signal from the original point to a neighboring point in signal space, the result is a meaningless combination if the exploitation is low, but will result in a different message if the exploitation is so high that the signal has been shifted to a point which is also occupied by a message. This happens comparatively often in English; a single misprint will often change the meaning of a message (*Wild wife league to meet tonight*). This also happens in other languages, but with a far smaller frequency than in English, as we shall see in more detail later. Similarly, the possibility of producing puns (*Two whites don't make a Wong*), where the shift is intentional rather than accidental, is much smaller in Russian or German than it is in English, though it is not totally absent.

The high exploitation of English signal space, then, is another reason for the compactness of English. It is, in fact, one of the four main causes of the high information density of English, at least it would appear so from arguments of the above types, though, of course, much statistical research is needed before such a statement can be established numerically and without guesswork, however obvious the guess may seem.

A third way of raising the transmission rate of a code is a method which, for artificial codes, is known as "extending the source." In coding the original source, we assign one code word to each member of the source alphabet; extending the source means assigning one code word to each *sequence* of *n* source alphabet members. Suppose the original source consists of the three elements *A, B, C*; then the second extension of the source consists of the nine elements (sequences) *AA, AB,*

$AC, BA, ...,$ and the third extension consists of the 27 elements $AAA,$ $AAB, AAC, ABA, ...,$ etc. The length of the code word assigned to a member of the nth extension of the source is shorter than the sum of the lengths of the n code words that would be assigned to the sequence in coding the original source, and this saving can be used to make a code as close to an optimum code as we please. It can be shown that in coding the nth extension of the source, the number of code words goes up as the nth *power*, but their average length increases only by a *factor* of n, and this is what the trick is based on. There is, however, a price to pay, and that is the increasing complexity of the code, since a very large number of code words becomes difficult to handle. To take a simple example, we could (theoretically) double the speed of a typist if we provided her with a typewriter whose keys activate two letters at a time; the keys would be labeled $SH, FF, SW, AT,$ etc. However, such a typewriter would not have the usual 40 keys, but about 1600 (actually, a little less, since some sequences, such as $QC, JX,$ etc., never occur in English). The complexity of such a typewriter would therefore be prohibitive, for the typist would have to be as deft as a piano virtuoso, even if she could memorize the 1600 locations on the keyboard.

If coding an extended source had an exact equivalent in Language, it would mean (in our model of the code) that we could code a sequence of two events by a single message (sentence) instead of a sequence of two sentences. There are, indeed, many examples of this, but they are hardly very important. (Example: The sequence of the two events coded by the two sentences *ABCD is a parallelogram. Its sides are equal* can be coded by the single sentence *ABCD is a rhombus.*) They are not important, because they concern particular words and sentences, not the general system in which languages are structured.

However, we meet the *principle* of coding an extended source in some languages, that is, the principle of coding a set of concepts or conditions by a single word at the price of higher complexity. This is what strongly inflecting languages do. True, we have not defined the source alphabet in terms of concepts or conditions; but the general idea is reminiscent of coding an extended source, because the code words are shortened by using a single code word to indicate an agglomeration of several conditions of the coded event, whilst other languages use simpler, but longer structures in which these conditions are indicated by strings of individual (grammatical) words.

Consider, for example, the English message or sentence

$$\text{They will be praised} \tag{5}$$

In our model of a code, this is one code word composed of whatever we choose as elements of the code alphabet (words, syllables, etc.). But there is a certain way in which this code word is structured from the words of the language. It is a form of the word *to praise*; but the third person, plural, future, and passive voice represents an agglomeration of conditions specifying the coded event, and this agglomeration can also accompany other actions than praising. On noting that this agglomeration of items occurs frequently, a code designer might decide to code such an event into a fixed modification of the corresponding verb. Although this does not exactly correspond to extending the source, it does represent the same idea of replacing a sequence of several code elements (grammatical words) by a single code element. But this is exactly what, for example, Latin does:

$$laudabantur \tag{6}$$

This Latin message codes the same event as the English message (5); but it is shorter (in graphemes or words), because it uses a single word where English uses a sequence of four words. The price paid is a greatly increased complexity of Latin grammar, or the rules of the code; this can be seen from the fact that the English verb *to praise* has only four morphological forms (*praise, praises, praised, praising*), whereas the Latin verb *laudare* has some 100 distinct forms.

The above example may not be convincing: It might be argued that (5) does not essentially differ from (6) in structure, since the spaces in (5) are a formality of orthography without equivalent in acoustically transmitted speech. But there are other examples. The verb in the Slavic languages is conjugated (in some persons and tenses) according to the gender of the subject; it is also conjugated as "perfective" or "imperfective," depending on whether the action is completed or not, so that, for example, *to crack* and *to break* are formed from the same root (since cracking means incomplete breaking). Thus, the English message *She finished reading* can be rendered by a single word in Czech (*dočetla*) or Russian (прочитала). This, surely, is no longer a question of single morphology.

Besides, one can go even further. Some languages have two plurals, one for two subjects, another for more than two; the first type is called a *dual*. There are also languages that have three futures: one for tomorrow, one for the day after tomorrow, and one for the future beyond that. If such a language also uses gender and dual, then the sentence

$$Two\ females\ will\ arrive\ on\ the\ day\ after\ tomorrow \tag{7}$$

can be rendered by a single word of that language (by corresponding modification of the verb *to arrive*); the transmission rate is greatly increased at the cost of a very complex grammar.

If coding extended sources were the only consideration concerning the rate of transmission of information, then we would expect the heavily inflecting languages such as Latin or the Slavic languages to be much shorter than English. To some extent this is true, namely to the extent that we compare a phrase that is rendered by a string of words in one language, and by inflection, conjugation or other modification of a single word in the other. Thus, the Czech sentence *dokouřila* is shorther than its English translation *She finished smoking* or *She put out her cigarette*, and the phrase *of the people, by the people* is longer than *populi, populo*. But if other languages have the edge over English in this respect, English more than compensates for it by other devices, such as its higher exploitation of signal space, compared to Latin or the Slavic languages. Moreover, there is also a "counterproductive" effect associated with shortening a language by inflections and other modifications involving the morphology of single words as against combining several words of fixed form: Once the function of a word is identified by its inflection (*dominus, dominum*), there is no need to identify it by its position in the sentence, as is the case in English (*The Lord is ..., to love the Lord*). But identification by position, i.e., by word order, is an extremely effective way of increasing the transmission rate, as we shall see. Nevertheless, the idea that underlies coding by extending the source is also an idea that underlies the structure of heavily inflecting languages, and there can be little doubt that it increases the transmission rate, i.e., shortens the language. In comparing the size of the code alphabet (in syllables) and the exploitation of signal space in English and Russian, we would expect English to be perhaps three or four times shorter than Russian, if this were the only consideration. The fact that Russian is only about 25% longer than English (in syllables per message) must therefore be due to devices which shorten Russian, but which English does not have. The device reminiscent of extending the source, i.e., the use of a complex morphology of single words rather than the use of a string of fixed words, is such a device.

4.3.1. HOMONYMITY

Let us now consider a fourth, and very effective, way of increasing the transmission rate. We have seen that the transmission rate can be increased by increasing the exploitation of signal space, but that at the same time the noise resistance of the code is necessarily reduced: Noise will distort the messages, so that the receiver will receive a signal that has been shifted from its original position in signal space. If there is no other message within the domain in which the signal has been shifted, then the original message can be easily restored (as is the case with the distorted sequence of graphemes *Pwograstination is tqe thief ov time*); but if the signal space is very crowded, the distortion may take the signal to a point where another message is located (*Crime among youth is growing* may be distorted to *Grime among youth is growing*). The fact that beyond a certain point, increased information density can be bought only at the price of lowered noise resistance is an insurmountable obstacle.

Or so it would seem at first sight. However, the above consideration applies only to *formal* decoding, which takes no account of the semantic significance of a message. We have seen an example (p. 74) where a message became ambiguous due to noise, and formal decoding could give us no clue as to whether the original message included the word *megahertz* or *gigahertz*; yet by semantic decoding, i.e., by examining the probabilities of the corresponding two events, the distorted signal could be decoded uniquely. The same is true of most other messages which are formally ambiguous, or even formally unique, but semantically improbable: They can usually be semantically decoded uniquely. Thus, the newspaper headline *Grime Among Youth is Growing* is formally unique, but we will usually assume that the original message was *Crime Among Youth is Growing*, and that *Grime* resulted through distortion (a misprint) of *Crime*. We know that crime statistics are being carefully recorded, which is not the case for grime statistics, and therefore there is a high probability that the message should start with *Crime* rather than *Grime*. (This is a case where we do not examine the probability of the coded event itself, but rather the probability that the newspaper coded it, i.e., the secondary information; but this is just as effective.)

For further examples, we may consult the regular column *Your slip is showing* of the *Reader's Digest*; almost all (and very often all) of the items represent messages that have been distorted into *other* messages (not merely into meaningless sequences), yet these messages can be semantically decoded, that is, the original messages can easily be restored: If this were not so, the item would not be funny, and would therefore not have been included in the column.

We may note in passing that English is a language with a signal space so crowded that it has kept this column of the *Reader's Digest* going regularly every month for many years, relying only on sentences that actually appeared in print, not on examples concocted for this purpose. The several editions of the *Reader's Digest* published in other languages lack this column. The obvious reason is that these "slips" are untranslatable; yet there is also another reason: Other languages have less crowded signal spaces, and therefore this type of "slip" does not occur as frequently as it does in English.

But let us return to the possibility of increasing the transmission rate of a code without endangering its noise resistance by applying semantic decoding. If semantic decoding makes it possible to separate two messages that have been merged into the same domain by noise so as to become indistinguishable formally, why bother to separate them by locating them at some distance from each other in signal space? Why not make that distance zero, so that they become formally identical? Why not, in other words, code two events by the same code word? The code word

will now be formally ambiguous even in the absence of noise; but since
we now rely on semantic decoding *exclusively*, it makes no difference
if two messages were merged by noise, or whether they were one and
the same message (coding two different events) to start with. We shall
call the application of this idea *homonymity*. Homonymity is the use of
a single code word for the coding of several events in the hope that the
ambiguity can be resolved semantically, that is, by examining the probabilities of the two or more events which this code word (a homonymous message) codes. There are several ways in which homonymity is
applied, but let us first give an example. The English word *calf* is a
homonym, which may refer to either a young animal or to a part of a leg.
It is not, by itself, a homonymous message, since grammatical words
are not, by themselves, code words or messages. But code words (sentences, messages) containing this word may be formally ambiguous, e.g.:

> *The rancher bought a brown calf*   (7)
> *The rancher was wounded in the calf*   (8)

Both sentences are formally ambiguous; for example, a computer
translating these two sentences into German would be unable to decide
whether to translate *calf* as *Kalb* or *Wade*, unless it was programmed to
decode semantically. At present, machine translation pays little or no
attention to semantics, and the dilemma is resolved by printing both as
KALB/WADE. (Actually, there are no English-German machines in operation to my knowledge, but the Russian-English machines treat Russian
homonyms in this fashion.) But if both messages are *formally* ambiguous,
they can be decoded semantically without ambiguity, for the probability
of the event that the rancher bought a brown part of a leg is negligibly
small; so is the probability that he was wounded during a stay in a young
animal. Thus, a homonym which is semantically decodable without ambiguity smuggles, in effect, an additional message into signal space, and
therefore shortens the code without lowering its noise resistance. As far
as coding theory is concerned, it is a waste of signal space to have two
words, *Kalb* and *Wade*, in German; one of them, say, *Wade*, could (in strict
theory) be used to replace a longer word, say, *Obergruppenführerstellver-
treter*, and thus make German a more economical language without lowering its noise resistance. The improvement would, of course, be negligibly small as far as all of the German language is concerned; indeed,
homonyms like *calf*, being a small fraction of the words of a language,
cannot play a significant part in raising the transmission rate, and the
example was chosen for explanatory purposes rather than for its significance. It is other uses of homonymity that are far more effective.

Let us therefore take a closer look at homonymity. We start by excluding certain related features from our present consideration. A message like *I am a liberal* is also ambiguous, since almost every speaker

transmitting this message assigns it to a different event. In this sense many, perhaps most or all, sentences of a language are ambiguous, but this is not what we have in mind here. To distinguish such cases from genuine homonymity, we define a homonymous code word as one whose ambiguity is entirely due to a *homonym*, that is, due to a (grammatical) word which has more than one well discernible meaning or more than one grammatical function. More generally, so as not to be limited to the code of Language, we shall understand a homonym to mean a member of the code alphabet for which the rules of the code allow different ways of being absorbed into a code word, the resulting code word having a different meaning for each such way, or no meaning for some ways.

There appear to be three types of homonyms in Language; we shall call them formal homonyms, semantic homonyms, and systematic homonyms. Only systematic homonyms have a significant effect on the transmission rate.

A formal homonym is a word that has two or more meanings or grammatical functions, but the ambiguity can be resolved without semantic considerations, merely from the structure of the sentence. The English word *to* is such a formal homonym, because it can be used either as a preposition or as part of an infinitive, but there is no need to understand the meaning of the sentence to decide which of the two functions it is performing. A computer that has access to a list of English verbs and adverbs can distinguish the two uses of *to* in the sentence *I went to my dentist to have a tooth extracted* simply by checking whether the word following the *to* is included in the list. It does not have to consider the meaning of the sentence, and it would do equally well with the sentence *He surrendered to my apotheosis so as to corrode her spleen*, which has no meaning at all.

Formal homonyms of this type are very common not only in natural languages, but also in artificial codes. In writing or printing (which are artificial codes), the period (.) may indicate the end of a sentence, or an abbreviation. Any American can resolve the two in Russian text without even knowing the Russian alphabet, let alone understanding Russian. In the computer language FORTRAN, the slash (/) may mean one of two instructions, either to divide two numbers, or to start a new line of the print-out. In the Morse code (when used in radio correspondence), dash-dot-dash may mean either the letter *K*, or, at the end of a message, "over to you." And so on.

Formal homonyms of this type use no semantic decoding, but they do shorten the code; if *to* were reserved for infinitives only, some other word, acting as a preposition, would increase the exploitation of the signal space of monosyllabic words, or it would have to have more syllables, thus lowering the noise resistance or increasing the length of the code.

Similarly, if the slash in FORTRAN were to be reserved for division only, a new and longer code word (e.g., two slashes) would have to be used. However, there are too few formal homonyms in natural languages to make them important for the transmission rate of the language as a whole.

A semantic homonym is a grammatical word (or in general, a member of the code alphabet) whose several functions can be discerned only semantically, that is, by considering the probabilities of the events coded by the resulting code word. An example is the English word *calf*, leading to ambiguous code words such as (7) and (8); the ambiguity is resolved semantically as discussed above. Semantic homonyms are particular words of the language, not large classes of words defined by a grammatical property. Semantic homonyms are quite common in natural languages. Examples in English are *calf, to sew/sow, to ring/wring, light* (adjective), and many others. Other languages also abound in such homonyms, e.g., the Russian word лицо may mean either *face* or *person*, the Czech word *zámek* may mean either *castle* or *lock* (which is also true of the German word *Schloss*, and the same two meanings of the Russian word замок are distinguished only by the stress on the first or second syllable). The German word *Rat* is a homonym just as its English equivalent *counsel/council*, and *wenn* may mean either *when* or *if*; the French word *tirer* may mean *to draw* or *to shoot*, and most languages have only one word for *to carry* and *to wear*. But again, if we consider the total number of words in the language (which we are now regarding as a code alphabet), then we find the fraction of semantic homonyms too small to have a significant effect on the transmission rate.

The application of homonymity that does make a difference to the transmission rate is the one based on *systematic homonyms*. By a systematic homonym we again understand a word that can be used in several senses or functions when absorbed into a code word (sentence); however, this time the multiple function is not limited to a particular word such as *calf* or *light*, but it applies to an entire class of words, in particular, to a grammatical species or to a part of speech. For example, in German, there is no difference (barring a handful of exceptions) between adjectives and adverbs; *gut* may mean either *good* or *well*, *glücklich* may mean either *happy* or *happily*, etc., and the double function is not limited to a few particular words, but applies to adjectives and adverbs *in general*. Since systematic homonymity occurs not occasionally for a few particular words, but throughout the language and frequently, it has an important effect on the transmission rate. Thus, every time English uses an adverb ending in -*ly*, it uses an additional syllable which, as shown by German (and quite often also by American colloquial speech), is quite redundant, and slows the rate at which information is transmitted. Similarly, French introduces an additional syllable by the suffix *-ment* to form adverbs from adjectives, in Latin there may be two additional syllables from the suffix *-iter*, and whilst the Slavic languages do not form adverbs by an additional syllable, they do modify the adjective and thus (from the narrow point of view of coding efficiency) they throw away the opportunity of shortening the code by using this modification for something else (say, to replace the word *very* preceding an adjective or adverb).

But this initial example has been taken from German, and this is misleading, for the adjective/adverb economy seems to be the only systematic homonymity in German. The language that abounds in systematic homonyms and, indeed, exploits them to an extent that often endangers its unique decodability, is English.

English packs no less than four distinctly different parts of speech into the same wordform: By adding the suffix *-ing* to *any* verb, it introduces a systematic homonym that can be a present participle (*it is growing*), an adjective (*a growing child*), a gerund *(to stop growing wheat)* or a nominalized verb (*to stop the growing of wheat*). Other languages use distinct word forms for these four functions (as far as they have them).

For all regular verbs, and for most irregular ones, too, English uses the same form as past tense (*I misunderstood*), as past participle (*I have misunderstood*), and as an adjective (*the misunderstood statement*). Here again, other languages often use different forms for these functions (as far as they have them). Moreover, English applies the same idea of using a past participle as an adjective to the past participle of non-existent verbs; thus the peculiarly English constructions (for which there seems to be no equivalent in other languages) *four-legged, cross-eyed, knock-kneed, underprivileged, oversexed, chicken-hearted, double-breasted,* etc., in which past participles are used as adjectives, are morphologically derived from the non-existent verbs *to four-leg, to cross-eye, to oversex, to chicken-heart,* etc.

If the above two systematic homonyms were the only ones used in English, they would (and probably do) by themselves account for a sweeping increase of the transmission rate, i.e., for the compactness of English. Where English uses a single form for present participle, adjective, gerund, and nominalized verb, other languages use four different forms, which leads to longer words either directly by adding an additional syllable, or indirectly by some other modification which takes up some point in signal space and makes it unavailable for an equally short word if the same noise resistance is to be maintained. Consider an example in two other languages:

English	German	Czech
to smoke	rauchen	kouřit
smoking, present participle	– – –	– – –
smoking, pr.p. as adjective	rauchend(e)(r)	kouřící
smoking, gerund	– – –	– – –
smoking, nominalized verb	Das Rauchen	kouření

We first note that neither German nor Czech (or French or Russian) have a present participle in the English sense; their present participles are not syntactically discernible from adjectives (*the smoking chimney*), and they make no difference between *I smoke* and *I am smoking*; if it is necessary to distinguish the two statements, they must be rendered as *I am a smoker* and *I am smoking just now*, thus again lengthening the code words (*je suis fumant* or *ich bin rauchend* are meaningless utterances or unexploited code words). These languages also have no gerund in the English sense; they cannot, for example, provide what is in effect a noun with an object (*breaking the sound barrier*) and instead have to use a nominalized verb (*the breaking of the sound barrier*) or an infinitive in a noun clause (*to break the sound barrier is...*), both of which English can do also. As for the remaining forms, they can be seen to be morphologically distinct, which leads to longer words either directly or indirectly as explained above.

But the story of systematic homonymity in English is far from finished. a vast number of English verbs can be used either as transitive or as intransitive verbs, very often corresponding to two different verbs in other languages. Thus, *to stop*, as an intransitive verb, means *to cease, to come to a halt*; but as a transitive verb it means *to prevent somebody or something from continuing an action*. The two meanings are different, and they are expressed by two different verbs in other languages. Similarly, *to run (down the hill)* and *to run (a business)* are expressed by different verbs, since the meanings of the transitive and intransitive verbs are different. Here are some examples:

English	French[1]	German[1]	Czech[1]
to stop (intr.)	cesser	aufhören	přestat
to stop (tr.)	arrêter	anhalten	zastavit
to leave (intr.)	départir	weggehen	odejít
to leave (tr.)	abandonner	verlassen	opustit
to run (intr.)	courir	laufen	utíkat
to run (tr.)	conduire	leiten	vést
to grow (intr.)	croître	wachsen	růst
to grow (tr.)	cultiver	anbauen	pěstovat
to decrease (intr.)	décroître	abnehmen	ubývat
to decrease (tr.)	diminuer	verringern	zmenšit

[1] Only one of several possible verbs has been given in each instance.

Hundreds of other examples could be given. True, other languages also sometimes use the same verb as a transitive or intransitive one. The French verb *brûler*, like its English equivalent, *to burn*, may mean either *to be on fire* or *to destroy by fire*, whereas German has two different verbs (*brennen, verbrennen*). The German verb *riechen*, like its English equivalent, *to smell*, may mean either to give off an odor, or to detect an odor, whereas French has two different verbs (*exhaler une odeur, flairer*). However, the transitive-intransitive homonymity is far less common in other languages than in English, and quite often the transitive verb in other languages is limited in meaning. Thus, the German verb *rauchen* (to smoke) can be used transitively for cigarettes and the like, but not for smoking meat or sausages, where a different verb (*räuchern*) is needed. The French verb *rouler* and the German verb *rollen* (to roll) can be used transitively for rolling a cigarette, but not for rolling (flattening) metals; a different verb must again be used (*laminer* in French and *walzen* in German). Moreover, there is a large number of English transitive verbs that have no transitive equivalent in other languages: The verb *to fly* in French, Latin, German, Czech or Russian can only be used intransitively; instead of *to fly a plane* one must say "to fly in a plane" or "to fly by plane;" the pilot can *control, pilot, lead,* or *drive* it, but the corresponding verb is not derived from the intransitive verb *to fly*. Many other such examples could be given.

In addition to these cases of transitive English verbs missing from other languages, there are also the English transitive verbs formed (homonymously) from nouns, such as *to sidetrack*. The statement "They subcommitteed the proposal to death" may not be grammatical, but the meaning of the transitive verb "to subcommittee" is easily understood even by those who have never heard it before. The possibilities of turning English nouns into transitive verbs seem limitless; or at least so it would appear on considering the exclamation "Don't gaslight me!" in which the transitive verb "to gaslight" is derived from the name of the film *Gaslight*, in which a man tries to make his wife believe that she is insane.

The peculiar English love for transitive verbs is also manifested in adjectives of the type *one-eyed, four-legged, chicken-hearted*, etc., which have already been mentioned in another connection. They are morphologically derived from the non-existent verbs *to one-eye, to chicken-heart*, etc., and these verbs, though non-existent, are (or would be) transitive. The coining of such adjectives is not possible in other languages. The German, Czech or Russian for *one-eyed* is an adjective which is labeled as such by its ending (the German *einäugig* or the Czech *jednooký* might be rendered in English as "one-eyish"), and in French either a totally new word must crowd signal space (*one-eyed* = *borgne*), or no way of constructing an adjective is available (*blue-eyed* = *aux yeux bleux*).

The ambiguity due to systematic homonyms may be resolved either formally (where possible) or, more often, semantically. The past tense can be distinguished from the past participle and from the past participle used as an adjective by the absence of the verbs *to be* or *to have* in the one or two words preceding it, but as a rule, the resolution must be performed semantically. This is so in the sentences

> *Growing wheat is green, maturing wheat is not* (9)
> *Growing wheat is profitable, burning wheat is not* (10)

A computer which is given no semantic information (e.g., probabilities of the coded events) could not possibly decide that *growing* in (9) is an adjective, whereas in (10) it is a gerund (similarly, *maturing* and *burning* are adjective and gerund, respectively), since the other words are, correspondingly, the same parts of speech. Both sentences are formally ambiguous, since (9) might also be equivalent to *The growing of wheat is green, the maturing of wheat is not*, and (10) might be equivalent to *Wheat which is growing is profitable, wheat which is burning is not*. However, the former is void of meaning (no event is assigned to this combination of words), and the latter, while meaningful, has a very small probability of being coded.

There is yet another systematic homonymity in English, though it is not as general as the present participle-adjective-gerund-nominalized verb economy or the past-past participle-adjective homonym. This is the use of the same word form for noun, verb, and adjective (or at least adjectival). The word *iron*, for example, can perform all three functions (*the iron, to iron, Iron Curtain*). This is not the case in other languages (French: *le fer, repasser, de fer*; German: *Eisen, bügeln, eisern*; Czech: *železo, žehlit, železný*; Russian: железо, глядить, железный). In English, however, this systematic homonym occurs very often, e.g. *water, to water, water colors; the light, to light, a light color*; and a very large number of others. Nevertheless, this homonym, just as the transitive-intransitive homonym, is not as general as the first two we have discussed, since in many cases noun, verb and adjective have three distinct forms (*gold, to gild, golden*). Often the noun and the verb differ in stress (*the present, to present; the increase, to increase;* etc.)

Another case of a systematic homonym in English is the same form of the verb for the indicative and subjunctive moods. Here one might object that the subjunctive has simply died out in English and only the indicative remains. However, it seems more logical to regard the subjunctive, by comparison with French or German, as distinctly present in such phrases as *lest he be, if I were, in order that we might, without requiring that it be,* etc, and to regard it as homonymous with the indicative in in other cases. Besides, far from dying out, the subjunctive is cropping up lately in places where it does not belong. Even a respected writer like Irvin Shaw uses sentences such as *He wondered if he were still in love with his wife.*

This remark, of course, strays from the use of systematic homonyms and their effect on the compactness of a language. But while we are digressing, we might also note that the German systematic homonimity of using the same form for adjective and adverb has left its mark on American English. Many differences between American and British English are evidently due to German influence on the former, as the following examples show:

American	German	English
on the street	*auf der Strasse*	*in the street*
the newest models	*die neuesten Modelle*	*the latest models*
to speak with	*mit ... sprechen*	*to speak to*
antenna	*Antenne*	*aerial*
(tax)wise	*(steuer)weise*	*in the way of (taxes)*
passport control	*Passkontrolle*	*passport check*
dumb (stupid)	*dumm*	*daft*
fresh (rude)	*frech*	*cheeky*

More important are the typically American colloquialisms in which an adjective is used (ungrammatically) instead of an adverb, surely under the influence of the corresponding German systematic homonym. Thus, *to do it good and proper* is an Americanism which an Englishman would express as *to do it well and properly*, and *May the Lord bless you real good* is an Americanism which an Englishman, most likely, would not use at all. The use of adjectives instead of adverbs in American colloquial speech (*do it good, tell me quick, go real quiet, aweful large, to look somebody square in the face, to play bad, to rest peaceful,* etc.) is so common that perhaps soon it will be regarded as grammatical, and perhaps it will penetrate (through TV and the movies) into British English also. Americanisms like *to take it easy* and *to play it cool* have already been absorbed into British colloquial speech, and it would be absurd to say *to take it easily* or *to play it coolly.*

It is, of course, a well known phenomenon that languages influence each other, especially where adopting words and phrases is concerned. Adoption of syntactic and grammatical features is perhaps less common, bu the adoption of the German homonimity for adjectives and adverbs appears to be such a case. There is also other evidence for syntactic and grammatical features having been taken over in certain dialects and colloquialisms in the American melting pot. Consider, for example, the following example of Brooklynese:

You want that I should accept a third-party check,
and made out to an unknown person, yet? That crazy
I am not. (11)

The word order and syntax of these sentences is Slavic. If a computer translated them by the word-by-word method into Polish, it would produce a grammatical Polish sentence. Interestingly enough, the syntax of (11) evidently did not creep into Brooklynese from Polish or Russian, but from Yiddish, whose syntax and grammar are essentially Germanic, even though it contains a large amount of Slavic and Hebrew words. But Yiddish did not only assimilate many Polish and Russian words, it also took over some syntactic features from the Slavic languages. For example, it did away with inversions, which is not surprising, since some of the conjunctions after which inversion is required in German are Slavic (e.g., *khoch*, which is Yiddish for *although*, is obviously related to the Polish *choć* and the Russian хотя). There is no inversion after the *that* in the first sentence of (11) as there would be in German (*du willst dass ich einen Scheck annehmen soll*). Thus, the syntax of (11), though it may have crept into Brooklynese from Yiddish, is Slavic rather than Germanic.

There are other examples of Slavic syntax having crept (through Yiddish) into American colloquialisms. In the phrases *I had myself a ball*, *go have yourself an apple*, the reflexive pronoun conveys a sense of indulgence and solitary pleasure; it does this quite grammatically in the Slavic languages, and it is also used in this way in Yiddish: *Er zang zikh a lid*, "he sang himself a song," means he sang a song just for himself, for his own pleasure; he indulged himself in a song.

Of course, Yiddish has received from, as well as given to, (American) English; there are many "Ameridish" words such as *di opstairsike* (the woman who lives upstairs).

4.3.2. EXPLOITING PERMUTATIONS

Homonimity essentially means assigning the same message to two or more events, the decoding being achieved semantically. Now consider the opposite case of assigning two or more messages to the same event, or *synonymity*. Sometimes synonymous messages are due to words that have the same meaning, or synonyms. As in the case of homonymity, synonymity can be particular or systematic. And just as homonymity will increase the transmission rate because it is a way of exploiting signal space more efficiently, so synonimity will lower the transmission rate because it wastes signal space by using some of its points for coding events that already have a message assigned, instead of using these points for coding some other events, and thus keeping the messages short.

Particular synonyms are particular words that have the same meaning; the synonimity resulting from them (in the sentences containing synonyms) cannot be generalized, and therefore particular synonyms are not important for affecting the transmission rate. The double ancestry of English has resulted in an appreciable number of synonyms such as *paternal* and *fatherly*; there is only one corresponding word in French (*paternel*) or German (*väterlich*).

As before, the feature of importance is systematic, rather than particular, synonymity. Consider, for example, the two messages *My father and mother are dead* and *My mother and father are dead*. They both code the same event and are therefore synonymous. If we were sufficiently unrealistic to examine languages only from the point of view of coding efficiency, this would be a waste, because we could assign these two equally long messages to two different events; we could use the two messages to convey more information (for example, we might "decree" that the first of the two subjects is the one who died earlier). The synonymity is systematic, because two subjects of a sentence joined by *and* can be interchanged without difference in meaning (with some exceptions which have no importance for the point we wish to make). There are very many cases of such systematic synonymity; e.g., in English, any adverb formed by adding -*ly* to an adjective can be replaced by the adverbial phrase *in a* [adjective] *manner*, and without substantial change in meaning. However, the synonymous messages *my father and mother are dead* and *my mother and father are dead* have an interesting property which (in other cases) becomes very important: The two messages are two different permutations of the same combination of words.

We have hitherto used the word *combination* rather loosely to denote any string of code elements. Mathematically, it means an *unordered* group of elements: The groups *AKM, MAK, KMA, AMK, KAM* are regarded as one and the same combination of the elements *K, M, A*. They are, however, six different permutations of these three elements, a permutation being an *ordered* group of elements. Two groups containing the same elements, but in different order, are two different permutations of the same combination. We shall have no need to go into algebraic details,* but the type of combination or permutation that is of interest here is a combination or permutation that allows repetition (e.g., *AVA, AAA, VVA*, etc., where a letter may occur more than once in a combination or permutation). Mathematics, incidentally, is very adept in coining words, but the type of combination or permutation we shall have in mind is one that is described rather clumsily as a "combination (permutation), *r* at a time, of *n* different things, each of which is available in unlimited supply." The points in a signal space using a code alphabet of words (along its

---

* For a popular introduction to combinatorics, see I. Niven, *Mathematics of choice*, Random House, New York, 1965.

coordinate axes) represent strings of words of a language. These strings are permutations, r at a time, of the n words in the language, each of which is available in unlimited supply (since Language allows the repetition of a word in the same sentence). Naturally, not all such strings are grammatical sentences constructed with r words; most of them are meaningless utterances, or "empty" points in signal space.

Now consider permutations of the same combination (of members of the code alphabet). Referring to Fig. 3.1, p. 56, it will be seen that such points are positioned with a certain regularity with respect to the main diagonal of signal space (e.g., CY and YC, or 001, 010 and 100), but this is not a point we wish to pursue here. What is of interest is that under otherwise equal conditions, a code using synonyms must have longer code words (on the average) than a code that does not. If we replaced the code of decimal notation by one in which 141, 114 and 411 denoted the same number, we would soon have to introduce longer and longer strings of digits to denote further numbers, because we wasted permutations of the same combination to denote only one number. Not even the Romans, who had a very cumbersome numbering system, did things as badly as that (IV was not the same as VI, and MCM was not the same as MMC). No competent code designer would leave the various permutations of the same combination unexploited. Yet some languages, in particular, the inflecting languages, exploit permutations comparatively rarely. On the contrary, English exploits permutations of the same combination superbly, even somewhat better than French, which essentially uses the same system.

Consider, for example, the two sentences forming two permutations of the same combination of words:

> *Cain killed Abel*   (12)
> *Abel killed Cain*   (13)

These two sentences code different events, whilst the remaining permutations, such as *Abel Cain killed*, are meaningless.

On the other hand, let us consider the first of these two events coded in heavily inflecting languages, such as Latin, Czech and Russian:

> *Cainus necavit Abelum*   (14)
> *Kain zabil Abela*   (15)
> Кайн убил Абеля   (16)

In (12), the subject and object of the sentence are identified by nothing but their position in the sentence: Whoever is named before the verb does the killing, and whoever comes after it is the victim. Not necessarily so in (14) to (16); here the subject and the object are not identified by their position in the sentence, but by the inflection of the corresponding noun: Abel is not the victim because his name follows the verb *necare*, but because it has the ending *-um*. The situation is analogous in Czech and Russian.

Now since the subject and object are already identified by their inflections, an additional identification by word order is not needed, and the three words of the combination can be permutated at will without loss of meaning, or even very significant change in meaning. For example, the six possible permutations of the words forming the message (15) are

Kain zabil Abela	(17)
Kain Abela zabil	(18)
Zabil Kain Abela	(19)
Zabil Abela Kain	(20)
Abela zabil Kain	(21)
Abela Kain zabil	(22)

All of these six sentences are grammatical, and they all essentially code the same event as (12) in English. True, they are not completely equivalent: For example, (22) has a slight flavor of "As for Abel, what Cain did to him was killing him," and (19) has a flavor of meditation, often rendered in English by the intonation recorded by three dots (*And so Abel killed Cain...*); (18) has a flavor of "Cain didn't play marbles with Abel; he *killed* him, " and so on. However, these differences are very slight, and to a close approximation, all six messages mean the same as the English message (12). A similar statement holds for the permutations of (14) and (16).

Quite similarly, the translation of (13) into an inflecting language also has six permutations, all of which are grammatical, and all of which mean more or less the same as the English message *Abel killed Cain*.

The example also shows why the messages in the inflecting languages are longer. The fact that *killed* is shorter (one syllable) than the corresponding words in Latin, Czech or Russian is, of course, accidental, and has nothing to do with the point under discussion. But the code is lengthened on two counts: first, by the additional syllable denoting the object (*-um* in Latin, *-a* in Czech, *-я* in Russian), and second, by the waste of signal space in alloting six points as messages to each of the two events coded in English by the two (and only two) messages (12) and (13). The second reason amounts to the signal space being filled up with messages very quickly, so that (for the same exploitation, and hence noise resistance) longer combinations of the code alphabet must be introduced by the inflecting languages long before English has run out of shorter code words (sentences).

As we have seen earlier, the inflecting languages have the capability of shortening the code by a method analogous to extending the source; but the waste of signal space due to failure to exploit permutations for coding

different events more than compensates for this. The Indo-European inflecting languages are all longer than English.

The identification of subject and object by word order, i.e., by the
position of the corresponding noun in the sentence, is probably the most
frequent and most important case of exploiting permutations. There are,
however, many other cases. *To have done something* is not the same as
to have something done, and this feature is again a systematic one, since
done can be replaced by the past participle of a very large number of
other transitive verbs (but not by all: *to have something despised* or *to
have something befriended* is hardly grammatical). Apart from such systematic exploitations of permutations, there are also particular messages
with which this can be done; they are often used in plays on words (we
reserve the term *pun* for a certain kind of play on words to be discussed
later). There is, for example, the advertisement for the hair lotion Silvi-
krine:

> *See how well your hair looks after Silvikrine —*
> *see how well Silvikrine looks after your hair*

There are hundreds more of these particular cases, but being particular, they cannot have the same effect on the transmission rate as the
systematic exploitations.

The systematic exploitation of permutations is an extremely ingenious device, for unlike crowding the signal space or using systematic
homonimity, it does not, in practice, lead to a loss of noise resistance.
Noise, as we have seen earlier, is a very general concept, and different
types of noise have different properties — statistical properties, for it
is the very essence of noise to be unpredictable. In designing an artificial code, the designer fortifies the code in a way that will protect its
messages against the type of noise most likely to be encountered in transmission. In sending a message by short wave radio, long strings of symbols may be lost due to fading, i.e., to the signal strength falling below
a minimum required level. On the other hand, the card reader of a computer is more likely to misread individual cards in long runs of correctly
read cards. A third type of noise is human error; for example, experience
has shown that in copying numbers, people often transpose digits, copying 4863 as 4683. Therefore, if a code is to be used in short wave transmission, the code designer will probably choose a burst-error-correcting
code, which is capable of having messages restored even when (fairly)
long strings of symbols have been mutilated. Card readers in computer
installations usually use parity error-detecting codes which are designed
to detect individual, isolated errors. To guard against errors by librarians,
the Library of Congress catalog card numbers use a code which will indicate most errors committed in copying them, including transpositions. In
all cases, the code designer must strike a compromise between efficiency

and noise resistance; every increase in efficiency will open the door to *some* kind of noise.

The same holds for languages. For example, a high exploitation of signal space will increase the transmission rate, but it will make the language vulnerable to acoustic noise, or to misprints in the case of the printed language. The two English messages *Crime among youth is growing* and *Grime among youth is growing* lie so close to each other in the crowded signal space of English that a single misprint will distort one into the other. Systematic homonimity also increases the transmission rate, but it opens the door to what we might call "semantic" noise; for example, the systematic gerund-adjective homonimity gives rise to ambiguities such as Chomsky's sentence *Flying planes can be dangerous.*

Now the exploitation of permutations, which once again increases the transmission rate or the compactness of a language, also opens the door to some type of noise, namely the noise responsible for changing the word order. But, and this is the beauty of exploiting permutations, *there is no such noise* in practice. If there were a plausible cause for distorting the message *Cain killed Abel* into *Abel killed Cain*, then English would have no protection against such a type of noise. Latin, Czech or Russian would be immune against such distortion, but since it has no significant probability, the inferior efficiency of these languages provides protection against a non-existent threat. English foregoes this protection, and thereby raises its information density without practical loss of noise resistance. Moreover, English is to some extent protected even against this type of distortion, since it leaves some of the permutations meaningless: *Abel Cain killed, Cain Abel killed, killed Abel Cain* and *killed Cain Abel* are all "empty" points in signal space, so that an error of this type can be detected, although it cannot be corrected. The inflecting languages, on the other hand, not only lose compactness by wasting the permutations on coding the same event, but they also lose noise resistance, for if these permutations are not assigned to different events, they might at least be left "empty" to provide protection against noise by facilitating the decoding of a mutilated message.

It has often been remarked that we recognize the parts of speech in Lewis Carroll's nonsense poem *T'was brillig and the slithy toves did gyre and gimble in the wabe...* We do this by recognizing the position of the individual words in the sentence with respect to the English words *T'was, and, the, did*; for example, *slithy* is an "adjective" attributed to the "noun" *tove*. But this is only half the story. We are also reassured by the fact that not all permutations of these "words" would correspond to to an English structure: *Gyre and gimble in did toves the wabe* is not a structure in which the genuine words *in, did, the* have a lawful position.

On the other hand, *Gyre and gimble did toves in the wabe* is a permutation allowed by English word order (the parts of speech are now different, the "sentence" being structurally akin to *Jack and Jill did push-ups in the kitchen*). Thus, we recognize the structure of the "sentences" in Lewis Carroll's poem by the word order, just as the structures of the sentences in a similar nonsense poem in Latin or Russian would be recognized from the inflections (or other endings) of non-existent words. Many years ago there was a song beginning with the ungrammatical question *Is you is or is you ain't mah baby*, whose meaning is quite obvious not only from the word order, but also, indirectly, from the fact that it is one of the few permutations of these words that corresponds to an English structure; the other permutations are "empty."

The fact that inflecting languages rarely distinguish permutations of the same combination of words, whereas English uses some, but not all, permutations to code different events and assigns no meaning to the remaining permutions, has an interesting and important consequence. This is a comparatively inflexible word order in English, even when at first sight there would seem to be no reason for such rigidity. For example, English grammar requires that information on place must precede information on time. Only foreigners use such ungrammatical sentences as *I was yesterday in Denver* or *I will be at two o'clock at home*. Similarly, English grammar forbids the separation of verb and object (except by an indirect object), so that *I gave him reluctantly the letter* is ungrammatical. Yet other languages do not have such rigid rules; in German, for example, both the English word order and the word order of the above examples is permitted (*Ich war gestern in Denver, ich werde um zwei Uhr zu Hause sein, ich gab ihm widerwillig den Brief*). Since the above ungrammatical English sentences involve no ambiguity, let alone the wrong message, it might seem strange that English does not allow them. Yet these rules serve a useful purpose as far as noise resistance is concerned, and the high information density of English (with the resulting low noise resistance) makes it advisable to use every available device increasing the noise resistance. These rules increase the noise resistance by keeping many points in signal space "empty" and therefore facilitating the decoding of mutilated messages. For example, the message *I was XXXXX in Denver*, where the *X*'s stand for one or more mutilated syllables, cannot be decoded uniquely, but in attempting to restore the original message, the word order rule limits the possibilities, and hence the value of the ambiguity [see formula (10), p. 71]; for example, the missing word could have been a past participle such as *born*, but not an indication of time such as *yesterday*. Other languages do not have such a high information density, and therefore they need less protection against noise: They do not need such a rigid word order.

Let us now consider how some other languages exploit permutations of the same combination. French runs a close second to English in this respect, since it also distinguishes the accusative and nominative of a noun only by its position in the sentence, i.e., by the word order (*le chien voit le chat, le chat voit le chien*). Particular permutable structures such as *to have done something* and *to have something done* occur in French also, although not in direct correspondence with English. *Tu as l'air perdue, tu as perdu l'air* (disregarding the orthography) is such a particular permutable structure.

However, the reason why French is second to English in this respect is that permutability is often destroyed by the rules of gender concord (which English does not have). Gender concord in French (and other languages) often leads to inefficient (needlessly long) constructions, such as

$$Le\ professeur,\ elle\ est\ charmante \qquad\qquad (23)$$

which means *The professor is charming*, but is literally constructed as *The professor, she is charming*. The feminine adjective *charmante* cannot be attributed to the masculine noun *le professeur*, and a lengthy construction has to be used to resolve the dilemma. The rules of gender concord often destroy the permutability of a message, e.g., *le prix soit déduit de la somme*, but *la somme soit déduite du prix*, where gender concord demands the words *déduit, déduite* (which differ not only in orthography), and gender also demands *du* or *de la*, so that the combination cannot be permutated like its English equivalent *Let the price be deducted from the sum* and *Let the sum be deducted from the price*.

German holds an intermediate position between English and the heavily inflecting languages as far as exploiting permutations is concerned. The accusative of a noun does not differ morphologically from the nominative, but the article and the adjective differ for masculine nouns in the singular (*der, den; ein, einen; schwer, schweren*). Where subject and object do not differ, German permutates in the same way as English, e.g., *Leute machen Kleider, Kleider machen Leute* means the same as *people make clothes, clothes make people*. But where there is a morphological difference, i.e., for masculine nouns with an article or adjective in the singular, the two permutations have the same meaning, e.g., *Die Katze hasste den Hund* (the cat hated the dog) and *Den Hund hasste die Katze* have, except for a difference in emphasis, the same meaning. *Den Hund die Katze hasste* would perhaps be permissible in poetry to achieve a rhyme, but would sound very cramped, much more so than in Latin, Czech or Russian, where the usual word order is readily abandoned in poetry or for any other purpose. The inversions required by German grammar after certain conjunctions represents a permutation of the words in the original sentence is the corresponding clause; this permutation is, of course, not merely permissible, but strictly required. Thus, after *weil* (because), the clause becomes *weil die Katze den Hund hasste*. The remaining permutations, *Hasste die Katze den Hund (?)* and *Hasste den Hund die Katze(?)* are exploited as questions, but have no meaning without interrogative intonation, or without a question mark in the written language.

German can also change the significance of certain words by the word order of the subsequent phrase. After *so* at the beginning of a sentence, inversion follows, as it does in English (*So great was his surprise that...*); but if *so* is not followed by inversion, its meaning is changed, which is the essence of exploiting permutations. Thus, if *so oft* is followed by an inversion, it means *so often*; but if it is followed by the regular word order, it means *as often as* or *whenever*. This device is used in a witty parody to be mentioned in Sec. 4.4.

The heavily inflecting languages such as Latin or the Slavic languages have a very flexible word order for the reasons already mentioned, and they exploit permutations comparatively rarely.

However, this statement, and indeed, most of the preceding considerations, are in need of some qualification. All languages, including the inflecting ones, make a difference between *the black cat saw the brown dog* and *the brown dog saw the black cat*, and these two messages are, strictly speaking, also permutations of the same combination of words. However, permutations of this type have little to do with syntax and structure of a language (as distinct from, say, *to have done something* and *to have something done*); such permutations are simply due to the component events of the semantic base having been permutated, and they would be used just as well in a flag code or a digital code which builds its code words by coding component events of a semantic base. The only type of code that would not do so would be one that "extends the source" by using four unrelated sequences of code alphabet elements representing, respectively, a brown cat, a brown dog, a black cat, and a black dog.

The permutations negating different words are also of this type, for example:

(English)	*I know what I do not want; I do not know what I want.*
(French)	*Je sais que je ne veux pas; je ne sais pas que je veux.*
(German)	*Ich weiss was ich nicht will; ich weiss nicht was ich will.*
(Czech)	*Vím co nechci; nevím co chci.*
(Russian)	Я знаю что я не хочу; я не знаю что я хочу.

It is interesting that these two sentences are not permutations of each other when translated into Latin, for Latin, in this rather unusual case, "extends the source;" it has a special word for "I want" (*volo*), and another for "I do not want" (*nolo*).

The above examples have been given to illustrate messages coding permutations of component events as distinct from genuine syntactic permutations. However, they can also be used to illustrate how "extending the source" can shorten a code. It will be seen that the Czech version of the two sentences is much shorter than the others, including English (8 Czech syllables compared with 14 English syllables). This is not typical of the two languages in general, as Czech is somewhat longer than English when long texts are compared for the number of syllables. But in the present case, Czech shortens the message at the price of a more complicated grammar, and English lengthens it by the use of a grammatical simplification. Czech "extends the source" by using a single word for the two English words *I know* and *I want*: The first person singular endings of the verbs make personal pronouns superfluous. This shortens the message at the expense of complicated conjugations, which are absent from English, but present in Czech, Russian or Latin. (Latin will replace the four English words *I do not want* by the single word *nolo.*) On the other hand, the English construction of questions and negatives by the use of the auxiliary verb *do* is the opposite of "extending the source;" it provides a stereotype or module into which the verb is simply "plugged in" in the infinitive. This "module" lengthens the code, but simplifies the grammar.

The reader may not immediately agree that the *do* constructions are simplifications of the grammar rather than complications. Students of English do not think so at first, either; however, when they get used to it, they are grateful for the trouble it saves with irregular verbs: *I did not sleep, eat or teach* is obviously simpler than *I slept, ate or taught not.* Perhaps the point is seen more easily in a foreign language. In French, a question is formed either by inversion, or simply by preceding the affirmative by *Qu'est-ce que*, which is again a standard routine reminiscent of the English *do* standard routine. If a student of French is required to put *Je ne m'en suis pas allé* (I did not go away) into the interrogative form, he has the choice of inverting the sentence in the hope of hitting on the right form (*Ne m'en suis-je pas allé?*) or simply preceding the whole sentence by the stereotype *Qu'est-ce que*, no matter how complicated the verb. This leaves little doubt that any stereotype construction, such as the *do* construction, is always a great grammatical simplification.

The Russian message is the longest of the five (16 syllables). This is because Russian (unlike Czech or Latin) inserts the pronoun even when the verb ending already identifies the person; also, the two verb forms have two syllables each.

4.3.3. RELATIVE INFORMATION DENSITIES

We have seen that English uses several devices to shorten its code words, and in Chapter 5 we shall meet one more such device. English is, in fact, a comparatively "short" language: If a large number of English messages, such as a long section of text, is compared in different languages (translations), English has less syllables than many other languages. Since all of the translations code the same events, this means that English has a higher average of information per syllable, or (if it is assumed that the duration of the average syllable in time is roughly the same for different languages) a higher transmission rate.

If $S(L)$ is the number of syllables in language L of the compared text, then for sufficiently long text the information density in that language is inversely proportional to $S(L)$. To measure the information density in semantic units per syllable is, for obvious reasons, difficult; but we can make the information density dimensionless by defining a *relative information density*

$$H_{rel} = S(E)/S(L) \tag{24}$$

where E is the language which acts as the standard for comparison, and whose relative information density is therefore 100%. A small test on English, French, Czech, German, and Russian yielded the following results:*

Language	Number of syllables	Relative information density in %
English	1693	100
French	1776	95.33
Czech	1811	93.48
German	1870	90.53
Russian	2214	76.47

The texts selected were different in character (from summaries of technical papers to the Lord's Prayer), and the language of the original text was not the same for all samples. It is not at all claimed that the length of the compared texts (1693 syllables in English to 2214 syllables in Russian) is sufficient to make the figures in the third column reliable. It is, however, believed that the order of the investigated languages, with English first and Russian last, would remain unchanged in a more ambitious experiment.

It is to be noted that these languages do not have wildly different information densities, which was to be expected, since each gains by some device of shortening the code and loses by failing to use another. Thus, the heavily inflecting languages Czech and Russian gain by "ex-

* P. Beckmann, *Versuch einer semantischen Informationstheorie mit Anwendungen auf gesprochene Sprachen,* Wiss.Z. d. Hochsch. Ilmenau, vol. 4, pp. 275-297 (1958).

tending the source" and lose by failing to exploit permutations or to use systematic homonyms; for English, the situation is reversed, but evidently English gains more by these devices than it loses by failing to extend the source.

The high information density of English is mainly due to its crowded signal space, the use of systematic homonimity, and the exploitation of permutations. A fourth major reason, to be discussed in Chapter 5, is a flimsy system of check morphemes. The fact that the exploitation of permutations has a significant effect on the information density can be shown mathematically (permutations and combinations are related to each other by a simple algebraic expression), but it is hoped that the qualitative arguments given earlier have convinced the reader of this fact. As for the exploitation of signal space and systematic homonimity, their effects on the information density are more easily judged indirectly from the loss of noise resistance, as we shall see in the next sections.

Russian is a heavily inflecting language, and as one would expect, its compactness is even lower than that of German, a weakly inflecting language. However, since Czech is also a heavily inflecting Slavic language, it is perhaps surprising that it is substantially more compact than Russian, and even exceeds the compactness of German.

The reasons why Czech is far more compact than Russian are a larger size of the code alphabet (in syllables), a higher exploitation of signal space, and more cases of extending the source.

Czech has a far greater supply of distinct syllables (a larger code alphabet) for two reasons. First, it can use the consonants *l* and *r* as so-called semivowels, that is, a syllable containing an *l* or *r* need not contain a vowel; for example, *prst, vlk, krk* are Czech words, but they are not even syllables in Russian. Second, Czech can multiply its basic store of syllables by four, since stress and length are independent (see p. 106), whereas in Russian, a stressed syllable is almost invariably lengthened as well. Although in Czech the stress is always on the first syllable of a word, Russian exploits distinctions in stress comparatively rarely; more often, both stress and morphology are used to distinguish two words (окн'о, 'окна), so that one of the two is "wasted."

The higher exploitation of Czech signal space can be seen in hundreds of Czech words which are shorter than the etymologically related Russian words due to the absence of the vowel and contraction of the consonants into a single syllable, which represents a saving of one or two syllables per (such) word. Some of hundreds of examples are *mléko-moloko* (milk), *mráz-moroz* (frost), *zdraví-zdorovije* (health), *čtu-čitaju* (I read), *brázda-borozda* (furrow), *král-korol* (king), etc. (The Russian words have been transliterated into Czech graphemes to make comparison easier.)

Finally, Czech extends the source in some cases where Russian does not, for example, like Latin, it uses the nominative of personal pronouns only for emphasis, not when the person is already identified by the verb ending.

All of these points make Russian look like a very inefficient language, and when its length is counted in syllables, this is no doubt true. However, if the compactness is measured per second rather than per syllable, then we must consider another device which is used in both English and Russian, but not in Czech or German. This is the quick and indistinct slurring over unstressed syllables, and pronouncing only the stressed syllables distinctly (*bread 'n BUtter, g'NIGHT, I've gotta TELLya*). In the English word *cooperation*, the stressed syllable *-ra-* is the only one which is pronounced distinctly. The Russian for *cooperation* is сотрудничество (*sotrudnichestvo*), with the stress on the syllable *-ni-*; the other syllables are pronounced rather indistinctly (*s'tr'dNIch'stvo*), so that Russian treats its unstressed syllables in a way reminiscent of English, though the unstressed syllables are not slurred quite as drastically as in English. On the other hand, Czech and German pronounce their unstressed syllables fairly distinctly.

The reason why Czech is shorter than German is again a far greater code alphabet of syllables (due to the semivowels and many sequences of consonants that German finds unpronounceable), greater exploitation of signal space (Czech has eight very frequent one-letter words, German has none, and most other Czech words are also shorter than their German equivalents); but above all, it needs no article. The definite article is the most frequent word in the languages that have one. *The* is the most frequent word in English, and *der, die, das* occur more frequently than any other German word (when the occurrence of any one of them is counted as one occurrence of the definite article). Russian and most other Slavic languages have no article, either, but Russian loses more by other wastes than it gains by the absence of an article, whereas Czech does not.

But the article is a feature which we shall describe as a check morpheme, and the effect of check morphemes on the information density of a language is a point which we postpone to Chapter 5.

4.4. Noise Resistance

An optimum code is one that maximizes the information density. A necessary (but not sufficient) condition for achieving this is a 100% exploitation of signal space, i.e., every point in signal space must be exploited as a message coding a different event. But this means that an optimum code is of little use for transmission through a noisy channel, since the slightest distortion will result in the wrong message being received. An example of a code that exploits every point of signal space is the decimal notation of numbers; no matter how the ten digits of the code alphabet are combined, they always designate some number. The sequence of digits 578 can easily be distorted in transmission by the change of a single digit to, say, 538; on the other hand, the sequence of graphemes *five hundred and seventy-eight* can easily afford the distortion of a single grapheme, or even several graphemes; for example, the sequence *fife gundrid ond zefemty-eeght*, in which 8 graphemes have been distorted, leaves little doubt as to the original number. The reason, as we saw in Chapter 3, is that this combination is an "empty" point in signal space, one to which no meaning is assigned, and when we receive such a sequence, we not only know that it corresponds to a distortion, but we can also correct the distortion by searching the neighborhood of this point in signal space for points occupied by messages, and, if there are several such points, by examining their respective probabilities.

This means that a noise-resistant code must necessarily be redundant; it must leave some points in signal space unexploited in order to facilitate restoration of the original message by the use of these "empty" points.

There are thousands of ways in which the redundancy of a code can be designed to facilitate restoration of an undistorted message, i.e., to make the code noise resistant. But they may be divided into two large categories. The first is to ensure that every message in signal space is well padded by a large neighborhood of "empty" points, so that noise will not distort the message beyond its protective padding. This might be called the "passive" method. The second, or "active" method is to introduce the redundancy in the form of clues that will show where a distorted message originally came from; these clues do not necessarily lie in the neighborhood of the original point in signal space. The second category is that of error-detecting and error-correcting codes. Language as an error-detecting code will be examined in more detail in the next chapter. Here we shall consider some features of Language which are characteristic of the first category, i.e., the padding of messages by a neighborhood of meaningless sequences of the code alphabet in signal space.

4.4.1. LENGTHENING

Let a sentence of a language consist of n code alphabet members (such as syllables or phonemes), so that this sentence is represented by a point in n-dimensional signal space whose coordinate axes bear the code alphabet (phonemes or syllables, say) of the language.

The redundancy (or one minus the exploitation) increases very rapidly with increasing length n of the message. This follows immediately from (13), p. 72; in fact, for any language, the redundancy increases much faster than would appear from that formula, which takes no account of codes whose code words are built up in hierarchies of sequences with increasing redundancy. Language is such a code: Sequences of phonemes form syllables, sequences of syllables form words, and sequences of words form sentences (code words); however, not all sequences of phonemes form syllables, not all sequences of syllables form words, and not all sequences of words form sentences [as implicitly assumed in (13), p. 72]. Hence the exploitation decreases much more rapidly than the nth power of the resolution D (a number smaller than one).

Thus, by coding an event of the semantic base into a longer sentence, the message becomes more noise resistant, because its padding in signal space becomes more voluminous.

The most primitive way of achieving a longer message is simply to repeat it. A typical example is "Will Mr. John Smith of Philadelphia, Mr. John Smith of Philadelphia, please come to the United Airlines desk, I repeat, will Mr. John Smith of Philadelphia, Mr. John Smith..." Introducing redundancy by repetition is useful when the noise level is not constant in time (or space); the hope is that the message will be received at least once during a time when the noise level is low.

A variation of this method is to repeat the message, or a sequence forming its part, by a synonymous sequence, e.g., *Pay $13.54 (thirteen dollars and fifty-four cents) to...*

Another method of lengthening is simply to avoid abbrevations. *Royal Air Force* is more noise resistant than *RAF*, which, in turn, is more noise resistant when pronounced *ar-ay-ef* than when pronounced *raff*. Similarly, on recalling that "noise" is not limited to acoustic noise, but denotes anything that will interfere with the correct decoding of a message, it is obvious that the abbreviation *SHEEP* is less noise resistant than *Society for Hysterical Ecology and Environmental Paranoia*. Also, as we have already noted in Sec. 3.3, the procedure of "explaining" a message (such as *white is stalemated*, or *23 is a prime*) almost invariably involves reducing the information density, and therefore lengthening the message. If insufficient training in chess or mathematics is considered a type of noise (and why not?), then "explaining" comes under this category also.

A third method is to substitute longer words for shorter ones. There are not many messages that consist of a single syllable, but two of them are very important: *yes* and *no*. In situations where the noise level is high, such as radiotelephony, they are often replaced by the longer words *affirmative* and *negative*. These two messages are not particularly suited, since their last syllables do not differ, so that the two messages are still close in signal space; *roger* and *negative* is a better choice.

Turning again from acoustic noise to other types of noise that might cause ambiguity, we find lengthening often used in law and mathematics, two fields where ambiguity is more dangerous than in others. In ordinary English, one says *I have two sons*, because in a simple statement of this type, people are not expected to distinguish between the truth and the whole truth (if I have six sons, I automatically have two sons also). But a mathematician, in similar circumstances, says *This equation has two, and only two, roots*. Similarly, a lawyer does not simply require the truth, but *the truth, the whole truth, and nothing but the truth*, and he uses phrases such as *for reasons of, but not limited to*. It is perhaps unnecessary to give more of these abundantly available examples.

Of course, not every lengthening of this type serves to avoid ambiguities. The use of phrases such as *at this particular time* instead of *now*, and *over and beyond* instead of *over* is not intended to reduce ambiguity and gives no additional information other than the secondary information that the speaker is inarticulate. On the contrary, people using such phrases as *the most essential part* (which is like *the most fifteenth part*) or *the true facts of the case* (as distinct from the fictitious facts?) throw doubt on the meaning of their statements, since they betray their incapability of coding correctly; and throwing doubt on the meaning of a message, or disturbing the single-valued correspondence between code words and source elements, is the very essence of noise.

As we have noted before, redundancy can be used to increase the noise resistance, but its mere presence will not guarantee a higher noise resistance. It is therefore possible to take the final step and to use redundancy to such an extent that the corresponding statements, though grammatical, are highly ambiguous, void of information, or trivial. This method is often used by diplomats, politicians and bureaucrats in an effort to be non-commital or to obscure embarassing facts.

Thus, a politician gives almost no information if, replying to newsmen, he states

> I am not, at this particular time, in a position to make a final statement that would do justice to all the numerous issues involved in this very complex problem; nevertheless, I can assure you that there is not the slightest doubt in my mind that, barring unforeseen developments for which we must, of course, always be prepared, this question will, with the help of not only myself, but also of all the other persons at present engaged in considering this problem from all its aspects, be resolved in due course one way or the other.

Similarly, bureaucratic obfuscation is evident in the following report published by the *Scotsman* and quoted by the *New Statesman* of 15 December, 1967:

> The man from the Ministry in Edinburgh confessed yesterday that it was a "gritty problem." He added: "We have not been able to make great progress. I can tell you, though, that we are at the moment stirring it up a bit. We are taking stock of the situation, but since we have not yet taken stock, I cannot say what we have taken stock of." It was, he said, "an urgent thing that we should want to see done, but on the longer-term basis of urgency."

The fact that bureaucratic gobbledegook is grammatical, but contains little information, makes it easy to spoof by a computer program, as we shall see in Chapter 6.

4.4.2. MINIMUM-RISK CODES

Lengthening, in particular, repetition, is a very crude method of increasing the noise resistance of a code; the waste of signal space is enormous. What would the designer of an artificial code do to improve matters? He would probably note that not all errors are equally probable; and even if equally probable in occurrence, they do not lead to the same consequences: Some errors can be disastrous, others are trivial. A more sophisticated approach would therefore surround the most probable and the most critical messages with the greatest volume of "padding" in signal space, and would not waste much redundancy on messages whose distortion does not lead to serious concequences.

We have defined and discussed the concept of risk on pp. 28-29; it equals the mean penalty in general, and in the present case, it corresponds to the penalties averaged over all errors. In many applications, such as telemetry, certain computer programs, etc., the penalties are well defined (or well definable), and it is possible to design a so-called minimum-risk code, which will minimize the quantity (20), p. 28.

In other cases, the penalties are too unpredictable to design a minimum risk code, but the idea of making particularly dangerous errors particularly improbable can still be used. Thus, the message to be sent by the President to unleash nuclear retaliation is (it is to be hoped) coded with greater noise resistance than the message wishing the Joint Chiefs of Staff a Happy New Year. If both had the same noise resistance, this would be a waste of signal space which could be put to better use by additional insurance that nobody will press the nuclear button on receiving a New Year card.

There may be certain features of Language that are to some extent based on this idea of keeping the neighborhood of a critical message empty, where "critical" means "whose misinterpretation may have serious consequences." The English message *Help!* is such a critical message; it is also short, and therefore liable to be distorted. Of course, the fact that in an emergency people do not call, but scream, for help, plays an important part in distinguishing this message from others; presumably any scream, whatever its articulation, comes from someone in need of help. (There is, incidentally, an analogy to this in artifical coding, too. Ordinary radio communications go through narrow channels, and no transmission may take up a wider frequency band than the allotted one. But a ship calling SOS uses a special transmitter calling attention to the signal by its incursion into other channels.) But in addition, the message *Help!* seems to be comparatively isolated in the otherwise very crowded English signal space. Most other monosyllabic English words have many others to rhyme with them (*cane, Dane, feign, gain, Jane, lane, mane, pain, reign, sane, vain, wane, train, swain, stain*), but the only word to rhyme with *help* that I can think of is the little used verb *whelp*. A rhyming word is, of course, only one of the words lying near in signal space (*held* is also near *help*), but even so, *help!* seems to be unusually isolated in English signal space. Perhaps this is not accidental, for the French *Aux secours!*, the German *Hilfe!*, the Czech *Pomoc!* and the Russian помогите! also appear to be comparatively isolated, although in the other languages this is less striking, since their signal spaces are less crowded, and therefore a word with few neighbors is less unusual.

The evidence presented here is admittedly flimsy, and it might well be that the comparative isolation of the point corresponding to a call for help in several languages is purely accidental. But perhaps it is a point inviting further investigation, and should the conjecture be confirmed, this would be an example where Language uses a principle on which minimum risk codes are based.

But if there is doubt as to this case involving only formal decoding, there can be little doubt as to a similar case appearing systematically in all languages and involving semantic decoding. A natural language is capable of coding infinitely many events; some of these are similar (*poppies are red — carnations are pink*), others very dissimilar (*poppies are red — better to have a smart enemy than a stupid friend*). Since Language makes up its sentences (code words) as sequences of words, which, most often, correspond to certain concepts or properties, we can define similar events as events involving similar concepts, and similar concepts as concepts belonging to a set of elements whose common characteristics severely limit the number of such elements in the set. Thus, *poppy* and *carnation* belong to the set of garden plants, a set with a limited number of members; but *poppy* and *friend* belong to the set of tangible objects, a set with a vast number of members. *Poppy* and *friend* are therefore dissimilar, or at least more dissimilar than *poppy* and *carnation*.

It is obviously the messages coding similar events that primarily need protection from being distorted into each other, for the distortion of a message into another message coding a dissimilar event can be detected, and usually corrected, by semantic decoding. This protection can be provided by separating words corresponding to similar concepts by large distances in signal space, that is, by making them sound very differently. Consider, for example, colors. The colors of the visible spectrum (seen in a rainbow) have the English names *red, orange, yellow, green, blue, indigo, violet*, and these exhibit a striking contrast in vowels alone, let alone consonants.

Although the names of the colors are widely separated from each other in signal space, they are very close to other words (*red-led, blue-flew, green-ream*, etc.) However, the resulting noise resistance is low only as far as formal decoding is concerned. The point mapping the message *Grass is green and poppies are red* is indeed close to the point corresponding to *Grass is mean and poppies are led*, and a computer programmed only to recognize grammatical English sentences would not be able to detect an error on receiving the second message, let alone correct it. But as soon as semantic decoding is used, that is, the probabilities of the two messages having been transmitted are examined, there is little doubt as to resolving the ambiguity even in such a short message.

Thus, by relying on semantic decoding, *it is only necessary to code similar events by dissimilar messages, for similar messages coding dissimilar events can be resolved semantically*, even if noise makes their formal decoding impossible. By assigning words of high acoustic contrast to similar concepts, the noise resistance is maintained without undue redundancy of the code. Semantic homonyms, such as *calf*, are merely the final step in following the rule of assigning similar words to dissimilar concepts: In a semantic homonym the two words are not merely similar, but they merge into identity. The names for the colors are not only widely separated from each other in signal space and near other words designating dissimilar concepts, but they are often themselves semantic homonyms (*He is too yellow to fight. I feel blue. Better dead than red. The black market. A white lie.*). The two concepts are mapped not merely by close points, but by identical points; however, semantic decoding resolves the ambiguity.

The principle of coding similar concepts by very differently sounding words, which results in the coding of similar events by dissimilar code words, or in large distances between the points mapping the corresponding messages in signal space, is one that is widely used in many languages; in fact, we shall shortly give reasons for believing that it is used in *all* natural languages. Consider these examples for colors:

English: *white, red, yellow, green, blue, brown, black*
French: *blanc, rouge, jaune, vert, bleu, brun, noir*
German: *weiss, rot, gelb, grün, blau, braun, schwarz*
Czech: *bílý, červený, žlutý, zelený, modrý, hnědý, černý*
Hungarian: *féher, piros, sárga, zölt, kék, bárna, fekete*

The application of this principle is not, of course, limited to colors. Here are some other examples:

English: *yes-no; left-right; big-small; war-peace; two-four*
French: *oui-non; gauche-droite; grand-petit; guerre-paix; deux-quatre*
German: *ja-nein; links-rechts; gross-klein; Krieg-Frieden; zwei-vier*
Czech: *ano-ne; levý-pravý; velký-malý; válka-mír; dva-čtyři*
Latin: *sic-non; sinister-dexter; magnus-parvus; bellum-pax; duo-quatuor*
Hungarian: *igen-nem; bal-jobb; nagy-kis; háboru-béke; kettő-négy*
Danish: *ja-nej; venstre-højre; stor-lille; Krig-Fred; to-fire*

It is easily seen that all these languages use very differently sounding words for similar concepts, and it is highly probable that the principle holds for all languages. The reason for this confidence is that the principle is self-adaptive: If a violation occurs, life simply forces the offending word to be abandoned. Thus, the word *propeller* was originally used (in the British RAF) for propellers made of wood; a metal propeller was called an *airscrew*. (Perhaps it was the other way round, I cannot remember.) But *airscrew* is quite close to *aircrew*, and the two concepts are similar in the sense that they both frequently occurred in aviation. The inevitable distortions in telephones, teleprinters, typists taking dictation, etc., caused misunderstandings so often that the word *airscrew* was finally abolished by official decree of the British Air Ministry.

Even more convincing is an example taken from German: The words *zwei, drei* (two, three) have a similar sound, although they are both numbers, and therefore similar concepts. The words survived until the twentieth century; but they did not survive the noise levels in telephones and the radio. Although *zwei* is still used in general speech, it has become *zwo* in giving a telephone number, or when the time of day is given over the radio. The word *zwo* is also used exclusively in the German military. The German names of the months *Juni* and *Juli* also differ only very slightly in sound, although they are words for similar concepts. To avoid misunderstandings, the latter is often pronounced as if it were spelled *Julei* (rhymes with English *July*).

Another case in point is the seeming violation of the principle in similar languages, such as American and British English. It is not a true violation, since these two languages are different codes which are sometimes erroneously assumed to be identical. (G.B. Shaw called Britain and the USA "two countries separated by a common language.") There are many examples of similar words, or even the same word, corresponding to two similar concepts. Thus, *napkin* in English means a diaper, an American napkin being called *serviette*. An English *subway* is a pedestrian underpass, an American subway being called an *undergound* or *tube*. *I am mad about this book* may mean the opposite in English and American. The British expression *I wasn't half angry* is often misunderstood by Americans to mean *I was only slightly angry*, whereas it really means *I was extremely angry*. When the same word corresponds to two dissimilar concepts, the probability of misinterpretation is small, and the penalty light. This is the case for words like *trolley*, which in American means an electric street car, and in English a serving cart. But when the same word corresponds to similar concepts, the probability of erroneous decoding is large, and the penalty may be large, too. During World War II, the British ordered several shiploads of *corn* from the US, and were very dismayed when the convoy brought what they called *maize* instead of the expected grain of wheat. I first learned English in England, where *pavement* means what Americans call *sidewalk*; my first drive in the US took me along a road in the Rockies past a sign saying "Pavement ends," and since the road had a sidewalk (or at least a shoulder), I took no notice of it. A few seconds later I found out quite dramatically that *pavement* does not mean the same in American and English; however, the word denotes two similar concepts in the two languages.

In all of these cases the error is not due to a genuine violation of the principle of using large distances to separate words corresponding to similar concepts, but to an insufficient knowledge of the code, i.e., to a mistranslation. The same type of error occurs in translations between other similar languages. Here are a few such pitfalls in the etymological similarity between German and English:

German	English
schlau	not *sly*, but *smart*
Zeit	not *tide*,* but *time*
schlicht	not *slight*, but *simple*
Knabe	not *knave*,** but *boy*
Knecht	not *knight*, but *underling*
Zoll	not *toll*, but *duty (tariff)*
zart	not *tart*, but *tender*
Hund	not *hound*, but *dog*
Dogge	not *dog*, but *hound* (usually *greyhound*)
heben	not *heave*, but *lift*

Very many other examples could be given. Note that in the above examples the words correspond to similar, but different concepts. A word

---

* Except in such words as *Yuletide*.
** Shakespeare still used *knave* in the sense of *boy*.

like *Gift* (which does not mean *gift*, but *poison*) does not belong in this group, because the meanings of *present* and *poison* are not very similar.

Similar examples occur in French and English:

French	English
joli	not *jolly*, but *pretty*
concurrence	not *concurrence*, but *competition*
contrôler	not *to control*, but *to check*
bref	not (usually) *brief*, but *short*
court	not (usually) *curt*, but *short*
assister	not *to assist*, but *to be present*
éventuel	not *eventual*, but *possible*
large	not *large*, but *broad*
étroit	not *straight*, but *narrow*
étage	not *stage*, but *floor (story)*
étape	not *step*, but *stage*

The Slavic languages are closer to each other than the Romance or Germanic languages. Thus, a Czech can get a fairly good idea of what a Pole is talking about, though he will not understand him completely; a German (let alone an Englishman) has only a vague idea what a Dutchman or Dane is saying. The Slavic languages are therefore particularly prone to mistranslation due to the seeming "violation" of the principle discussed above. Examples of similar, but different meanings in Czech and Russian corresponding to etymologically similar words are *shroud-shirt, tomb-grave, nation-people, brief-short, to chat-to speak, to twist-to turn, institute-constitution, lukewarm-moist, castle-town, astonishment-terror, thumb-finger, lip-mouth, snout-lip,* and hundreds of others. Sometimes the meanings and the etymology are strangely interwoven, although a little etymological investigation can clear up the puzzle. Thus, the word *život* means *life* in Czech, but *stomach (belly)* in Russian. However, the roles are interchanged in the Russian for *alive* and the Czech for *corset* (a garment covering the stomach). The explanation is that the word meant *womb* in ancient Slavic; the Czechs generalized this to the life giving organ, and the Russians to the region of the body in which it is contained. Both have abandoned this word in the sense of *womb*; the modern Russian word for *womb* is related to *mother*, and the modern Czech word is related to *child*.

Another Russian word, красный, has given rise to a universal mistranslation. The reader may be under the impression that Red Square in is "Red" because the Communist government named it that way. Not so. It had the same name in Tsarist Russia, long before Lenin was born. But the word originally meant *beautiful* rather than *red* (it still means *beautiful* in Czech). The Russians seem to associate beauty with color, at least they have a homonym meaning both *flower* and *color*, and the root of the word *beautiful* also appears in *paint*. In any case, for reasons that have nothing to do with politics, the Russian word красный changed its meaning from *beautiful* to *red* long before the revolution and long after Beautiful Square had been laid out in Moscow. Many Russians also think that Red Square is named in honor of communism. It is not; Red Square is a universal mistranslation of what should really be Beautiful Square.

Etymological similarity is a major cause of mistranslations. A host of examples could be given, such as the yarn about the school boy who translated *Tant pis, tant mieux* as "Auntie is leaving the room, auntie is feeling much better," or the German who asked the waiter "How long must I wait before I become a beefsteak?" (*bekommen = to get*). Mistranslations in general, not necessarily caused by etymological similarity, could fill a whole book, and a very amusing one. There was, for example, the sign in a Swiss hotel which read "Visitors are preyed not to enter the ballroom in boots of the ascension." But the winner of them all is probably a British Member of Parliament who went to France not long after World War II to give a lecture on his life. Using the wrong word for *past*, he opened the lecture with the following sentence: *Chaque fois que je regarde mon derrière, je vois qu'il est divisé en deux parties.*

4.4.3. VULNERABILITY OF MESSAGES IN OVERCROWDED SIGNAL SPACE

We have seen in the preceding paragraphs how a message can be made noise resistant by padding its neighborhood in signal space with meaningless strings of code elements. Let us now consider what happens when this condition is not satisfied, and the neighborhood of the message contains many other messages. We have already seen what will happen in general: Even a slight amount of noise will distort the message into another message, leaving only semantic decoding to detect, and possibly correct, the error. At this point we will consider some examples.

It has already been noted that English has a very crowded signal space, due to such causes as a high exploitation of syllables, use of systematic homonimity, and (as we shall see later) due to a very flimsy check system. Examples of ambiguities due to lack of check morphemes will be considered in Chapter 5, and exploitation of permutations does not, in practice, lower the noise resistance of English, since there is no plausible noise that will change the word order. We shall therefore only briefly examine the loss of noise resistance caused by high exploitation of signal space and by the use of systematic homonimity.

The high exploitation of syllables has previously been pointed out by noting the large amount of monosyllabic English words formed by the phoneme sequence *b*, vowel(s), *t* or *d* (p. 107), and the large amount of monosyllabic English words that will rhyme. Only one example of each such case was given, but it would be easy to give other examples, and to compare them to the smaller set of such examples in other languages. There is, however, an easier method of demonstrating the comparatively high density of messages in English signal space, and that is to note how frequently and how easily English messages are distorted into different messages, often requiring only distortion of a single phoneme or grapheme; as for the use of systematic homonimity, the message is quite often ambiguous to start with, without the intervention of noise or the presence of a grammatical error.

Consider first distortions of messages into other messages due to insufficient distance between them in signal space. This is usually caused by insufficient distance between words (*last-least, same-some, crime-grime, window-widow*); typical examples are a misprinted advertisement for Ford cars,

YOUR FIRST COST IS YOUR LEAST COST

or a misprinted line in an advertisement by a mail order business,

ORDERS RECEIVED BEFORE NOON SHIPPED SOME DAY

In both cases the error can be detected and corrected semantically, because the events coded by these messages have a negligible probability of being advertised. Errors of this type occur in all languages, because all languages have similarly sounding (or printed) words in some parts of signal space, even if the average density of messages in their signal space is low. For example, the signal space of German has a fairly low exploitation, but it is not immune to distortions like *Wir bitten diesen Dreckfehler zu entschuldigen* (please excuse this dirty mistake) due to the small distance between *Druckfehler* (misprint) and *Dreckfehler* (dirty mistake, lousy mistake); similarly *bodenlos* (abysmal) and *hodenlos* (without testicles). However, such errors do not occur with anywhere near the frequency caused by the crowded signal space of English. Consider, for example, the following distortions in newspaper headlines which actually appeared in print:*

GRIME AMONG YOUTH GROWS
FLIES FROM GEORGIA TO SEE FRIEND INJURED IN CRASH
WALWORTH COUNTY FARMER DROPS HEAD WHILE PLOUGHING
MAN FALLS IN SOUFFLE, BREAKS ARM
LIVE WIFE STRIPS CLOTHES FROM ORGANIST IN STREET
CLEANING WIDOWS CAN BE FUN
MOTHER AND DAUGHTER ARRESTED FOR SHIP LIFTING
ENTOMOLOGISTS FIND UNKNOWN SPECIES OF WORM IN
ANCIENT EGYPTIAN'S WOMB

* E. Tempel, *Humor in the Headlines,* Pocket Books, New York, 1969.

WILD WIFE LEAGUE WILL MEET TONIGHT
GOON MANNERS ARE A SOCIAL ASSET ANYWHERE
LIBRARY TO STORE BORE BOOKS
FOURTH NAVEL WINS ACCLAIM FOR WRITER
SETS FIRE, DIETS IN IT
COOKING GARBAGE CAN BE FUN AND TASTY
ARMY TO BUILD HUG LABORATORY
NEW PASTOR TO BE PICKLED BY CHURCH COMMITTEE
DEAD CAN HEAR MUCH BETTER WITH NEW HEARING AID

The list of such examples, involving only the change, omission, or addition of one or two graphemes, could be continued endlessly. Yet the above examples are only a few of a set limited by the following properties: 1) They appeared in print as headlines in American newspapers, 2) The distortion has not only resulted in another message, but a funny message, 3) the error is easily detected by semantic decoding.

For additional support of the claim that the signal space of English is more crowded than that of other Indo-European languages, we note that the *Reader's Digest* has been running a column called "Pardon, your slip is showing" every month for many years, and the restrictions are, in effect, just as severe as for the above examples, except that the "slip" need not be a newspaper headline. The column is not present in the other editions of 13 other languages in which this magazine is published, although one would assume that it is just as easy to request readers' entries, since translation is not feasible. There are, of course, many times more American newspapers than, say, German ones being published, which in itself ensures an abundant supply of such "slips" in English; but why is there (as far as I know) no such German column published less frequently, or with fewer entries, to compensate for the difference?

The answer, surely, is that English signal space is much more crowded, so that a "slip" slips more often into a neighboring message, and not just into the meaningless "padding" of the message.

Moreover, the above examples are based on graphemes, not phonemes; yet English orthography is highly redundant, and therefore highly noise resistant. (The redundancy of printed English is 50%, that is, if half of the letters of English text are removed at random and independently by letters, the text is still readable; *y cn rd ths, cnt y?*) Czech, which is some 9% longer than English when measured in spoken syllables, is some 15% shorter when measured in graphemes (because its orthography is close to phonetic). Thus, the examples of low noise resistance in printed English indicate an even lower noise resistance of the spoken language (though not, of course, for each specific example).

Let us next consider the loss of noise resistance due to homonimity, the device raising the transmission rate as discucced in Sec. 4.3.1. The loss of noise resistance is basically due to the same reason as before, except that now the message does not have to be shifted through small distance in signal space to become ambiguous; it need not be shifted at all, because it may already be ambiguous to start with, in which case only semantic decoding can resolve the ambiguity.

Particular homonyms can lead to ambiguities in all languages, but the two meanings of the homonym are usually such that decoding is quite easy. Thus, the particular homonym *case*, two meanings of which (eventuality and container) are rendered by the separate French words *cas* and *étui*, lead to the ambiguity of the following headline, which appeared in print:

TWO GIRLS, DAD ALL JAILED IN WATCH CASE

Similarly, the particular homonym *pat/Pat* caused the following ambiguous headline:

IKE SAYS NIXON CAN'T STAND PAT

Sometimes two particular homonyms can cooperate to form an ambiguity, e.g.,

WIFE CHARGES BATTERY

or

RUBBER FARMERS TURN TO COCOANUTS

the latter containing the homonyms *to turn to* (change one's interest, be transformed) as well as *rubber farmer* (farmer growing rubber, farmer made of rubber).

The prize in the category of particular homonyms should perhaps go to the *Florence* (Colorado) *Citizen*, which printed a story under the following headline:

BEATS ASS OFF HUSBAND WITH PITCHFORK
Heroic Woman Saves Husband's Life

Note that this headline, unlike the preceding ones, needs the subcaption to be semantically decoded without ambiguity.

More important than homonymous nouns are the many meanings of the verb *to have*. In other languages, the corresponding verb is mainly used to denote possession, although other uses are also quite common in French (*avoir froid, avoir envie*), German (*Hunger haben, Lust haben*), and others; but English puts this verb to particularly many uses (*to have a baby, to have guests, to have a good time, to have the house painted,* etc.), not counting its uses as an auxiliary verb (*to have gone*). This means that if we traverse signal space along a coordinate of *have*, we will run through clusters of messages, including some ambiguous ones, such as the following newspaper headlines:

AVOID HAVING BABY AT DINNER TABLE
TIRED WIFE HAS HUBBY FOR LUNCH
ATTORNEY SAYS HE'LL HAVE BABY IN COURT
VFW TO HAVE NEEDY CHILDREN FOR DINNER

Consider next the effects of systematic homonimity. Systematic homonymity applies to entire parts of speech, not merely to particular words; therefore the ambiguities due to systematic homonyms are far more frequent than those due to particular homonyms. Consider first the noun-adjective-verb homonymity in English, which is not truly systematic, because it applies to many, but not all nouns. *Talk* is such a homonym, and it has lead to ambiguous newspaper headlines such as

DEALERS TO HEAR CAR TALK FRIDAY
POULTRY MEN TO HEAR EGG TALK

in which *car* and *egg* contribute to the ambiguity for the same reason, since they can act either as nouns or as adjectivals.

Similarly, the noun-verb *run* and the noun-adjectival *maiden* yield the ambiguity in

GLASS DOMED CAR MAKES MAIDEN RUN

The presnt participle-adjective-nominalized verb-gerund homon:mity is truly systematic, since any verb with the ending *-ing* can be used in these functions. In Chomsky's well known sentence *Flying planes can be dangerous*, the word *flying* is a gerund in one meaning, and an adjective in the other. One could make up an endless list of other examples, e.g.,

REVOLTING FOREST RANGERS PROTEST THE PLIGHT
OF HUNTING VICTIMS

where the ambiguity is sextuple, since the forest rangers might be either in revolt or revolting others, and the plight could concern the victims of hunting, or the hunting of victims, or victims engaged in hunting. As usual, only one of the six events coded by this message has a high probability, the event that forest rangers in revolt protest the plight of the victims of hunting. Also, the ambiguity is sextuple only in print; in speech, the ambiguity of *hunting victims* is partially resolved if the stress is on *victims*, and totally resolved if the stress is on *hunting* (as it probably would be in the present case).

The past-past participle-adjective homonymity is also systematic for all English regular verbs. *Uncovered* can be an adjective or the past tense of a verb, *remains* can be a noun or a verb, and *Indian* can be a noun or an adjective in the following ambiguous headline:

ANCIENT INDIAN REMAINS UNCOVERED NEAR ROSWELL

However, in this case, the ambiguity is also cause by the omitted check morpheme *are*.

The homonymity of using the same verb transitively and intransitively is one of which English is particularly fond. Like other homonymities, it can endanger the protection from ambiguity; for example, the two meanings of *stop* resulting from this homonimity (see p. 117) give rise to the ambiguity in

OWNERS CANNOT BE REQUIRED TO STOP BARKING

The device of exploiting permutations is one that does not usually lead to ambiguities, for reasons that have already been discussed. Thus, the headline

WOMAN HURT WHILE COOKING HER HUSBAND'S BREAKFAST
IN A HORRIBLE MANNER

is, strictly speaking, not ambiguous; by the rules of English grammar and word order, it means that the woman cooked the breakfast in a horrible manner and nothing else. By semantic decoding, i.e., comparing the probabilities of the corresponding events and of their being coded as a headline, we easily ascertain that the woman was *hurt* in a horrible manner; however, in this case the fault lies not with the structure of English, but with the editor who chose the wrong permutation to code the information he intended to convey.

But in all the other cases discussed above, the cause lies with the structure of English: The various devices used to make English a highly compact language are also the very devices that make it highly vulnerable to ambiguity.

Other languages are, of course, also vulnerable to ambiguity, but only to the extent that they use devices raising their information density. All languages have particular homonyms, and these, like all other compactness-raising devices, can lead to ambiguity. The intentional ambiguity of the title of Oscar Wilde's play *The Importance of Being Ernest* has been translated into German as *Ernst sein* (being Ernest), and into Czech as *Jak je důležité mít Filipa* (How important it is to have Philip = to have one's wits about him). Similarly, the ambiguity of

ACTRESS UNVEILS BUST AT CEREMONY

also translates into German, since the German homonym *Büste* (bust) has the same two meanings.

However, other languages, being more redundant, give more protection against ambiguity. More evidence for this statement will be given in the next chapter, but it also follows from the absence of systematic homonymity in some languages, and from the absence of certain particular homonyms. For example, the English preposition *with* is a particular homonym, since it is used both in the sense of *accompanied by* and *by means of*. (The same is true for the German preposition *mit*.) Other languages distinguish the two meanings either by different words (French:

avec and *par*) or by different constructions (Latin: *cum* or solely the ablative case; Czech, Russian: *s*, or solely the instrumental case). This prevents ambiguities of the type

NIXON FISHES WITH CUT FOOT

in Latin or in the Slavic languages, but not in English or German (*Nixon fischt mit verwundetem Fuss*).

Another redundancy that many languages have is gender; it is present in English only to a very minor extent (*he, she, it; waitress, widower*), and with some minor exceptions, it is entirely determined by biological sex. The ambiguity of the headline

HORSE BITES OFF BABY'S FINGER AS IT SITS IN BUGGY

is resolved in all languages assigning a different gender to *baby* and *horse* (Czech, Russian, but not German or French).

The vast number of ambiguities that can result from the device of systematic homonymity is, of course, prevented in languages which do not use this device. *To hear a car talk* cannot be ambiguous in a language that does not use the same form for adjective, noun and verb (*ein Auto sprechen hören; einen Autovortrag hören*); *growing flowers* cannot be ambiguous in a language that does not use the same verb transitively and intransitively (*fleurs croissantes, cultiver les fleurs*), nor in a language that does not have a gerund (such as French, German, Czech or Russian, where only *to grow flowers* or *the growing of flowers* has an exact equivalent); and the ambiguity of

BARONESS TO DISCUSS AFRICAN ADVENTURES
WITH CHIMPANZEES

is resolved in languages in which *to discuss* is not a transitive verb (such as French, German, Czech, Russian or Latin).

On the other hand, where other languages have devices of increasing the information density that are absent from English, they may give rise to ambiguous messages, the ambiguity being resolved in each of the English translations. Thus, the nonexistence of articles in Latin and most Slavic languages can occasionally lead to ambiguities; *soror mea iit in scholam* may mean *my sister went to school* (to be educated) or *my sister went to the school* (to a PTA meeting) or *my sister went to a school* (to learn driving). However, as we shall see in the next xhapter, ambiguities of this type are rather rare, since the article serves a more important function than to distinguish between definite and indefinite objects.

It should also be noted that all of the above ambiguities are due to the particular structures of particular languages. More often, ambiguities arise from the very character of Language as a code for the transmission of information in general, and these ambiguities are common to all lan-

guages. We have already noted that a statement like *Grass is green,* let
alone more complicated statements, is highly ambiguous. It is, in fact,
characteristic of Language to code very many events by a single message. In most cases, such as the particular spectral curve described by
the word *green*, the distinction is unimportant. In other cases, the ambiguity is resolved by semantic decoding. For example, the statements
The convict hit the guard in the stomach and *The convict hit the guard
in the court room* are only formally ambiguous, since in each case the
"other" event has zero probability. But in some cases semantic decoding
does not yield a zero probability for all but one of the coded events; the
resulting ambiguity might then be called semantic rather than formal.
Some semantic ambiguities are common to Language as a code in general,
and such ambiguities will not be resolved by translation. For example,
the following ambiguous headlines can be translated into other languages
without eliminating the ambiguity:

> STREETWALKER HURT IN BUSINESS SECTION
> (Gassenmädchen im Geschäftsviertel verletzt)
> BRITISH POLICEMAN SLAIN FOR FIRST TIME IN 7 YEARS
> (Policier britannique assassiné pour la première fois en 7 ans)
> ACCIDENT CAUSED BY BEE IN PYJAMAS
> RATTLESNAKE HUNT INCLUDES WOMEN
> BABIES FLY BEST AT NIGHT
> HOSTESS NEVER BOTHERS TO DRESS FOR CARD PARTY
> ACCUSED SAYS DEAD MAN THREATENED HIM WITH RAZOR
> GRANDFATHER AND GRANDSON BORN ON SAME DAY
> 11 MEN NEEDED TO FEED PYTHON

In resolving ambiguities, we often examine (unconsciously, of course)
the probabilities of events that are not explicitly coded by the message.
For example, two messages following each other are often associated
with two events denoting cause and effect, although the cause-effect
relationship is not explicitly stated, e.g.,

> FLOODS CONTINUE; FIVE PERSONS DROWNED

This can lead to ambiguity by associating the effect with the wrong
cause, as in

> FATHER OF 10 SHOT; MISTAKEN FOR RABBIT
> FATHER OF 11 FINED $200 FOR FAILING TO STOP

or to ambiguity by assuming a cause-effect relationship where none is
intended, e.g.,

> WAR HERO DECORATED FOR BRAVERY TO WED LOCAL GIRL

Negation is also often ambiguous, as we noted in the example *You
do not have an inferiority complex* (p. 95). Often it is left to the receiver

to decide what part of a statement is to be negated. There is, for example, the story of the man who said "Half the city council are idiots," and being forced to retract the insult, he amended this to "Half the city council are sane."

A major, and perhaps the greatest, cause of ambiguity in Language is the failure to draw a distinction between the truth and the whole truth. We have already remarked that the message *I have two sons* is generally understood to mean the same as *I have two, and only two, sons.* The distinction between the truth and the whole truth can often be found absent in many other hazy statements of Language; and it is particularly often intentionally abused in political propaganda and commercial advertising. Thus, the USSR boasts of the enormous sales of novels by Tolstoi, Dostoyevsky, Hugo, Balzac, Dickens, Twain, and other classics. This is the truth; but the whole truth is that modern writers are, for the most part, either prohibited or unreadable. Similarly, the claim that Brand X is America's best selling brand may be true; but the whole truth might be that Brand X has 0.1% of the market, and the next best selling brand has 0.09%.

The difference between the truth and the whole truth is perhaps best illustrated by the story according to which the captain of a ship entered the statement "The first mate was drunk today" in the log book, and remained adamant to the first mate's pleas to strike the entry. The following week, the first mate kept the log, and avenged himself by the entry "Today, the captain was sober all day."

4.5. The Pun and the Parody

Let us define a pun as a message lying close in signal space to another message whose meaning is different from that coded by the pun. The two messages may be separated by a small distance, or by no distance at all; in the latter case the pun is homonymous. There is only a small difference between the pun and the "slip;" the slip is accidental, the pun is intentional.

Thus, *Pedestrians should be seen and not hurt* is a pun, because its meaning differs from that of *Pedestrians should be seen and not heard*, which differs only by a single phoneme. Similarly, *Two Wongs don't make a white* is a pun, because its meaning is very different from the message *Two wrongs don't make a right,* which lies very close in signal space, in fact, since it differs by only two phonemes (assuming the h in *white* is not sounded), the distance is exactly $d\sqrt{2}$ units in n-dimensional space, where d is the distance between the phonemes w and r along one of the n coordinate axes, and n is the number of phonemes in each of the two messages (20).

For an example of a homonymous pun, consider the following story. Two brothers started a cattle ranch and asked their mother for a suggestion how to name it. "Focus;" said the mother, "where the sun's rays meet." The pun is phonetically homonymous, although there is some distance of separation in the signal space based on graphemes ("where the sons raise meat").

This is not the place to list puns, which are abundantly available elsewhere, for example, in the issues of the news magazine *Time* until a few years ago (*the enterporneurs of Grove Press; but Sartre was smartre*) Our interest in the pun concerns the light it throws on the structure of Language. In particular, we shall be concerned with two points: It is not particularly easy to code an event by a pun, and it is easier to do so in English than in other languages. The first point testifies to the low exploitation of signal space in all languages, and the second to the higher exploitation in English than in other languages.

The fact that a pun is a relatively rare type of message is confirmed by the circumstance that a pun is always an attention-getter. It is therefore extensively used in advertising. The trucks of a Denver garbage collection company carry the sign *Satisfaction guaranteed or double your trash back*; this is, by our definition, a pun, since the message differs only by a single word (*trash* instead of *money*) from the usual guarantee statement. Other examples of puns used in advertising are *Half-price sale — Exmas candy* (advertisement displayed one day after Christmas); *You cannot buy better peas than we can* (advertisement for canned peas); *Do you have a drinking problem?* (advertisement for distilled water); etc. Sometimes an advertiser will capitalize on the slogan of another by making a pun on it. Capitalizing on Avis' slogan *We try harder*, a Denver news station displayed a billboard *We pry harder*; in Britain, the slogan of a detergent is *Persil washes whiter*, and this was pirated by a Manchester church, which displayed a sign *God washes whitest*.

The fact that puns are widely used by comedians (*That hairpiece makes you look 20 years sillier*) is a further indication that puns are rare, and therefore funny.

All this indicates that the signal space of a language is not densely exploited. If it were, there would always be another message nearby, and puns would be so commonplace as to lose their value as attention getters or as humorous items.

But puns can be made more frequently in English than in less efficient languages, precisely because English signal space is more crowded, as we have seen from many aspects now. The contention that puns are more easily made in English than in less efficient languages is not easy to demonstrate directly, but perhaps the following can be offered as evidence: *Time*, while it still "went in" for puns, had many puns on each page every week, evidently finding little difficulty in finding appropriate ones. However, the German newsmagazine *Der Spiegel*, which is quite obviously fashioned after *Time* in every respect, also attempts to use puns in its articles — but with nowhere near the success and frequency of *Time*. On the other hand, puns are quite common in French; but then, the efficiency of French is quite close to that of English.

The parody is a special type of pun; as with any pun, its message lies close to another message in signal space, but the meaning of the parody is a satire of the other message. Thus, *Vietnam — love it and leave it* is a parody of *America — love it or leave it*. Because the parody is a satire of the original message, it is often used as a political slogan, as in the example just given.

This is also true in other languages. The Germans like to think of themselves as

> *Das Volk der Dichter und Denker*

(the nation of poets and thinkers). The Austrian-Jewish journalist Karl Kraus, who wrote in the early decades of this century and was fiercely opposed to German influence, turned this into

> *Das Volk der Richter und Henker*

(the nation of judges and hangmen).* He was also opposed to the Hapsburg monarchy, and turned the first line of the Imperial Austrian anthem

> *Gott erhalte, Gott beschütze, unsern Kaiser, unser Land!*

(God save, God protect our emperor, our country) into

> *Gott erhalte, Gott beschütze vor dem Kaiser unser Land!*

(God save, God protect our country from our emperor).

The parody was also used by the Czechs as a way to ridicule their various oppressors. Not more than 24 hours after the Germans occupied Czechoslovakia in 1939 and proclaimed a protectorate, in Czech, *protektorát*, the Czechs changed this into *pro tentokrát*, meaning "just for this one time."

In German, there is a witty parody (nonpolitical) of Göthe's poem *Der König von Thule*. It uses no more than the interchange of two words (see p. 129 for the meaning of *so oft*). The poem relates of a King of Thule, to whom a lover had given a golden cup on her deathbed; the king cherishes this cup, and

> *Die Augen gingen ihm über*
> *so oft er trank daraus.*

(his eyes went dizzy whenever he drank from it). The parody is

> *Die Augen gingen ihm über*
> *so oft trank er daraus*

(his eyes went dizzy, because he drank from it so often).

---

*The parody is actually more successful than it sounds in the English translation, because *Richter* (judge) has a rather sinister sound. The German verbs *richten* (to judge) and *hinrichten* (to execute) are closely related, so that the parody has a flavor of "The nation of executioners and hangmen."

The pun is closely related to another curiosity, the play on words. During World War II, an Englishman was asked why the GI's were not very popular in Britain; he answered "They're overbearing, overpaid, overfed, oversexed, and over here." This is not, by our previous definition, a pun, since it does not involve similar sounding messages coding different events; it simply mixes the prefix *over-* with the preposition *over*. We shall call a message of this type a play on words.

Heinrich Heine thought up this clever play on words: *Eifersucht ist eine Leidenschaft, die mit Eifer sucht, was Leiden schafft* (Jealousy is a passion which eagerly seeks what causes suffering).

The play on words is an amusing curiosity which, like the pun, is a humorous attention-getter; however, it does not, as far as I can see, throw light on the structure of Language to the same extent as the pun does. It does not, for example, require a crowded signal space.

The tongue-twister is, in a sense, a play on words; it is a message with its phonemes so arranged that they are difficult to pronounce. It is of some interest, since it is very easy to program a computer to generate millions of tongue twisters at the rate of several a second, as we shall see in Chapter 6.

The trick that will cause difficulties in pronunciation (in all languages) is to include similar sequences of phonemes and to let them alternate as often as possible. If only similar words are included in the message, it is not very difficult to pronounce (*How much wood would a woodchuck chuck if a woodchuck could chuck wood?*) The alternation of similar sequences of phonemes is much more deadly: *A skunk sat on a stump; the skunk thunk that the stump stank, but the stump thunk that the skunk stank*. Or: *Three sixths of thirty-six sixteenths exceed six sixths of this thistle.*

The same principle also produces tongue twisters in other languages, e.g., in German: *Fischers Fritz fängt frische Fische; frische Fische fängt Fischers Fritz* or *Der Kotbuser Postkutscher putzt den Kotbuser Postkutchkasten*, or in Czech: *Nenaolejuji-li já Julii, naolejuje Julie mne.*

5

Language as
an Error-Detecting Code

5.1. Error-Detecting and Error-Correcting Codes

We have seen in the previous chapters that the only way to protect coded messages from noise of all types is to keep the exploitation of signal space low, i.e., to make the code redundant. But this still leaves us with a choice as to what to do with the redundancy, that is, what to do with the "empty" points in signal space, representing sequences of code elements to which no meaning is assigned. We have so far examined only the "passive" method, in which nothing in particular is done with the empty, redundant neighborhood of the messages; it forms a padding or protection of the messages, preventing (one hopes) the noise from shifting the signal beyond this protective neighborhood into the domain of another message, facilitating semantic and formal decoding to restore the original message.

However, in a way, this is a hap-hazard approach; one simply provides the messages with an unexploited neighborhood, and then hopes for the best. The "active" approach also leaves the neighborhood of messages redundant (there is no other way of achieving noise resistance), but instead of leaving the points of this neighborhood totally empty, it furnishes them with labels showing what their location is, in other words, with labels identifying the original message, if it was distorted into this point of its neighborhood.

Consider an example. Suppose we wish to code 16 different events, or members of the source alphabet, by using a binary digital code (whose

code words are sequences of the digits 0 and 1). Let us compose the
code words as four-digit sequences; there are $2^4 = 16$ such sequences,
and we can therefore assign one such code word to each of the 16 source
elements (events) to be coded; if we are lucky with the source probabilities, we may even achieve an optimum code. However, this code is
entirely without noise resistance. If any one digit is distorted to another,
a false message is received. To give the code some noise resistance,
we must introduce some redundancy. Let us do this by making the code
words five, instead of four, digits long. This yields $2^5 = 32$ different
sequences (from 00000 to 11111), twice as many as the 16 source elements to be coded. The exploitation of signal space is now reduced from
100% to 50%. In the "passive" method, we would simply intersperse the
16 messages with the 16 meaningless points to give a fairly uniform density of the signal space, and then hope for the best. If a meaningless
sequence is received, the signal must have been distorted, and one can
guess (examine the corresponding probabilities) what the original message might have been. However, if a meaningful message is received,
there is no guarantee that this was the message that was actually transmitted: It could be the result of noise which has distorted the original
message into another message.

In the "active" method, we put the redundant parts of the code to
use as identifiers or check digits. A simple way to do this is to use a
parity code, which works as follows. We use the first four digits as "information" digits coding the sixteen source elements as before. But now
we add a fifth, redundant digit, not as hap-hazard padding, but to check
whether distortion has set in during the transmission of the signal through
the channel. This check digit checks on the information digits by checking their parity, that is, whether the binary number of the information digits is odd or even. If the sum of the information digits is even, the
check digit is made a zero; if it is odd, the check digit is made a one.
The sixteen messages of the code now look as follows:

source element	information digits	check digit	code word
1	0000	0	00000
2	0001	1	00011
3	0010	1	00101
4	0011	0	00110
5	0100	1	01001
6	0101	0	01010
7	0110	0	01100
8	0111	1	01111
.... etc			
15	1110	1	11101
16	1111	0	11110

For example, source element no. 8 would (in a non-redundant code) be coded by the information digits 0111; the sum of the digits is 3, an odd number, and therefore the check digit is 1; the code word is therefore 0111 supplemented by a 1, that is, 01111.

If we now receive the sequence 01011, we know immediately that an error has occurred: The check digit does not match the information digits. The code contains no such word, and therefore distortion must have set in. Note that the check digit checks not only the information digits, but also itself; this is quickly established by distorting a check digit, or by noting from the above coding table that all code words have an even sum of digits.

A code of the above type is called an error-detecting code; the specific code given above is a binary parity code (binary because it uses two symbols for a code alphabet, and parity code because it checks whether a number is odd or even). It can be shown that the noise resistance of this specific code is no greater than if we had added the fifth digit by the hap-hazard method; however, on receiving a sequence of digits, we no longer have to go through the entire coding table to see whether such a message exists or not, because the sequence now carries a label saying, in effect, "I am a genuine code word" or "I have been distorted." Also, in more sophisticated codes of this type, the noise resistance can actually be increased.

There are two things to be noted in connection with the above code. First, it is an error-detecting code, not an error-correcting code. If we receive the sequence 10110, we know that an error has occurred, because the check digit is wrong, but we cannot say which one of the digits is in error, and therefore we cannot correct it.

Second, it is evident that the code will detect an error if one (or three, or all five) digits have been distorted; but this code will give no warning if two or four digits are in error. More sophisticated (and also more redundant) codes can take care of this, and by making the code words sufficiently long, it is possible to design error-detecting codes that will detect errors up to any prescribed order (simple, double, treble, etc.). Since the length of the code words increases faster than the order of the error that can be detected, it can be shown that it is impossible to construct a code that is immune to *all* possible errors; however, this is a highly theoretical problem, for in practice the probability of an $n$tuple error diminishes very rapidly with growing n (if the errors are independent, not "burst errors"). In contemporary electronic channels, even simple errors have a probability of only 10^{-3}, and often as low as 10^{-6} or 10^{-7}. (If the channel has an error rate of more than 10^{-3}, it does not need an error-detecting code, but a repairman.) Thus, double errors are extremely improbable, and quadruple errors virtually impossible.

By making the code more redundant, that is, by adding more check digits to the information digits, we can not only detect an error, but also pin-point the digit that has been distorted (no matter whether it was an information digit or a check digit), so that the error can be corrected. To correct all possible simple errors in a code with four binary information digits (coding 16 different messages), we need three check digits. Each check digit checks the parity of the sum of four digits in the resulting 7-digit code word (e.g., the first digit might check the parity of the sum of the first three information digits and the second check digit). By ascertaining which of the three checks are wrong, the erroneous digit can be located, and therefore corrected. Exactly how this is done need not concern us, since we are interested in languages, and not in digital codes;* but it should perhaps be added that the detection and correction of errors by such codes is usually automated. A computer using an error-detecting code in some part of its equipment (such as a card reader) will, on having detected an error, stop its work and print, for example, PARITY ERROR IN CARD READER; the operator will then correct the error (resubmit the misread card to the reader) and start the computer again. But if an error-correcting code is involved, the computer will correct the error without outside assistance and continue working without interruption.

The parity code described above is not, by any means, the only type of error-detecting code. As we have seen, it is used only in cases where the noise distorts the digits independently, and in the form described here, it will not detect double errors in the same code word. Double errors are, however, quite common when the noise distorting the digits is due to human error. For example, in transcribing Library of Congress catalog card numbers (which are widely used by librarians for indexing books), it is quite common for librarians, editors, type composers, etc. to interchange two digits (7531 instead of 7351), and interchanging two digits is a double error. Credit card numbers, account numbers, and other numbers subject to automatic processing must also be protected from errors of this type. In December 1968, the Library of Congress therefore introduced a numbering system which amounts to an error-detecting code. On the verso of this book (back of the title page), the reader will find its Library of Congress catalog card number. At the time of writing it is not yet known what it will be, but it begins with a seven, and the hyphen after the second digit is followed by a number of up to six digits. This number is the actual, nonredundant number of this book; the digit preceding the hyphen and following the 7 is a check digit; the 7 only identifies the number as one of the "seven series." This series is used in all books published after 1968, so that if it is known that the book was published

*See W.W. Peterson, *Error-Correcting Codes*, Wiley, New York, 1963.

in 1972, the 7 has a probability of one, and therefore carries no information. To check whether the number printed on the verso has not been distorted (by transposition or otherwise), multiply the digits from left to right, respectively, by 7, 8, 4, 6, 3, 5, 2, 1 (if the check digit is a 0, treat it as a 10). Add the resulting products, and divide the sum by 11. If there is a remainder, i.e., if the sum is not an integral multiple of 11, then somebody has goofed either at the Library of Congress, or at Golem Press.

Beyond that, the details of the Library-of-Congress code need not interest us; it is simply another example of an error-detecting code.

To see that natural languages are error-detecting codes, we need not go into the details of digital error-correcting codes, and the reader who may not have completely understood the details of the two digital codes described above need not worry about them, for the only important point is the *principle* of error-detecting (or error-correcting) codes. This principle is the following: *We may assign the information digits of an error-detecting code in whatever way we wish* (depending on what we want to communicate); *but once we have made this decision, we are required to insert the check digits strictly by the rules of the code.*

The rules of the code (or the grammar of the code) always require the the insertion of the check digits as follows:

1) Each error-detecting code applies some criterion to the information digits; it asks, as it were, a test question. The parity code asks whether the sum of certain digits is odd or even. The Library of Congress asks whether the sum of the appropriately weighted digits is divisible by 11. Many other criterions can be used.

2) When the test question has been answered, the check is implemented accordingly. In the parity code, a 1 is added if the tested sum is odd, and a 0 is added if it is even. In the Library of Congress code, the check digit equals the lowest multiple of 8 that will make the sum divisible by 11.

Other implementations are possible, for the implementation is not uniquely determined by the check criterion. For example, in a parity code, we might agree to insert a 1 for even sums, and a 0 for odd sums; the code would work just as well (provided, of course, that the receiver was aware of this unusual implementation). Similarly, it is merely a convention where to insert the check digits. It is usual to insert them after each group of information digits, but they might equally well be inserted before them (as is done in the Library of Congress code), or they might equally well be interspersed with the information digits, again provided that the receiver knows the rules of the code, i.e., how to find the positions of the check digits.

Let us now return to the binary parity code as given by the coding table on p. 156. A string of code words will have the following form (the check digits are flanked by hyphens for better visual readability only; no hyphens are used in fact):

0011-0-1110-1-0110-0-1011-1-1000-1-00001-1-... etc.   (1)

The difference between an error-detecting and an error-correcting code, as we have seen, is not very drastic; an error-correcting code simply has more check digits per group of information digits, enabling the error not only to be detected, but to be located within a code word, so that the offending digit can be automatically corrected. An error-correcting code using four information digits followed by three check digits then gives rise to sequences of code words which might look like this (the hyphens would, again, not be used):

0001-011-1111-111-0011-100-0010-111-0000-000-... etc.   (2)

Although it may seem strange at this point, the strings (1) and (2) are very much like sentences of a natural language, for in natural languages, too, the informational items alternate with check items.

5.2. Language as an Error-Detecting Code

The basic principle of error-detecting and error-correcting codes is this: The user (transmitter) of the code can use the information digits in whatever way he pleases, but once he has made the decision, he must insert the check digits dictated by the rules of the code accordingly.

Applied to Language, this means: A speaker can say whatever he pleases, but once he has decided what to say, he must insert the check features dictated by the grammar of the language accordingly; as in digital codes, the insertion is dictated by a check criterion and by a check implementation. This assertion is the basic topic of this chapter, in which we will investigate the character of the information and check features of natural languages. In the next chapter, we will furnish an experimental proof of the above assertion by describing a computer program which chooses what it wants to say at random (by making random choices of words and, if the option is open, of answers to check criterions) and then inserts the check features as dictated by (English) grammar in much the same way as the insertion of check digits in a digital code can be computerized .

The two types of codes show far reaching analogies. In both digital error-correcting codes and natural languages, informational items alternate with check items. In both cases, the information items are optional, and the check items are prescribed. In both cases, distorted, ambiguous, or even totally missing information items can be restored from the check items; this is frequently done in languages with a very redundant check system (Latin, Russian), but difficult in a language with only a flimsy check system (English). In both cases, the check items are redundant and can therefore be omitted; this violates the rules of the code (the grammar), and is therefore usually met in slang, colloquialisms and dialects, but it transmits the information just as a non-redundant digital code would do. In both cases, the code becomes very vulnerable to ambiguities if the check system is not fully implemented; in both cases, the more redundant code can afford the loss of check items with less risk of ambiguity than the less redundant code (e.g., Russian versus English). In both cases, the insertion of check items requires two steps: a check criterion and a check implementation. In both cases, the same code element (a digit, or a morpheme) is sometimes used as an information item, and sometimes as a check item.

One would be tempted to say "and so on," but there seems to be nothing left of the properties that make a code an error-detecting or error-correcting code.

Of course, in a digital code the check digits are more easily defined than the check items in Language. In the Library-of-Congress code, the check digit is the one following the initial 7; in the binary parity code described in the previous section, every fifth digit is a check digit. Language has no such simple rules, and there are, in fact, cases when it is difficult to decide whether a morpheme or word represents an information feature or a check feature, or perhaps both at the same time. However, such cases are surprisingly few, and in any case, we must not expect Language to be structured with the precise (and boring) regularity of an artificial code; but to abandon the concept of Language as an error-detecting code because of a few exceptions would be like condemning the concept of grammar because of a few irregular verbs.

Let us first examine the information items of a language. We know that if Language is to satisfy the definition of a code, its messages or code words must be equated to the sentences of that language. We also know that what is to be regarded as the code alphabet (whose elements are combined into code words) is simply a matter of convenience. We can regard sentences as made up of words, syllables, morphemes or phonemes (graphemes in the printed language). We have, in fact, used all of these for different investigations as code alphabet members. In the present instance, it is most convenient to regard the code words (sentences) as composed of morphemes of the corresponding language. Words and phrases are then simply fixed sequences of morphemes that form parts of a sentence, but not, in general, an entire sentence or code word. A morpheme is usually defined as the smallest meaningful unit of a language; a word, prefix, suffix, or other unit that cannot be broken down any further, such as *lid, swim, -able, -er, -est, in-, pre-, be-*. This definition is adequate for our purposes, except for the word "meaningful," which we understand in the sense of "corresponding to a member of the source alphabet (an envent of the semantic base)." The morpheme *lid* is not meaningful in this sense, nor is the string of morphemes *lack of judgement* (unless it codes an event in answer to a question, e.g.,"What is his biggest handicap as an executive?"). But with this reservation concerning the term *meaningful*, we can accept the usual definition of a morpheme.

Let us now examine some non-redundant English utterances composed of information morphemes only. If English and other natural languages are structured like error-detecting codes, then the absence of check morphemes will usually violate the rules of the code, that is, the resulting utterance will be ungrammatical. Such utterances are often found in slang and colloquial language; but at present we shall consider some utterances made by children and foreigners, where the absence of check morphemes is due to lack of knowledge of the code.

Thus, a child who has not yet learned to code in English properly, will produce utterances such as

$$\textit{Annie want milk} \tag{1}$$

or

$$\textit{Flower, pretty} \tag{2}$$

These utterances are not grammatical sentences, yet it is perfectly clear what the child means, that is, there is no doubt what events the child is coding by these sequences of English morphemes. The messages are non-redundant, but ungrammatical; the rules of the code (English grammar) would require the insertion of the redundant check morpheme *-s* after *want* in (1), and the insertion of the redundant check morphemes *the* and *is* in (2) so as to form the English sentence *The flower is pretty*. Russian does not use either of these check morphemes: There are no articles, and the word *is* is omitted (in all but mathematical, legal and other statements requiring unusual precision). Since the Russian equivalent of (2) (цвет красивый) is grammatical, the morphemes *the* and *is* are evidently redundant. However, Russian has other check morphemes; *flower* is masculine in Russian, and the rules of the code require the check morpheme -ый to be used with the Russian adjective for *pretty* to achieve gender concord. Conversely, the Russian check morpheme is again redundant, as shown by English, which does not modify its adjectives according to gender (and by Hungarian, which has no gender at all).

Another case of a speaker who will leave out check morphemes because he has not yet mastered the code is the foreigner speaking in "broken" English. Suppose, for example, that a driver addressed somebody in a heavy foreign accent with the following words:

*Please — want go Rochester — lose road — no map — please
show Rochester.* (3)

The only thing that is broken in this message is the grammar; the
meaning is perfectly clear. It is a non-redundant message without check
morphemes. It can equally well (or badly) be coded in French, German,
or any other language.

These examples show that the roots of nouns, verbs and adjectives
are usually (strings of) information morphemes; they are not, however,
the only examples. Similarly, articles, conjugation endings, inflections
of adjectives and auxiliary verbs are generally (strings of) check morphemes, but they are not the only ones. Moreover, check morphemes are
only one kind of check feature, though by far the most common kind. In
some cases the tense of a verb can be exclusively used as a check feature, furnishing no other information of any kind.

Natural languages have a large number of check criterions, and each
check criterion has a large number of implementations. We shall examine
these criterions and implementations in more detail later, but a simple
example should make it clear at this time what we have in mind.

Consider a simple event that involves a doer, an action, and an object on which the action operates (or fails to operate), that is, an event
which in the Indo-European languages is coded by the grammatical structure subject-verb-object. Let us take the event which is coded in English as *Napoleon did not visit England* and in Latin as *Napoleonus non
visitavit Angliam.* One could imagine an artificial language in which this
information was coded as *Napoleon-doer, visit-action, England-object,
time-past, negative.* The structure of such a language would essentially
be non-redundant, although, of course, it could be made much more efficient by encoding the functions of the words and their identities into
shorter forms. Up to a point, this is what natural languages do. English
identifies the subject by putting it at the beginning of the sentence (or
more generally, before the verb), Latin identifies it by adding a nominative case ending to the root of the word.

But both English and Latin now pose the redundant check criterion
or test question "One or many?" and implement it by the corresponding
check morphemes (or their absence); in this case, the answer is "one,"
which means that English will add no -s to *Napoleon*, and Latin will use
the nominative singular ending.

The next check criterion is one that Latin does not have; namely,
the criterion determining the article in English. It is convenient (especially for computerization) to consider the English article as having four
forms: *a, an, the,* and its absence. The criterions governing the choice
of these articles are complicated (more so than, say, in French), and
there is a number of criterions, some of which can overrule others

(definite or indefinite, singular or plural, countable or not countable, abstract or concrete, and many others). In the present case, the check criterion "Is it a proper name or not?" overrules the others and results in the absence of the article; that is, the absence of the article is the implementation of the check criterion testing whether *Napoleon* is a proper name.

The time of the (negated) action is in the past, which offers a choice of six past tenses for the English verb: past, perfect, pluperfect, and each of these may or may not be continuous (*visited, has visited, had visited, was visiting, has been visiting, had been visiting*). The answer to the (English) check criterion "Was the action being performed concurrently with some other named action or at a specific time?" is *no*, which rules out the continuous forms for implementation; similarly, the answer to the check criterion "Did the action take place before some other stated time in the past?" rules out the pluperfect for implementation. The choice between the two remaining tenses (past or perfect) depends on the answer to the check criterion "Was the action performed (a) in the past with no relation to the present, or (b) does it continue into the present, or was it performed recently, or – if negated – may it yet take place?" If, as we assume, *Napoleon* means Napoleon Bonaparte (and not a dog named Napoleon on the Calais-Dover channel ferry), there is no chance of Napoleon ever visiting England in the present or future, and therefore the criterion must be implemented by the past tense (preterite) of the verb. The negation in this tense is implemented by *did not* plus infinitive, yielding *Napoleon did not visit...*

Note that this criterion does not exist in Latin (or most other languages). But Latin has another criterion to form the check morphemes of the verb, namely, "Is it first, second, or third person?", a criterion which is never tested in the English past tense (except for the verb *to be*). Depending on the outcome, Latin would implement the check morphemes *-vi, -visti* or *-vit*.

The object is identified in English by its position following the verb, in Latin by the accusative case ending.

Other languages would have checked criterions which are not checked by either English or Latin. The Slavic languages would have tested the gender of *Napoleon* and would have implemented the test by adding check morphemes of gender to the past tense of the verb. Hungarian would have asked whether the verb is followed by a direct object, and if so, would have modified the verb ending accordingly. German would have asked whether the verb (*besuchen*) has a separable prefix, and if so, it would have put the prefix at the end of the sentence. (Had the verb been *aufsuchen*, the sentence would have resulted in *Napoleon suchte England nicht auf*.)

All of the morphemes in the string making up a sentence are, of course, selected by some criterion. But the implementation is optional in some cases, and obligatory in others. "Who or what is the subject?" might perhaps be regarded as a criterion for implementation, but it is not a check criterion, because the speaker is entirely free to choose the implementation — *Napoleon, mouse, plague*. What makes a criterion a *check* criterion is 1) it asks a redundant test question, and 2) the answer to the question determines the implementation, leaving the speaker no option.

Thus, the criterion of gender is obviously superfluous in the above sentence; English does not ask for the gender of *Napoleon*, and it does not implement the gender by morphemes appearing in the verb or anywhere else in this sentence. The (English) criterion "completed or not completed in the past" is superfluous (Latin or German do not ask such a test question); so is the criterion "proper name or not" (Latin and the Slavic languages do not need it). Moreover, the implementations leave the speaker no choice: English grammar forces him to omit the articles and to use the past (preterite) tense; it prohibits utterances like *The Napoleon has not been visiting England.*

But when is a criterion "superfluous"? When do the check morphemes inserted as its implementation convey no essential information, i.e., no information that the speaker would have chosen to transmit if the grammar of the language had not forced him to do so? That question is not as easily answered as in an artificial error-detecting code. In some cases, the answer is obvious. The word *not* in the sentence *I was not here* is an information morpheme, conveying essential information. The morphemes appearing at the end of a Slavic verb in the third person past tense, which ensure gender concord with the subject, are obviously redundant check morphemes, since the Germanic and Romance languages get on well enough without them, and so do the Slavic languages themselves in other persons and tenses. The *her* in *She nodded her head* is obviously quite redundant.

But how about the article in *a school, the school, school*? Let us take a closer look at some check morphemes.

5.2. Check Morphemes

5.2.1. THE ARTICLE

The fact that the article (e.g., in English, French, German or Hungarian) is a redundant check morpheme can be established in several ways, two of which seem particularly striking.

First, some languages, such as Latin, Czech or Russian, have no articles, yet there is no difficulty in communicating in these languages without their benefit. These languages never ask the test question "Is the object described by the noun definite or indefinite?" (Czech and Russian pose different test questions, e.g., "Is it animate or inanimate?" which English does not pose or implement.)

Second, the article is discarded as unnecessary and wasteful in newspaper headlines and telegrams, even when the grammar of the language would require its use. Thus, a headline such as

MAN KILLED IN CAR CRASH NEAR CITY LIMITS

leaves out the articles in *a man, a car crash, the city limits* (as well as the check morpheme *was*). Similarly, no articles are used in telegrams such as

ACCEPTANCE OF OFFER TO BUY COMPANY NOT
RECOMMENDED. BUYERS CREDIT DUBIOUS. HIGH RISK
OF LAWSUIT.

(This telegram also omits other check morphemes, such as *is, there is*.)

In spite of these arguments, the reader may be reluctant to regard the articles, one of which is the most frequent word in the English language, as something redundant. He may object, for example,

(a) that the article is an essential word in a statement like "This used to be *the* hotel of Watford,"

(b) that there is a difference between *school, the school* and *a school,* and between *the wife of Egypt's prime minister* and *a wife of Egypt's prime minister,*

(c) that there is a substantial difference between *He bought paper* and *He bought a paper.*

Objection (a) is disposed of very quickly, because it is not really relevant. The *the* does not really have the function of an article, although it is an article formally; it means *the only hotel of any significance,* and as such has to be emphasized in speech, or printed in italics in print; it functions as an adjectival or as a demonstrative adjective rather than an article.

The difference between *school, a school* and *the school* is more to the point. There is admittedly a difference. But it is usually a difference so slight that other languages can do without it; there is no exact equivalent for the three in Russian or Latin. Moreover, the difference is in almost all cases self-evident; if it is not, some other construction that does not merely rely on the article is brought to use. Thus, *school* without an article comes under the category of nouns expressing an association with the object denoted by the corresponding noun rather than denoting the object itself. In the case of *school,* the associated concept is *learning;* similarly *bed-sleep, church-praying,* etc. English grammar rules that if the association rather than the object itself is implied, the article must be omitted; hence *to go to school, to bed, to church*, but *the bus stops at the school and at the church, the lamp stands by the bed*. But is this distinction essential? If one says *The bus goes to the school and to the church* in Russian or Latin, i.e., without the articles, no one will (due to semantic decoding) assume that the bus goes to the school to learn and to the church to pray; and if one says *Jack went to bed with Jill* in Czech, no one will interpret this to mean that Jack and Jill took up a location in the neighborhood of the bed.

A similar state of affairs holds for the messages *The bus stops at the school* and *The bus stops at a school*. The equivalent statement in Czech or Russian makes no difference between the two, because usually it is not important. If it is important, then the point is made in the same way as in English: Instead of *a school* one says *some school, one of many schools, a school of some kind or another*, etc; instead of *the school,* one says *this school, the school on 42nd street, the school I have mentioned,* etc. In other words, the difference made by the definite and indefinite article, or by the absence of either, is either unimportant, or it is stressed by some other construction involving more than merely the article. *The wife of Egypt's prime minister* and *a wife of Egypt's prime minister* is just another example of this, and we might repeat the same type of arguments as for *the school* and *a school*; however, here we have an additional argument: Suppose the prime minister's name is Ali; how do we tell the difference in *Ali's wife*? There isn't any; Ali's wife might be his only wife or one of Ali's wives, and we say so only if the difference is important.

Moreover, we do not have to examine the article, or any other check morpheme for that matter, case by case to convince ourselves that it is redundant. All languages have some check criterions, and they vary from language to language. To an American, the difference between a definite and indefinite object may seem important, because he is used to distinguishing between them by means of the article; a Czech, who is not used to this criterion, will consider it redundant. On the contrary, in Czech (and the other Slavic languages) a verb is conjugated in a manner depending on whether the action is completed or not, and to a Czech the message *He rode a bicycle* is ambiguous, because it does not say whether he rode it just once, or whether he was in the habit of riding it. But, an American will say, that is unimportant; if I want to distinguish the two, I will say so by additional words. Precisely. And the same is true for the article. Both articles and conjugations in perfective and imperfective aspects are implementations of redundant check criterions. In either case the receiver obtains some additional information in one language that he would not obtain in the other, but it is not essential information.

Here again we can use the analogy of error-detecting digital codes. The check digits of these codes are not void of information, either. The check digit of the binary parity code gives the information that the sum of the remaining digits is odd or even, but this is not the information the receiver is waiting for. The Library-of-Congress check digit gives information on the remainder when the remaining digits are divided by 11; but this is not what the librarian needs when she goes to look up the number of a book. The analogy goes further: Given (only) the check digit of a Library of Congress number, there is no way of telling whether the sum of the digits is odd or even, and given (only) the check digits of a binary parity code, there is no way of telling whether the sum of the weighted digits is divisible by 11 without remainder. Similarly, there is no way of telling whether the Czech word *škola* means *school, a school* or *the school*; and there is no way of telling whether *to smoke a cigarette* means *to be in the process of smoking* or *to finish the cigarette and grind it out.* The meaning is, most often, evident from the context of the entire sentence. But then, given the entire code word in the Library of Congress code or the binary parity code, we can also (if we care to do so) ascertain whether the former has an even sum of the digits, and whether the latter is divisible by eleven.

The last two paragraphs apply to any check morpheme, not necessarily the article, and the reader is asked to recall them when we discuss other check morphemes. However, we still have to explain a further objection, the difference between *paper* and *a paper*. This is indeed a different case from the preceding ones, namely, a case of restoration, which we will discuss more fully later. Restoration essentially amounts to restoring the meaning of ambiguous information morphemes from given check morphemes, which is the original purpose of an error-detecting code. This is precisely what is happening here. When *paper* has no article, it must be a collective noun, i.e., a material. When it has an (indefinite) article it must be countable, i.e., it must be a newspaper or a scientific paper or some other countable object made of paper. This form of restoration is, of course, not possible in languages that have no article, and they must use different words for the two concepts. Thus, Russian has a different word for *paper* (бумага) and *a paper* (газета), and a different word for *glass* (стекло) and *a glass* (стакан). But English, French or German can use the article as a check morpheme to restore the wanted meaning of the ambiguous words *glass, verre* or *Glas*. Conversely, the Slavic languages can use their check morphemes to modify the same root of a verb where two verbs are needed in English. Thus, *to vote* and *to elect* are, to a Czech, two aspects of the same action, since electing is simply the successful completion of the action of voting, and the two are therefore formed from the same root (*volit, zvolit*). In somewhat rarer cases, German can do this, by the use of prefixes, also (*schiessen,* to shoot; *er-schiessen,* to shoot to death; *trügen,* to be deceptive, *betrügen,* to cheat).

Restoration, then, is why the presence or absence of the article in *(a) paper* significantly changes the meaning of the word. However, this reason does not contradict the assertion that the article is a check morpheme; on the contrary, it supports it.

Now all of the foregoing discussion only makes the point that the article is redundant. But, as we know from our discussion of codes in general, including languages, redundant does not mean useless. The main purpose of a check morpheme is to prevent ambiguity, and that, in my opinion, is the main purpose of the article; the indication whether a certain object is definite or indefinite is, as the foregoing arguments show, entirely secondary. Consider what often happens in newspaper headlines, where articles are usually omitted:

MAN REFUSES TO GIVE UP BITING DOG (1)

The message is ambiguous; it could code one of the two events which are coded less ambiguously as follows:

MAN REFUSES TO GIVE UP THE (a, his) BITING DOG (2)
MAN REFUSES TO GIVE UP BITING THE DOG (3)

The article identifies the word *biting* as an adjective in the first sentence, and as a gerund in the second, as reliably as the check digit in a digital code identifies the sum of the digits as being odd or even. Whatever comes between the article and the next noun must be an adjective (or at least an adjectival); but the absence of an article is one of the characteristics of a gerund. And this is what the article (in English) is for: It primarily acts as a marker or pointer indicating the function (part of speech) of the words that follow. (In other languages it performs an additional check on the gender of the following noun). Whether it was *a, the* or *his* dog is quite unimportant as far as the coded event is concerned; what is important is whether the man refused to give up a dangerous dog, or whether he insisted on remaining a dog-biter.

In most cases, the check performed by the article is redundant, e.g.,

MAN REFUSES TO GIVE UP DOG (4)

and it is therefore omitted as superfluous in headlines. But in some cases, such as (1), it resolves an ambiguity. The editor who let (1) go into print, did not realise that this was such a case, or he would have inserted a check morpheme before *biting* to resolve it.

Yet this editor is also my witness in claiming that it is not important whether the man refused to give up *a* biting dog or *the* biting dog or *his* biting dog: He would not have omitted the corresponding word if he had thought this specification important.

5.2.2. PLURAL OF NOUNS

It is hoped that the reader, after reading the preceding section, has accepted the fact that the articles are redundant check morphemes; yet he may consider it going too far if we contend that the plural ending of nouns (such as -s and its allomorphs in English) is a redundant check morpheme also. Surely, he may object, there is an essential difference between *boy* and *boys.*

Hardly ever. If the difference is essential, it is usually made abundantly clear by additional words in the sentence (e.g., numerals, *many, few, a single,* etc.). Two arguments appear particularly persuasive to make this point.

First, there are some nouns that do not differ for singular or plural. In English, *sheep* and *aircraft* are two of several such nouns. In other languages, nouns having the same (nominative) singular and plural are even more common. If it were so critical to distinguish singular and plural by the ending of a noun, these words would give rise to ambiguities, and the evolution of Language would surely force a change. But this has not happened; *sheep* and *aircraft* live in English as happily as the words taking a plural ending, furnishing a demonstration that this ending is unnecessary.

Second, and probably more important, the distinction between one object and two or more such objects is historically understandable, but it is totally arbitrary. Why should one be distinguished from all other integers? Why not have a plural ending when the number of objects exceeds 117, and a singular ending otherwise? Apart from the historical evolution of numbers in human consciousness, the number 117 is no more arbitrary as a dividing point (if there must be one) than the number 1. Indeed, not all languages restrict such a criterion to the number 1 as a dividing point. Czech uses different forms for the noun depending on whether the number of corresponding objects is 0, 1, 2 to 4, or 5 and greater: For zero (*no*), the noun is often (and in Russian, almost invariably) in the genitive singular or plural, for 1 it is in the nominative singular, for 2 to 4 it is in the nominative plural (genitive singular in Russian), and for 5 or more it is in the genitive plural. In addition, Czech used to have an additional form called the *dual* until the late middle ages; this was used for two objects (as distinct from more than two), and it has left traces in modern Czech in the peculiar declensions of some objects that come in pairs (eyes, ears, pants, etc.). Such complications are obviously redundant, since English does very well without them. Why, then, should the distinction between 1 and more than 1 be any less redundant? What is the difference between *no train* and *no trains*? How fateful is the ambiguity in *The sheep died* or *The aircraft crashed*?

As in the case of articles, the ambiguity is either unimportant or it
can be resolved from the context in which these messages appear; for
if this is not so, then we take the trouble to say *one sheep died* or *all
the sheep died* (for example); *this aircraft crashed* or *both aircraft crashed*
(for example). Similarly, the difference between *He loved his daughter*
and *He loved his daughters* is either obvious from the context, or it is
unimportant; if it is important, the *s* of *daughters* is rarely relied on to
stress the point, and a more emphatic construction such as *He loved his
only daughter* or *He loved all of his daughters* is used.

In English, there is only a handful of words such as *sheep, aircraft,
fish,* which do not differ in singular and plural (there are a few more ungrammatical ones such as the now widely used *one media, one data*).
But other languages have them by the hundreds. In French, any noun ending in *-ou* (*bijou*) and most nouns ending in a consonant (as a grapheme)
such as *part, pied, baron, loup, son,* distinguish between singular and
plural only in spelling, and the ambiguity is resolved only by the preceding article, another check morpheme. In German, the hundreds of nouns
ending in *-en* (Wagen) or *-er* (Fleischer), provided they do not change the
preceding vowel (*Böden, Väter*), are the same for singular and plural,
and the ambiguity can be resolved only by the *gender* of the article,
which is an additional check feature. The reader familiar with Russian
will be aware of the vast number of Russian nouns ending in -ие, an ending which is used, among other nouns, for all nominalized verbs, so that
it frequently corresponds to the English ending *-ing*. In Russian, this
ending changes into -ия in the plural; but the corresponding Czech ending is *-i,* and this is the same for both singular and plural. Some of the
hundreds of Czech words that fall into this category are the equivalents
of *letter, sign, blasphemy, invitation, exercise, solution, eqrthquake,
transmission, performace, spice,* which perhaps cannot easily be ima-
gined as having the same form in singular and plural, yet the Czechs
have no difficulty in using many hundreds of these words, although admittedly the check is often performed by the qualifying adjective or by
the verb.

But let us return to English for some more examples of the relative
unimportance of the plural as an item of information. As in other languages, there are the *plurale tantum* nouns, which are always in the plural, regardless of whether they denote one or many countable objects:
glasses, trousers, overalls, etc. (True, they consist of two parts; but
so does a bicycle, and a pair of bicycles does not correspond to a pair
of glasses). Then there are the nouns with a plural ending, but always
used in the singular: *news, optics, mathematics,* etc. Then there are the
nouns used as singular in American English, but as singular or plural
in British English (*the government is/are, the enemy has/have,* etc.).

These examples are, of course, special cases where the distinction between singular and plural is particularly unimportant and blurred. Let us therefore perform a little experiment in more general cases. The language used in the articles of the *Scientific American* is neither particularly simple, nor particularly complex. The first sentence of each article relies on no specific previously transmitted information (except perhaps the title of the article). Let us see whether we have difficulties in deciding whether the meaning of these first sentences (October 1971 issue) can still be decoded when the plural check morpheme (or its absence) is rendered ineffective. This is done by giving both singular and plural forms of each noun (where both forms exist), and asking the reader to choose, if possible, the form that was used in the original. The title of the article is also given, since it might yield specific information needed for decoding.

(The Physiology of Starvation:) The human body/bodies has a remarkable capacity/capacities for surviving without food/foods for long period/periods.

(Cable Television:) At the beginning/beginnings of 1952, when reliable statistic/statistics on the three-year old cable television industry/industries in the United State/States were assembled for the first time/times, 70 operating system/systems were serving a total/totals of 14,000 subscriber/subscribers.

(The Object in the World of the Infant:) According to most traditional theory/theories of how we come to perceive the world/worlds around us, the quality/qualities of solidity belongs to the sense/senses of touch/touches in the same way/ways that the quality/qualities of color/colors belongs to the sense/senses of vision/visions or the quality/qualities of pitch/pitches to the sense of hearing/hearings.

(The Lunar Rocks:) The opportunity/opportunities to examine rock/rocks collected on the surface/surfaces of the moon/moons has been an intellectual challenge/challenges of the first magnitude/magnitudes.

(Carbon 14 and the Prehistory of Europe:) Our knowledge of European prehistory is currently being revolutionized.

(How Living Cells Change Shape:) Single-cell animal/animals such as the amoeba/amoebae are not the only cell/cells that are capable of self-propelled movement/movements.

(Mössbauer Spectroscopy:) One of the most useful tool/tools available to the chemist/chemists for the study/studies of molecular structure/structures and molecular bonding is a form/forms of spectroscopy based on the Mössbauer effect/effects, for which Rudolf L. Mössbauer was awarded the Nobel prize/prizes in physics in 1961.

(The Measurement of the "Man-Day":) Until well into the present century/centuries a significant part/parts of all mechanical energy/energies was supplied by man's/men's muscle/muscles, even in the technologically advanced country/countries.

In these eight sentences by different authors, there is perhaps only only one case among the 47 nouns where the choice of singular or plural is difficult or important: *the Mössbauer effect/effects*. This is a relativistic effect (singular) in atomic physics, and the term is hardly a household word outside the scientific community.

In one or two cases, it is not easy to decide what the original was, but this is primarily so because it does not matter much anyway: The two phrases *to examine rock collected on the surface of the moon* and *to examine rocks collected on the surface of the moon* do not significantly differ in meaning; had the author wished to stress that the material, and not individual pieces were important, he would have done so more elaborately than by the mere omission of the check morpheme -*s*.

In all other cases the ambiguity can easily be resolved by formal or semantic decoding. *Has a remarkable capacity/capacities* is resolved in favor of the singular, because it is literally being double-checked by the check morpheme *a* (the indefinite article); *color/colors belongs* is double-checked by the check morpheme-*s* indicating the third person singular of the verb. This is analogous to the check digits of a digital error-correcting code, which not only check the information digits, but also each other.

But even if these check morphemes fail to protect the meaning of the message formally, there still remains semantic decoding, that is, comparison of the probabilities of the events coded by an ambiguous message. This is why *the television industries in the United State* is rejected in favor of *the television industry in the United States*, although both phrases are formally grammatical.

It is, no doubt, possible to construct sentences, and perhaps even to find them in real life, where the plural of nouns is important, semantically not obvious, and expressed by no more than the plural ending of the noun. Such exceptions should not be surprising, for Language cannot be expected to exhibit the precise regularity of artificial codes. However, the great majority of cases shows that the singular-plural distinction is either double-checked by check morphemes other than the plural ending of the noun, or semantically obvious, or unimportant.

In English, the implementation of the plural check for nouns is very simple: Except for a handful of irregular nouns (*teeth*), the plural is formed by adding an *s* (corresponding most often to the phoneme *z*) with some small variations (*boxes, loaves*). In other languages, the implementation is often combined with the implementation of another check criterion, namely, gender; and most Slavic languages combine this with the implementation of a third check criterion (for masculine gender), namely, whether the object described by the noun is animate or inanimate.

In summary, the information given by the plural endings of nouns, namely, whether a number of objects is or is not greater than one, is of the same type as the information given by the Library of Congress check digit, namely, whether a certain number is or is not divisible by eleven. The structure of the sentence is checked by the plural check morpheme, just as the actual number of the book is checked by the check digit; both facilitate correct decoding by preventing ambiguity, but neither carries the information that is of primary interest to the receiver.

This concludes our discussion of the one-or-many check morpheme or (in the Slavic languages) the one-or-two-to-four-or-five-and-more check morpheme. But it seems a good place where to digress to a point that may be of interest, namely, the light thrown by linguistics on the early history of mathematics. The fact that the names of the numbers correspond to a decimal system (or, as in French and Danish, to a vigesimal system) is, of course, due to the number of fingers on man's hands, and proves nothing beyond the fact that Nature is a poor mathematician, because 10 is a very disadvantageous number to have as a base, compared to 12 and some other numbers.* However, Language has given clues to more subtle points. The irrational, negative, complex, transcendental and transfinite numbers were discovered (in that order) comparatively late in man's history; but the rational numbers were known long before recorded history. There is some evidence to suggest that people learned to count to two long before they discovered the other integers, and that they were familiar with the number 1/2 before they had learned to count beyond two, and long before they understood the concept of a ratio and a reciprocal. The evidence is, in part, anthropological. Some tribes of Australian aborigines can still only count to two; by repeated counts they can tell whether the number of sheep in a flock is odd or even. If one sheep is stolen, they will detect the loss, but not if two (or an even number) is stolen;** this is reminiscent of the check digit in the binary parity code, which can detect one error, but not two (or an even number of) errors in a code word. But the aborigines are familiar with the concept of one half. However, the evidence is also linguistic: The word for 2 is unrelated to the word for ½ in many (all?) languages, whereas from 1/3 onwards, the name of the fraction is derived from the name of the reciprocal integer, as evident from the table on p. 175.

This, together with the existence of a dual (a special plural for two objects) in several languages, suggests that the order in which the rational numbers were discovered was 1, 2; ½ ; 3 and the other positive integers; 1/3 and the other reciprocals of integers; the other rational numbers.

---

* The reader interested in this point can obtain more information from the Duodecimal Society of America, 11561 Candy Lane, Garden Grove, CA 92640.

** T. Danzig, *Number: The Language of Science*, Macmillan, New York, 1943.

Language	½, 2	1/3, 3	1/4, 4
English	*half, two*	*third, three*	*fourth, four*
German	*halb, zwei*	*Drittel, drei*	*Viertel, vier*
French	*moitié, deux*	*troisième, trois*	*quart, quatre*
Czech	*půl, dva*	*třetina, tři*	*čtvrtina, čtyři*
Latin	*semi-, duo*	*tertia pars, tres*	*quarta pars, quatuor*
Hungarian	*fél, kettő*	*harmád, három*	*négyéd, négy*
Russian	пол, два	третья, три	четверть, четыре

But all this is noted here only parenthetically in connection with the plural check criterion; it does not concern the check itself.

5.2.3. GENDER

It is probably not difficult to persuade the reader whose native language is English that gender and the rules of gender concord (there are no such rules in English) are redundant; the corresponding morphemes are check morphemes, used quite rarely in English.

Gender is only very weakly present in English, and with only a few minor exceptions it is entirely determined by biological sex. It makes an appearance in English in the pronouns *he, she, it*, and in a few suffixes and prefixes (*waitress, widower, she-wolf*). The cases where gender is not determined by sex are also very few: ships, countries, and machines with which the speaker feels a personal involvement (cars, planes, machine tools, etc.), in which case they become feminine. Gender introduced by personalization (*nature — she, the moon — he*, etc.) is not really an exception, since it agrees with the sex of the metaphorical person. Strangely enough, the computer has remained neuter, though it is a machine, and personal involvement is probably stronger than with other machines ("It doesn't like my statement; it kicks; I can't make it understand; it's talking back at me instead of running the program," etc.).

If gender is only weakly present in English, it is totally absent from Hungarian, which makes no difference between *he, she, it*; there is only a single third-person-singular pronoun (*ő*).

The fact that gender is only weakly present in English, and totally absent from Hungarian, shows that it is redundant in the languages that make strong use of it. It is a check criterion, whose implementation can sometimes prevent ambiguities.

As in the case of other check morphemes, a gender check morpheme, such as the suffix *-ess* in *waitress* or *actress*, conveys information that is unimportant; indeed, if the sex of the corresponding person is important, then we can, and do, state the sex in more explicit constructions. This is easily demonstrated by the vast majority of other English nouns denoting a person, such as *teacher, driver, employee, epileptic, communist, penny-pincher* or *prime minister*. The essence of epilepsy, for instance, has very little to do with the sex of the stricken person, probably no more than his or her weight or size. There is no reason to give information on the sex of an epileptic every time he or she is referred to, and no sex is indicated in English. Other languages do give a gender, and this is then a check morpheme; theoretically there might also be a check morpheme giving other irrelevant information, e.g., whether the epileptic has brown hair or not. In contrast to other languages, English also uses no check morphemes (suffixes) of gender where the sex is obvious from the meaning of the word (*father, brother, boxing champion, rapist; mother, aunt, Lesbyian, nanny*).

All this is very different from other languages, e.g., Latin, French, German, Czech, Russian. When a noun in these languages denotes a person, it is the exception rather than the rule not to use a check morpheme of gender. The French *le professeur* may mean either a male or a female professor, and *l'ami, l'amie* are not phonetically discernible; but in the majority of cases, the gender *must* be indicated by the article, or a suffix, or both. In German or Czech, this leads to words which might be rendered in English as "driveress, employee-ess, ministress, chairwoman, studentess, consumeress, secretary-ess," and many hundreds of others. These words have check morphemes of gender either in the form of the article, or a suffix, or both (*die Sekretärin*). In addition, the gender is checked by a check morpheme ensuring gender concord with the adjective in French, Latin, German or the Slavic languages, and the Slavic languages have check morphemes of gender concord in the past tense of the verb as well. Since French has some nouns which have the same gender for male and female persons (*le professeur*), yet gender concord by sex is required, the result is a contradiction, from which French extricates itself as in the following example:

Le professeur, elle est charmante.

However, all this concerns only the cases where gender is tied to sex. More often, the languages using gender extensively assign it quite independently of sex. Thus, the word for *letter* is masculine in Czech and German, feminine in French and Latin, and neuter in Russian; the word for *apple* is masculine in German, feminine in French, and neuter in Latin, Czech and Russian.

Languages using gender extensively also usually have one or two "hermaphrodites" among their nouns, nobody being very sure what their gender should be. To give but one example, the French for *enzyme* is *l'enzyme*, and nobody was very sure whether it should be masculine or

feminine (i.e., how the gender concord for adjectives should be formed).
The French Academy of Letters ruled that it should be feminine; but
this was ignored by French advertisers of laundry detergents, who needed
to create an image of virile, robust enzymes eating up all the dirt, and
who therefore made it masculine. An academic body is, of course, no
match against the onslaught of TV and the press, and *l'enzyme* is now
apparently masculine. The existence of such "hermaphrodites" in many
languages is another demonstration of the redundancy of gender.

In some cases, the gender is in contradiction to sex; e.g., in German,
der Backfisch (female teenager), *die Wache* (guard), *das Mädchen* (girl).
In several languages, titles of the type *Your Majesty, Excellency, High-
ness*, etc. are feminine, and gender concord is governed by the gender
of the title, even if this contradicts the sex of the person who bears it.
The prize for gender-sex contradiction must surely go to French: The
impolite words for the male and female sex organs, respectively, are
la queue and *le cont*.

Check morphemes of gender appear not only in the article and suffixes or other endings of nouns, but also in adjectives *(magnus, -a, -um)*,
relative pronouns *(qui, quae, quod)*, interrogative pronouns *(quis, quid)*,
demonstrative pronouns *(hic, haec, hoc)*, personal pronouns and possessive adjectives (as in English), emphatic pronouns (French *lui, elle*),
and in the Slavic languages, even in the verb (the past tense ends in
-l, -la, -lo if the subject is singular and masculine, feminine or neuter,
respectively). Ordinal numerals are essentially adjectives, so that it
is not surprising that they may be required to obey gender concord, but
some languages required gender concord even for cardinal numerals:
Czech and Russian have two words for *two*, though they distribute the
two words over the three genders differently. Thus, gender makes an appearance in almost every sentence in languages using it extensively,
and usually it makes an appearance several times in each sentence. For
example, the English sentence *The little girl loved both dogs* carries no
information on gender (there is no formal indication that *girl* is feminine);
but the corresponding sentence in Czech has a gender morpheme in each
of these words (except the article, which Czech does not have). *Girl* and
dogs are identifiable as feminine and masculine, respectively, *little* and
loved is in gender concord with *girl*, and *both* is in gender concord with
dogs.

The purpose of a check morpheme is to protect messages from ambiguity, and that is what gender morphemes do quite frequently. English,
which has no gender morphemes of any systematic significance, can produce ambiguous messages, whose ambiguity is resolved by translation
into a language using systematic gender check morphemes. Consider,
for example, the trebly ambiguous sentence

They were not allowed to appeal the verdict or the sentence, which was unjust.

What was unjust, the verdict, the sentence, or the denial to appeal them? In a language in which *verdict* and *sentence* do not have the same gender, the pertinent noun is identified by the gender concord of *which* and *unjust*. The German for *which* is *welcher, welche, welches,* and the Latin for *unjust* is *injustus, injusta, injustum.* In addition, many languages distinguish between *which* as a relative pronoun referring to a noun, and a relative pronoun referring to an entire clause (*qui, ce qui; welches, was;* которое, что), and though this has little to do with gender, it performs an additional check, i.e., it is the implementation of yet another check criterion. Latin does not have this additional safeguard, and since *judicium* (sentence) is neuter, it can resolve only two of the three ambiguities:

Non licuit iis appelare contra sententiam neque judicium,

$$\left(\begin{array}{l} quae\ injusta \\ quod\ injustum \end{array}\right) erat.$$

On the other hand, German (also Czech and Russian) can resolve all three ambiguities:

Es war ihnen nicht erlaubt sich gegen das Urteil und den

$$Strafsatz\ zu\ berufen,\ \left\{\begin{array}{l} welches \\ welcher \\ was \end{array}\right\} ungerecht\ war.$$

Of course, the gender check is not foolproof, for the two nouns to which a relative pronoun might refer need not have different genders in a particular language; nevertheless, the system improves the chances of protection from ambiguity (by 2/3 for each double-valued ambiguity, assuming a uniform distribution of genders over the noun population).

There are other cases where gender resolves potential ambiguities. Sometimes a homonym is resolved by gender, as in German *der Tor* (the fool) and *das Tor* (the gate), but this is a case where German uses gender to resolve an ambiguity of its own making, so to speak. Other cases of resolving ambiguities by gender are obvious and need no discussion, but the gender and type of relative pronoun is a particularly effective way of protecting a message from ambiguity (as in the example above). In translating from Russian to English, it is very common to meet a sentence which is perfectly clear in Russian due to gender (and case) concord of the relative pronoun, but which must be translated into English by special artifacts (such as breaking up the Russian sentence into two English sentences and repeating the relevant noun) in order to avoid ambiguities or sometimes even utter unintelligibility.

The rules of gender concord (and other redundancies) give Russian, Czech and Latin a very flexible word order, since gender concord is an indicator tying various words together even though they may be separated by their position in a sentence or a phrase (*summa cum laude*, "the highest with praise"). Since English lacks this redundancy, it cannot afford to change the word order significantly; "the highest with praise" would usually be misunderstood or not understood at all, but it would scarcely be equated to "with the highest praise."

It is also to be noted that the gender check is, by itself, not a very efficient check: It invests an enormous amount of redundancy by burdening every noun, adjective, and some other parts of speech with redundant check morphemes, but the check enables only three genders to be distinguished, which will resolve ambiguities in some, but not all, cases. At first sight, the system would be more efficient if there were more genders. However, when gender is combined with other check criterions to determine different paradigms, the check becomes efficient, because the number of paradigms (in languages that have them) is usually far greater than three.

5.2.4. CASE ENDINGS

The only case ending in English is the Saxon genitive (*my father's car*); after the Norman conquest, when English was spoken only by the Anglo-Saxons and developed unimpeded by literature or education for more than a century, the Anglo-Saxon serfs made a superb job of discarding the other redundant inflections for case endings, and they discarded the Saxon genitive for most inanimate nouns, too (why they kept it for statements of time, such as *in three weeks' time* or *half an hour's journey*, and for some other exceptions, is not clear to me). The genitive and dative are formed by the prepositions *of* and *to* , although the nomenclature seems to stem from comparison with other languages only; *of* and *to* are not really different from other English prepositions, all of which are followed by the accusative. (If *of* and *to* were followed by a genuine genitive and dative in the sentences *They took care of the children* and *We must put an end to wars*, it would hardly be possible to transform these sentences into the passive voice: *Wars must be put an end to; the children were taken care of.* The logical classification is to regard *to take care of* and *to put an end to* as transitive verbs *en bloc*, which means that *of* and *to* are followed by the accusative like any other English preposition.)

The accusative is distinct from the nominative in English only for personal pronouns (*I, me*), and for the relative or interrogative pronoun *who/whom*; in all other cases the English accusative can be discerned from the nominative only by the position of the corresponding word in the sentence (*which killed Jim, which Jim killed; Jack loved Jill, Jill loved Jack*) or, in relative clauses, by the presence or absence of a subject (*which was growing, which he was growing*), or by other devices not relying on a case ending.

Not so in other languages. The agglutinative languages (such as Hungarian) add a suffix to the nominative to express the case, the inflecting languages (such as Latin) add a different ending to a common stem. Thus, the Hungarian word *ember* (man) adds -*nek* to form the dative *embernek* (to the man); Latin inflects *homo* to *homini* for the same purpose. (Hungarian also agglutinates suffixes where the Indo-European languages use possessive adjectives or prepositions.)

Here again, the English speaking reader will have no difficulties in realizing that case endings are redundant check morphemes, since English does not need them. (The other languages have prepositions as well, so that the case endings are in most instances an additional feature.) As in the case of gender check morphemes, the case ending can avoid ambiguities, particularly by indicating which noun a relative pronoun refers to. The Latin relativ prounoun *quam* refers to a previous noun in the feminine singular, and it is itself in the accusative; no such pinpointing is possible with the English *which*.

The prevention of ambiguities by check morphemes of case is achieved in the same way as by check morphemes of gender. Thus, the headline

MAN HIT BY AUTO STEPPING FROM CURB

remains ambiguous even after the check morphemes usually omitted in headlines are replaced: *A man was hit by an auto stepping from a curb.* Except by comparison of the corresponding probabilities, i.e., by semantic decoding, it is not possible to say whether the man or the auto stepped from the curb. However, *man* is in the nominative, whereas *auto* is in the accusative (in English; it would be in the ablative in Latin, and in the instrumental in Russian), and if English had case endings and rules of case concord, then *stepping* would have the case ending of the case of either *man* (nominative) or *auto* (accusative, ablative, instrumental, etc.), and the ambiguity would therefore be resolved.

However, once again English is saved by its rules of inflexible word order, and the editor who wrote the above headline violated these rules (see p. 148 for a similar case involving cooking in a horrible manner). The correct word order for the event the editor intended to code would have been

MAN STEPPING FROM CURB HIT BY AUTO

though this would have been out of keeping with the journalistic custom of putting the items with the highest information (lowest probability) at the beginning of the headline.

Apart from the obvious checks performed by case endings, of which the above headline is a typical example, case endings can also often be used to distinguish two meanings by the presence or absence of a preposition. Thus, the English preposition *with* may mean either *by means of*, or *accompanied by, in the presence of*, and this can lead to ambiguities such as

POLICE SEARCHING FOR CAR WITH DENTED FENDER

POLICEMAN SHOOTS BOY WITH KNIFE

NIXON FISHES WITH CUT FOOT

The same ambiguities occur in German, since *mit* has the same two functions as the English *with*. On the other hand, languages that have an ablative or instrumental distinguish the two by using the equivalent of *with* only when it denotes company, but using the bare ablative or instrumental when it denotes means. Thus, the two meanings of *with... foot* are rendered in Latin by *cum piede, piede*, and in Czech by *s nohou, nohou*. Of course, a simpler way is not to use *with* as a homonym; in French, the two meanings are usually distinguished by the two prepositions *avec* and *par*.

When *with* is used with the verb *to play*, it has yet a third meaning, so that the following headline contains a treble ambiguity:

MAYS PLAYS WITH INJURED FINGER

(does Mays play inspite of his injured finger, or by means of his injured finger, or has he given up playing with toys and plays with his injured finger instead?) The treble ambiguity translates into German: *Mays spielt mit verwundetem Finger*. The case check morpheme will resolve one of the three ambiguities by excluding the instrumental possibility, but the sentence remains ambiguous in Russian. Czech can resolve all three ambiguities, but the ambiguity remaining in Russian is resolved by making the verb reflexive (for playing with a toy) rather than by the case check. The case check criterion is a very powerful one, but the above example shows that it is not unlimited in its capabilities.

In the inflecting languages, the same preposition can often govern different cases, a different meaning corresponding to each case. Location is often distinguished from motion in this way, e.g., in Latin, *in ecclesia* (in church), *in ecclesiam* (into the church), with analogous examples in the Slavic languages. This may be regarded as another instance where the case ending acts as a check morpheme to resolve an ambiguity. A non-inflecting language such as English, or a weakly inflecting language such as German need different prepositions (or other parts of speech) to distinguish between location and motion. However, the redundancy of this check criterion is demonstrated by the fact that many words associated with motion are dying out in English, showing that the distinction is superfluous. The English words *hither, whither,*

thither, hence, whence, thence are more or less archaic, and few people
bother to use *into* instead of *in*, or *onto* instead of *on*, in such statements
as *He inserted the coin in the slot* or *I put it on the table.*

Whilst there are only three genders, there are usually more than three
cases, and still more paradigms in a language. Therefore a case ending,
especially when determined by gender, is far more effective in avoiding
ambiguities than gender alone, since the word on which the check is performed is now pinpointed by many more characteristics than by only three
genders.

Thus, Latin has six cases (the usual four plus vocative and ablative), Czcech has seven (the ablative is replaced by prepositional and
instrumental), and Russian has six (same as Czech, minus the vocative).
In each case, this number must be multiplied by two, corresponding to
singular and plural. But the paradigms of an inflecting language are also
determined by several other criterions, of which gender is usually one.
Apart from gender, Czech and Russian use such criterions as whether
the noun is animate or inanimate, and whether it ends in a "hard" or
"soft" consonant. In Czech, this results in four paradigms for each gender, each having seven cases singular and plural, or a total of 168 func-
tionally different case endings, although they are not necessarily phonetically discernible – but that covers only the regular nouns. To this
must be added the paradigms for adjectives, participles, personal, possessive, interrogative and relative pronouns, and numerals of all types.
It is obvious that Czech is well protected from ambiguity, and that Czech
comedians have a harder time making puns than their English colleagues.
(They succeed, but not with the same ease or frequency).

It is interesting to note that if a language does not have check criterions and the corresponding implementations of one kind, it usually has
some of another kind; it simply protects its messages from ambiguity in
a different way. Bulgarian, for example, is a Slavic language, but it inflects only weakly. (The reasons are similar to those in English; it was
the Turks rather than the Normans who caused the cessation of the standardizing influence of education and literature, and the language therefore developed rapidly and freely). But Bulgarian is also the only Slavic language using articles (they developed from demonstrative pronouns,
this, that). When one check system was discarded, another evidently had
to develop, or the language would have been (or perhaps was) too vulnerable to ambiguity and distortion.

Similarly, Hungarian has only four cases and no gender. This would
yield only a relatively small number of paradigms with correspondingly
few case endings or case check morphemes. Nor could one count on the
compensating effect of the article, for Hungarian has only a definite article; the indefinite article is absent, and therefore grammatical Hunga-

garian cannot distinguish between *school* and *a school* (unless, as in other languages, the difference becomes important, in which case a more emphatic construction is chosen). By comparison with other languages, this would call for an additional check criterion to yield more case endings, and hence better protection against distortion. Hungarian has such an additional check criterion: The vowels are divided into three groups, two of which must not occur in the same word, whereas the third may be mixed with the other two. Thus, for each case there are two suffixes to be agglutinated, and the check implements the one in harmony with the vowels of the preceding stem. For example, *á* and *é* are not permitted to occur in the same Hungarian word (*kávé*, meaning coffee, can therefore immediately be spotted as a foreign word). This multiplies the number of case endings by two: The dative of *ember* is *embernek*, but the dative of *alma* is *almanak*. All other suffixes, such as the equivalents of prepositions and possessive adjectives, also have the two forms ("high" or "low" vowel).

Compared to the article, suffixes determined by case, number, gender and other criterions such as dead or alive, hard or soft consonant, high or low vowel, etc., are both more complicated and more effective as protection against distortion and ambiguity, which is the usual case of getting more returns on a bigger investment. One might compare this to the simplicity of the check system in a binary parity code and the complexity of calculating the check digit in the Library of Congress code. However, the binary parity code (in the version previously given) will detect only simple, not double, errors, whereas the Library of Congress code will detect virtually all types of reasonable errors.

5.2.5. *CONJUGATION MORPHEMES*

The various conjugation morphemes denoting the tense, mood, voice, etc., of a verb are not, of course, all redundant. Whether something was done in the past or will be done in the future may contain essential information that needs itself protection; it is not information whose primary purpose is merely to protect other information from ambiguity or distortion. However, there are many other redundant features appearing in the conjugation of a verb.

One of such obvious redundancies is the use of both a personal pronoun and a conjugation morpheme showing the person. Latin and Czech, for example, use only the verb ending to indicate the person: *laudo, laudamus* means *I praise, we praise*; the endings *-o, -amus* are sufficient to show the first person singular or plural, and it is unnecessary to precede the verb by a personal pronoun as well (*ego laudo* means *It is I who praise*). Similarly, Czech adds personal pronouns only for particular emphasis. Conversely, the Danish verb does not change with person, nor does it need to, since it is preceded by a personal pronoun (or other subject) making it abundantly clear who is performing the action. But some languages, e.g., German and Russian, use both a personal pronoun and a verb ending to indicate the person (*ich liebe, du liebst, er liebt,* etc.); one of the two is therefore redundant and acts as a check on the other. As a matter of fact, German does omit the personal pronoun in telegrams, where this redundancy costs additional money.

Except for the irregular verb *to be,* modern English has only one such verb ending, the *-s* for the third person singular. Since English uses personal pronouns even when no emphasis is intended, this ending is a redundant check morpheme. Its redundancy can be demonstrated not only by referring to the Danish verb, but also by noting that many auxiliary and defective English verbs (*will, shall, would, should, may, might, ought, can, could, must, need not*) do without it, and do without it very well. An additional demonstration of the redundancy is provided by the English past tense (*he played, he ate*), where the third person singular is not treated differently from the other persons.

The check morpheme *-s* attached to a verb can resolve some minor ambiguities, such as *the sheep sleeps* or *the sheep sleep*; for regular plurals it acts as a double check, as in *my son sleeps* or *my sons sleep*; but the distinction is one of little importance, since there is nothing to resolve the ambiguity of *the sheep slept*, whilst *my son slept* and *my sons slept* do not need the double check. (The difference between *he sets, puts* and *he set, put* is, like the irregular plural of *sheep,* limited to a few words, not systematic.)

Many languages, including English, have several past and future tenses. The check criterions they use for the choice of a particular past tense are very different in different in different languages, and since the criterion used in one does not exist in another, it must be redundant, or the other language could not do without it. The criterion for choosing the pluperfect is the same for most languages that have the tense, namely, whether the action took place before another named, past action. But Czech, for example, no longer has a pluperfect (it died out in the last century), and the fact that the Czechs experience no difficulty in communicating without it shows that it is redundant. In English, too, most people will not bother to insert the *had* in a sentence like *After I had locked up, I went to bed*; the *after* is sufficient to indicate the sequence of actions.

The criterions for choosing among the other past tenses vary widely in different languages. In English, which has six indicative past tenses (*I slept, I have slept, I had slept, I was sleeping, I have been sleeping, I had been sleeping*) as well as a past infinitive (*to have slept*) and two past conditionals (*I would have slept, I would have been sleeping*) and some more idiomatic past tenses (*I may have slept, I may have been sleeping*, etc.), the choice between general and continuous tense is governed by the criterion whether the action was performed at a specific time or not; this criterion, which is absent from many other languages, is not limited to the past tense. The choice between past and perfect is governed by the criterion whether the action was finished in the past (*I was in Denver yesterday*) or whether it continues to the present or to the very recent past (*I have not been to Denver today; I have just returned from Denver*). Other languages do not use this criterion, for example, there is no such difference between *Ich war in Denver* and *Ich bin in Denver gewesen*. The fact that the criterion is redundant is demonstrated not only by its absence in other languages; it is equally persuasive that we have no difficulty in understanding what a foreigner means by the ungrammatical statements *I have been in Denver yesterday* and *I was not yet in Denver today*.

That English should have such a criterion to distinguish past and perfect seems just as strange to students of English as the criterions for conjugating verbs in other languages seem strange to English speaking students. The Slavic languages also have several past tenses, but the criterion for choosing the tense (past or other) is whether the action was completed or not, whether it was performed once or several times, or whether it was performed habitually (like the English *I used to go*). In Hungarian, the verb is conjugated differently depending on whether it is followed by a (possibly implied) direct object or not. In German, some prefixes are separable from the verb, others are not (*schneiden,* to cut; *aufschneiden,* to cut open; *zerschneiden,* to cut to pieces; the past tenses are *ich schnitt, ich schnitt auf, ich zerschnitt*). In each case, the criterion is a redundant check criterion implemented by the conjugation which is prescribed by the rules of the code, that is, by the grammar of the language.

5.2.6. PRESCRIBED SEQUENCE OF TENSES

We now come to a check feature (an implementation of a check criterion) which is not a morpheme: a prescribed sequence of tenses. Many languages have such prescribed sequences, usually following a certain conjunction. In English, the temporal conjunctions *when, after, before, until* require certain tenses determined by the tense in the main clause (for example, the future is prohibited in the subordinate clause initiated by one of these conjunctions); the tense in a subordinate clause initiated by the conjunction *if* is governed by one set of rules if the *if* expresses a condition, and by another set of rules if it expresses a supposition (*if it is sufficient, if it were sufficient*).

Consider an example of a prescribed sequence of tenses in more detail. The English rules for indirect speech, which are given here only in part, say the following: If the introductory verb (*to say, allege, claim, think,* etc.) is in the present, any tense can follow in the subordinate clause (*he says he agrees, will agree, agrred, would agree,* etc.). If the introductory verb is changed from present to past, then in the subordinate clause present changes to past, past changes to pluperfect, future changes to present conditional, and present conditional changes to past conditional (*he said he agreed, would agree, had agreed, would have agreed*). These rules are waived when the subordinate clause expresses a generally accepted truth (*he said that still waters run deep*).

Now these prescribed tenses are, by the very fact that they are prescribed, a check feature. This can be shown in two ways. First, since they leave little option, and in some cases no option at all, the probability of a certain tense following the critical conjunction, introductory verb, etc., is very high, or even unity. This means that the corresponding tense carries very little information, or no information at all. *I shall wait until...* contains the conjunction *until*, and the tense of the main clause is future; this predetermines the tense of the following verb, which must be present (in some cases, the perfect is allowed). The present then has probability one (or almost one), and the information conveyed by it is zero. The rules of the code forbid a continuation resulting in *I shall wait until you will come back* or *I shall wait until you came back*. Similarly, *He said that...* must be followed by one of four tenses, drastically increasing their probabilities, and therefore reducing their information. Moreover, the meaning of the verb increases the probability of the tense: *He claimed that he* [to be] *innocent* virtually rules out anything but *was* or *had been*, and even this uncertainty is usually resolved by the remaining context.

Second, a prescribed tense gives little or no information on the time of the action, because quite frequently it contradicts that time. Thus, *till death do us part* is present tense, as required after the temporal conjunction *till*; but this is semantically absurd, since death is not expected during the wedding ceremony, but in the distant future. The perfect tense, *till death has parted us*, is also grammatically correct, but semantically even more absurd. The phrase *till hell freezes over* refers to the future so distant that it will never arrive, but *freezes* is present tense. *Get out of here before I call the police* is a threat to call the police in the future; *You will be sorry if I call the police* is a conditional prediction which can only come true in the future, because the condition can only be satisfied in the future. *If he had not got out, I would have called the police* exhibits the tenses dictated by grammar for two actions, neither of which took place. What reason is there for the pluperfect in the subordinate clause? None whatsoever, except the arbitrariness with which check criterions must be implemented: French, German or Czech would use the past conditional, and other languages might prescribe yet another tense with equal arbitrariness.

A grammatically prescribed sequence of tenses is therefore a check feature. However, in many cases a tense whose choice is not dictated by grammar can also be redundant. There is no tense indicated in the headline *Check Forger Sentenced to Three Months*, and none is needed because it is obvious; but by formal grammar, *will have been* or any other tense (or mood) of the verb *to be* would be equally acceptable for insertion before *sentenced*. Similarly, there is no tense indicated in the telegram

ARRIVING THURSDAY FOUR PM

because it is obviously future; but by formal grammar, it would be perfectly acceptable to precede the telegram by *I would have been*.

The corresponding German telegram

ANKOMME DONNERSTAG 16 UHR

not only uses the present tense, but it also identifies some other German redundancies by their (ungrammatical) absence: the omission of the personal pronoun *ich*, made superfluous by the verb ending, the omission of the preposition *um* (at) before the time, and the failure to separate the prefix (*ich komme an*), for this check feature costs the price of an additional word.

There is another case of a tense that does not indicate the time of action. Grammar rules that a verb must have a tense (with the debatable exception of the infinitive), but sometimes, in general statements, no tense is wanted. In such cases the present acts as a "non-tense." If the present tense in the statement *The sun sets in the west* were taken in its usual time connotation, the statement would be false, since the sun set in the west (yesterday) or will set in the west (tomorrow); even in the unlikely event that the speaker is communicating this message during sunset, he has to say *The sun is setting in the west*. When the present substitutes for such a "non-tense," it carries no primary information on time.

5.2.7. *THE VERB* TO BE

The verb *to be* means *to exist* in certain cases (*I think, therefore I am*), but our concern with it is its use as an auxiliary verb and as a tense marker. A regular verb indicates both the type and the time of an action; the two are combined, for example, in *I slept*. But in many cases, only an indication of the tense, no specified action, is needed. There is only a tense, no action, in the statements *It is worthless, they were furious, you will be sorry, he would be a fool*, etc. When the verb *to be* plays this role of an empty tense marker indicating no action, it loses a significant amount of the information usually carried by a verb. If the tense is unimportant (*grass is green*), it loses even that information and becomes a redundant check morpheme, a filler for a verb whose action is absent, and whose tense is unimportant. In that case it is left out in telegrams and newspaper headlines (*Boulder Man Arrested for Bigamy*).

Russian, which is heavily fortified by other check morphemes, leaves out all forms of the verb *to be* in the present tense, thus demonstrating its redundancy. (In printed Russian, its absence is often indicated by a dash, but this does not correspond to a pause in spoken Russian.) There are Russian words for *is* (есть) and *are* (суть), but they are used only where maximum precision is required, e.g., in mathematical theorems or legal definitions. The word for *am* is archaic and is now practically met only in the Bible (*I am who I am*). Sometimes the verb являться is used where other languages use the verb *to be*, but it is not an exact equivalent, as it is close to the verb *to appear*.

The English words *is* and *are* are also redundant, as shown by newspaperheadlines, but since English has a much flimsier check system, these check morphemes are sometimes required to resolve an ambiguity, for which they are the sole prevention. The check morpheme *are* before *women* would have resolved the ambiguity of the following headline:

FRENCH ARMY COOKS WOMEN

This is a typical case where the check morpheme *are* acts as a pointer indicating that the following word *cooks* is a noun, and not a verb. This function is performed very often by the verb *to be*, and when it is not an auxiliary verb forming the tense of another verb, this function of identifying the part of speech of the following word appears to be the main function of the verb *to be* in English, as we shall see more clearly on examining the ambiguities caused by its omission. This pointing function appears to be at least as important as that of an "actionless" tense marker.

The verb *to be* is not the only pointer of this kind in English; this function can also be performed by other check morphemes, e.g., possessive adjectives, as we shall see below.

5.2.8. POSSESSIVE ADJECTIVES

In most languages, but not in English, possessive adjectives are used exclusively to indicate to whom or what a certain object or person is to be attributed, or to whom it belongs. If this information is not important, then the speaker usually does not give it.

In English, the situation is different. Possessive adjectives can, of course, be essential in English just as they usually are in other languages. But English uses possessive adjectives to a far greater extent. There is, for example, the rule that parts of the body must be attributed to their owners, if the latter are known (the owner is unknown in a sentence such as *The photograph showed a hand clutching a thigh*). Thus, in English one says *She shrugged her shoulders*, although she could not possibly have shrugged anybody else's shoulders; the German translation, *Sie zuckte die Achseln*, does not use a possessive adjective, nor would one be used in French, Czech, or Russian. The possessive adjectives are similarly redundant in the statements *I waved my hand, you lost your head, she had her face lifted, we had a lot of trouble on our hands, they nodded their heads.*

On the other hand, the possessive adjectives give essential information in the sentence *She put her hand on his shoulder*, and the corresponding information is given in other languages also. Curiously, other languages seem reluctant to attribute parts of the body to their owners by a possessive adjective; a literal translation of the above sentence would result in the German *Sie legte ihre Hand auf seine Schulter*, which is perhaps not ungrammatical, but usually gives away the speaker as an English speaking foreigner. The usual construction is *Sie legte ihm die Hand auf die Schulter*, "she put to him the hand on the shoulder," and exactly the same curious construction would be used in French, Czech and Russian.

English is very fond of using possessive adjectives also in other cases where they are redundant. Attributing the ownership of articles of clothing (*he took off his shirt*) is perhaps merely an extension of the part-of-the-body rule, but there are other cases where a possessive adjective, though optional, is almost invariably inserted: *Don't forget to do your homework, he has no time for his family life, he knows on which side his bread is buttered,* etc. In some colloquialisms the use of a possessive adjective seems no less than absurd to foreigners: *...and that's why your infant mortality has gone up; ... that's where your solar energy comes in.*

The reason for this abundance of possessive adjectives in English is evidently due to the lack of other check morphemes (such as gender), and the possessive adjective is in these redundant applications used as an operator whose function is not primarily to indicate the owner, but to flash the warning "noun coming." Once again, possessive adjectives are usually omitted in newspaper headlines as superfluous, but whilst it is true that they are usually superfluous for identifying ownership, they are not always superfluous in preventing ambiguities. The ambiguity of the headline

>   OWNER CANNOT BE REQUIRED TO GIVE UP BITING DOG

would immediately be resolved if the possessive adjective *his* were inserted in one of two positions:

>   OWNER CANNOT BE REQUIRED TO GIVE UP HIS BITING DOG
>   OWNER CANNOT BE REQUIRED TO GIVE UP BITING HIS DOG

Obviously, it is not important to whom the dog belonged (my witness is the editor who omitted the *his* in this headline), but whether *biting* is an adjective or a gerund. Since other languages do not use systematic homonimity to the extent English uses it, they need no protection from the ambiguities caused by it; they therefore use possessive adjectives to denote possession, not to implement a check. But English needs the extra protection, and accomplishes it, in part, by using possessive adjectives as check morphemes. Parts of the body, for example, are frequently used as verbs without morphological identification (*to head, to hand, to foot, to eye, to stomach, to elbow, to shoulder, to neck, to nose, to mouth, to finger, to toe, to palm, to back*, etc.; all of these can also be used as adjectives). Like the article, a possessive adjective used as a check morpheme has the function of identifying the grammatical significance of its neighbors, and therefore clarifying the meaning of the message. (In fact, the definite article could be used just as well to resolve the ambiguity of the above headline.) To whom the dog belongs is just as unimportant as whether it is a definite or indefinite dog; the check morpheme, whether article or possessive adjective, has an entirely different function in the above messages. Czech, for example, would not use a possessive adjective in this case, and it could not use an article (it has none); its message coding the same event is protected from ambiguity by check morphemes of case, gender, adjective ending and nominalized verb ending (it has no gerund).

It is interesting to note in this connection that a possessive adjective often fails to do what its supposed purpose is, namely, to identify the owner. The possessive adjective in *Jack took Jim home in his car* gives no indication whether the car belonged to Jack or Jim; on the other hand, *Jack took Jill home in his car* is unambiguous due to the gender check. This type of ambiguity is quite common also in other languages that have no additional check on ownership, e.g., French and German, and special constructions must be used if the ambiguity is to be avoided (*the latter's car, dessen Auto,* etc.). The Slavic languages have all the possessive adjectives of English and French, but in addition, they have one meaning "belonging to the subject of the sentence" (свой in Russian). This system is also used in some other languages, though not as consistently. In Latin, the difference can be made in the third person singular: *suus* attributes to the subject, *eius* (his) to someone else, so that if the car is *suus*, it belongs to Jack, but if it is *eius*, it belongs to Jim. There is a similar difference between the German *sein* and *dessen*, but the use of *dessen* is optional, and therefore it does not perform a reliable check if absent.

5.2.9. RELATIVE PRONOUNS

Relative pronouns are redundant markers indicating (and quite often, failing to indicate) to what noun a certain phrase is to be attributed. The fact that they are redundant can, as usual, be demonstrated by their omission in headlines, telegrams and other messages that do not waste space or time on redundancies: *Man Seen Near Burglary Denies Involvement* means *Man who was seen...*; *Woman Born in USA Is...* means *woman who was born in the USA is...*; *Funds Alloted by Congress are...* means *Funds which were alloted by Congress are...*; etc.

Sometimes it is not easy to decide whether a relative pronoun (and other check morphemes) has been omitted, or whether a relative clause has simply been replaced by an adjectival phrase, which is "legal" not only in English, but also in other languages. Thus, most people would consider it grammatical to say *He identified the man seen near the burglary; she was not the only woman born in the USA; he misused the funds alloted by Congress.* However, it matters little whether the relative pronoun was omitted in such a case, or whether the entire relative clause was replaced by an adjectival phrase, for both methods show the relative pronoun to be redundant.

There are two peculiarities associated with relative pronouns in English, and once we regard a relative pronoun as a check morpheme, we can easily see the connection between them.

First, an English relative pronoun is not very successful as a check morpheme. It is supposed to act as a pointer indicating to which noun the relative clause is to be attributed. If there is only one noun, such a pointer is obviously superfluous; if there are several, an English relative pronoun quite often fails to identify the required one. In Latin, the relative pronoun indicates the gender and number (but not the case) of the corresponding noun; in the Slavic languages, in addition, it may indicate whether the corresponding noun is animate or inanimate, in other words, the relative pronoun in these languages gives more information on the noun that is to be pin-pointed. Thus, the Latin relative pronoun *quas* is feminine, accusative, plural, and refers to a noun which is feminine plural (the cases need not agree). The Russian relative pronoun которого is accusative or genitive singular; if it is accusative, it refers to a masculine, animate noun in the singular. The relative pronoun is thus provided with a virtual arrowhead pointing to the noun to which it refers. Ambiguities are possible, but not very probable. On the other hand, the

English relative pronoun has few such characteristics, and they are often blurred in any case. Thus, *who* an *which* may distinguish between an animate and inanimate noun; but the distinction is lost in the relative pronoun *that*, which can often be grammatically applied to either, and whilst *which* does not refer to an inanimate noun, it may refer to either a noun or to an entire clause (*He lied, which was despicable*). The latter function is one to which other languages assign a special relative pronoun. Similarly, *who* and *whom* distinguish the nominative from the accusative, but *which* and *that* have no such distinction, and to many people the difference between *who* and *whom* is not very clear; others know the difference, but sometimes consider it snobbish (*I don't know whom you think you are kidding* does sound strange). The net result is that English relative pronouns quite often fail to perform their primary function of pointing out what they refer to; they are not, as in Latin or Russian, arrow heads, but more like unmarked circular discs, not pointing in any direction, and giving rise to ambiguities such as the treble ambiguity in *They were not allowed to appeal the verdict or the sentence, which was unjust.* As we have seen on p. 178, other languages can resolve the ambiguity partially or totally, and they do so by the use of relative pronouns.

The second peculiarity of English relative pronouns is that their omission is quite often legal (grammatical), even when replacement by an adjectival phrase is not involved. This is, at first sight, an unusual phenomenon: Check morphemes are omitted in all languages, but this is a violation of the rules of the code (the grammar), so that omission of check morphemes usually occurs only in ungrammatical sentences. The omission of check morphemes in English is, as a rule, also ungrammatical; headlines, for example, are usually ungrammatical, though they are generally quite easy to understand. But English grammar does permit the omission of relative pronouns in certain cases; for example, *whom* and the relative pronoun *that* in the accusative may be omitted whenever they (might) occur: *The car I drove, the man you saw,* etc. Other languages do not permit this.

Once we regard relative pronouns as check morphemes, the reason why English permits the omission is quite evident: The relative pronoun is not very effective in avoiding ambiguities, as it is not often equiped with the morphemes identifying the item to which it refers; and since it is not much use in this respect, it might as well be discarded. But more than that: Its omission can in itself act as a check feature. The relative pronoun *that* can be either nominative or accusative, but grammar permits its omission only in the accusative (*the car that crashed; the car I bought*). The omission of *that* is therefore an indication of the accusative, so that the omission does more for the protection of the message than insertion might perhaps do.

As noted earlier, other languages can sometimes also avoid relative clauses; however, they cannot merely discard the relative pronoun as in *the car I bought*, but they can replace a relative clause, as English can, by an adjectival phrase. *The book which is lying on the table* is equivalent to *the book lying on the table*, and this phrase can be translated almost word for word into French, Czech or (with commas inserted) Russian. German puts the adjectival phrase between the article and the noun: *Das auf dem Tisch liegende Buch*, literally "the on-the-table-lying book," and though this construction is considered ugly by many people (including many Germans), this is, after all, where an adjectival logically belongs. Russian can use this construction also (на столе лежащая книга).

It is also interesting to note that whilst the English relative pronouns *which* and *that* do not implement check criterions used by other languages, such as gender, case, animate-inanimate, noun-clause, etc., they do implement some check criterions absent from other languages. If the relative clause specifies a part of the whole or extracts a specific object from a set of similar objects, the relative pronoun is *that* (*the town that has no cinema*); if the relative clause merely describes the noun in more detail, the relative pronoun is *which* (*the town, which has no cinema, is one of the biggest in the state*). Unfortunately, this is not the only criterion dictating the choice between *which* and *that*, nor are the two possibilities always mutually exclusive. The reader familiar with English grammar will recall the numerous set of rules governing the use of *which* and *that*, and the fact that none of them is without exceptions.

When a relative pronoun is omitted in a newspaper headline, the verb *to be* is usually omitted as well. Sometimes this results in an ambiguity, e.g.,

MAN CAUGHT CHOKING WOMAN KILLED BY POLICE

This headline was evidently intended to mean *A man who was caught choking a woman was killed by the police.* Yet the restoration of the relative pronoun is unnecessary to resolve the ambiguity, for the check morpheme *was* will do this by itself: *Man choking woman was killed by the police* or *Man was choking woman killed by the police* give either of the two meanings unambiguously. The English relative pronouns, therefore, are in a sense even more redundant than the other check morphemes.

5.3. Vulnerability of Non-Redundant Language

The check morphemes or other check features of a language serve the purpose of avoiding or resolving ambiguities in the messages (sentences) of a language. They have the same function as the check digits in an error-detecting or error-correcting digital code. In the preceding section we investigated the methods by which the check morphemes do this; let us now examine what happens if they are omitted.

The omission of check morphemes generally violates the rules of the code, that is, sentences omitting certain or all check morphemes are generally ungrammatical. This most often occurs in colloquial language, slang and dialects, and we shall consider this case in the next section. But check morphemes are also omitted in telegrams and newspaper headlines, in both cases for reasons of economy. A study of newspaper headlines is particularly useful for appreciating the significance of check morphemes, and in the following we again use examples from Tempel's collection.*

The great majority of newspaper headlines are unambiguous, showing that check morphemes are indeed redundant and unnecessary in most cases. But often the missing check morpheme will result in an ambiguous headline, although even then the message can usually be correctly decoded by semantic decoding, that is, by comparing the probabilities of the two or more coded events. It is also to be noted that newspaper headlines do not omit *all* types of check morphemes, but only those that take up significant space, particularly the words *he, she, it, they,* the various forms of the verb *to be,* articles, and possessive pronouns; they do not omit morphemes that form part of a word, such as the ending -s either for the third person of verbs or the plural of nouns.

We have already met some examples of ambiguous headlines resulting from the omission of check morphemes, and we shall now consider some others. Consider first some ambiguities caused by the absence of the verb *to be*:

```
HARTFORD SURGEON HUNTING VICTIM
YOUTH BORN IN USA IN SWEDISH UNIFORM
MAN CAUGHT CHOKING WOMAN KILLED BY POLICE
MAN THOUGHT HURT BUT SLIGHTLY DEAD
ANCIENT INDIAN REMAINS UNCOVERED NEAR ROSWELL
FIGHT TO AID CATTLE TO GO TO CONGRESS
MAN KICKED BY COW IN HOSPITAL
FRENCH ARMY COOKS WOMEN
```

We note three points about these ambiguous messages. First, they are only formally ambiguous; each can be decoded semantically without

---

*E. Tempel, *Humor in the Headlines,* Pocket Books, New York, 1969.

ambiguity. Semantic decoding, as we know from Chapter 3, involves a comparison of the probabilities of the two or more events coded by a formally ambiguous message. In all of the above cases, the ratio of the probabilities of the two events coded by the corresponding message is never near one; one of the two events has a very much higher probability than the other. It is highly improbable that a surgeon was hunting a victim, that a person was born in Swedish uniform, that a man was choking a woman who had been killed by the police, that a man was slightly dead, that an Indian remained uncovered, that cattle is to go to Congress, that a man was kicked by a cow while he was in hospital, or that the French army cooks women. This is not peculiar to the above examples; it is the rule rather than the exception. There are, no doubt, sentences that are not only formally ambiguous when their check morphemes are removed, but that cannot even be decoded uniquely by semantics. But such sentences usually have to be invented for the purpose of demonstrating that this is possible; they do not often occur in real life, unlike the examples given above, which actually appeared in print.

Second, none of the above sentences remains ambiguous when translated into a foreign language, even when the check morphemes corresponding to *is* and *are* (as well as articles and possessive adjectives) are omitted. There are two basic reasons for this. One is that the check system (check criterions and their implementations) is different in different languages, so that it is not to be expected that an ambiguity due to the absence of a check morpheme in one language will translate into another, especially when it is recalled that ambiguities of this type are the exception rather than the rule. The other reason is that English has a rather flimsy check system compared with other languages; whilst other languages can usually afford the loss of a single check morpheme, English cannot. Thus, Russian does not even have words for *is* and *are*, but none of the above sentences would be ambiguous; Russian has too many check morphemes of gender, case, etc., to need these two check morphemes. Nor do other languages use systematic homonymity, such as the adjective-participle homonymity in *hunting victim*. The two parts of speech are rendered by different words, for example, in German, *Hartforder Chirurg Jagdopfer* and *Hartforder Chirurg jagt Opfer*. In both cases the German translation lacks the check morphemes of the verb *to be* and the article (as is customary in German newspaper headlines also), but there is no ambiguity in either; German lacks the efficient device of systematic homonymity, and is more noise resistant as a consequence.

One might continue from example to example in this way, identifying the cause of the ambiguity and noting that in other languages the cause is either absent, or the ambiguity is resolved by additional check criterions and their implementations. Thus, the ambiguity in *Man thought*

but slightly dead is (after the *is* has been removed) due to the English
particular homonym *but*, which can act as an adverb or a conjunction
(in other cases, also as a preposition). This cause is absent from other
languages: French distinguishes these two functions by different words
(*ne ... que* and *mais*), and so do other languages.

The ambiguity of *French Army Cooks Women* is an interesting one;
not only is the cause of the ambiguity (verb-noun homonymity in *cooks*)
absent from other languages, but other languages often have an additional gender check (female cooks) to protect the message from ambiguity.
But this very check ruins the point of the headline. Every editor strives
to make his headlines interesting, unexpected, sensational, in other
words, high in information content. But what, then, is the point of a headline saying, in effect, "French female army cooks are women"? That is
what a literal translation into German or Russian would amount to (*Fran-
zösische Armeeköchinnen sind Frauen;* Французские военные поварихи
– женщины). In practice, no German or Russian editor would write such
a headline; he would make it *French Women Serve as Cooks in Army*, or
something else where *women* hits the reader first, and the female check
morpheme in *cooks* follows quite naturally.

Third, as is the case with practically all check morphemes, the word
is (*are*) does quite a different job than one might at first expect. In none
of the above headlines (if it were inserted) does it mean *exists*, or for
that matter anything else; it is not even needed as a tense marker. It has
no meaning of its own; it is a marker saying "Subject or subject clause
is over, predicate coming." This is easily verified in the above examples.

The story of ambiguity due to missing check morphemes in other
cases, such as omission of articles, possessive adjectives, etc., in
headlines is much the same, and will not be continued here for fear of
becoming repetitious. The reader is referred to Temple's collection (see
p. 194) for hundreds of other examples. Let us just take one more headline which illustrates several of the points made here,

USED GIRLS TO FORGE CHECKS

in which the subject (*he*) is missing; if we did not know better through
semantic decoding, it could also be that the check morpheme *are* is missing, which on restoration would yield the grammatically correct message
Used girls are to forge checks. The missing check morphemes *he* or *are*
resolve the ambiguity, which is due to the English systematic homonimity of using the same form for past tense, past participle, and adjective, in this case for *used*. Other languages do not have this systematic
homonimity, and therefore no ambiguity results when the subject of the
sentence is omitted. The heavily inflecting languages have a different
ending for the past tense and the past participle (used as an adjective
in the second unambiguous message). In German, *benützte* can, as in

English, be either the past tense of *benützen* (to use) or the plural of the past participle used as an adjective. However, this homonym is neither systematic, nor applicable in the present case. It is not systematic, because past participles are more often formed in German by the prefix *ge-*, and it is not applicable because in the present case *to use* means *to exploit*, in which case the German verb is *ausnützen*, whereas *benützt* means *used* in the sense of *not new*. There is therefore no ambiguity in German.

. Additional protection in other languages is ensured by two different constructions which are both rendered by the infinitive in English. The construction *to be* + infinitive, meaning to be predestined, dutybound, intended, etc., is expressed by a special ending or by a special verb in other languages (*-ndus* in Latin, *devoir* in French, *sollen* in German, etc.), whereas final clauses are usually initiated by a special marker (e.g., *um zu* in German, *pourque* in French, чтобы in Russian, corresponding to the English *in order to*), or, as in English, a final clause can be replaced by a construction using a preposition (*used girls for check forging*).

But the interesting point is that if the subject were given in the above headline, its importance would not lie in identifying who the subject is, but in the fact that a subject is present before the word *used*. It would flash a warning "verb coming" and thus identify the function of the word *used*. The identity of the subject, as is always the case with check morphemes, is of secondary importance. Thus, the following sentences are unambiguous, because a subject is present; the identity of the subject is so insignificant that the editor, overlooking its marker function, left it out:

He used girls to forge checks
She used girls to forge checks
They used girls to forge checks
Someone used girls to forge checks
An unknown person used girls to forge checks
John Smith used girls to forge checks
They used girls to forge checks

This is, of course, typical of check morphemes. Their presence, and the fact that the check criterion is satisfied, is what is important; the actual information given by the check morpheme (definite-indefinite, animate-inanimate, etc.) is of secondary significance. This is again in correspondence with digital error-detecting codes. For example, in a binary parity code, the important point is whether the check agrees or not; if the check digit satisfies the check criterion, it is entirely uninteresting whether it satisfies it with an even digit or with an odd one.

Our last example of what the absence of a check morpheme can do
in English is Chomsky's well known sentence

FLYING PLANES CAN BE DANGEROUS

which is truly ambiguous, because the ambiguity cannot even be resolved
semantically: Neither of the probabilities corresponding to the events
that planes in flight can be dangerous and that the flying of planes can
be dangerous, is negligible. The cause of the ambiguity, as so often in
English, is the systematic homonymity for gerund, nominalized verb, present participle, and adjective; in this case, *flying* can be either a gerund
or an adjective. The check morpheme that would normally resolve the
ambiguity is the third-person ending -*s* of the verb, and Chomsky's ambiguity is entirely based on the defective verb *can*, which (like *may, must,
ought*, and others) lacks the -*s* in the third person. As soon as the defective verb *can* is replaced by a regular verb, say, *to appear*, the ambiguity
is resolved by the check morpheme -*s*:

FLYING PLANES APPEAR TO BE DANGEROUS
FLYING PLANES APPEARS TO BE DANGEROUS

Chomsky's sentence is also one of many examples where an English
sentence is protected from ambiguity by a single check morpheme; as
soon as the sole protector disappears (as it does in the defective verb
can), the sentence becomes ambiguous. This is one more example of the
flimsy check system in English, resulting both in its high information
density and in its low noise resistance. In other languages, Chomsky's
sentence is protected by more than one check morpheme, so that the loss
of only one of them would not result in an ambiguity. In German, the two
meanings are coded by the following two distinct messages (the check
morphemes are printed in capitals):

FliegenDE FlugzeugE kÖnnEN gefährlich sein
DAS Fliegen von FlugzeugEN kAnn gefährlich sein

German has no systematic homonimity for adjectives and gerunds;
it does not even have a gerund, only a nominalized verb (*das Fliegen*,
the flying of). Nor is the verb *fliegen* (to fly) transitive; in German one
can fly only *with* something, one cannot fly *something*. In addition, the
meaning of the message is protected by the presence or absence of the
article, the differing endings of the present participle used as an adjective or a nominalized verb, the inflection of the noun *Flugzeug*, and the
conjugation of the verb *können*.

All of these are also used in Czech, but in addition, the adjective
dangerous ends in one more check morpheme of case, number and gender:

LétaJÍCÍ letadlA mOHOU být nebezpečnÁ
LétáNÍ letadlY mŮŽE být nebezpečnÉ

Russian follows a similar pattern with only a slight difference in the inflection of the adjective (since Russian uses the instrumental case in this instance, the adjective ending indicates the number, but not the gender of *plane* or *flying*):

Лета**ЮЩИЕ** самолеты мо**ГУТ** быть безопасн**ЫМИ**
Лета**НИЕ** самолет**АМИ** мо**ЖЕТ** быть безопасн**ЫМ**

5.4. Omission of Check Morphemes in Ungrammatical Language

We have hitherto confined our attention to newspaper headlines to study sentences with missing check morphemes. Let us now examine some other cases. With a few minor exceptions, the omission of check morphemes violates the rules of the code, so that the resulting sentences are generally ungrammatical (as are newspaper headlines as a rule). Sentences with missing check morphemes will therefore typically occur in slang, colloquial language, and dialects.

The exceptions, that is, cases where omission of check morphemes is permitted by the grammar of the language, are not very significant. We have met the example of the English relative pronoun *that*, which may be omitted if it is in the accusative; *that* may also be omitted when it is a conjunction (*He says he loves me*). Similarly, the suffix *-to* denoting motion in the prepositions *into, onto* is often (legally) omitted. There are several other cases of legal omission of check morphemes, but they are equally petty.

More interesting is the omission of check morphemes in slangs and other ungrammatical forms of language. We have so far stressed the similarities between Language and other error-detecting codes, and we have emphasized the aspects of Language which can be examined by the methods of coding theory. We now come to a point that distinguishes Language from other codes: It is self-adaptive. We have seen that information density and noise resistance are contradictory requirements; the information density of a code can be raised only by impairing its noise resistance, and the noise resistance can be raised only by increasing the redundancy. A well designed code strikes an acceptable balance between efficiency and redundancy for the application in which the code is to be used. For example, a card reader in a computer installation is a mechanical device, and it is therefore not very reliable: It may feed two cards instead of one, or dust particles may prevent a punched hole to be missed, etc. On the other hand, the electronic parts of a computer are much more reliable. The code used in the card reader should therefore be more redundant than the one used in the central processor. A librarian copying a Library of Congress catalog card number is apt to interchange two neighboring digits, but this is virtually impossible when the number is transmitted by teleprinter (once it has been typed correctly by the operator). The code in the former case therefore includes redundancies to detect transpositions; the redundancies of teleprinter codes check only for independent, simple errors. But when these teleprinter signals are transmitted by short wave radio, another type of error will distort the messages: The perturbations of the ionosphere will cause the signal strength to fall below the receiver sensitivity, and the resulting fade will extinguish or distort long strings of code elements. In that case a "burst-error correcting code" is used whose redundancy is so designed that it will restore the string of signals distorted or extinguished by the fade. Thus, it is possible to design codes to protect messages from particular types of noise. But the code is quite different in each case, and no one (to my knowledge) has yet designed a universal code that can be instantly adapted to the conditions in the transmission channel.

However, natural languages do just that. The same language, say, English, is adapted to form highly redundant, and therefore noise resistant messages when ambiguity is probable or might entail serious consequences, but it is made highly efficient, and therefore highly prone to ambiguity, when no such dangers threaten. To take a drastic example, consider the two English messages

> *John Ferdinand Paul Smith feloniously, wilfully, and of his malice aforethought, did kill and murder one Elizabeth Evelyn Brown*
> (1)

and

> *He offed her*
> (2)

The two statements are coded in two different sublanguages of English: (1) is British legal usage, (2) is American ghetto slang. The extreme redundancy of (1) and other legal usage is, no doubt, often a mere tradition; however, that tradition is fed by the desire to keep legal statements unambiguous, because ambiguity in legal matters is particularly dangerous. On the other hand, the message (2) would be used when such safeguards are unnecessary, because the receiver would be familiar with American slang, and also quite clear as to the persons "he" and "her" refer to. In that case identification by several given names is unnecessary, and the verb *to off* implies murder, not manslaughter, so that the additional information "feloniously, wilfully," would be superfluous (even if comprehensible to the receiver); if the distinction between murder on impulse and premeditated murder is not important in the corresponding conversation, the phrase "with malice aforethought" is redundant also.

But this example is rooted quite deeply in the semantics of the communicated message. More important from the point of view of the formal structure of language are the cases when check morphemes are systematically omitted in ungrammatical, but frequently used language. For example, the distinction between *who* and *whom*, both for relative and interrogative pronouns, is often omitted in colloquial speech, demonstrating that the check morpheme *-m* indicating the accusative is quite redundant. There are some other examples in English, but as English has a very flimsy check system to begin with, there are not many check morphemes to be omitted, and the omission of check morphemes is more common in languages that have more of them.

Here it should once more be pointed out that whilst we are going to consider cases of omitted check morphemes resulting in the shortening of language, it is not at all claimed that this is the only motivation for the use of slang or the only driving force in its development. Indeed, there are many cases when slangs introduce redundancies not found in grammatical language, although, as a rule, they do not compensate for the omission of grammatical redundancies, and the net result is usually a slang that is more efficient and less noise resistant than the grammatical language.

The slangs and dialects of all languages contract quite radically, and thus make transmission more efficient (*gonna* instead of *going to*, with analogous examples in other languages). They also use other devices for raising the efficiency of the language; the English ungrammatical homonym *ain't* replaces no less than five morphological forms (*am not, is not, are not, have not, has not,* not counting the subjunctive *be not*). However, slangs and dialects also use redundancies lengthening the language. The insertion of *got* after every *have* not followed by a past participle is a redundancy of colloquial language only; *I ain't got no nutt'n* is longer than the grammatical *I have nothing*; and the words *went and* convey no information in sentences like *He went and spilled the coffee again*. British West-country (Gloucestershire) dialect omits the third-person ending *-s*, but gains nothing, because that ending is added to the other persons instead (*I goes, you goes, he go*). The use of profane words like *bloody, goddam*, etc., lengthens the language and conveys no information when used so often that it loses its value of shock or emphasis. (I knew a corporal who had been in the British RAF for 15 years, and who would not only say *two o' bloody clock*, but also *Liver-bloody-pool*.)

The situation is similar in other languages. The slangs and dialects also, for the most part, contract words and raise the efficiency of the language, yet they also use ungrammatical redundancies. Contractions are very common in all languages. In French slang, the two syllables *t'as qu'ta* (*gueule à fumer*, for example) stand for the four grammatical syllables *tu n'as que ta*; in German slang, *hammernich'* stands for *haben wir nicht*; in Czech slang, *pá* stands for *povídá*. Most slangs have a universal homonym which can stand for any inanimate noun; in English, it is (the unusually long) *thingamybob* or *whatchemacallit*; in French, it is *le truc*; in German, it is *das Zeug*; in Russian it is вот эта штука; in Czech it is *tentononc*; and in Hungarian, it is *izé*, which can also be turned into the universal verb *izélni*. On the other hand, there are (much rarer) cases of ungrammatical redundancies and dialect expressions longer than the grammatical word. For example, some German dialects replace *nicht wahr?* (isn't it? didn't you? etc.) by the longer *gelloka?*, although most dialects contract it to *newa?* or *noa?* or use a shorter dialect word such as *gelt?*

In general, slang, colloquial language and dialects use both efficiency-raising devices and ungrammatical redundancies; but the net result is a faster transmission of information. This is evidently true even in English, though here it is less evident than in other languages, because English slang only contracts, but does not shed check morphemes, of which it has only a small supply in the grammatical language. But even in English it is evident that ungrammatical language is shorter than educated speech, mainly due to contractions (*gonna, whazza, how d'ya*), and due to a vocabulary limited to short words, for words like *procrastination, to premeditate* or *metamorphosis* are not usually used in slang and other ungrammatical language.

The use of professional jargon is another case where the code is adapted to the decoding capability of the receiver, and where the transmission of information is greatly speeded up by words with high information densities. Thus, the monosyllabic verb *to dump* is used in computer operation for the action of making the computer print out the information stored at each location of the core memory, and some such long phrase would have to be used in talking to a layman.

But the main point of interest for us is the omission of check morphemes and the drastic simplification of the check criterions and their implementations. This can, of course, be done only in languages that have so many check morphemes that they can easily afford the loss of some of them. English is not such a language.

In French, the negative is formed by inserting the verb between the words *ne...pas, ne...personne, ne...rien, ne...que*, etc. (not, nobody, nothing, nothing but = only). Since French, like English, has a fairly inflexible word order, it is only the second part of the construction that carries any information; the *ne* is the same for all negatives, and therefore redundant. Accordingly, it is omitted in French slang (*j'sais pas, j'ai rien, il a que*). English has no redundancy to drop in the negative (although it does contract: *I do' want, I dunno*).

Gender morphemes, which are always redundant, are also simplified and sometimes omitted in the slangs of some languages. In the Prague

dialect of Czech, no difference is made between neuter and masculine
adjectives, and the genders are not distinguished in the third person
plural of verbs.

Case endings are also radically simplified in slangs and dialects.
The vocative of masculine nouns has virtually died out in Czech colloquial speech, though it remains in the written and printed language. (The
vocative has already died out in Russian, where its only remnant is
Господи! = *Lord!*) Other case endings are drastically simplified. For
example, the instrumental plural is formed correctly according to one of
twelve paradigms if the noun is regular, and by special rules if it is not.
But in colloquial language, the instrumental plural is formed by a single
universal ending, regardless of gender or other criterions determining
the proper paradigm. On studying this and other cases of declensions
being simplified in Czech slang, one can vividly imagine what the Anglo-
Saxons did to English in the 11th century; probably the main difference
is that there were no teachers, editors, linguistic institutes, books, journals, libraries, radio stations, TV programs or other standardizing influ-
ences to obstruct their good work.

In German, personal pronouns have different morphological forms in
the nominative, genitive, dative, and accusative (*du, deiner, dir, dich*);
but Berlin dialect uses only the nominative and the dative forms, the
latter being used for a universal "non-nominative" case (*ick hab' dir
jesehn*). The genitive is avoided not only in Berlin, but in most German
dialects (*wegen dir* instead of *deinetwegen*).

Here again, English has only two forms (and only one for *you* and *it*),
so that there is little left to drop or simplify. The English colloquialism
It's me, it's him is *not* a case in point. The form of the pronoun does not
omit or simplify anything, and it is used for emphasis, not for speed or
simplicity. Besides, it is debatable whether the structure is ungrammatical. The usual objection that the pronoun is in the wrong case (accusative instead of nominative) is flawed: One could quite logically regard
the *me* or *him* as the nominative of an emphatic pronoun in analogy with
the French *c'est moi, c'est lui.*

One could give many more examples of the omission of check morphemes in languages that have them in abundance. English, as already
pointed out, does not have an abundance of redundant check morphemes,
and it therefore does not have many that it can shed in slang or dialects.
In fact, newspaper headlines are, in English, a much more fertile source
of messages lacking (some) check morphemes than is the case for ungrammatical speech. However, if we search hard enough, we find such cases
even in English. The omission of the *-m* in *whom* has already been mentioned. Another case is the failure to implement the singular-plural check
with some words borrowed from Latin. What we have in mind here are not

plurals of the type *radiuses, formulas, matrixes*, for the check morpheme of the plural is not omitted, but "incorrectly" implemented.* But the noun *medium*, plural *media*, is one which in ungrammatical language is used with the plural ending for either singular or plural. This occurs not only for news media, but also in professional jargon for media of propagation (for media in which waves propagate); physicists and engineers quite frequently slpeak about *a refractive media, a turbulent media*, etc. This is a case where the singlular-plural check criterion is ignored, and the implementation by a check criterion is not carried out in ungrammatical language. Closely related is the ungrammatical use of *data*. This was originally a past participle, whose plural (like that of *visa*) was taken over as a *plurale tantum* noun; but in colloquial language it is often used in the singular (*the data is ...*).

Another case where a check criterion is ignored in English is the use of *whose* and *of which*. The criterion is (or used to be) the animate-inanimate criterion, with the implementation *whose* for the former, and *of which* for the latter. The criterion is ignored so often in American English that the replacement of *of which* by the shorter *whose* can probably no longer be considered ungrammatical (*a parallelogram whose sides*), though British English apparently still insists on implementing the criterion in print (*a parallelogram, the sides of which*). Colloquial British English follows the American pattern of using *whose* in the genitive in all cases.

Another criterion which is often ignored in colloquial English is the one requiring *among* if many items are involved, but *between* if only two are involved (*among people, between heaven and earth*). But in colloquial language, *between* is often substituted for *among*; the "mistake" is so common that *Time* recently made it in an article bemoaning the incorrect use of words in English.

Time, incidentally, is quite good at these pot-calling-the-kettle-black errors. It quite often uses phrases like *the most essential part* (which is as absurd as *the most twentieth part*), and remarking on Senator Mansfield's bad English, *Time* wrote (November 1971):

> His syntax slightly awry, he addressed the chair. "Mr. President," said Mansfield, "an event of unusual occurrence has just taken place in the Senate this evening."

Time never noticed that there was nothing wrong with the *syntax* of the senator's statement.

---

*I have put the "incorrectly" in quotation marks, because I am not persuaded that these forms are wildly wrong. It seems inconsistent to insist on *radii, formulae* and *matrices*, but not on *elevatores* and *translatores*; and if the "correct" plural of *formula* is *formulae*, then the "correct" plural of *polka, robot, sputnik,* and *Volkswagen* should be *polky, robotove, sputniki*, and *Volkswagen*. Besides, if you are willing to treat *affidavit* (a verb) or *visa* (a past participle) as nouns, what is so revolting about *formulas*, a genuine noun?

5.5. Omission of Information Morphemes: Restoration

In a digital error-correcting code, strings of information digits are followed by strings of check digits (the check digits could also, as in Language, be interspersed with the information digits, but this is not customary). The check digits are redundant; if no noise threatened, they could be omitted. But it is equally fair to say that the information digits (or some of them) are redundant, and only the check digits are necessary: If no noise threatened, the information digits (or some of them) could be omitted, because they could be restored from the check digits.

The second alternative is, for obvious reasons, never used in digital coding; but its analogy is extensively used in Language. To omit the check morphemes of a Language violates the rules of the code (the grammar), and this method is mainly used in slang, dialects and colloquialisms, as well as telegrams and newspaper headlines. The result is, with a few minor exceptions, an ungrammatical message.

On the other hand, the grammar of a language very often permits the omission of strings of information morphemes (words) when they can be restored from the check morphemes contained in the remaining sentence. This can, of course, only be done if the language has such an abundance of check morphemes that restoration of the information morphemes is possible. English, with its flimsy check system, does not fall in this category, and only a handful of examples of genuine restoration can be found in English. In contrast, the heavily inflecting languages use restoration abundantly; Latin and the Slavic languages use restoration more often than French and German, and French and German use it more often than English, where the phenomenon is very rare.

Consider, for example, the Latin phrase *inter pares alias*, which literally says "among other equal," but gives no noun to which the adjectives "other equal" are to be attributed. Any noun could follow in English, but the ending -*as* of the Latin adjective *alias* indicates that the missing noun is plural, accusative, feminine; that is, the check morpheme -*as* implements the criterion of concord with the number, case and gender of the (missing) noun. Theoretically, this still leaves thousands of Latin feminine nouns that could be restored, but in practice the phrase is so frequent that the receiver has little difficulty in restoring the plural accusative feminine noun *conditiones*; thus, *inter pares alias* means *under otherwise equal conditions*.

The Slavic languages, having more check morphemes than Latin, can practice restoration to a greater extent; French and German, whose check systems are much simpler, can do this only to a limited extent. However, restoration is quite common even in French and German. Unlike the English adjective, the French or German adjective is usually well discernible from a noun, and unlike the English adjective, it usually includes, or is preceded by, a check morpheme of gender. This is often sufficient to omit the following noun altogether: *la pauvre* or *die Arme* means *the poor girl* or *the poor woman* – it does not matter which; if it did matter, the speaker would not have chosen this construction. In certain contexts, the phrase might even mean *the poor cow* or it might imply any other feminine noun which is either known or unimportant to the receiver. The phrase is often mistranslated into English as *the poor one*, a construction which is unnatural in English (in this case), and which is far more ambiguous than the original. *The miserable ones* is a mistranslation of *les misérables*; a better translation would be *the wretches*.

There are cases in English, too, where the noun can be omitted after an adjective; but the possibilities are, naturally, far more limited. In the plural, the noun missing after an adjective preceded by *the* is *people*: This is what is implied by *the poor, the French, the meek, the downtrodden,* etc. But whereas this can be done in French and German (let alone the heavily inflecting languages) systematically with any adjective, English uses this type of restoration only with certain adjectives; it would not be possible to use *the Boston, the epileptic* or *the Jesus* in the sense of the constructions *the English, the deaf* or *the religious*. As one would expect, this is because the corresponding adjectives cannot be identified as such. *Boston, epileptic* and *Jesus* can be used as adjectives (*the Boston Symphony Orchestra, an epileptic fit, the Jesus people*), but unlike *English, deaf* or *religious*, they cannot be unambiguously identified as adjectives when the noun is omitted. In German and Latin, an adjective can usually be identified unambiguously, and in the Slavic languages this is virtually always possible. The identification is made not only semantically (as with the English adjective *deaf*), but also by the check morpheme labeling the adjective.

The unambiguous identification of an adjective appears to be necessary for this type of restoration in English, but it is by no means sufficient. *Wild* and *golden* are unmistakably adjectives, but *the golden* or *the wild* is apparently never used in the same construction as *the blind* or *the affluent.*

There are also some genuine cases of restoration involving the English past participle used as an adjective, e.g., *the accused* means the accused *person.* The check morpheme -*ed* identifies the word as a past participle used as an adjective (since it follows the article); this adjective is nominalized when the following noun is omitted. But again, this is not a systematic rule; it is not possible to say, for example, *the elected is...* in analogy with *the accused is...*

In short, the construction *the* followed by an adjective without a noun is a case of restoration. It is severely limited, since no gender or other check for the missing noun is supplied by the adjective, and only one type of noun can be restored — *people* or *persons*. Moreover, this type of restoration cannot be used systematically, but only with particular adjectives. Nevertheless, it is a genuine case of restoration.

There are some cases that are close, but do not represent genuine restoration. For example, the adjective *primary* often precedes the noun *election* or (in electrical engineering) the noun *winding*. In politics and electrical engineering, the corresponding noun is often omitted (*to enter a primary; to short a primary*). This looks like restoration, but it differs from the case of *the poor, les pauvres, die Armen, pauperi*, etc. The difference is that *primary*, if used as a noun, is a genuine noun, whereas *the poor* is merely a nominalized adjective, which acts as a noun syntactically, but retains the morphological characteristics of an adjective; it does not take an -s in the plural. *Primary* is a genuine noun (when it is used as a noun); its plural is *primaries*. If restoration were involved, the plural would be *the primary* in analogy to *the poor*.

The situation is analogous in other languages. When a noun is omitted after an adjective and the receiver is left to restore the missing noun, the adjective becomes nominalized; syntactically it acts as a noun. (In German, this is recognized by giving *die Arme* a capital *A*.) But a nominalized adjective is only masquerading as a noun; it retains its adjectival morphology. In German or French, it can still take any gender, as is usual for adjectives, but (with only a handful of exceptions) impossible for a noun. In addition, the difference will often show up in the case endings in the inflecting languages. In the Slavic languages, adjectives have paradigms differing from those of the nouns, which usually makes the distinction quite evident. For example, the Russian for *the miserable ("ones")* is бедные, whereas *wretches* is бедники ; both are formed from the same root, but one has the ending of an adjective, the other that of a noun.

In English, an adjective that has become a genuine noun can always be distinguished from an adjective with the following noun omitted by looking at the plural. The adjectives *primary, liberal, variable, epileptic, differential* can be used as genuine nouns, because their plurals are *primaries, liberals, variables, epileptics, differentials*. On the other hand, the nominalized adjective *the accused* does not take an -s in the plural, and therefore represents genuine restoration. Whether *the Almighty* is a nominalized adjective or a genuine noun is hard to say; final judgement would have to be made by heathen usage (*the Almighty are* or *the Almighties are*).

But by and large, restoration is an insignificant phenomenon in English. On the contrary, English often goes out of its way to avoid it; it insists on the word *one* in the sentence *The blue book is heavier than the brown one* (obviously, to prevent *brown* from being mistaken for a noun), and it usually repeats a verb in sentences such as *I am bigger than you are* or *I arrived earlier than you did.* This is only natural for a language which has only a flimsy check system to protect its messages from ambiguity.

On the other hand, it is only natural for languages with a complex and abundant check system to practice restoration, that is, to omit information morphemes which are sufficiently well indicated for restoration by check morphemes. Indeed, if these languages did not use restoration, their information densities would not be 15% or 25% smaller than that of English, but a great deal smaller still.

As a typical case of restoration in such a language, consider the following example taken from Czech. An aria in the Bartered Bride starts with the verse

> *Každý jen tu svou*
> *má za jedinou.*

The words of this sentence are *every, only, his, regards, as, only.* (The word *tu* is a redundant demonstrative adjective and will be ignored in the following.) The string of English words *Every only his regards as only* is not only ungrammatical, but also totally void of meaning. Yet in Czech, the check morphemes of part of speech, gender and case are quite sufficient to restore the missing information morphemes (a Czech would rarely think of them as missing, any more than an American would think of anything missing in *the poor*). The sentence means *Every man regards his sweetheart [wife] as the only woman in the world.* This may look as if the Czechs were a nation of puzzle solvers, but the restoration is actually quite natural and easy. First, *only* is an adverb-adjective homonym in English, but not in Czech; it is *jen* as an adverb, and *jediný* as an adjective. The gender of *každý* (every) is masculine, singular, nominative, so that it must mean *every man* (just like *jeder* in German or *chacun* in French); *svou* is not the exact equivalent of *his*, but a possessive adjective meaning "belonging to the subject of the sentence" (see p. 190), and since it has a feminine, accusative, singular ending, it is obvious that what every man cherishes above all other items described by a feminine singular noun must be his sweetheart or wife. Finally, *to regard one's wife as the only one*, where *only one* is feminine singular, must mean *to regard one's wife as the only woman in the world.* I repeat that a Czech, on hearing such a sentence for the first time, solves no puzzles and does not mentally run through the various possibilities presented by, say, a feminine noun; he grasps the meaning of the sentence as soon as he hears it. He does not literally restore *sweetheart* or *wife* any more than an American literally restores *people* or *citizens* after hearing the expression *the affluent*.

Hundreds of other examples might be given, especially for the heavily inflecting languages. However, they all rest on the same principle, namely, the omission of information morphemes (words) whose identity is sufficiently clear from the check morphemes to which they give rise even in their absence. This is perhaps one of the strongest analogies of Language with a digital error-correcting code, where some information digits could also be omitted if the check digits contained sufficient information to restore them at the receiving end of the channel. The reason why this is not done in practice is that an artificial code is never made so redundant as to make systematic restoration possible: If the redundancy is not needed to combat noise, it is easier to transmit only the information digits and not to bother with any check digits at all. English, incidentally, comes close to realizing this philosophy.

Let us return once more to the verse of the aria from the "Bartered Bride." As an example of restoration, it is nothing extraordinary; however, it is also the subject of a striking parody. We have, in Sec. 4.4, defined a parody as a special case of a pun, in which one of the two messages lying close to each other in signal space satirizes the other. In the case of the verse from the "Bartered Bride," the change of a single letter (or phoneme) will turn the sublime into the obscene: The parody

> Každá jen tu svou
> má za jedinou

differs from the original only by the last letter in the first word, changing the ending of *every* from masculine to feminine; but whilst the original meant *Every man thinks his sweetheart is the only woman in the world,* the parody means *Every woman thinks her vagina is the only one in the world* (as the reader can check out fairly easily by the previous explanation of how the information morphemes are restored).

The beauty of this parody (and I do think it is beautiful) is twofold: It is hard to beat on a "cost-effectiveness" basis, for it changes only a single phoneme; and it uses no off-color words of any kind — the obscenity is restored by the receiver, and is therefore literally in the mind of the beholder.

6

Computerized
Sentence Synthesis

6.1. Purpose of Computerized Sentence Synthesis

There is a number of reasons why it is useful to computerize the construction of grammatically correct sentences from a given lexicon of unprocessed words, particularly if the sentences can be made not only grammatically correct, but also meaningful, true and interesting (these requirements are successively more difficult to achieve). The applications to linguistics, computer programming, and artificial intelligence will be discussed in more detail later.

However, as far as the structure of Language (and also the author) is concerned, the main point of computerizing sentence construction is the experimental proof that the model of Language as an error-detecting code is a workable one.

It is extremely easy to computerize the insertion of check digits to re-code messages from a non-redundant code to an error-detecting or an error-correcting code. The computer need only be programmed to test the check criterion and to implement it accordingly. Thus, for the binary parity code given in Sec. 5.1, it would simply add four successive digits of the given string of information digits, check whether this sum was even or odd, and insert a 0 or 1 accordingly. It is equally easy to insert the check digit in the Library of Congress code; the insertion of the check digit following the first 7 is, in fact, done by computer.

If, then, Language is an error-detecting code that does not, in principle, differ from digital error-detecting codes, the construction of code words (sentences) in that code by computer must be possible by the same principles: Program the computer to test in accordance with the check criterions of the given language, and then implement them by the rules of the code, i.e., by the rules of the grammar of the given language.

The author has written such a program for English; it can construct some 100 billion grammatically correct English sentences from a lexicon of less than 100 unprocessed words. A second program will produce not only grammatically correct, but also meaningful sentences, and a third program will produce not only meaningful, but also true statements. These programs will be discussed in later sections.

Theoretically, the construction of grammatical sentences can be computerized by basing the computer program on *any* generative grammar, for this is what a generative grammar, almost by definition, is supposed to do. In practice, however, some generative grammars are far more easily computerized than others, and most of them are very difficult to use as a basis for a computer program. Chomsky's grammar, which is evidently the most widely accepted and most developed generative grammar, has been used to computerize sentence synthesis,[1] but the results were in most cases more limited, and in all cases attained with less ease, than the results produced by the present approach. The ultimate reason for this is that Chomsky's grammar has two types of rules, the rules of phrase structure and transformational structure on one hand, and the morphophonemic rules on the other.[2] [3] The former are general re-write rules, the latter rules depend on lexical information. The actual generation of sentences by computer needs both types of rules, but the morphophonemic rules do not follow a general system in the way that Chomsky's re-write rules do. This is understandable, since Chomsky's grammar is aimed at syntax more than at morphology. It is primarily a derivative and transformational grammar; it is also generative, but this is not its primary purpose. The grammar based on the model of an error-detecting code is primarily a generative one; it cannot detect syntactic ambiguities or transform, at least not as simply as Chomsky's, but it can do some things that Chomsky's grammar cannot do. For example, in Chomsky's grammar, the terminal symbols are selected only after the phrase structure has been constructed; in the generative grammar to be described below, the selection of a word from the lexicon may significantly alter the phrase structure of the (remaining) sentence. But even at this early point I would like to stress that the generative grammar to be described below does not attempt to reject, improve, or replace Chomsky's grammar; the two grammars are suited to different purposes.

[1] V.H. Yngve, *Random generation of English sentences,*Memo 1961-4, MIT Machine Translation Group, RLE, Cambridge, Mass., 1961.

[2] N. Chomsky, *Syntactic Structure,* Mouton, The Hague, 1957; p. 33, 45-48.

[3] N. Chomsky, *Aspects of the Theory of Syntax,* MIT Press, Cambridge, Mass., 1965; Chapter 2, Secs. 4.1 - 4.4.

There are also hundreds of other applications involving computerized language processing. Some of these, such as the various question-answer systems (in which the question is usually posed in a fairly small subset of English, and answered by a computer) come quite close to what we are interested in here. However, these systems usually couple a restricted subset of English with some other purpose; they do not attempt to deal with the structure of English as a whole and as an end in itself. The reader interested in these applications should consult the volume edited by Borko,* even though this is now five years old (a long time in the rapid development of computer science and its applications).

6.2. Computer Programming

The reader who has programmed a computer, even if only by typing on a time-sharing terminal, is invited to skip this section and to go on to Sec. 6.3. The present section is intended for linguists who have not had any contact with computers, and for people who are under the false impression that to program a computer takes as much training as, say, to drive a car.

A computer is a machine, just like an automobile is a machine. Like any other machine, it will do exactly what it is instructed to do, which can be quite exasperating, because very often what the programmer tells it to do is not exactly what he wants it to do. It is possible to drive a car without having the faintest idea what goes on under the hood, but it helps to have a rough idea what a carburetor does and what the spark plugs are for. Similarly, it is possible to program a computer without having the faintest idea what goes on inside the computer, but it helps (especially for language processing, which is not what a computer was primarily made for) if the programmer has a rough idea what the computer does when it is executing his instructions.

The most striking difference between a computer and any other machine is its ability to obey logical instructions, in particular, conditional transfers. An automobile obeys, in a sense, the driver's instructions also; as long as he depresses the accelerator, it will keep going, and if he steps on the brake, it will stop. But he cannot tell it "Keep going at this speed until you come to a traffic light; if it is green, ignore it, if it is red, stop and continue after it has turned green; however, these instructions are to be overruled if an obstacle appears in your immediate path ahead, in which case stop."

A computer, on the other hand, is capable of obeying "if...then" instructions, that is, it will test whether a certain condition is satisfied, and it will then proceed with its work accordingly, doing one thing if the condition is satisfied, and another if it is not. A washing machine ("if the water reaches the specified level, turn off the water and start agitating") is therefore nearer to a computer than an automobile, but its programs are very primitive and inflexible.

The other two characteristic properties of a computer are speed and memory. It can perform an elementary operations such as adding two numbers in much less

---

* H. Borko (ed.), *Automated Language Processing — The State of the Art*, Wiley, New York, 1967.

than a millionth of a second. It can also store vast amounts of information in its memory, each item so stored being ready for use when needed. It can also erase specified items of information from its memory within a millionth of a second (which cannot be done by a library, a photograph or the human brain).

The basic element of a computer is a memory location (also called an address) consisting of several cells. Each cell is in one of two states (it does or does not carry a current, it is or is not magnetized, etc.). The number nine can therefore be stored in binary code as 00001001, where successive digits are the states of successive cells of the address. In this way, a memory location can store a number. Since letters or words can be coded by numbers, a computer can store letters, words and sentences as well. A sentence is stored by a string of addresses, each of which stores one letter or one word.

Now the computer can do several things with the numbers thus stored in its memory locations. First, it can shift the number stored at one address to another address. It is useful to think of the addresses as mail boxes, and the numbers stored in them can be regarded as letters (epistles, not graphemes). Each address contains either one letter or none. If it receives a letter when it already contains one, the old one is thrown out, and the new one taken in. But when it "sends" a letter, it only sends a copy, keeping the original until it is replaced by a received letter.

Before the computer receives instructions from the program, the mailboxes or addresses are empty. They are filled by assignment statements. Thus, in the language Fortran, $X = 3.17$ means: Take an address and call it X; store the number 3.17 in it. Similarly, $Y = 0.25$ means: Store the number 0.25 at address Y.

To shift numbers about in the memory locations is done by similar instructions. What is to the left of the equal sign is the address, what is to the right of it is the number to be stored in it. Thus, in Fortran, $X = Y$ means: Store the number Y at the address X ("the number Y" is really the number stored at the address Y). Throw out from X whatever was in it before.

The second thing a computer can do with the numbers stored in its memory locations is the performance of arithmetical operations. It can add two numbers, and since all other operations are essentially derived from addition, it can also subtract, multiply, divide, exponentiate, find the trigonometric functions of a number, etc. The (Fortran) instruction $X = Y*Z + SQRT(1.8)$ means: Take the numbers stored at the addresses Y and Z, multiply them, subtract the square root of 1.8 from the product, and store the result at the address X. The (Fortran) instruction $N = N + 1$ (which would be absurd if it were regarded as a mathematical equation) means: Take the number stored at N, increase it by one, and store it at the address N. In other words, increase the number stored at N by one.

The third thing a computer can do with the numbers stored at its addresses is to subject them to logical operations. It can be told "If X is greater than Y, continue to the next instruction; but if X is less than, or equal to, Y, jump to instruction no. 257 of the program, and continue from there." In the language Fortran, this is expressed by the statement IF (X.LE.Y) GO TO 257. The computer will then compare X and Y (that is, the numbers stored at X and Y); if the specified condition is not satisfied, it will ignore the statement, but if it is satisfied, it will look for instruction no. 257, execute it, and continue with the instructions following no. 257. Another example is the Fortran statement GO TO (5, 7, 189, 45), K. This tells the computer to look at the number (stored at) K; if that number is 1, it will jump to statement 5; if it is 2, it will jump to statement 7; if it is 3, it will jump to statement 189; if it is 4, it will jump to statement 45; if it finds a number other than 1,2,3, or 4 at the address K, it will not know what to do, so it will print EXECUTION DELETED and refuse to do anything at all.

The computer logic is the heart of the computer. It was the same man, Claude Shannon, whose name we have so often met in connection with information theory, who was responsible for a break-through in synthesizing logic circuits. A mathematical discipline called Boolean algebra can be used to solve logical puzzles of the following type:

> Exactly two of six suspects must be guilty of a crime. Miller says it was Smith and Jones. Brown says it was Williams and his wife. Williams accuses Smith and Mrs. Williams. Jones says it was Miller and Smith. Smith accuses Brown and Williams. If one of these accusations is totally false, and the others blame one innocent and one guilty person, who are the guilty two?

Boolean algebra can find the solution quickly and without trial and error. What Shannon discovered as a graduate student at M.I.T. was that if electrical switches (in those days, they were relays, today they are semiconductors) are arranged in a certain way, then an open switch corresponds to a false statement, and a closed switch to a true one. It is possible to construct a circuit corresponding to the above puzzle and to look for a solution in the form of a current flowing through certain branches corresponding to the suspects. Such a circuit would immediately indicate that the guilty parties are Smith and Brown. In practice, there is no need to build a special circuit for this puzzle; Shannon's basic idea is realized in a number of standard elements (or-gates, and-gates, nor-gates, nand-gates) which can be so combined as to provide a certain output for a given input and a given logical requirement.

The part of the computer that ultimately executes the instructions of the program by processing (arithmetically or logically) the numbers stored at the various addresses is the central processor. The peripheral equipment includes the input and output equipment, i.e., the parts where the instructions are fed in, and where the results of the computation are communicated. The input can be (among others) a typewriter terminal or a card reader which converts the holes punched in cards into electrical signals. The output can be a print-out, obtained from a line printer, which prints a line of 150 characters at one time.

The instructions are fed to the central processor, or the "hardware," in "machine language." An instruction given in machine language differs for different computers. An IBM computer will not understand CDC machine language, and machine language also differs from model to model made by the same company. Also, machine language usually needs several statements for what, from the programmer's point of view, is a single instruction. Obviously, machine language is best left to the computer experts. The programmer need only program his instructions in a machine-independent "source" language, which is then translated into the required machine language by a special program, called a compiler. This is part of the "software," or programs supplied with the machine. Typical source languages are Fortran, Basic, Algol, Cobol, Snobol, Lisp, and many others.

Each such computer language has special advantages and disadvantages, and is therefore particularly suited to certain applications. Simscript is particularly suited for comuter simulations, Cobol is particularly suited for accounting and other business applications, Lisp is a list-processing language. A computer expert will often invent a language for a particular type of problems, and he will write a compiler for it. At present computer languages are being invented at the rate of one a day in the United States. The beginner will obviously do better by selecting one of the standard languages for which textbooks and compilers are widely available. Theoretically, he ought to choose a language suited to his needs; for the linguist, this would be a language such as Snobol, Lisp or Comit. Unfortunately, in practice his choice is often severely restricted by the software available at the installation to which he has access. A Snobol compiler is usually available only at large and expensive installations, and Comit compilers are quite rare.

Under these circumstances, I would recommend Basic as the first language to learn. It is probably the easiest computer language; it makes no difference between integer and real variables, the loops are very easy, and the output statement is not much more than simply PRINT, whereas in Fortran and other languages the output statement can be quite difficult . It is also widely available, since most time sharing computers (terminals for the users, with a central processor at a distant installation) accept Basic. Textbooks are also available if needed, but the rules can be stated on only a few pages, and the computer will teach the student the rest by typing the reasons why it cannot accept an illegal instruction, and the statement can be corrected as often as necessary until the computer accepts it. A further advantage of ("extended") Basic is that it has string variables, enabling letters and words to be concatenated, which is particularly useful for the linguist.

Once the student has mastered Basic, he will have mastered the essential points of computer programming in general, and it will be quite easy to learn another computer language. This will sooner or later be necessary, since Basic is not suited for more complex, non-numerical programs.

Computers are primarily made for numerical processing; the hardware is usually unable to process anything but numbers. However, nondigital or alphanumeric processing is also possible. The input and output is supplied in letters (or words); the computer processes these by coding the letters into numbers, processing the numbers, and then reconverting them into letters. The programmer does not even have to know how this is done.

Several languages particularly suited to nondigital processing are available. For linguistic processing, Snobol appears particularly powerful, and textbooks for this language are available.* But Snobol compilers are usually found only at very large computer installations, where processing time runs from $300 to $1,000 an hour, and the student may have to settle for Fortran. This is a language primarily used for numerical processing; it is very flexible, but also rather cumbersome for linguistic processing — laborious subroutines must be written for instructions that Snobol gives with a single statement. However, Fortran has one overwhelming advantage: A Fortran compiler is available at most computer installations.

To learn Basic or Fortran is a matter of a few evenings with a textbook; the computer will teach the student the rest. What separates the boys from the men are the control cards, the cards inserted before the main program and each subroutine indicating who pays the bill, what compiler is to be used, whether the program is to be listed, etc. The control cards vary from one computing center to another; the only thing they seem to have in common is a conspiracy

---

* E.g., A. Forte, *Snobol 3 Primer*, MIT Press, Cambridge, Mass., 1968.

to keep the system obscure. Corner anybody you can get hold of and try to sort out their conflicting advice. If the computer refuses to execute the program because the student number is missing, you cannot tell it that you are not a student and have no student number. Ask how many digits student numbers have; if six, try 999999 or 123456. Computers are very stupid, and they are easily outfoxed.

The first programs of a beginner will probably come back as unexecutable, and he will have to debug them. This is quite usual; even old hands rarely write a program that will run first time, unless it is very simple. A single dot instead of a comma is enough to make the computer refuse the entire program. However, it will give an indication where the mistake is to be found. Unless the programmer has at least a slight idea how a computer works, this can be very infuriating, because it can indicate first one mistake, and when that is corrected, it may indicate another mistake, and after that is corrected, it may say NO ERRORS IN ABOVE COMPILATION, yet on the third try it will "kick" about the first mistake again. This may look as if there was something wrong with the computer, but that is extremely unlikely, for computers have a very high reliability. A typical example how this can happen is the following. The compiler first works through the program, then lists the errors in it and, because of the errors, refuses to execute it. Suppose one of the errors listed says ILLEGAL STATEMENT in line 116. The programmer looks up line 116, which says GO TO (10, 15, 43) N. The compiler could not understand the statement, because a comma was missing before the N. When this is corrected to GO TO (10, 15, 43), N , the computer still does not like it, because the programmer made no difference between "oh" and "zero." When this is corrected to GO TO (10, 15, 43), N , the computer will accept it, and if there are no other errors in the program, it will print NO ERRORS IN ABOVE COMPILATION after listing the program and it will start executing it; but it may come back once more with ERROR IN LINE 116. Since the compilation went through without objection, there can be no formal error in line 116; *how* the programmer said it was correct (the compiler understood it), but *what* he said was wrong (the central processor found it impossible to carry out the command). Line 116 assumes that N will assume the values 1, 2 or 3, and the computer found some other number at the address N. The compiler had no way of knowing that this would happen, and therefore gave no warning; the error was found only during the execution of the program. The programmer must now examine all lines where the variable N is changed to see where the wrong value crept in. The program may then still come back with further errors that it encounters on execution. Even when the program runs its whole course without a hitch, the programmer's troubles may not be over; he may get a blank sheet of paper instead of a print-out. Perhaps the computer performed all the complicated computations just as instructed by the programmer, but then it erased the results from its memory for ever, because the programmer forgot to tell it to print them. In its exasperating stupidity, a computer does exactly what the programmer tells it to do; it takes nothing for granted.

It is well to remember that computer programming needs no mathematical ability and almost no mathematical knowledge. It requires a little common sense and a capacity for logical thinking, and a lot of meticulous attention to detail. But it is really much closer to law than to mathematics, for the rules of programming are not natural laws; they were drawn up by mortal computer scientists just like city ordinances were drawn up by mortal lawyers.

6.3. Two Examples of Computerizing Error-Detecting Codes

If Language is structured like an error-detecting code, then the computerized synthesis of grammatical sentences must be possible in the same way as the generation of a digital error-detecting code can be computerized. To see this, let us first consider how one would go about generating a digital error-detecting code. The non-redundant digits would ordinarily be selected by the transmitter in accordance with what he wishes to communicate; but the output of such a transmitter can also, for our purposes, be simulated by a generator which selects information digits at random. The job of the computer program is then to convert the string of non-redundant information digits (whether produced by a genuine transmitter or simulated by random choice) into a string of messages coded in an error detecting code.

Let us take the simple case of a binary parity code, which can be summarized as follows:

Code elements: the digits 0 and 1.

Check criterion: parity of the sum of four successive digits.

Check implementation: Insert a 0 if the sum is even, insert a 1 if the sum is odd.

Note that we need not know how the original, non-redundant messages are structured. Perhaps a string of four digits is a non-redundant code word; perhaps messages are transmitted as code words of 64 digits each; perhaps the code words vary in length. This makes no difference to the insertion of the check digits.

Fig. 6.1 shows a flow chart of the program. The input is obtained from a genuine transmitter or by simulation; in either case the input is a string of 0's and 1's. Four successive digits at a time are then added and the check criterion "odd or even?" is applied to the sum; depending on the outcome, a 0 or a 1 is inserted as a fifth digit after every four information digits.

The flow chart is a general diagram of the sequence of computations which are to be performed. It is used only as an aid by the programmer; each part of the flow chart must then be spelled out in statements which the computer can understand. For example, the parity check, i.e., the determination whether the sum of the digits is even or odd, can be performed in many ways. In the present case, the only odd numbers that can occur for the sum of the digits are 1 and 3. If the sum of the digits is denoted by K, then the check digit M could be simply determined (in Fortran) as follows:

$M = 0$

IF $(K.EQ.1.OR.K.EQ.3)$ $M = 1$

The first statement assigns the value zero to the variable M. The second statement is ignored by the computer if the condition (in the

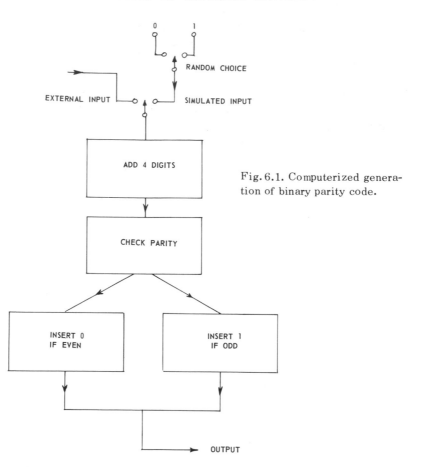

Fig. 6.1. Computerized generation of binary parity code.

bracket following the IF) is not satisfied, so that M stays equal to zero.
But if the sum K equals 1 or 3, then the value of M is changed to 1.

Of course, this method would be cumbersome if the parity of a very
large number were to be determined. In that case one can use the fact
that an even number has no remainder when divided by two. Basic, for
example, has a function INT(X), which is equal to the integral part of
the number X, so that in Basic, the statement

LET E $= X/2 - \text{INT}(X/2)$

can be used to find out whether X is even or odd: If X is even, E equals
zero, if X is odd, E equals 0.5. The check digit M could therefore be
computed by the instruction

LET M $= 2*(X/2 - \text{INT}(X/2))$

where X is an arbitrarily large number, corresponding to the sum of many
information digits (not just four, as in our case).

This example was given only to indicate to the reader who is not familiar with programming how a part of the flow chart is actually implemented in writing a program. However, in the following, we will not usually bother with these details; with a little experience, any programmer knows (or quickly discovers) how to make the computer determine whether a number is even or odd.

Similarly, there is no need to discuss how the computer is programmed to add four digits at a time or how to insert the check digit it has computed. Even without these details it is obvious that if the input string of digits is 00110111..., then the output string will be 0011001111 ..., etc., where every fifth digit is a check digit, and every group of five digits has an even sum.

Now let us do the same thing for Language. As a simple example, we begin with a program that will produce English sentences of two words, namely, a pronoun and a verb in the present tense, so that it will construct sentences of the type *They sing. It dries. We perspire. He must.*

Such a program is very simple, since it can merely choose a personal pronoun and a verb from the lexicon at random; except for the third person singular and the verb *to be*, it will simply separate the pronoun and the verb by a space, add a period, and print the resulting sentence. It can then start from the beginning and construct, say, 50 sentences of this type, and then stop.

For simple sentences of this type, English has essentially only one check criterion: Is the subject in the third person singular or not? If not, no check morpheme is added to the infinitive form. If the check is positive, further check criterions follow: Is it

1) a verb ending in *y*?
2) a verb ending in a sybillant (*-s, -z, -x, -sh, -ch*)?
3) a defective verb (*can, may, must,* etc.)?
4) an irregular verb?
5) none of the preceding?

The implementation of the check criterion is then carried out, respectively, by

1) deleting the last letter and adding *-ies*,
2) adding *-es*,
3) making no changes,
4) modifying the verb according to instructions contained in a lookup table,
5) adding *-s*.

This program would not handle the verb *to be* correctly (it would produce *I be* instead of *I am*), and since we wish to keep this initial example very simple, we will (for the time being) simply not include the verb *to be* in the lexicon.

The lexicon is a set of words stored in the memory of the computer in unprocessed form (i.e., only the form *think* is stored, not the forms *thinks, thinking, thought*), and it should be independent of the program that actually constructs the sentences; that is, if different words (but the same part of speech) are substituted, the program must still produce grammatical sentences. In the present case, it must form the third person singular correctly for any verb. In general, the lexicon will contain not only words, but also their morphological and grammatical characteristics. For example, the verb *to have* will have some code warning the computer that the verb is irregular: If its third person singular is required, this code will send the progeam to a look-up table, where it will find *has*; without this warning, the computer would form the third person by the usual rules, which would result in the incorrects *haves*.

The flow chart of a program which will construct English sentences consisting of a pronoun and a verb in the present tense is shown in Fig. 6.2.

The program first chooses one of the seven English personal pronouns at random. Although we do not intend to spend much time explaining the details of how the program is actually written in a certain computer language, a way to choose words stored in a lexicon at random will be briefly described. A computer can always be made to produce a random number with a specified probability distribution. Usually a function producing a six-digit number between 0 and 1 with uniform probability is already available. In Basic, it is already contained in the language as $RND(X)$; Fortran does not have such a built-in function, but it can usually be called from the library of the computer installation. The uniform distribution from 0 to 1 can easily be transformed to any other desired probability distribution. In the present case, we need an integer equal to at least 1 and at most 7 with equal probability. Multiplying the available random number $RND(X)$ by 7 and adding 1 will result in a uniform distribution from 1 to 8 (actually, from 1.000000 to 7.999999); the integral part of this will therefore be a random integer from 1 to 7. Thus, the Basic statement

LET R = INT(7*RND(X) + 1)

will yield a random integer R assuming a value from 1 to 7 with equal probability.

To save storage space, the pronouns can be put into a single array (or string) in the form

IYOUHESHEITWETHEY

The pronoun YOU is then chosen as the 2nd to 4th element of the array. The unequal length of the pronouns (or other words) may complicate the random selection routine; an easier way to store the pronouns is

I$$$YOU$HE$$SHE$IT$$WE$$THEY

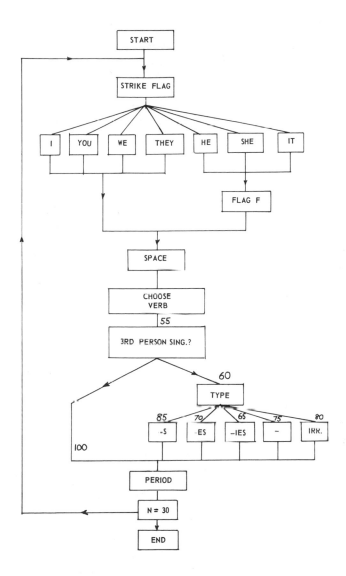

Fig. 6.2. A program for constructing two-word sentences
of the type *It dries*.

in which every fourth element is the beginning of a new pronoun, and all the words are four letters long (e.g., HE$$). The word then goes through a subroutine which looks for dollar signs and discards them before the word is made available for further processing. The same subroutine can also easily measure the length of the original word in letters, which is needed for concatenating the word with the previous words of the sentence. Many other methods can be used; the programmer selects one by his personal preferences and wits.

After the program has chosen a pronoun, say, WE, it puts it into an array reserved for the final sentence, using up the first two elements of this array for the word WE. It then concatenates a space as the next element and chooses a verb, say, SING. Verbs and pronouns must be stored in different arrays, or otherwise identified in the lexicon, so that the program will choose a verb, and not another pronoun. Now the program goes through the check criterion "Third person singular or not?". Since WE is not third person singular (we shall see in a moment how the computer knows this), it concatenates the verb without change, then adds a period and prints the entire sentence array, resulting in

WE SING.

The number of periods is counted; if the number is less than (say) 30, the program is sent back to the beginning to construct a further sentence. When 30 sentences have been constructed and printed, the program reaches the end of the execution.

If the verb has *he*, *she* or *it* for a subject, the program takes a different path, as shown in Fig. 6.2. This, as always, is done by making the program test the check criterion ("Is it 3rd person singular or not?") and to provide the answer. In a very simple program like the one now under consideration, this could be done by a statement expressing the idea "Is the word preceding the verb *he, she* or *it*?" There are, however, several reasons why this is not advisable. First, this idea is not easily expressed by a statement in most computer languages (it is easy in list-processing languages, but not in others). Second, the rule would work for this simple program, but it is, in general, wrong: It would not work for constructions like HE RARELY SINGS. Third, the check criterions of a natural language are often quite complicated; they ask for information contained in "distant" parts of the sentence, or they combine with each other to require a certain implementation. For example, the indefinite article *a* is an implementation of five check criterions: indefinite, singular, countable, but not proper, and followed by a consonant phoneme. Often one check criterion can cancel or take priority over another; for example, the definite article *the* is implemented when the noun is definite, but if the noun is qualified by a possessive adjective, the article is omitted.

To program all this explicitly would obviously be a stupendous task and for all practical purposes quite out of the question. A much simpler and far more efficient method is the use of "flags." A flag is a variable that assumes two values, 0 ("struck") or 1 ("hoisted"). These flags are placed in various branches of the program, and all flags are struck (set equal to zero) when the program starts on its course; as it passes through certain branches, it hoists the flags in those branches, leaving a track marked by hoisted flags, just like a dog leaves his tracks in the snow.

In the present case, we need only one such flag, to indicate whether the program selected one of the third-person pronouns. Let us call this flag F. At the beginning of a sentence, i.e., before a pronoun is chosen, F is set equal to zero. If the chosen pronoun is *he, she* or *it*, the program passes through the branch where the flag is raised, i.e., F is set equal to one. If it passes through any other branch (i.e., if it chooses any other pronoun), F remains equal to zero, because there is nothing to change its initial value.

It is now very easy to program the check criterion. If $F = 1$, then the pronoun is *he, she* or *it*; if $F = 0$, it is another pronoun. No searching for specific words is needed, and the criterion would stay in force if the program were to construct more complicated sentences, such as *He occasionally, though very rarely, sings.* After a verb has been chosen in its unprocessed form from the lexicon in the present program, the 3rd person check criterion looks like this (in Fortran):

55 IF(F.EQ.0.) GO TO 100

The 55 is the statement number. Statements with numbers from 56 to 100 are statements adding the 3rd person singular ending to the verb, in particular, statement no. 60 (see Fig. 6.2) is the criterion deciding what the third person ending should be. If $F = 0$, i.e., if the pronoun is not third person singular, then the above conditional transfer causes the program to bypass all this and to jump to statement no. 100 (see Fig. 6.2), where the verb is concatenated in its basic form. But if $F = 1$, that is, if the condition (following the IF in the brackets of statement 55) is not satisfied, the program will ignore the statement, and proceed through the regular order of statements in which the programmer has originally arranged them; in this case, it will go on to statement no. 60 to process the third person ending of the verb. In other words, a flag being up or not decides which of two possible branches of a fork the program is to take.

Statement no. 60 (Fig. 6.2) is again a fork; this time it has more than two branches, and the decision which branch to take depends on the verb that has been selected. If it is *to fly*, we need the branch beginning with statement no. 65, where the last letter is removed and the letters -*ies* are added. In a language like Snobol, one can (in effect) say "look at the last letter, and if it is a *y*, go to statement no. 65." But a language not primarily designed for nondigital processing, such as Fortran, the corresponding routine would be time consuming in both programming and execution, and it is easier to code the applicable morphology directly in the lexicon. That is, verbs like *fly, carry, cry*, are followed by a code number indicating that they form the third person by dropping the last letter and adding *-ies*. Verbs taking *-es* (*catch, rush, box, buzz*, etc.) will have another code number. These numbers are then used in the decision which branch of the fork to take. Irregular verbs will send the program to a look-up table, where it will find *has, goes*, etc.

It is hoped that the reader can see from this example how simple the system is. There is, for example, no longer any need to exclude the verb *to be*: All we need are two more flags, one (say, F1) in the branch of the pronoun I, and another (F2) in common to the branches YOU, WE, THEY; the lexicon code of *to be* and the flag F1 would then decide on the implementation AM, and the lexicon code and F2 would determine the implementation ARE. (The implementation IS is already covered by the original version of the program.)

The same system of forks and flags would require only a few additional statements to make the program produce archaic forms such as *thou singest, thou art, he hath, she perspireth*, etc.

There is, however, one more thing to be done to ensure that the program will produce only grammatical two-word sentences. Sentences such as *he can, we may, it flies* are grammatical, because they could be produced in answer to a question. However, English has a number of transitive verbs which are not allowed to be used without an object, such as the verb *to like*. The utterance *He likes* is not a grammatical sentence; even in answer to a question, the code word would be *He does* or *He likes it*. There are many other such verbs demanding some object, e.g., *deny, cross, attain, overthrow, defeat*, etc. (The verbs *overcome* and *enjoy* would normally also belong to this group; however, *overcome* is used without an object in the civil rights song *We shall overcome*, and *enjoy* is sometimes used as an intransitive verb in hip language, e.g., *Let's split for a week and just enjoy*.) Such transitive verbs must therefore be excluded from the present program. This can be done simply by excluding them from the lexicon used in this program, or coding them by a special number; a conditional transfer after the verb choice will then tell the computer to reject such a verb and to pick another one.

To summarize this section, we can say that a program constructing messages in an error detecting code (whether a digital code or a natural language) alternates between the optional and the required; the optional elements (whether digits or words) are chosen at random. (They could also be chosen with a definite purpose, but we leave this for later.) When a choice has been made, the program checks whether a certain criterion is satisfied (Is the sum even or not? Is the pronoun third person singular or not?). Depending on the outcome, the check criterion is implemented with a check digit or a check morpheme. The implementation is not optional, but dictated by the rules (the grammar) of the code.

The flag system traces the path of the program and radically simplifies the programming of the check criterions and their implementations; however, it is only a very convenient aid for the programmer, not an essential part of the structure of the code (language).

The flag system, incidentally, has another potential advantage. The grammatical rules which decide what branch of a fork is to be taken by the program can be quite complicated, and since flags have only two possible values, 0 or 1, they can be used as Boolean variables, and the grammatical rules can be expressed as Boolean functions. For example, the presence or absence of the definite article in the expressions *The Kremlin, Buckingham Palace, the Louvre, Windsor Castle, the Boston City Hall, Grand Central Station, the Denver Station,* etc., is governed by the following complicated rule: Nouns denoting definite objects are preceded by the definite article, unless they are proper names; however, if the proper name denotes a building, the definite article is retained unless the name includes the word *Palace* or *Castle*; if the name includes other words denoting a building, such as *hall, stadium, auditorium, depot, station,* the article is retained if the proper name is identified by a geographical location or by an equivalent qualification, and omitted otherwise.

A rule of this type is not unlike the puzzle on p. 214, and the presence or absence of the article can be computed from the values of the flags indicating whether or not the noun is definite, proper, denoting a building, etc., by Boolean algebra. The use of Boolean algebra can occasionally be advantageous for programming complicated grammatical rules, but the reader is not encouraged to learn it if he expects to have no other use for it.

6.4. A Generative Grammar Based on Choice and Check

The little program for constructing two-word sentences given in the preceding section chooses freely among options left open by English grammar; and after it has chosen, it tests a check criterion to add check morphemes to the chosen word as dictated by the grammar.

This principle can be extended indefinitely to form more complex sentences. There is presumably no reason why the principle should not be extended to include all possible structures of a language, so that any grammatical sentence of a language can be produced.

The basic element of such a program is a fork or branch point (Fig. 6.3), at which the program is offered a choice of several words or grammatical features (parts of speech, tenses, moods, singular or plural, definite or indefinite, etc.). More often than not, the choice of words is unhampered by grammatical rules; but the choice of grammatical features is often limited by the choices made in previous parts of the program. For example, if the program has chosen an uncountable noun, such as

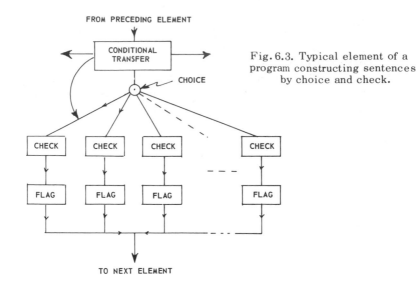

Fig. 6.3. Typical element of a program constructing sentences by choice and check.

milk, it no longer has the choice of singular or plural, but must take the singular branch. This is accomplished by a conditional transfer before the fork, which will prohibit some of the branches (or all but one branch) of the fork to be taken by the program if this is required by the rules of the grammar or the previous choices. As a rule, a fork represents a check criterion. After a branch has been chosen by the program, the implementation of the check (such as concatenation of a check morpheme) is carried out. The branch taken by the program is flagged, since the present choice may affect future choices. This flag will then be involved in future criterions, i.e., in the conditions of some future conditional transfers.

A typical element of the program is shown in Fig. 6.3. The program enters this element through a conditional transfer (IF...THEN...). If the condition posed by the conditional transfer is not satisfied, the transfer is ignored, and the program is free to choose one of the several branches offered by the fork. This choice is made at random (but not necessarily with equal probabilities for each branch); it is also possible to force the program to choose a certain branch (by assigning a probability of one to the desired branch, and a probability zero to all others). Such a forced decision, however, is made by an external source, not by the program itself. If, however, the condition of the conditional transfer is satisfied, the conditional transfer may force the program into a particular branch, or it may prohibit the use of some branches, or it may send the program to a different element altogether. When the program has chosen a branch (whether at random or by direction), it implements the

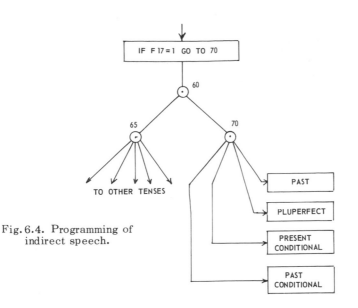

Fig. 6.4. Programming of
indirect speech.

check required by the grammar of the language (English, in all of the
following). If it is a plural branch, it will add an -s or its allomorphs to
the noun, or form an irregular plural. If it is the past branch of a tense
fork, it will form the past of the corresponding verb, etc. It then proceeds
to raise the flag in the same branch; this flag will be used in the conditional transfers of coming elements, provided the present choice can affect future choices in other elements.

Consider an example. The rules of indirect speech have been briefly
outlined on p. 186; for our present purposes we can simply say that if the
introductory verb is in the present, any tense can follow in the subordinate clause, but if the introductory verb is in the past, the subordinate
clause must be in one of only four tenses: past, pluperfect, present conditional, or past conditional. These rules are enforced by the conditional
transfer and the forks shown in Fig. 6.4. The fork is made up of three individual forks with statement numbers 60, 65, and 70. Before the program
arrived at this part of the program, it chose (we will assume) a pronoun,
say, *he*, and an introductory verb, e.g., *to say*. It then chose a tense for
the introductory verb. In the past tense branch of this verb, there was a
flag called F 17, which was raised if the program passed it. It then chose
another pronoun, say, *she*, and a verb, say, *to agree*. At this point the
program arrives at the part of the flow chart shown in Fig. 6.4. Suppose
it previously chose the present tense for *to say*, so that the sentence
so far is *He says she...*, to which the verb *agree* is to be added in a
tense chosen by the program. Since the program did not go through the

past tense branch of the introductory verb, the flag F 17 is not hoisted, the conditional transfer shown in Fig. 6.4 is ignored, and the program will decide at random whether to continue to statement 65 or 70, and in either case, it will again decide at random which of the available tenses to choose; all tenses are open to it. Suppose it decides to go to the fork in statement 65, and then to choose the future tense. The check implementation of the future tense (not shown in Fig. 6.4) is *will* plus infinitive; the resulting sentence is therefore

HE SAYS SHE WILL AGREE

which is grammatically correct.

But suppose that the program chose the past tense for the introductory verb (*he said she...*). Then in going through the past tense branch of the introductory verb *say*, the program hoisted the flag F 17, which is located in that branch. The condition of the transfer shown in Fig. 6.4 is now satisfied, and the program is sent to statement 70; the tenses connected to the fork of statement 65 (which are now ungrammatical) cannot be reached by the program, and it can only choose from the (grammatical) tenses accessible through the fork in statement 70. If the program chooses the past conditional whose implementation (not shown in Fig. 6.4) is *would* plus *have* plus past participle, the resulting sentence is

HE SAID SHE WOULD HAVE AGREED

The conditional transfer also allows *he said she would agree, he said she agreed, he said she had agreed*; however, it prohihibits ungrammatical statements of the type *He said she will agree* or *He said she has agreed*.

It is hoped that the preceding examples have made it obvious that any grammatical feature, whether morphological or syntactical, can be handled by means of forks posing an option or testing a check criterion and the corresponding implementations in the branches of the fork. Let us now formulate general rules how to construct sentences of a language (English or other) from the unprocessed words in a lexicon. These general rules will form a generative grammar of the language.

1. Start with the base of a kernel sentence (in Chomsky's sense), or with a fork offering a choice of such bases, e.g., noun phrase plus verb phrase or (for a question) verb phrase plus noun phrase, etc.

2. Insert a fork whenever there is a choice, i.e.,

     (a) wherever the rules of traditional grammar offer a choice. For example, the subject noun phrase may be composed of a pronoun or a phrase containing a noun as a subject; we therefore insert a fork which offers a choice between the two. In the former case, grammar allows any pronoun, so we insert a fork offering all the pronouns of the language, etc. Similarly, grammar does not (usually) prescribe whether a verb is to be negated or not; so we insert a fork with an affirmative and negative branch; and so on. Among the choices left open by the grammar of a language is not only whether to choose this or that part of speech, grammatical form or word, but quite often also whether to choose anything at all. Thus, in the noun phrase *the two happily smiling brothers*, not all parts of speech are required; *the brothers* will grammatically function equally well as a noun phrase. The choice of whether or not to include an optional part of speech, an optional subordinate clause, etc., is again accomplished by a fork, a double-pronged fork in which one branch "short-circuits" the other. This type of fork quite often corresponds to a node in Chomsky's phrase marker tree (a re-write rule).

(b) wherever the particular language poses a check criterion of the type described in Chapter 5. Typical check criterions in English are "singular or plural?" "definite or indefinite?" "third person singular or not?" Other languages have other check criterions, e.g., in the Slavic languages the singular-plural (one or many) criterion is replaced by the criterion "one, two to four, or more than four?"

3. Insert check morphemes or other implementations of the choice criterions as dictated by

    (a) the result of a check criterion,
    (b) the lexical data (type of paradigm, type of conjugation, etc.),
    (c) the branch taken in a previous fork.

4. Insert flags in the branches of the fork in order to facilitate conditional transfers and check implementations in subsequent forks. This is not an essential part of the grammar, but drastically simplifies the method of expressing conditional transfers.

5. Precede each fork by conditional transfers expressing pertinent rules of traditional grammar. For example, the singular-plural fork will be preceded by the conditional transfers "If noun is non-countable, take singular branch" and "If noun is *plurale tantum*, take plural branch."

6. Prevent recursive transfers from looping. A recursive transfer is one that sends the grammar back to a fork through which it has already been once. For example, we can construct a double subject of the type *My father and I* by letting the grammar generate a subject, concatenating *and*, and sending it back to generate a second subject. Unless proper precautions are taken, this could result in an unlimited number of subjects, all joined by the conjunction *and*. This can be prevented, for example, by assigning a sufficiently small probability of recursion (if that probability is p, the probability of an $n$tuple subject is only p^{n-1}) or allowing a maximum number of multiple subjects.

The actual grammar engendered by these rules will, of course, differ from language to language, since the check criterions are different (which simply means that different languages have different grammars). It is believed that these rules are complete, i.e., that they can be used to produce all possible structures of a language.

6.5. The Biased Fork

It is evident that the fork (see Fig. 6.3, p. 226) is an element of central importance in any program based on the generative grammar outlined in the preceding section. Its purpose is to give the program an option as to which path it is to take.

However, it should have two additional properties to make it flexible and efficient: First, the alternative paths should not necessarily be offered with equal probabilities, and second, these probabilities should be accessible for assignment through the data cards, and should not form a rigid part of the actual program.

A program for synthesizing grammatically correct sentences has many applications, not all of them linguistic, and a change in the probabilities with which the program will take certain branches results in a change of style of the constructed sentences. For example, the choice of a subject as either a noun or a pronoun (or both, linked by a conjunction) is, in general, not equiprobable. In colloquial speech, pronouns are very frequently used as subjects; in legal documents and scientific literature, they occur as subjects rather rarely. In a program designed to spoof legalese gobbledegook to be described below, they were eliminated altogether. More important, in many applications the program will not make its selections at random, but will be controlled by an intelligent agent (such as a human, or another program endowed with artificial intelligence), and this agent will wish to force the program through quite definite branches. This can be done by assigning a probability of one to the desired branch of the fork, and a probability of zero to all other branches, which is therefore merely a special case of controling the probability distribution over the branches of the fork. By assigning probabilities to the branches of the fork, we bias the fork; the program is biased toward taking the branches with the higher probabilities and against those with lower probabilities.

The bias, i.e., the probability distribution, associated with each fork will differ for various applications, including the extreme case when only one branch is open and all others are prohibited. To re-write the program for each application would, however, be a considerable chore, and it is therefore more advantageous to leave the probabilities unspecified, and to read them in as data. This means that the main program stays intact for each application, and only the data cards need be changed (just as the main program stays intact when the lexicon is changed).

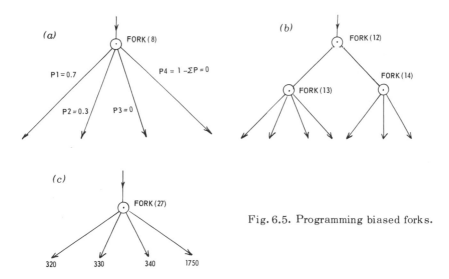

Fig. 6.5. Programming biased forks.

There are many ways of achieving the above two objects. The method given below has been tried and therefore should need no debugging.

The forks are standardized to have four branches. The probabilities of only three branches need be specified, since the fourth probability equals one minus the sum of the others. If less than four branches are needed, zero probabilities are assigned to the unwanted branches (Fig. 6.5.a), and if more than four branches are needed, several forks can be combined (Fig. 6.5b, showing a fork with 7 open branches).

Let FORK(K) be a random function equal to 1, 2, 3, or 4, which assumes these values with specified probabilities as is to be shown in a moment. K is the number of the fork as marked by the programmer on the flow chart. If FORK(17) has the same probability distribution as FORK(8), the programmer can avoid duplication of the necessary data by calling the function FORK(K) with argument 8 rather than 17.

The probabilities with which the forks are to be biased are read into an array called BIAS(N), in which the first three elements (say, 0.7, 0.3, 0.) are the probabilities P1, P2, P3 of the first three branches of the first fork, the next three elements are the probabilities P1, P2, P3 of the first three branches of the second fork, and so on.

The random function FORK(K) is then produced by a subroutine shown in Fig. 6.6. It is written in Fortran; the COMMON statement includes all common addresses, even those not used in this subroutine (such as SENT). The function RNDMU(X), in which X is a dummy argument, is a library function producing a number from 0 to 0.999999 with uniform probability; this function is almost always available at a com-

```
INTEGER FUNCTION FORK(I)
COMMON SENT(600), BIAS(90)
J=3*(I-1)
P1=BIAS(J+1)
P2=BIAS(J+2)
P3=BIAS(J+3)
S2=P1+P2
S3=S2+P3
R=RNDMU(X)
IF(R.LT.P1) GO TO 10
IF(R.LT.S2) GO TO 20
IF(R.LT.S3) GO TO 30
FORK=4
RETURN
10 FORK=1
RETURN
20 FORK=2
RETURN
30 FORK=3
RETURN
END
```

Fig. 6.6. Fortran subroutine for biased fork.

puter installation, but does not necessarily go by this name. The value of FORK(K) is thus equal to 1, 2, 3, or 4 with the probabilities specified in the array BIAS (actually by the triplet of probabilities indicated by the pointer K).

In the main program, the fork is programmed as follows. Suppose that, as shown in Fig. 6.5c, fork no. 27 is to have four branches, leading to statements no. 320, 330, 340 and 1750, respectively. The choice between the four branches is then accomplished by the (Fortran) statements

I = FORK(27)

GO TO (320, 330, 340, 1750), I

These two statements, realizing the fork no. 27, stay in the main program for good. The bias of the fork can be manipulated as desired, from equiprobability of the four branches to prohibition of all except one branch, by reading the corresponding probabilities into the array BIAS. This is done by the data cards, and involves no modification of the main program or its subroutines.

6.6. The Lexicon

The lexicon stores unprocessed words and is quite separate from the program containing the grammar. If the program is to show that it is possible to construct sentences from the words stored in the lexicon, it must be able to use the lexicon when the words are changed for different ones without being manipulated; otherwise the construction of sentences might not amount to much more than the "construction" of the sentence *Make another selection* which lights up on a vending machine when a certain product is sold out.

Apart from the words themselves, some of their grammatical properties must be stored in the lexicon, or the computer would have no way of knowing that a certain verb is irregular, or that the indefinite article before *usurer* is *a*, whereas before *urn* it is *an* (if the lexicon stored words in phonemes rather than graphemes, this might not be necessary).

The easiest way to store the grammatical information is by digital codes, i.e., by a number following the word. A certain number following a noun might mean "forms the plural by adding *-es*" (as in *boxes*), another number might mean "forms the plural by deleting the last letter and adding *-ves*" (as in *loaves*), and so on. An address quite often stores the equivalent of an eight-digit decimal number plus algebraic sign, which allows 20 million different codes to be used per address, so that the codes can be used quite lavishly, although the programmer may run out of addresses (rather than the numbers stored in them). However, the lexicon need not be stored "in core" (in the memory locations of the central processor); it can also be stored externally in the peripheral equipment, on magnetic tape or on magnetic disks. This will, in fact, have to be done if the lexicon contains many thousands of entries (words), for which the internal storage of the computer might not be sufficient.

The lexicon can be arranged in any manner the programmer finds convenient. In the following, we will describe the method used in the program MORON (so called because its grammatically correct sentences are meaningless gibberish). This program was written as a sample program to demonstrate the possibility of constructing grammatical sentences by the choice-and-check method based on the premise that Language is an error-detecting code. It contained sufficiently many structures to make it clear that any other structure could also be programmed by this method, but it did not, by any means, contain all English structures. Similarly, it could handle the irregular verbs *teach, eat, understand, feel, weep* and *fight* to demonstrate how irregular verbs are handled, but no provision was made to handle the other irregular verbs, since this can be done by the same methods.

The lexicon used in the sample program MORON contained room for 20 nouns (at a time), 20 adjectives, 20 verbs, each of these words and their grammatical codes being punched on one card; one card each was used for 7 personal pronouns, 7 possessive adjectives, 6 cardinal numerals, and 7 ordinal numerals or words having the same distribution as ordinal numerals (*last, next, only*).

Nouns were stored in an array called NSTR (for "noun store"), adjectives in an array called ADJSTR ("adjective store"), and so on. The part of speech was thus given by the corresponding store and did not have to be coded in the lexicon.

Adjectives had only a single code, indicating whether the indefinite article preceding the adjective was *a* or *an*, denoted by 0 or 1, respectively. A more ambitious program would also have to indicate how the adverb is formed from the adjective (*slowly, happily, fast, in a silly manner*, etc.), but MORON did not use adverbs. It is also advantageous for random selection of a word from the adjective store or any other store to have all words of equal length, so that a pointer can simply point at random to one of the regularly spaced points within an array where a word starts. This was done by making all adjectives 15 letters long, the unused letters (if any) being replaced by dollar signs. Thus, typical cards for adjectives would look like this:

```
NEW$$$$$$$$$$$$ 00000000
OBSOLETE$$$$$$$ 00000001
AD HOC$$$$$$$$$ 00000001
LOWER$$$$$$$$$$ 00000000
RE-ELECTED$$$$$ 00000000
INTERCOLLEGIATE 00000001
```

(The space between the word and the code has been inserted here only for better legibility; the actual columns punched are 1 to 23.)

The adjective chosen from the adjective store is later processed by a subroutine called CLEAN, which examines each letter of the word until it meets a dollar sign; it then discards the dollar signs and notes the length (in letters) of the word. (These tricks would not be necessary in a language like Snobol.) Thus, NEW$$$$$$$$$$$$ returns from the subroutine CLEAN as the word NEW, and the subroutine also measures the length of the word (IL) as 3 letters.

Nouns are stored and cleaned in the same way. The noun code is an 8-digit number, but only the first four digits are used as follows:

1st digit (type of noun)	2nd digit (plural)	3rd digit (irr. plural)	4th digit (indef. article)
0 countable	0 regular	0 regular	0 *a*
1 (not used)	1 adds -*es*	1 *men*	1 *an*
2 proper	2 deletes last letter and adds -*ies*	2 *teeth*	
3 collective		3 *mice*	
4 abstract		4 *children*	
	3 deletes last letter and adds -*ves* (*loaves*)		
	4 deletes last two letters and adds -*ves* (*knives*)		
	5 irregular, consult 3rd digit		

Gender and other grammatical characteristics were not used in this program. Here again, a more suitable language than Fortran would not need all the information contained in the second digit; it could, for example, express the idea "see if the last two letters are FE" quite simply.

Typical noun cards are shown below (there is again no blank, the punched columns are 1 to 23).

```
GADFLY$$$$$$$$$$ 02000000
CHILD$$$$$$$$$$$ 05400000
THEODORE$$$$$$$$ 20000000
HOGWASH$$$$$$$$$ 30000000
ILLNESS$$$$$$$$$ 01010000
AUTOBIOGRAPHY$$ 02010000
STEERING WHEEL$ 00000000
UNDERTAKER$$$$$ 00010000
MEAT LOAF$$$$$$ 03000000
```

The verb code consists of two four-digit numbers; the first determines how the past tense and the past participle are formed, the second
determines whether the verb is transitive or intransitive, or whether it
requires a certain preposition.

The first verb code is arranged as shown below:

1st digit	2nd digit	3rd, 4th digit
0 adds -*ed*	0 regular	not used
1 adds -*d*	1 *felt, felt*	
2 deletes last *y*, adds -*ied*	2 *understood, understood*	
3 doubles last consonant and adds -*ed* (*rammed, squatted*)	3 *ate, eaten*	
	4 *taught, taught*	
4 irregular, consult next digit	5 *wept, wept*	
	6 *fought, fought*	

The second verb code is more easily explained by introducing the
terms "semi-transitive" and "quasi-object." On comparing the constructions *to see somebody — to rely on somebody, he was seen — he was
relied on*, etc., it will be seen that there is no important syntactic difference between the verbs *to see* and *to rely on* (provided we consider
the verb *to rely on* as a single verb *en bloc*, not as a verb *to rely* plus
the preposition *on*). The verb *to see* is transitive in *He saw Jill*, and
Jill is its object; it therefore seems logical to call *to rely* a semitransitive verb, and to call *Jill* its quasi-object in the construction *He relied
on Jill*. Thus, a semitransitive verb is one that is followed by a preposition and a noun phrase, and that noun phrase is its quasi-object. Although I believe this terminology could simplify the expression of some
rules of English grammar, the reader who disagrees need not be discon-
certed: We only need these terms as descriptive names here and in the
following.

The second verb code, then, is arranged as shown in the table on
the next page.

1st digit	2nd digit	3rd,4th
(transitive, intr., or semitransitive)	preposition	not used
0 trans. only (*to like*)	0 none	
1 trans. or semitr. (*to fight*)	1 *from*	
2 intrans. only (*to perspire*)	2 *for*	
3 semitransitive (*to rely*)	3 *at*	
	4 *about*	
	5 *on*	
	6 *to*	
	7 not used	
	8 *against*	
	9 *with*	

Hundreds of other constructions could be added; not only further prepositions, but also other constructions following the verb, such as the infinitive of a verb (*to learn to read*) and others (*to know how to, to prevent from* plus gerund, etc.). Further possibilities could also be added in the first digit, e.g., intransitive or semi-transitive (*to talk, to talk about*) or transitive or intransitive (*to smoke, to smoke a cigarette*).

Typical verb cards read into the verb store are (no blanks, columns 1 to 23):

```
CONDEMN$$$$$$$$ 0000 0000
SNEEZE$$$$$$$$$ 1000 3300
EAT$$$$$$$$$$$$ 4300 0000
DEFY$$$$$$$$$$$ 2000 0000
SURRENDER$$$$$$ 0000 3600
THEORETIZE$$$$$ 1000 3400
UNDERSTAND$$$$$ 4200 0000
PERSPIRE$$$$$$$ 1000 2000
FORNICATE$$$$$$ 1000 3900
FEEL$$$$$$$$$$$ 4100 0000
```

The other stores were not coded. In Snobol, a string of letters (e.g., a word) can easily be inserted by the program where desired. In Fortran, this is usually more cumbersome, and for longer words such as *against* or *understood* it is easier to store such insertions in a special array, from which the program can draw them when needed; in MORON, these little bits and pieces were stored in arrays called JUNK and JUNK2. From *understood*, incidentally, one can also obtain other words if needed, such as *under, stood, too, to,* or the prefixes *un-, erst-*.

For the benefit of readers who want to play with the program MORON, the uncoded arrays appear below.

Possessive adjectives (POSSTR):

```
MY$$$YOUR$HIS$$HER$$ITS$$OUR$$THEIR
```

Possessive adjectives (POSSTR):

    MY$$$YOUR$HIS$$HER$$ITS$$OUR$$THEIR

Cardinal numerals (CARSTR):

    TWO$FOURFIVESIX$NINETEN$

Ordinal numerals (ORDSTR):

    FIRSTTHIRDONLY$LAST$NEXT$FIFTH

Pronouns (PRNSTR):

    I$$$YOU$HE$$SHE$IT$$WE$$THEY

Auxiliary verbs (AUXSTR):

    MIGHT$MAY$$$WILL$$COULD$WOULD$SHOULD

Array JUNK:

    CHILDREN$TEETH$ANDORWITH

Array JUNK2:

    FELT$UNDERSTOOD$ATE$EATEN$TAUGHT$WEPT$FOU
    GHT$DID NOTFROMFORATABOUTONTOAGAINSTWITH

JUNK2 consists of two data cards, of which the second contains only the last letter H of the above string.

6.7. The Program MORON

The base structure of the sample program MORON is

   Subject clause + Verb + Object (+ subordinate clause)

The subordinate clause is optional; the program may or may not decide to continue after the main clause. The object is replaced by a quasi-object if the verb is semitransitive, and it is, of course, absent if the verb is intransitive. The subordinate clause has the same structure as the main clause; it is, in fact, generated by a second run through the part of the program that generates the main clause, after a conjunction has been concatenated.

The verb may or may not be negated, and it may have one of several tenses.

The subject is built up as follows:

   [Article] + (possessive adjective) + (cardinal or ordinal numeral)
   + (adjective) + (, adjective) + noun

where the parts of speech in parentheses are optional; the article (or its absence) is computed. The entire subject clause can also be replaced by a personal pronoun, and a second subject may or may not be added after the conjunctions *and, or* or *with*; after *and* and *or*, the program runs through the subject routine a second time, but after *with* it runs only through the noun clause branch of the subject routine (for simplicity, so as to avoid accusatives of personal pronouns).

Given this base structure and its many optional modifications, the program is written along the principles outlined in the previous sections. It will thus produce sentences such as

> *They could not have seen the green tree.*
> *The malicious child and the third officer ate two big, green gadflies, because my two small dogs did not surrender to an ugly, paranoic cat.*
> *You with his ridiculous children should not have relied on the undertakers, regardless of whether Theodore perspired.*
> *She perspired.*
> *The three officers and my four white calves sneezed at her stupendous autobiography, although I should have mesmerized the four libraries.*
> *He died.*

In this state of the program, with the decisions quite random and unguided by semantic coding in the lexicon, these sentences are, of course, quite meaningless.

Fig. 6.6 shows the flow chart of the program. The conditional transfers are marked by small crossed boxes, the numbers are the statement numbers, and W(1), W(2), ... are flags.

After declaring integer variables, assigning dimensions and reading the data cards, the actual program starts with statement 600. Fork (1) decides whether the subject (or the first of two subjects) is to be a noun or a pronoun. If a noun, the program first srikes all flags W in the noun clause in the DO loop 701, and then selects a noun from the noun store at random. Fork (2) is a check criterion deciding whether the noun is to be singular or plural, but if the selected noun is not countable (i.e., collective, abstract or proper), the conditional transfer 721 will transfer the program to the singular branch. Fork (3) and Fork(4) decide whether the noun is to be definite or indefinite, and a provisional decision on the article is made (1 corresponds to *a*, 2 to *an*, 3 to *the*, and 0 to the absence of an article). The decision is provisional, since a possessive adjective, if selected, will delete all articles, and an adjective, if selected, may change *a* to *an* and vice versa. Fork (5) decides whether to include a possessive adjective; but the choice is offered only if the noun was chosen as definite in the previous procedure. Fork (6) decides whether to include a numeral; if so, it may be either cardinal or ordinal.

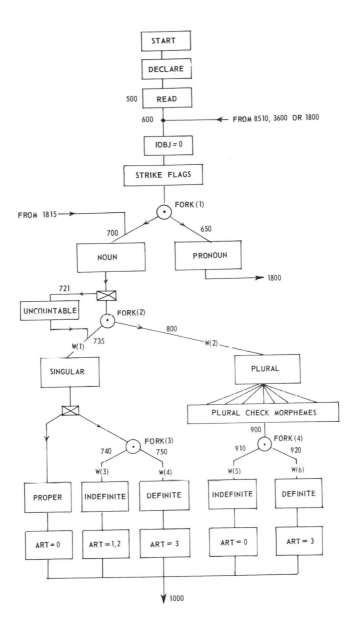

Fig. 6.6. Flow chart of the program MORON
(continued on the following pages).

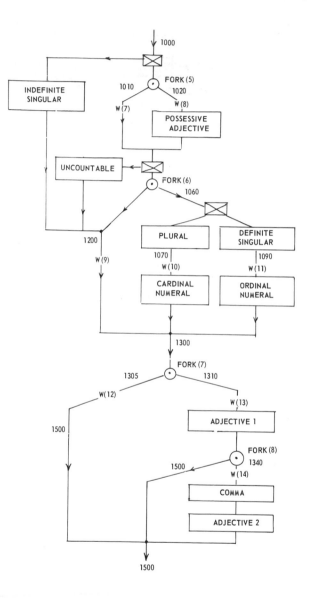

Fig. 6.6, continued.

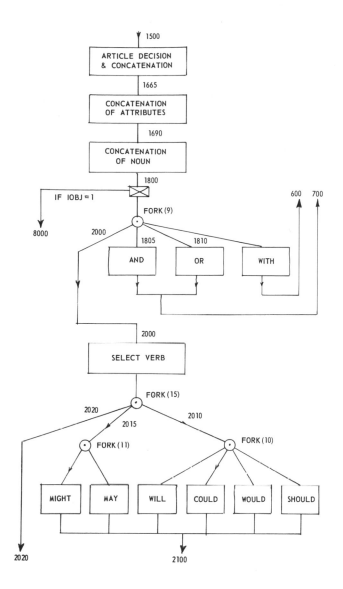

Fig. 6.6, continued.

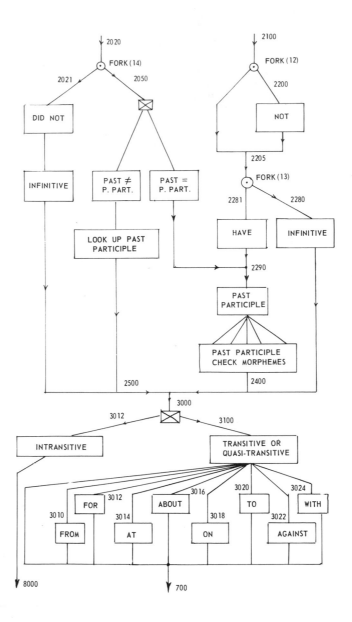

Fig. 6.6, continued

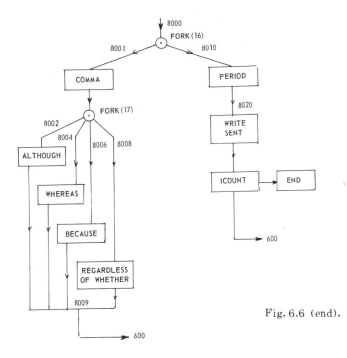

Fig. 6.6 (end).

Fork(7) decides whether to include an adjective, and Fork (8) decides whether to include a comma and a second adjective.

All the information needed to compute the article is now known. The statements following 1500 either leave the provisional decisions intact or change them as necessary in accordance with the flags that have been raised since the provisional decisions were made.

The hoisted flags also show which parts of speech are included in the noun clause, and these are cleaned from dollar signs in the subroutine CLEAN and successively concatednated, i.e., inserted in the array SENT (for *sentence*) in the subroutine CONCAT.

Fork (9) decides whether to continue to the verb or to insert *and, or* or *with* and to run through the subject routine a second time. The counter NS does not permit more than one recursion through the subject clause.

The program then proceeds to the verb; it is hoped that the flow chart from statements 2000 to 3000 is sufficiently clear and does not require further explanations. The program makes use of the fact that the past tense and the past participle are identical not only for all regular verbs, but for many irregular verbs as well. The past tense, therefore, need be looked up only for "doubly" irregular verbs such as *eat, shake, write,* but not *teach, fight, set, weep*, and most others; the irregularity is looked up only once in the past participle.

In the branch following statement 3000, the program checks whether the selected verb is intransitive or (semi)transitive. In the latter case it concatenates the required preposition (if any) before proceeding to the (quasi)object, which is produced by a second run through the subject routine. The counter IOBJ prevents loops by forbidding a second verb.

Fork (16) decides whether to continue with a conjunction and a subordinate clause (in which case the program starts from the beginning, with the counter ICONJ preventing a loop), or to finish the sentence by a period and print it. The counter ICOUNT will end the program when a prespecified number of sentences, say, 300, has been constructed.

If the program is run again, it will produce the same sentences, because the random routine in a computer is really a "quasirandom" routine, producing the same sequence of random numbers. If a different set of sentences is desired, this can be accomplished by seeding the random routine, or simply by shuffling the data cards of the noun store, verb store and adjective store (each separately, not with each other).

The number of different sentences that can be produced by the program from a lexicon of 20 nouns, 20 adjectives, 20 verbs, 7 pronouns, 7 possessive adjectives, and 7 numerals can be estimated as follows. Each of the 7 possessive adjectives can combine with any of the 7 numerals (7×7), and each such combination can combine with any of the 20 adjectives $(7 \times 7 \times 20)$, then with any of the 20 adjectives used as a second adjective, and so on. Continuing to the verb and object plus subordinate clause, this yields

$$[(7 \times 7 \times 20 \times 20 \times 20)^3 \times 3 \times 20]^2 \times 4 \approx 6 \times 10^{38}$$

(a six with 38 zeroes). True, the above calculation applies if all verbs are (semi) transitive; however, the presence of intransitive verbs is probably more than compensated by the fact that the above calculation does not consider the sentences omitting some of the optional parts of speech, nor does it consider the choice of pronouns, auxiliary verbs, tenses, negatives, plurals or articles. In any case, who wants to quibble about a few powers of 10 in an astronomical number like 10^{38}?

Obviously, the chances of the same sentence occurring in the same run, or in any reasonable number of runs, is virtually zero.

Fig. 6.7 shows a listing of the program MORON.

In connection with the listing of the program, I would like to observe the following. There are few things as boring and confusing as reading someone else's program, and I had originally not planned to include the program statement by statement in this book. However, after the recent publication of two articles,* so many people wrote for a copy of the program "to play with" that

---

* See footnote on opposite page.

I decided to include it. The user should note, however, that the program is not in its simplest form. There are three reasons for this: 1) the logical OR and logical AND were out of order on the machine on which the program was run; hence, for example, the three transfers to 1600 below statement 1500, where ordinarily a single statement would do. 2) Debugging often involves several trial modifications, and the successful one may eliminate the error in a complicated way. An ideal programmer will then rewrite the originally faulty part in the most elegant way, but a lazy programmer like the author will let the modification stand as long as it works. 3) The program grew by successive additions of grammatical constructions, resulting in a less perfect program than one with all the possibilities planned from the outset. And, of course, no program is so good that it could not be improved.

The array SENT is dimensioned for 600 letters (A1 charcters), or up to five lines of the print-out. It was not considered worth while to write a subroutine breaking a line at the end of a word, and not in the middle of one; the program will therefore print, say, CONSPICUOU at the end of one line, and S at the beginning of the next, if the U in CONSPICUOUS is the 125th character of the sentence (or a multiple of 125).

The subroutines that have not yet been explained are the function LENGTH which measures the length of a word in letters, and the subroutine UNPACK, which extracts the individual digits of an eight-digit (decimal) number, so that the program can look at the individual grammatical properties of the lexicon entries.

```
      INTEGER FORK
      INTEGER SENT,ADJSTR,ADJCOD,POSSTR,CARSTR,ORDSTR,PRNSTR,PRON,W,
     1ART,POSS,CAR,ORD,ADJ1,ADJ2,POSSC,ORDC,CARC,ADJ1C,ADJ2C
      INTEGER VRBSTR,VRB,VRBC,VRBK1,VRBK2,AUX,AUXSTR,PP,PPC
      DIMENSION NSTR(300),NCOD(20),ADJSTR(300),ADJCOD(20),
     1POSSTR(35), CARSTR(24), ORDSTR(30), PRNSTR(28),PRON(4),NOUN(20),
     2POSS(5),ORD(5),CAR(4),ADJ1(15),ADJ2(15),W(40),KODE(8),JUNK(100),
     3INSRT(20), PRONC(4),NOUNC(20), POSSC(5),ORDC(5),CARC(4)
      DIMENSION VRBSTR(300),VRB(20),VRBC(20),VRBK1(20),VRBK2(20),
     1AUX(6),AUXSTR(36),AUXC(6),KODE2(8),JUNK2(100),PP(20),PPC(20),
     2ADJ1C(15),ADJ2(15)
      COMMON SENT(600),BIAS(90)
      READ(5,501) (BIAS(I), I=1,45)
  501 FORMAT(3(20F4.3),/))
      DO 520 J=1,20
      I1=15*(J-1) + 1
      I2=I1 + 14
      READ(5,510)(NSTR(I),I=I1,I2),NCOD(J)
  510 FORMAT(15A1,I8)
  520 CONTINUE
      DO 525 J=1,20
      I1=15*(J-1)+1
      I2=I1 + 14
      READ(5,524)(ADJSTR(I),I=I1,I2),ADJCOD(J)
  524 FORMAT(15A1,I8)
  525 CONTINUE
      READ(5,530)(POSSTR(I),I=1,35)
  530 FORMAT(35A1)
      READ(5,535)(CARSTR(I),I=1,24)
  535 FORMAT(24A1)
      READ(5,546)(ORDSTR(I),I =1,30)
  540 FORMAT(30A1)
      READ(5,545)(PRNSTR(I),I=1,28)
  545 FORMAT (28A1)
      READ(5,546)(JUNK(I),I=1,80)
  546 FORMAT(80A1)
```

Fig. 6.7. Listing of the program MORON (continued on the following pages).

* P. Beckmann, *Natural languages as error-correcting codes*, Lingua, vol.28, no. 3, pp.251-264, (1971).

P. Beckmann, *Computerization of English*, IEEE Spectrum, vol. 8, no. 12, pp. 20-27 (1971).

```
      DO 548 J=1,20
      I1=15*(J-1)+1
      I2=I1+14
      READ(5,547)(VRBSTR(I),I=I1,I2),VRBK1(J),VRBK2(J)
  547 FORMAT(15A1,2I4)
  548 CONTINUE
      READ(5,550)(AUXSTR(I),I=1,36)
  550 FORMAT(36A1)
      READ(5,552)(JUNK2(I),I=1,100)
  552 FORMAT(80A1,/,20A1)
      WRITE(6,553)
  553 FORMAT(X,*FORKS ARE BIASED AS FOLLOWS*)
  555 CONTINUE
      DO 570 J=1,350
  570 SENT(J)=1H$
      LS=0
      MZ=0
      ICOUNT=0
      NS=0
      IOBJ=0
      ICONJ=0
  600 CONTINUE
      I=FORK(1)
      GO TO (700,650),I
  650 R=7.*RNDMU(X)
      IR=R
      DO 651 J=1,4
      I=4*IR + J
  651 PRON(J)=PRNSTR(I)
      CALL CLEAN(PRONC,IL,PRON,4)
      CALL CONCAT(LS,PRONC,IL)
      LS =LS + IL + 1
      GO TO 1800
  700 CONTINUE
      DO 701 J=1,40
  701 W(J) = 0
      R=20.*RNDMU(X)
      IR=R
      KI=15*IR
      NK=NCOD(IR+1)
      DO 720 J=1,15
      I=KI+J
  720 NOUN(J)=NSTR(I)
      CALL UNPACK(KODE,NK)
      IF(IOBJ.EQ.0) GO TO 721
      IF(KODE(1).EQ.4) GO TO 700
  721 IF(KODE(1).NE.0) GO TO 735
      I = FORK(2)
      GO TO (735, 800),I
  735 W(1)=1
      IF(KODE(1).EQ.2) GO TO 744
      I = FORK(3)
      GO TO (740,750),I
  740 W(3)=1
      IF(KODE(1).NE.0) GO TO 744
      IF(KODE(4).NE.0) GO TO 742
      ART = 1
      GO TO 1000
  742 ART = 2
      GO TO 1000
  744 ART = 0
      GO TO 1000
  750 W(4)=1
      ART = 3
      GO TO 1000
  800 W(2) = 1
      L=LENGTH(NOUN)
      I=KODE(2)+1
      GO TO (835,830,825,820,815,805),I
  805 IF(KODE(3).EQ.2) GO TO 810
  806 DO 807 J=1,9
  807 NOUN(J)=JUNK(J)
      GO TO 899
```

```
  810 DO 811 J=1,6
  811 NOUN(J) = JUNK(J+9)
      GO TO 899
  815 NOUN(L-1)=1HV
      NOUN(L)=1HE
      NOUN(L+1)=1HS
      NOUN(L+2)=1H$
      GO TO 899
  820 NOUN(L)=1HV
      NOUN(L+1)=1HE
      NOUN(L+2)=1HS
      NOUN(L+3)=1H$
      GO TO 899
  825 NOUN(L)=1HI
      NOUN(L+1)=1HE
      NOUN(L+2)=1HS
      NOUN(L+3)=1H$
      GO TO 899
  830 NOUN(L+1)=1HE
      NOUN(L+2)=1HS
      NOUN(L+3)=1H$
      GO TO 900
  835 NOUN(L+1)=1HS
      NOUN(L+2)=1H$
  899 CONTINUE
      L=LENGTH(NOUN)
      I=L+1
      DO 5000 J=1,20
 5000 NOUN(J)=1H$
  900 I=FORK(4)
      GO TO (910.920),I
  910 W(5)=1
      ART=0
      GO TO 1000
  920 W(6)=1
      ART=3
      GO TO 1000
 1000 IF(W(3).EQ.1) GO TO 1200
      I=FORK(5)
      GO TO (1010,1020),I
 1010 W(7)=1
      GO TO 1050
 1020 W(8)=1
      R=7.*RNDMU(X)
      IR=R
      DO 1025 J=1,5
      I=5*IR+J
 1025 POSS(J)=POSSTR(I)
      ART=0
 1050 IF(KODE(1).NE.0) GO TO 1200
      I=FORK(6)
      GO TO (1200,1060),I
 1060 IF(W(2).EQ.1) GO TO 1070
      IF(W(4).EQ.1) GO TO 1090
 1070 W(10)=1
      R=6.*RNDMU(X)
      IR=R
      DO 1075 J=1,4
      I=4*IR+J
 1075 CAR(J)=CARSTR(I)
      GO TO 1300
 1090 W(11)=1
      R=6.RNDMU(X)
      IR=R
      DO 1095 J=1,5
      I=5*IR+J
 1095 ORD(J)=ORDSTR(I)
      GO TO 1300
 1200 W(9)=1
      GO TO 1300
```

Fig. 6.7, continued.

```
1300 I=FORK(7)                          1805 INSRT(1)=1HA
     GO TO (1305,1310),I                     INSRT(2)=1HN
1305 W(12)=1                                  INSRT(3)=1HD
     GO TO 1500                               CALL CONCAT(LS,INSRT,3)
1310 W(13)=1                                  LS=LS+4
     R=20.*RNDMU(X)                           GO TO 600
     IR=R                               1810 INSRT(1)=1HO
     KA=ADJCOD(IR+1)                          INSRT(2)=1HR
     DO 1320 J=1,15                           CALL CONCAT(LS,INSRT,2)
     I=15*IR+J                                LS=LS+3
1320 ADJ1(J)=ADJSTR(I)                        GO TO 600
     I=FORK(8)                          1815 INSRT(1)=1HW
     GO TO (1500,1340),I                      INSRT(2)=1HI
1340 W(14)=1                                  INSRT(3)=1HT
1341 R=20.*RNDMU(X)                           INSRT(4)=1HH
     KR=R                                     CALL CONCAT(LS,INSRT,4)
     IF(KR.EQ.IR) GO TO 1341                  LS=LS+5
     DO 1345 J=1,15                           GO TO 700
     I=15*KR+J                          2000 CONTINUE
1345 ADJ2(J)=ADJSTR(I)                        R=RNDMU(X)*20.
     GO TO 1500                               IR=R
1500 CONTINUE                                 K1=VRBK1(IR+1)
     IF(W(8).EQ.1) GO TO 1665                 K2=VRBK2(IR+1)
     IF(W(12).EQ.1) GO TO 1600                DO 2005 J+1,15
     IF(ART.EQ.0) GO TO 1600                  K=15*IR+J
     IF(ART.EQ.3) GO TO 1600            2005 VRB(J)=VRBSTR(K)
     IF(KA.EQ.0) ART=1                        I=FORK(15)
     IF(KA.EQ.1) ART =2                       GO TO (2020, 2015,2010),I
     GO TO 1600                         2010 IR=FORK(10)-1
1600 I=ART+1                                  DO 2011 J=1,6
     GO TO (1665,1620,1630,1640),I            K=6*IR+J
1620 INSRT(1)=1HA                        2011 AUX(J)=AUXSTR(K)
     IL=1                                     GO TO 2100
     GO TO 1650                         2015 IR=FORK(11)+3
1630 INSRT(1)=1HA                             DO 2016 J+1,6
     INSRT(2)=1HN                             K=6*IR+J
     IL=2                               2016 AUX(J)=AUXSTR(K)
     GO TO 1650                               GO TO 2100
1640 INSRT(1)=1HT                        2100 CONTINUE
     INSRT(2)=1HH                             CALL CLEAN(AUXC,IL,AUX,6)
     INSRT(3)=1HE                             CALL CONCAT(LS,AUXC,IL)
     IL=3                                     LS=LS+IL+1
     GOTO 1650                                IF(MZ.EQ.1) GO TO 2205
1650 CALL CONCAT(LS,INSRT,IL)                 I=FORK(12)
     LS=LS+IL+1                               GO TO (2205,2201),I
1665 IF(W(8).EQ.0) GO TO 1670           2201 INSRT(1)=1HN
     CALL CLEAN(POSSC,IL,POSS,5)              INSRT(2)=1HO
     CALL CONCAT(LS,POSSC,IL)                 INSRT(3)=1HT
     LS=LS+IL+1                               CALL CONCAT(LS,INSRT,3)
1670 IF(W(9).EQ.1)GO TO 1680                  LS=LS+4
     IF(W(10).EQ.1) GO TO 1675          2205 CONTINUE
     CALL CLEAN(ORDC,IL,ORD,5)                I=FORK(13)
     CALL CONCAT(LS,ORDC,IL)                  GO TO (2280,2281),I
     LS=LS+IL+1                         2280 CALL CLEAN(VRBC,IL,VRB,15)
     GO TO 1680                               CALL CONCAT(LS,VRBC,15)
1675 CALL CLEAN(CARC,IL,CAR,4)                LS=LS+IL+1
     CALL CONCAT(LS,CARC,IL)                  GO TO 3000
     LS=LS+IL+1                         2281 INSRT(1)=1HH
1680 IF(W(12).EQ.1) GO TO 1690               INSRT(2)=1HA
     CALL CLEAN(ADJ1C,IL,ADJ1,15)            INSRT(3)=1HV
     CALL CONCAT(LS,ADJ1C,IL)                INSRT(4)=1HE
     LS=LS+IL+1                               CALL CONCAT(LS,INSRT,4)
     IF(W(14).EQ.0) GO TO 1690               LS=LS+5
     SENT(LS+1)=1H,                     2290 CONTINUE
     LS=LS+1                                  L=LENGTH(VRB)
     CALL CLEAN(ADJ2C,IL,ADJ2,15)            I=K1/1000+1
     CALL CONCAT(LS,ADJ2C,IL)                GO TO (2300,2301,2302,2303,2304),I
     LS=LS+IL+1                         2300 VRB(L+1)=1HE
1690 CALL CLEAN(NOUNC,IL,NOUN,20)            VRB(L+2)=1HD
     CALL CONCAT(LS,NOUNC,IL)                L=L+2
     LS=LS+IL+1                               GO TO 2400
1800 IF(IOBJ.EQ.1) GO TO 8000
     NS=NS+1
     IF(NS.EQ.2) GO TO 2000
     I=FORK(9)
     GO TO (2000,1805,1810,1815),I
```

Fig. 6.7, continued.

```
2301 VRB(L)=1HI                        3018 INSRT(1)=1HO
     VRB(L+1)=1HE                           INSRT(2)=1HN
     VRB(L+2)=1HD                           IL=2
     L=L+3                                  GO TO 3500
     GO TO 2400                        3020 INSRT(1)=1HT
2303 VRB(L+1)=VRB(L)                        INSRT(2)=1HO
     VRB(L+2)=1HE                           IL=2
     VRB(L+3)=1HD                           GO TO 3500
     L=L+3                             3022 DO 3023 J=1,7
     GO TO 2400                             INSRT(J)=JUNK2(J+70)
2304 I=K1/100-40                            IL=7
     GO TO(2311,2322,2333,2344,2355,2366),I GO TO 3500
2311 DO 2312 J=1,5                     3024 DO 3025 J=1,4
2312 VRB(J)=JUNK2(J)                    3025 INSRT(J)=JUNK2(J+77)
     GO TO 2400                             IL=4
2333 DO 2334 J=1,6                          GO TO 3500
2334 VRB(J)=JUNK2(J+20)                3500 CONTINUE
     L=6                                    CALL CONCAT(LS,INSRT,IL)
     GO TO 2400                             LS=LS+IL+1
2344 DO 2345 J=1,7                     3600 IOBJ=1
2345 VRB(J)=JUNK2(J+26)                     GO TO 700
     L=7                               8000 IF(ICONJ.EQ.1) GO TO 8010
     GO TO 2400                        C THIS IS FORK(16) ON FLOW CHART
2355 DO 2356 J=1,5                          I=FORK(6)
2356 VRB(J)=JUNK2(J+33)                     GO TO (8001,8010),I
     GO TO 2400                        8001 SENT(LS+1)=1H,
2366 DO2367 J=1,7                           LS=LS+1
2367 VRB(J)=JUNK2(J+38)                     NS=0
     L=7                                    IOBJ=0
     GO TO 2400                             ICONJ=1
2400 DO 2401 J=1,L                     C THIS IS FORK(17) ON FLOW CHART
2401 PP(J)=VRB(J)                           I=FORK(10)
     PP(L+1)=1H$                            GO TO(8002,8004,8006,8008),I
2410 CALL CLEAN(PPC,IL,PP,20)          8002 DO 8003 J=1,8
     CALL CONCAT(LS,PPC,IL)            8003 INSRT(J)=JUNK(J+15)
     LS=LS+IL+1                             IL=8
     GO TO 3000                             GO TO 8009
2020 I = FORK(14)                      8004 DO 8005 J=1,7
     GO TO(2021. 2050),I               8005 INSRT(J)=JUNK(J+23)
2021 DO 2022 J=1,7                          IL=7
2022 INSRT(J)=JUNK2(J+45)                   GO TO 8009
     CALL CONCAT(LS,INSRT,7)           8006 DO 5555 J=1,21
     LS=LS+8                           5555 INSRT(J)=JUNK(J+37)
     CALL CLEAN(VRBC,IL,VRB,20)             IL=21
     CALL CONCAT(LS,VRBC,IL)                MZ=1
     LS=LS+IL+1                        8009 CALL CONCAT(LS,INSRT,IL)
     GO TO 3000                             LS=LS+IL+1
2050 I=K1/100                               GO TO 600
     IF(I.EQ.43) GO TO 2500           8010 SENT(LS+1)=1H.
     GO TO 2290                             LS=LS+1
2500 CONTINUE                               NS=0
     DO 2520 J=1,4                          IOBJ=0
2520 PP(J)=JUNK2(J+16)                      ICONJ=0
     GO TO 2410                             ICOUNT=ICOUNT+1
3000 CONTINUE
     I=K2/1000
     IF(I.EQ.0)GO TO 3600
     IF(I.EQ.2)GO TO 8000
     I=K2/100-30
     GO TO(3010,3012,3014,3016,3018,3020,3600,3022,3024),I
3010 DO 3011 J=1,4
3011 INSRT(J)=JUNK2(J+52)
     IL=4
     GO TO 3500
3012 DO 3013 J=1,3
3013 INSRT(J)=JUNK2(J+56)
     IL=3
     GO TO 3500
3016 DO 3017 J=1,5
3017 INSRT(J)=JUNK2(J+61)
     IL=5
     GO TO 3500
```

Fig. 6.7, continued

```
      J1=LS+1
      DO 8015 J=J1,600
8015  SENT(J)=1H
      WRITE(6,8020) (SENT(I),I=1,125)
8020  FORMAT(X,125A1)
      IF(LS.LE.125) GO TO 8500
      WRITE(6,8025) (SENT(I),I=126,250)
8025  FORMAT(X,125A1)
      IF(LS.LE.250) GO TO 8500
      WRITE(6,8030) (SENT(I),I=251,375)
8030  FORMAT(X,125A1)
      IF(LS.LE.375) GO TO 8500
      WRITE(6,8031)(SENT(I),I=501,600)
8032  FORMAT(X,100A1)
8500  IF(ICOUNT.EQ.300) GO TO 9000
      SENT(1)=1H
      LS=1
      DO 8510 J=2,350
8510  SENT(J)=1H$
      GO TO 600
9000  STOP
      END


      FUNCTION LENGTH(PARS)
      DIMENSION PARS(20)
      K=0
      DO 10 J=1,20
      IF (PARS(J).EQ.1H$) GO TO 20
      K=K+1
10    CONTINUE
20    LENGTH=K
      RETURN
      END


      SUBROUTINE CLEAN(PARSC,IL,PARS,N)
      INTEGER PARS, PARSC
      DIMENSION PARSC(20), PARS(20)
      IL=0
      DO 10 J=1,N
      IF(PARS(J).EQ.1H$) GO TO 20
      IL=IL+1
10    PARSC(J)=PARS(J)
20    CONTINUE
      RETURN
      END
```

```
      INTEGER FUNCTION FORK(I)
      COMMON SENT(600), BIAS(90)
      J=3*(I-1)
      P1=BIAS(J+1)
      P2=BIAS(J+2)
      P3=BIAS(J+3)
      S2=P1+P2
      S3=S2+P3
      R=RNDMU(X)
      IF(R.LT.P1) GO TO 10
      IF(R.LT.S2) GO TO 20
      IF(R.LT.S3) GO TO 30
      FORK=4
      RETURN
10    FORK=1
      RETURN
20    FORK=2
      RETURN
30    FORK=3
      RETURN
      END


      SUBROUTINE UNPACK(KODE,K)
      DIMENSION KODE(8)
      DO 10 J=1,4
10    KODE(J)=MOD(K/10**(8-J),10)
      DO 15 J=1,4
15    M=K-KODE(J)*(10**(8-J))
      DO 20 J=1,3
20    KODE(J+4)=MOD(M/10**(4-J),10)
      KODE(8)=MOD(M,10)
      RETURN
      END


      SUBROUTINE CONCAT(LS,INSRT,IL)
      COMMON SENT(600),BIAS(90)
      INTEGER SENT
      DIMENSION INSRT(20)
      SENT(LS+1)=1H
      DO 10 J=1,IL
      M=LS+J+1
10    SENT(M)=INSRT(J)
      RETURN
      END
```

Fig. 6.7 (end).

6.8. Some Compositions by MORON

Since MORON in the state described in the preceding section produces only meaningless (albeit grammatical) gibberish, it does not have many important direct applications; it is a stepping stone for more sophisticated programs.

The most important application of MORON is the experimental demonstration that the model of Language as an error-detecting code with check criterions and check implementations is a viable one, and that a computer instructed on this basis will actually produce grammatically correct sentences from a lexicon of unprocessed words, no matter how the words are chosen by the random routine. The program was written as a sample program demonstrating this assertion, and therefore it contained only a limited amount of grammatical structures, though this number was (it is hoped) sufficient to make it evident that any other English structure could equally well be included and based on the same principles.

The program, as it stands, can also be used as a subprogram of another program biasing the probabilities of the fork branches in such a way as to produce desired sentences. The meaning would then be inherent in the commands of the main program, and the subprogram would simply express this meaning in grammatical English sentences. We shall have more to say about this in the next chapter; for the time being we will note that by biasing the corresponding forks with probabilities one and zero, and loading the dictionary with the necessary words, the program could be made to produce meaningful sentences such as

MARY AND HER THREE SISTERS LONGED FOR THEIR OLD GRANDFATHER, ALTHOUGH THEY COULD NOT REMEMBER HIS KIND, BESPECTACLED FACE.

A program of the MORON type could also be written for other languages, though this would be more complicated than for English. In French, gender and gender concord would have to be introduced, and the verb would require more forks for conjugations in general, and for conjugations of different types. German, with inflexions, inversions and separable prefixes, would presumably be more difficult than French. Latin would presumably more than offset the advantage of no articles by its conjugations and paradigms. The Slavic languages would be even more difficult to program. However, the difficulty is only one of increased effort and complexity, not one of principle, for the same system of check criterion and check implementation can be used in any of these languages.

Apart from its demonstrational value for throwing light on the structure of Language, MORON and similar programs producing meaningless sentences can also be used for a number of pastimes. Some of these were tried.

When the lexicon was loaded with words beginning with the same phoneme, Moron produced alliterations at the rate of about two sentences per second. Samples are shown in Fig. 6.8. The run through a subordinate clause was suppressed (by biasing FORK(17) with probability zero for continuing, and probability one for a period), since the alliterations sound better as short sentences.

MORON can also talk with a German accent when the lexicon is loaded with appropriately misspelled words. Samples are shown in Fig. 6.9. BIK, ACH SO BIK was stored as a single adjective; so was PLUE OR PLACK.

A spoof on legalese gobbledegook was also attempted. The lexicon was loaded with legal terms, and also some nonexistent words (*intrajudicial, extraparental, to redisestablish*). Pronouns were inactivated, all possessive adjectives were replaced by SAID (which deletes the articles just like a possessive adjective would), cardinal numerals were inacti-

```
THE FORCEFUL FIN FUMBLED WITH A FOLDER.
A FLABBERGASTED PHILOSOPHER MAY HAVE FASCINATED A FROG.
15 PHILOSOPHERS OR PHILIP DID NOT FORFEIT THE FASTIDIOUS,
    FINGER-LICKING PHOTOGRAPHER.
A FOUL PHILOSOPHER WITH THE 45 FATEFUL, FAST FIREFLIES WILL HAVE
    FLATTERED THE FRIVOLOUS FIRE FIGHTERS.
54 FINS DID NOT FRY THE FLAMING FIREFLIES.
THE FLABBERGASTED, FLAMING FROGS WOULD FOOL THE FRUITFUL
    FOREFATHERS.
FOUR FRUSTRATED PHARAOES FUMED.
15 FISHWIVES MAY NOT HAVE FORNICATED WITH THE 54 FORSAKEN,
    FEARFUL FIRE FIGHTERS.
THE PHOTOGRAPHERS WOULD HAVE FRATERNIZED WITH THE 15TH
    FOREFATHER.
A FANFARE WILL NOT HAVE FANNED A PHILATELIST.
FRUSTRATED PHILIP WITH THE FEARFUL FRAUD WILL NOT HAVE FOOLED
    PHILOSOPHERS.
FABULOUS FRANCES MAY NOT FUME.
FLUFF MIGHT NOT FLIP THE FIRE FIGHTER.
FIVE FRIVOLOUS FILATELISTS MIGHT NOT PHOTOGRAPH FIVE
    FOREFATHERS.
A FICKLE FANFARE WILL HAVE FRUSTRATED FRUITFUL FIREFLIES.
54 FATEFUL FRIGATES MIGHT FORNICATE WITH A FORSAKEN, FOUL FIN.
THE FINAL FABULOUS FRIGATE OR 54 FILATELISTS SHOULD HAVE FOOLED
    THE PHILOSOPHER.
A FISHWIFE MAY HAVE FRUSTRATED THE 500 FORCEFUL, FRIVOLOUS
    FRIGATES.
A FUMBLING, FEARFUL FIREFLY FELT FOR THE FATEFUL FLUFF.
THE FABULOUS FRAULEIN FETCHED FOUR FIENDISH, FLAMING FIREFLIES.
45 FIRE FIGHTERS DID NOT FULFIL THE FISHWIFE.
FLUFF AND THE FINS FRUSTRATED A FRAUD.
54 PHARAOES FUMBLED WITH 54 FATEFUL FILATELISTS.
A FIN OR A FRAULEIN MAY HAVE FANNED THE FORCEFUL PHARAOES.
FRANCES OR FIREFLIES FORNICATED WITH THE FIVE FRUITFUL FRAULEINS.
THE 50TH FOUL, FICKLE FILATELIST WILL NOT FRUSTRATE FIREFLIES.
FROGS OR THE FASTIDIOUS, FATEFUL FORGERS SHOULD FEEL FOR A FROG.
THE FIRST FORGER AND A FORCEFUL FROG SHOULD HAVE FRUSTRATED
    A FLAMING FRIGATE.
A FIRE FIGHTER DID NOT FUMBLE WITH A FRUSTRATED FANFARE.
A FIENDISH PHILOSOPHER SHOULD NOT FASCINATE 500 FISHWIVES.
FRANCES AND THE FIREFLY FUMED.
THE FOUL PHILANTROPIST DID NOT FULFIL FRANCES.
FRIVOLOUS FRAUDS AND 45 FANFARES DID NOT FETCH THE FINS.
FIVE FRIGATES WOULD FORFEIT A FICKLE FOREFATHER.
```

Fig. 6.8. Alliterations
(see opposite page).

```
THE THIRD CHOYFUL ZUBMARINE WILL NOT HAVE SHTIMULATED A
    GESCHWUMPUNG.
THE ZUPERZONIC ZUBMARINES SHMILED AT THE THIRD HEDCHEHOK.
THE HEAFFY CHENERATOR DID NOT SHPECULADE ABOUT THE SHPITEFOLL
    WORDTS.
THE WATCHDOK COULD NOT ENCHOY THE BATH TUP.
A MANADCHER PULFERISSED THE DEUTSCHE ORANCHE CHUICE.
THE LIPRARY SHOULD HAVE SHNEEZED AT THE SHNOW-WEISSE PIK.
THE BIK, ACH SO BIK DOK WILL HAVE SCHEISSED ON THE ZENTIMENTAL
    LIPRARY.
A GESTRUTZVOLLE EQUASHION PROTESTED AGAINST GOODT ORANCHE CHUICE.
THE MANADCHER WILL SHWAMP THE PLUE OR PLACK HEDCHEHOKS.
THE FIFE SHWINGING CATALOKS DID NOT EMERCHE FROM THE ZUBMARINE.
A CHERMAN CATALOK AND FIFE SHWINGING, REDT DOKS EMERCHED FROM
    THE BATH TUP.
A DEUTSCHE FISHING RODT SHOULD NOT FIGHT AGAINST A GESCHWUMPUNG.
THE PLUE OR PLACK HEDCHEHOK ANALYSSED A ZUPERZONIC ZAGRIFICE.
THE CHERMAN CATALOK WILL ZURRENDER TO THE CANDIDT PLEASHURE.
THE HEAFFY MANADCHER WILL NOT ZUBMERCHE THE SHTERN ZUBMARINE.
A CHOYFUL HEDCHEHOK DID NOT ANALYSSE THE ORANCHE CHUICE.
```

Fig. 6.9. MORON talks with a German accent
(see opposite page).

SAID EXTRAPARENTAL, REACTIVATED SUBSECTION C AND/OR THE FORMER
RETROACTIVE BRIEF REFERRED TO THE JUDICIAL PARAGRAPH 144/2,
REGARDLESS OF WHETHER SAID PRECEDENTS WOULD, POST EJACULATIONEM,
CONTRADICT SAID INTERCOLLEGIATE PRECEDENTS.

SAID ZONING LAWS AND/OR A PREJUDICIAL CITY ORDINANCE MAY HAVE
ANULLED PARAGRAPH 144/2, ALTHOUGH AN EXTRAPARENTAL PROCRAS-
TINATION MAY NOT, PER ONANIAM, HAVE IGNORED THE SUBSECTIONS.

A DEFINITION DID NOT, EX DEFINITIONE, DISCUSS SAID COUNTY COURTS,
WHEREAS SAID INJUNCTIONS AND/OR UPPER FEDERAL COURTS CONTRA-
DICTED SAID OBSOLESCENT, BINDING PARAGRAPHS.

A PROCRASTINATION SHOULD EXONERATE A PRECEDENT, REGARDLESS OF
WHETHER SAID BRIEFS AND/OR A DEFINITION MIGHT, PRIMA FACIE,
HAVE APPLIED TO AN OBLIGATORY VERDICT.

THE REACTIVATED FEDERAL COURT AND/OR SAID JURISDICTIONAL
DECISIONS WILL NOT, PRIMA FACIE, HAVE APPLIED TO AN APPEAL,
BECAUSE RETROACTIVE DEFINITIONS, CUM FECIBUS TAURI, INVALI-
DATED THE SUBSECTION.

SECTION A WOULD IGNORE SAID INTERCOLLEGIATE VERDICTS, ALTHOUGH
THE REACTIVATED, TACIT VERDICT COULD NOT, SUB JUDICE, REACTI-
VATE A PROCRASTINATION.

THE DISPUTE AND/OR SAID EXTRAPARENTAL APPEALS COULD HAVE REJECTED
A BINDING DECISION, BECAUSE A LEGALISTIC ZONING LAW DID NOT,
EX DEFINITIONE, REDISESTABLISH THE OBLIGATORY, LOWER ZONING
LAWS.

THE VERDICT AND/OR A NEW, EXTRAPARENTAL PRECEDENT MIGHT NOT, PER
ONANIAM, HAVE REACTIVATED SAID BINDING VERDICTS, WHEREAS
SUBSECTION C, PRIMA FACIE, CONTRADICTED THE OBSOLESCENT
DISPUTE.

THE EXTRAJUDICIAL, OBSOLESCENT INJUNCTION AND/OR SAID AD HOC,
JURISDICTIONAL FEDERAL COURT DID NOT, AB INITIO, REDEFINE
THE VERDICTS.

SAID JURISDICTIONAL PRECEDENT AND/OR CITY ORDINANCES MAY HAVE
DISQUALIFIED SAID CITY ORDINANCE, ALTHOUGH UPPER, OBLIGATORY
FEDERAL COURTS DID NOT, DE JURE, OVERRULE THE EXTRAPARENTAL
TESTIMONIES.

A COUNTY COURT AND/OR SAID VERDICT MIGHT HAVE ANNULLED THE CITY
ORDINANCES, WHEREAS SAID SUBSECTION C DID NOT, AB INITIO,
DISQUALIFY A TACIT SUIT.

THE INTERCOLLEGIATE PRECEDENTS AND/OR FORMER SECTION A, POST
EJACULATIONEM, ANNULLED SAID EXTRAJUDICIAL, REACTIVATED
CITY ORDINANCE, WHEREAS THE ZONING LAWS AND/OR THE RETROACTIVE
DISPUTE, DE JURE, EMPHASIZED SECTION A.

A LEGALISTIC VERDICT AND/OR FORMER FEDERAL COURTS WOULD VOID THE
INTERCOLLEGIATE CITY ORDINANCES, ALTHOUGH A SUIT AND/OR SAID
COUNTY COURT COULD HAVE, PER ONANIAM, REVERSED SAID OBSOLESCENT
DECISION.

AN APPEAL, POST EJACULATIONEM, VOIDED SAID RETROACTIVE DEFINITION,
REGARDLESS OF WHETHER THE INJUNCTION AND/OR A DISPUTE WOULD
HAVE IGNORED THE PRECEDENT.

SAID RETROSPECTIVE, AD HOC DECISION AND/OR SAID PROCRASTINATIONS
DID NOT, AB INITIO, DISQUALIFY SAID MISINTERPRETED SUBSECTIONS,
ALTHOUGH THE DISPUTES AND/OR OBLIGATORY PARAGRAPH 144/2 DID NOT
REDEFINE SAID REACTIVATED FEDERAL COURTS.

A FORMER COUNTY COURT AND/OR AN EXTRAPARENTAL DECISION INVALIDATED
SAID REACTIVATED PROCRASTINATIONS, BECAUSE THE CITY ORDINANCES
MIGHT NOT, DE JURE, HAVE DISCUSSED EXTRAPARENTAL INJUNCTIONS.

SAID DECISIONS SHOULD REFUTE THE OBSOLESCENT ZONING LAWS, REGARDLESS
OF WHETHER SAID PARAGRAPH 144/2 AND/OR A RETROSPECTIVE ZONING
LAW WOULD HAVE, SUB JUDICE, REDEFINED THE AD HOC PRECEDENT.

SAID RETROSPECTIVE, JUDICIAL SUBSECTIONS AND/OR THE MISINTERPRETED,
TACIT DEFINITIONS MIGHT NOT, PRIMA FACIE, REDEFINE SAID
JURISDICTIONAL SUBSECTIONS, REGARDLESS OF WHETHER A BINDING,
EXTRAPARENTAL DISPUTE MAY HAVE, DE JURE, INVALIDATED SAID
INTERCOLLEGIATE TESTIMONIES.

Fig. 6. 10. A spoof of legalese gobbledegook (see pp. 250, 253).

vated, and all ordinal numerals were replaced by *aforementioned*. All of these changes can be made in the data cards, but the program was also slightly modified to concatenate certain Latin phrases *en bloc*. Before FORK(13), before the past tense, and before the infinitive following DID NOT, the program was given a choice whether to concatenate a Latin phrase. If it chose to do so, it was given a choice of the following eight Latin phrases, inserted in the sentence between commas:*

> PRIMA FACIE
> SUB JUDICE
> DE JURE
> EX DEFINITIONE
> AB INITIO
> POST EJACULATIONEM
> PER ONANIAM
> CUM FECIBUS TAURI

Samples of the resulting print-out are given in Fig. 6.10.

Other pastimes are, no doubt, possible. One only has to look for a sublanguage with a style so distinct that when it is recognized, the meaning does not matter very much. Apart from the cases actually programmed, this would seem to include tongue twisters, poetry and political speeches.

For tongue twisters, one could load the lexicon with words containing similar phonemes, such as *thistle, sixth, thousand, seethe, this, these, soothe, sing, thing, sink, think*, etc.; the program will then produce billions of tongue twisters at the rate of about two per second. (This is roughly the speed of the line printer; the construction of the sentences is very much faster.)

For poetry, or rather lyrics, the lexicon should be loaded with words considered poetic by the programmer (perhaps *to soar, to dwell, rosy, star, dawn, twilight,* etc.) with occasional ugliness thrown in for contrast (*slimy earthworm, running sore*, stored as single nouns). All punctuation should be deleted, and the lines of the print-out should be broken in random places. Do not aim at rhyme, rythm or meaning, which are alien to modern poetry.

For political speeches, load the lexicon with nouns such as *people* (always "the"), *justice, freedom, peace, ecology, environment,* adjectives such as *American, noble, just, freedom-loving, vigorous, effective, responsible, forward-looking,* and verbs such as *to pledge, promise, challenge, revolutionize,* etc. Only the future tense should be kept active.

---

*Samples of the print-out were given in the two articles mentioned on. p.245, but where the program had concatenated one of the last three phrases, they were retouched, as they might not have been accepted for publication by these respected journals. I am grateful to the editor of Golem Press for being less prudish.

This is, of course, intended to produce American-style campaign promises. For Soviet-style speeches, the lexicon should be loaded with
*banner of marxism-leninism, people's democracy, cadres, glorious, in-
vincible, victorious, vigilant, toiling masses* (store as a single noun),
etc., and about half the lexicon should be loaded with invectives such
as *imperialist henchman, political double-dealer, reactionary saboteur,
fascist lackey, bourgeois objectivist, butchering bloodhound,* etc. Flags
should be used to prevent mishaps like *glorious imperialist* or *our fascist
Soviet fatherland.*

Perhaps the UN could escape from its financial straits if it computerized its speeches in this manner. Its present effectiveness would
hardly be affected.

6.9. Synthesis of Meaningful Sentences

The program MORON does not, in general, produce meaningful sentences, and would not do so regardless of the number of basic grammatical structures added to its present state. MORON produces merely
grammatical sentences. But linguists have no unanimous opinion as to
what constitutes a grammatical sentence. Personally, I agree with Chomsky* that "the notion of 'grammatical' cannot be identified with 'meaningful' or 'significant' in any semantic sense," and that the meaningless sentence *Colorless ideas sleep furiously* is grammatical.

As far as MORON is concerned, its sentences satisfy the following
definition of a grammatical sentence: A sentence is grammatical if it
can be converted to an "undisputedly" grammatical sentence by substituting words with identical grammatical properties. An "undisputedly
grammatical" sentence is one that is grammatical by any current definition. For example, the sentence *The boy was plagued by loneliness* is
surely considered grammatical by any definition. The above definition
then says that the sentence *The boy was belittled by jealousy* is also
grammatical, although it is obviously meaningless. Similarly, the sentence *Colorless green ideas sleep furiously* can be converted, by substitution of words with the same grammatical properties, to *Odorless
green peas sell quickly,* which is undisputedly grammatical.

There is also little agreement as to what constitutes a meaningful
sentence. Books have been written on the meaning of meaning, and it is
not proposed to make them all obsolete with a two-line definition. However, as far as the program to be described below is concerned, a fairly
satisfactory definition is the following: A meaningful statement must
be either true or false; if it is inherently impossible to establish whether it is true or false, then it is meaningless. Thus, *Fir trees are*

---

*N. Chomsky, *Syntactic structures*, Mouton, The Hague-Paris, 1969; p. 15.

purple is a meaningful statement, because it is false; but *Fir trees are monogamous* is meaningless, for if it were merely false, then *Fir trees are polygamous* would be true.

A somewhat more general definition along the same lines, which also matches the theory outlined in Chapters 2 and 3, is the following: A meaningful statement is one that codes an event to which a probability can be assigned; all other statements are meaningless. This does not limit the statement to true (probability one) and false (probability zero). Meaningless statements either do not correspond to any event (e.g., *Cats are multiple-valued*), or if they do correspond to an event, it is inherently impossible to assign a probability to it (*The hovnotron is a particle that has no mass, charge, or other property rendering it capable of detection*). Also, the assignment of probabilities is performed, as usual, by the receiver, so that the same sentence can be meaningful to one person, but meaningless to another: The sentence *Prsi* is meaningless to all but those who understand Czech; and the sentence *An entire function can have no essential singularities* is meaningful only to those familiar with functions of a complex variable.

As far as writing a program producing only meaningful sentences is concerned, these definitions amount to prohibiting certain combinations of words in a grammatical sentence. This was done by additions to the program MORON. The lexicon entries were supplemented by semantic codes, and the program rejected words that would make the sentence under construction meaningless.

For reasons to be explained below (that is, essentially, for reasons of simplicity), the subordinate clause sometimes produced by MORON was inactivated, so that the program would produce only main clauses of the type

> *Three big, small frigates multiplied an extreme, algebraic waitress.*

The sentence is grammatical, or as grammatical as *Colorless green ideas sleep furiously*, but both sentences are meaningless because of unacceptable combinations of words. Both sentences have contradictory adjectives (*big-small, colorless-green*), both use adjectives to attribute properties which the object described by the noun does not have (*extreme, algebraic waitress — green ideas*), both use a verb denoting an action which the subject is incapable of performing (*frigates multiply — ideas sleep*), and the action operates on an incompatible object (*to multiply a waitress*) or in an incompatible manner (*to sleep furiously*). As far as the basic grammatical structure of MORON is concerned, only four combinations need be avoided to prevent meaningless sentences:

1. Contradictory adjectives (*big, small*);
2. Incompatible noun and adjective (*algebraic waitress*);

3. Incompatible subject and verb (*frigates multiply*);
4. Incompatible verb and object (*to multiply a waitress*).

These four requirements are far simpler than grammatical rules, and they are therefore much easier to program — at least in principle, though, of course, the sheer quantity of required codes becomes prohibitive if the universe of concepts becomes too large. Indeed, one of the first things to note is that whilst it is believed that there are no insurmountable difficulties involved in enlarging a program of the MORON type to cover the entire grammar of a language, no such claim is made with respect to ensuring meaningful sentences, particularly if they are involved and contain clauses beginning with *if, because, although*, etc. But the simple structure yielding only a main clause of the above type can easily be made meaningful. For example, all contradictory adjectives are coded by the same number; the program then tests these numbers of two adjectives attributed to the same noun for equality, and if they are equal, one of the adjectives is rejected, and a different one selected; the process is repeated until a suitable adjective is found. Similar provisions are made for the other three incompatibilities.

The program to be briefly described below was again a mere demonstration, and therefore nouns were divided into only five categories:

1 persons,
2 animals,
3 concrete objects,
4 emotional states,
5 mathematical functions.

Also coded were some properties with respect to which the noun can or cannot be modifed, namely, color, size, weight, intensity, mathematical property, and character or emotional state. The corresponding semantic code, which is entered in the dictionary in addition to the grammatical code described earlier, is an 8-digit number, of which the first digit gives the category, and the other digits (except the 8th which was not used) are used for the properties; a 0 or 1 means that the noun cannot, or can, be modified with respect to that property. Typical semantic noun codes are shown below.

	Ccswime-
WAITRESS	10110010
LIBERAL	10111010
CHIMPANZEE	21110010
MILK	31010000
TOOTH	31110000
JEALOUSY	40001010
POLYNOMIAL	50000100

The letters above the individual columns have the following meaning: C category of noun; c color; s size; w weight; i intensity; m mathematical property; e emotional state.

The other codes are geared to this semantic noun code. The semantic adjective code is an eight-digit number, of which the first seven are used. The first digit (labeled I below) prevents contradictory adjectives being attributed to the same noun; the same digit is given to incompatible adjectives (*sad-merry, heavy-light*). Adjectives compatible with any other adjective in the lexicon (*malicious, discontinuous, paranoic*) have a zero as the first digit. The remaining digits indicate what property the adjective may modify. The properties follow the same scheme as in the noun code, and a 1 or 0 corresponds to ability or inability, respectively, of modifying the pertinent property. Typical adjective codes are

```
            Icswime-
SAD         50000010
MERRY       50000010
IRRATIONAL  00000110
CONSPICUOUS 01111010
GREAT       11111010
HEAVY       30100000
```

When the program attributes an adjective to a noun, it multiplies the ith digit of the adjective code with the ith digit of the noun code, where i equals successively 2 to 7; if none of the six products differs from zero, the adjective is rejected as incompatible, and another adjective is selected from the lexicon until at least one positive product is encountered. Thus, *the extreme waitress* would be rejected, but *the extreme liberal* accepted; *the irrational waitress* and *the irrational derivative* will both be accepted, since *irrational* is entered under both emotional state and mathematical property. *Her white jealousy* is rejected, but *her extreme, paranoic jealousy* is accepted, and so on.

If a second adjective is chosen, its compatibility with the first adjective (as well as its compatibility with the noun) is checked by multiplying the first digits of the two adjective codes; if the product equals the square of one code and differs from zero, the adjective is incompatible. In that case (just for "show"), the program does not reject the adjective, but prints the sentence up to the following noun and gives the reason for rejecting the combination.

The verbs are very easy to code, since it need only be decided who or what can perform the action, and on whom or what it can be performed. Accordingly, verbs have two semantic codes, a subject code and an object code. Both are 8-digit numbers; the first five digits correspond to the noun categories, the remaining three are not used. A 1 or 0 in the subject code indicates whether the action can be performed by the subject of the corresponding category or not; in the object code it denotes whether the action can be performed on the object. Thus, *to kill* can have a person, animal or concrete object as a subject, but only a person or an animal as an object; *to differentiate* can only have a person as a subject, and only a mathematical function as an object; *to enrage* can have anything or anybody as subjects, but only persons or animals as objects.

Typical verb codes are the following:

		subject code	object code
	category	1 2 3 4 5 - - -	1 2 3 4 5 - - -
VANISH		1 1 1 1 1 0 0 0	0 0 0 0 0 0 0 0
FETCH		1 1 0 0 0 0 0 0	1 1 1 0 0 0 0 0
ENRAGE		1 1 1 1 1 0 0 0	1 1 0 0 0 0 0 0
DIFFERENTIATE		1 0 0 0 0 0 0 0	0 0 0 0 1 0 0 0
HATE		1 1 0 0 0 0 0 0	1 1 1 1 1 0 0 0

The program ascertains the category of the noun by looking at the first digit of its semantic code; if that digit is i, it looks at the ith digit of the verb code to check whether it is a 1; if not, the combination is incompatible and the offending word is rejected and another is selected until a compatible combination is found. The rejection proceeds in the order in which the sentence is constructed, i.e., if subject and verb are incompatible, the verb is rejected, but if verb and object are incompatible, the noun is rejected.

The method uses trial and error only in each successive step, i.e., for each new word with a semantic code to be concatenated; it does not use trial and error by constructing an entire sentence first, and then checking whether it is meaningful, which would result in an enormous number of errors with rare cases of success, and therefore in very slow processing. The step-by-step method is systematic and results in the construction of meaningful sentences at a rate much faster than they can be printed (about two per second). The grammatical structure allows about 1.3 billion sentences differing in semantically coded words (not counting variations in tense, number, negative, etc., nor the uncoded parts of speech such as pronouns, numerals, possessive adjectives, etc. etc.). How many of these are meaningful will, of course, depend on the words entered in the lexicon.

Fig. 6.11 shows samples of the print-out. It will be seen that the sentences are always meaningful. However, they are not always true. For example, the statement *The imaginary polynomial diverged* is certainly false, since a polynomial, whether real or imaginary, must be finite and cannot diverge. *The red chimpanzee sneezed at the conspicuous tooth* codes an event with very small probability, but the very

```
WE DID NOT RELY ON ALUMINUM.
THE LIBERAL DID NOT TALK ABOUT THE THIRD DISCONTINUOUS POLYNOMIAL.
WE TREMBLED.
THEIR FIVE MALICIOUS CHIMPANZEES MIGHT DIE.
A SMALL CALF SNEEZED AT THE TEN PARANOIC CHILDREN.
I WOULD NOT HAVE QUARRELED WITH A LIBERAL.
HER JEALOUSY VANISHED.
THE WHITE THUMB TACKS KILLED THE DOG.
THE POLYNOMIAL COULD DIVERGE.
THE DISCONTINUOUS INTEGRAL DID NOT DIVERGE.
AN EXTREME LIBERAL WOULD HAVE VOMITED.
THEY WILL HAVE FETCHED A SMALL, BIG MEAT LOAF...***STOP*** MEAT
    LOAF EITHER SMALL OR BIG, BUT NOT BOTH.
THE FIFTH SINGLE-VALUED, IMAGINARY DERIVATIVE COULD HAVE ENRAGED
    THE SMALL UNDERTAKER.
HER IRRATIONAL JEALOUSY ENRAGED THE THIRD OFFICER.
THE IRRATIONAL INTEGRAL MIGHT VANISH.
THE EXTREME LIBERAL HATED HER EXTREME, PARANOIC MELANCHOLY.
A TRANSCENDENTAL, DISCONTINUOUS DERIVATIVE COULD ENRAGE A SMALL
    CHIMPANZEE.
SHE FETCHED THE DOG.
THE SMALL, RED MEAT LOAF COULD NOT HAVE KILLED THE CHILDREN.
THE PARANOIC WAITRESS WOULD NOT HAVE TALKED ABOUT YOUR MERRY,
    CONSPICUOUS CHILDREN.
MY SAD, MERRY CHILDREN...***STOP***CHILDREN EITHER SAD OR MERRY,
    BUT NOT BOTH.
SHE MAY NOT HAVE PLAYED WITH VERY LIGHT ALUMINUM.
I MIGHT NOT FETCH THE CONSPICUOUS DOG.
WHITE MILK COULD HAVE TREMBLED.
THE TWO MERRY OFFICERS SHOULD NOT HAVE PLAYED WITH THE THIRD TOOTH.
THEIR DISCONTINUOUS POLYNOMIALS COULD NOT HAVE ENRAGED THE
    PARANOIC CHILDREN.
OUR AVARICE MAY NOT ENRAGE THE WAITRESSES.
THE FIVE SAD OFFICERS COULD NOT HAVE EATEN ALUMINUM.
THE FIVE IRRATIONAL LIBERALS CALCULATED.
HER FIFTH DOG SHOULD NOT HAVE ENRAGED THE BLACK CALVES.
YOU MAY HAVE MATRICULATED.
YOUR MALICIOUS AVARICE WOULD NOT HAVE VANISHED.
SHE VOMITED.
THEIR BLACK ALUMINUM DID NOT KILL OUR DOG.
THE NEXT IRRATIONAL, DISCONTINUOUS INTEGRAL COULD NOT HAVE
    DIVERGED.
HE DIED.
```

Fig. 6.11. Meaningful (but not necessarily true)
sentences.

fact that a probability can be assigned makes the sentence meaningful.

It will also be seen that semantic coding and the construction of
meaningful sentences is, in the above case, quite simple, certainly much
simpler than the underlying program producing grammatical sentences in
the first place. However, this simplicity is deceptive, for there is an
essential difference between the presently discussed program and the
original program MORON. There seems to be no reason why the latter
should not be enlarged to include all possible grammatical structures
of English, or, for that matter, why the method should not be used on a
language with much more complicated grammar than English. Given enough
time and resources, there appears to be no reason why such a program
could not be written for all possible structures of, say, Czech, with its
many paradigms, cases, conjugations, and exceptions.

No such claim, however, can be made for semantic coding. The coding was easy in the above case, because the semantic ties were very

close — from adjective to noun, from noun to verb, and from verb to object. Since a semantic code of eight decimal digits allows for 20 million different numbers, the method could also be extended to include many more categories (the verb *to corrode* would require a category of metals, and the verb *to wilt* a category of flowers), including overlaps and exclusions. However, as the semantic ties become more distant — from subordinate clause to main clause or from sentence to sentence — the difficulties of semantic coding will rapidly increase until they become prohibitive. A subordinate clause beginning with *because* implies a reason, and one beginning with *although* makes an objection; even if we require only meaning, not truth, this means an enormous amount of information to be stored by the computer, enough to recognize such relationships as cause and effect, obstacles to an ocurrence, and many others for *if, when, before, after, until, regardless of whether*, etc. For semantic ties between different sentences, the situation is even worse. Consider the phrase *at either of the above two addresses*, which is meaningful only if there are two addresses in the previous print-out. Whilst it is conceivable to write a subroutine that will search for, recognize, and count strings of words forming a postal address, it is clear that there is an unlimited number of analogous cases, each of which would need an equally complicated routine, and the work involved (as well as the necessary storage) would quickly become prohibitive.

The method of semantic coding described above can therefore be used only to a limited extent and is incapable of coping with meaning where more complex relationships are involved. However, this is not to say that it is impossible to make a computer construct meaningful sentences of arbitrary complexity. The storage capacities of computers are now approaching and surpassing that of the human brain; the access times are shorter, and within the next decade the physical dimensions of such vast memories will probably be reduced to those of the human brain, too. The field of Artificial Intelligence is also rapidly advancing, and there are already such things as programs to write programs, and programs that will learn either from a teacher or from their own experience. It is therefore quite conceivable that a computer will eventually learn to "talk" in the same way as a human child — by learning through listening to others and by experience, by grasping the meaning of statements, and thus learning to code events in natural Language. But this is an entirely different method from the mechanistic coding used in the above program.

Even so, the above program may have some practical applications. In machine translation, for example, all meanings of a homonym are usually printed, separated by slashes. Thus, in translating from Russian, the print-out will contain such words as LOCK/CASTLE,   FACE/

PERSON, CARRY/WEAR, etc. A human editor then deletes the inapplicable meaning, which he recognizes, as always with homonyms, by semantic decoding. The method fo semantic coding described above could probably automate the decision which of the two meanings is applicable. For example, the Russian noun лицо means either *person* or *face* in English; these two nouns would, even in the primitive code described above, have different semantic codes:

```
            Ccswime-
PERSON      10110010
FACE        31100010
```

In phrases like *his pale person/face, a heavy person/face, a person/face sneezed*, the program, even as it stands now, would make its own decision whether *person* or *face* is applicable. The expression *a jealous person/face* would not allow an unambiguous decision based only on these two codes, but there are not many verbs that can equally well have *a jealous face* and *a jealous person* as a subject, and probably even fewer verbs that can have both as an object. A further refinement would replace the 0's and 1's in the digits coding compatibility by the statistical probabilities of occurrence; the sophisticated methods of statistical inference and decision theory could then be used to resolve the ambiguity.

Another possibility of using semantic coding arises in the files of medical and legal case histories, which are being computerized with increasing frequency by legal firms and medical centers. Ambiguous words and abbreviations may cause erroneous processing, and though a computer might not yet be trusted to make its own decision on how to process the ambiguous information on the basis of semantic codes, it could at least signal a request for clarification if it finds a discrepancy in processing the semantic codes of the offending words in a lexicon.

6.10. Synthesis of True Sentences

To decide whether a meaningful sentence is true or false, a computer, just like a human being, needs at least one of two assets: a sensor (measuring instrument) or knowledge stored in its memory. In a small demonstration program, only the latter was used.

Let us return to MORON for a moment. This program can be regarded as one with many forks which are so interlocked by conditional transfers that no matter which way they are switched, the constructed sentence must be grammatical. It is therefore possible to switch the forks at random to produce any amount of grammatical sentences. Now suppose that the forks are not switched at random, but that they are controlled

by some source which "knows what it wants to say." For example, if
that source is a human being, he could switch the forks in such a way
as to produce the sentence

YOUR AUNT SHOULD SEE A DOCTOR, BECAUSE
HER COUGH DISTURBS THE CHILDREN.

No semantic coding is needed to produce such a meaningful sentence:
The meaning is guaranteed by the intelligence of the operator who throws
the switches (forks) meaningfully, and not at random so as to produce
only grammatical gibberish.

Moreover, the above sentence might not be merely meaningful; it could
even be true. It could be produced by a person who is asked to make a
true statement about someone's aunt, and who knows how to control the
program MORON. Instead of saying the sentence aloud or writing it on
a typewriter, he would feed the computer a few numbers instructing it
how to make its choices (at the forks and other points where decisions
were formerly made at random), and the computer would construct the required sentence.

A human who produces this sentence acts as an agent who 1) knows
how to control the program MORON, 2) knows "what to say," i.e., knows
how to select the event that is to be coded in English.

A computer program can, in principle, perform both of these functions.
The first, to control MORON or a similar program is trivially easy. The
whole program constructing grammatical sentences can be run as a subroutine whose arguments are the desired states of the forks. This subroutine will then print the desired sentence after adding the required
check morphemes (which are required by the grammar of the language and
implicitly determined by the operator's choices without special instructions). In the program to be described below, for example, this subroutine
was called

SUBROUTINE ENG(A,B,C,D,E,F,G,H,I,J,K,L,M,N,O,P,Q,R,S,T,U,V,Y)

where ENG is short for English, and A,B,C,... are the designations of
the forks in the subroutine. Setting, say, $D = 3$ instructs the subroutine
to take branch 3 of fork D. The main program determines the branches of
each fork (the values of each argument) and then calls the subroutine
ENG, which will print the corresponding sentence; it supplies the required
check morphemes automatically (on the principles of MORON, though the
grammar is very much simpler).

To determine how the forks are to be switched, i.e., what the values
of the arguments are to be, the computer must have some knowledge. To
produce a sentence like *Your aunt should see a doctor, because her cough
disturbs the children* needs quite a lot of knowledge (and observation or
measurement as well). It would have to sense that children are being dis-

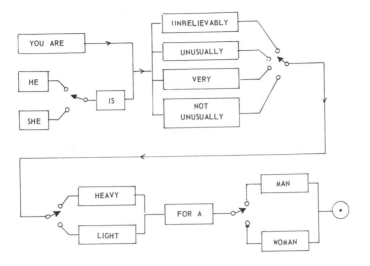

Fig. 6.12. Part of the subroutine ENG. The
switches are thrown by command of the main
program.

turbed, that they are being disturbed by coughing, who is doing the coughing, what the coughing person's relationship to the receiver is, and that
one goes to see a doctor to cure the cause of the cough.

But consider a simpler example. Suppose someone were asked to
comment on the statement "My wife weighs 180 lbs." He might comment
"She is very heavy for a woman." For such a statement, very little knowledge is needed: One only has to know 1) that wives are women, 2) the
usual weight of women, 3) the significance of the deviation of the stated
weight from the average weight of women.

All three items of knowledge are very easy to store in a computer.
The subroutine can actually produce the sentence *She is very heavy for
a woman* as a comment on the statement *My wife weighs 180 lbs*, and it
will produce the sentence by selection of words, not by storing the entire sentence *en bloc*. Fig. 6.12 shows how the forks of the subroutine
are switched to produce the sentence; also shown are some, but by no
means all, alternatives.

It will be seen that no matter how the forks are switched in Fig.
6.12, the result will be a meaningful sentence. This, however, is accidental, because the figure shows merely a small part of the possibilities; if the subroutine were called with inept arguments, the resulting

sentence might not only be false, but also meaningless. (It will, how-ever, be grammatical, since the check impementations are produced auto-matically.)

On establishing that WIFE is a woman, the program sets the first fork shown in Fig. 6.12 to SHE IS and the last fork to WOMAN. (The check morphemes are already built into the subroutine; *she are* or *you is* are not possible.) On receiving the information *180 lbs*, the program compares this to the average weight of the American adult woman (142 lbs) and ascertains whether the given weight is above or below the aver-age. It will then throw the fork to HEAVY or LIGHT, respectively. It then examines the absolute value of the deviation (the difference between the given value and the average); if this is not greater than 20 lbs, it sets the fork to NOT UNUSUALLY; from 20 to 30, it sets the fork to VERY; from 30 to 50, it chooses UNUSUALLY; from 50 to 70, it selects UNBELIEVABLY; and if the absolute deviation is greater than 90 lbs, the subroutine selects, at random, one of several statements such as *You are a liar* or *Don't try to kid a computer.*

In similar fashion, using the same sentence-constructing subroutine, the program comments on age, size, number of children, and times for a 100 yard run. Apart from statistical knowledge, it also stores information on the size, weight, age and number of children of Mr. Nixon (who was chosen simply as a person whose physical characteristics are well known to everybody). When the sentence to be commented includes YOU or YOUR, the program constructs a sentence expressing that it does not have human properties.

The sentences to be commented simulate a human being. They are produced by a program constructing a limited number of sentences with simple grammar, as can be seen from the samples of the print-out shown in Fig. 6.13. These statements are constructed at random. The numeri-cal value is selected with a probability distribution (normal for weight and size, shifted exponential for speed, age and offspring) whose mean is realistic, but whose standard deviation is much greater than the true standard deviation. This occasionally results in sentences like *My sis-ter is 4 inches tall*, giving the other program an opportunity to reply in a way showing that it will not be fooled.

The simulation program prints its statements on the left side of the print-out; the "intelligent" program, which formulates its findings by constructing English sentences, comments on each such statement on the right. Samples are shown in Fig. 6.13.

The point of this program was to show how stored knowledge can be used to construct meaningful and true sentences; the complexity of the grammar is not interesting here, and therefore it was made quite primi-tive.

```
LEFT SIDE IS SIMULATED HUMAN       RIGHT SIDE IS COMMENT BY PROGRAM
*****************************       *********************************

MR NIXON IS 92 YEARS OLD.
                                   HE IS NOT AS OLD AS THAT.

YOUR LAWYER IS 62 YEARS OLD.
                                   I AM A COMPUTER PROGRAM, I HAVE
                                   NO LAWYER.

MY MOTHER IS 67 INCHES TALL.
                                   SHE IS VERY TALL FOR A WOMAN.

MY WIFE WEIGHS 104 POUNDS.
                                   SHE IS VERY LIGHT FOR A WOMAN.

MY AUNT CAN RUN 100 YARDS IN
UNDER 11 SECONDS.
                                   SHE IS UNUSUALLY FAST.

MY FATHER IS 18 INCHES TALL.
                                   DON'T TRY TO KID A COMPUTER.

YOU WEIGH 105 POUNDS.
                                   I AM A COMPUTER PROGRAM, I HAVE
                                   NO WEIGHT.

MY LAWYER HAS 13 CHILDREN.
                                   HE IS UNBELIEVABLY FERTILE.

MR NIXON HAS 5 CHILDREN.
                                   HE HAS 2 CHILDREN.

I CAN RUN 100 YARDS IN UNDER
9 SECONDS.
                                   YOU ARE A LIAR.

MY BROTHER WEIGHS -24 POUNDS.
                                   WEIGHT IS NONNEGATIVE.

MR NIXON IS 51 YEARS OLD.
                                   APPROXIMATELY.

I AM 113 YEARS OLD.
                                   OH YEAH?

MY UNCLE IS 79 INCHES TALL.
                                   HE IS UNUSUALLY TALL FOR A MAN.

I AM 98 INCHES TALL.
                                   BOLONEY.

MR NIXON WEIGHS 124 POUNDS.
                                   HE IS HEAVIER THAN THAT.

MY SISTER WEIGHS 473 POUNDS.
                                   HUMANS MAY BELIEVE IT, I WON'T.
```

Fig. 6.13. Construction of true sentences by a subroutine
steered by the main program on the basis of
its knowledge.

As can be seen from the print-out, the knowledge stored in the memory of the computer (such as the average height of American men or Mr. Nixon's age) is extremely small, and by itself, the program proves no more than what has always been known to politicians, advertisers, salesmen and all types of quacks, namely, that to be impressive, one need not know much; it is sufficient to be able to talk well.

Nevertheless, the program contains the germ of an important application. A computer can have many types of output: It can draw curves, or produce a regulating voltage, or play music, or control machine tools, etc. The most widely used output is the print-out, and this usually takes one of two forms. Either the otput is digital, with the results of the computation stated in numbers, or it prints a message in a natural language. However, in the latter case, it is not really the computer that produced the message; the programmer put it there *en bloc*, just like the designer of a vending machine arranged for the message *Please make another selection* to light up when required. A vending machine knows no more English than the usual program which produces English sentences in the print-out. The present program shows that it is possible to use English (or other languages) as an output — not prefabricated English sentences stored *en bloc*, but sentences which the program constructs from stored words by using its knowledge and judgement.

This has, in a sense, been done before in question-and-answer systems such as BASEBALL, SAD SAM, and in other logical inference and text based programs.* However, in most of these the output sentence is either formulated by (more or less) copying the syntax of the question, or by selecting a prefabricated, or almost fully prefabricated answer. For example, in a system called "The Conversation Machine," which allows a computer to carry on a seemingly intelligent conversation about the weather,* only the words in italics are inserted in the otherwise pre-stored sentence "Well, we won't usually have *rainy* weather in *July*, so you will probably not be disappointed." More recent systems are much more complex and sophisticated, but neither complexity nor sophistication is the issue here: None of these programs (as far as the author is aware) have a simple and general system of converting numerical or other knowledge into the sentences of a natural language by building them up from unprocessed words stored independently of the program.

The above program, primitive as it may be, does have this property. The main program signals the results of its work in the form of a string of numbers to a MORON-type subroutine, which converts the string into an English sentence by choosing the fork branches in accordance with the received numbers and implementing the check criterions as demanded by the grammar of the language. The same main program could also steer a subroutine constructing French or Russian sentences coding the same events as an English subroutine. Conversely, the English subroutine is entirely independent of the main program: If its syntactic structures and vocabulary were enlarged (which would involve more time and effort, but no new principles), the subroutine could be called equally well by a program analyzing the case histories recorded by a dog psychiatrist, or a program processing mediaeval Turkish poems; in both cases, it would

---

* H. Borko (ed.), *Automated Language Processing*, Wiley, New York, 1967. R. Gunzenhäuser (ed.), *Nicht-numerische Informationsverarbeitung*, Springer Verlag, Wien-New York, 1968.

merely re-code the signals received from the main program into English, just like a Fortran compiler re-codes Fortran into machine language. The same English subroutine (provided with sufficiently versatile syntax and abundant vocabulary) can be called by any program switching its forks to produce an output in English, just like the same Fortran compiler is used for any program written in Fortran.

This idea has already been put to use in producing the error diagnostics of a compiler by syntactical construction from a limited number of words rather than by storing hundreds of complete sentences, as we shall see in the next chapter.

Although it is the English subroutine constructing sentences that is primarily of interest here, the main program also throws some light on the structure of Language. Even in the above primitive example, the main program must reduce the information, or coarsen the event to be coded, before it is ready to be re-coded into a natural language, for Language is a rather hazy and ambiguous code.

We have noted several times that Language is a "doubly" ambiguous code: The same code word (sentence) codes a multitude of events, and the same event can be coded by many code words (by many sentences in the same language). The same is true of grammatical words, which often specify a certain aspect of the coded event. The word *red* is used for infinitely many colors, each one defined by the corresponding spectral curve specifying the contributions of the various wavelengths from a wide range of waves forming the mixture called "red." Yet *red* denotes a simple physical property that can be accurately measured, even if it is very coarsely described by Language. This cannot be done with most other concepts, such as *just, jealous, beautiful, democratic, lovable*, and the haziness and ambiguity of such concepts is even more apparent. Sometimes, of course, a very precise statement can be made by Language; but usually it involves specialized language (such as mathematical diction) with which only experts are familiar.

If, then, a precisely defined event is to be coded by Language, in particular, non-numerical language, the information associated with that event must first be reduced; the precise information must be replaced by the coarse events coded by the hazy and ambiguous code words of Language. The precise event coded by a spectral curve, for example, has to be replaced by the coarse event "the radiation has a maximum somewhere near 6,000 angstrøms" before it can be coded into an English statement containing the word "red." Under what conditions a word like *justice* or *love* is to be selected by the subroutine will have to be determined by the programmer of the main program quite arbitrarily; but then, people select these words in real life with the same degree of arbitrariness; there is no known measurable parameter associated with justice or love, and everybody uses his own standards for their presence or absence. The only difference is that the programmer must express these standards explicitly. He need not, however, define them uniquely or elegantly; he can program, in effect, "childish" definitions of the type "Justice is when..."

It is perhaps no exaggeration to say that the only precisely defined knowledge is numerical knowledge (such as the probability distributions associated with the occurrence of events or states). Perhaps this is too sweeping a statement, but digital computers must ultimately store their knowledge in numerical form. This is a form which codes the corresponding events much more finely than language does. The first requirement for expressing the knowledge stored in a computer by a natural language, therefore, is to coarsen the stored information. The method of choosing the words *not unusually, very, unusually,* or *unbelievably* in the program mentioned above (see Fig. 6.12 and text on p. 264) is therefore not accidental; it represents a typical case of "data reduction" from a known probability distribution with infinitely many numerical values to four coarse, arbitrarily selected, and hazily defined concepts.

7

APPLICATIONS

7.1. Linguistics

The application of information theory to linguistics is nothing new; after Shannon's classic paper was published in 1948,* a voluminous stream of papers and books appeared on the application of information theory to linguistics and related subjects.** However, whilst Shannon's information theory gave a certain stimulus to statistical linguistics, it did not produce a major advance in understanding the structure of Language, at least not one comparable to, say, the introduction of Chomsky's transformational grammar.

The reason for this is not the inapplicability of Shannon's basic ideas to Language, but rather the fact that Shannon's theory, as used (and intended) for technological channels of communication, is more suited to the formal and microscopic structure of signals rather than to large, interdependent blocks such as words and sentences. The theory outlined in Chapters 2 and 3 is based on Shannon's fundamental ideas, but modified to treat signals with respect to their functions, not merely with respect to their formal structure. The applications of treating Language as a code in general, and as an error-detecting code in particular, have already been discussed in Chapters 4 and 5. It would appear that such an approach to Language can provide new insights, such as what the *her* is doing in *She shrugged her shoulders*, and why English, in con-

---

* C.E. Shannon, *A Mathematical Theory of Communication*, Bell System Technical Journal, vol. 27, pp. 379-423 and 623-656 (1948).

** E.g., J.R. Pierce, *Symbols, Signals and Noise*, Harper, New York, 1961; C. Cherry, *On Human Communication*, 2nd ed., MIT Press, Cambridge, Mass., 1968.

trast to other languages, insists on inserting it, or why English makes
less use of restoration than German, and German makes less use of it
than Russian. The computer programs composing sentences as described
in Chapter 6 are a linguistic application in the sense that they are intended to demonstrate the viability of the idea that Language is an error-
correcting code.

Beyond these applications that have already been discussed in the
preceding chapters, the error-correcting code aspect of Language may
prove useful not only for giving insight into the structure of any particular language, but also for comparing different languages.

For example, English and Bulgarian are two languages that can
hardly have had any appreciable effect on each other. Yet they have
something in common: Neither language inflects significantly, and both
languages have articles, although the other Germanic and Slavic languages do inflect, and no other Slavic language has articles. The obvious common historic reason for the absence of a significant inflection
system is that in both cases the language developed rapidly and its grammar was drastically simplified during periods of foreign domination, when
there was little or no native literature or education to standardize, and
hence impede the simplification of, the corresponding language. English
went through such a period after the Norman Conquest, and Bulgarian
during the Turkish occupation. But this would only explain why both
English and Bulgarian discarded inflections, or at least drastically simplified them; it does not explain why Bulgarian introduced articles.
Could it be that without either articles or inflections the noise resistance of a language becomes so low that additional check morphemes
must be introduced to keep it from becoming unreasonably ambiguous?
The many examples of ambiguity occurring in English newspaper headlines, which are also without inflections (grammatically) or articles (ungrammatically), would suggest that this is so. We have already seen that
the English article, contrary to accepted beliefs, provides no significant
primary information, but that it is a check morpheme preventing ambiguities, mainly by acting as a noun-identifying marker. If articles served no
purpose at all, they would, presumably, have been discarded along with
inflections (which often also served as identification markers of nouns).
The fact is that no Indo-European language has both articles and a heavily inflecting check system; the heavily inflecting languages such as
Latin, Russian, Polish or Czech have no articles, and the modern Romance languages have articles, but inflect weakly or not at all. The
Germanic languages inflect weakly, and all have articles (including Danish and Norwegian, which insert them after the noun).

It is therefore possible that excessive ambiguity forced Bulgarian to develop articles (from the roots of words which are used as demonstrative adjectives in the other Slavic languages). The almost total disappearance of Latin inflections, together with the emergence of articles, in Italian, French, Spanish, Portugese and Romanian is a similar example. Since the simplification of grammar took place in periods lacking literature, the metamorphosis is difficult to investigate; nevertheless, it is hoped that historical linguists will find food for thought in the suggestion that articles developed as ambiguity-reducing noun markers when the language lost its check morphemes of inflection.

Another possible application to comparative linguistics is the introduction of numerical values to characterize certain properties of different languages. It has already been described how the information density of a language (with respect to some reference language) can be measured (p. 131). To measure the noise resistance is more difficult, but one could perhaps increase the noise level of a channel until the messages in various languages become undecodable; a language with a very crowded signal space (such as English) would presumably be rendered ineffective earlier than one with a lower efficiency (such as German or Russian). It is noteworthy in this connection that the US telephone network uses a bandwidth of 4 kHz per telephone channel, whereas in Germany 3.5 kHz (which results in more distortion) is considered sufficient. Whether this figure was chosen after intelligibility tests, or whether no such reasons were involved is not easily investigated; certainly there were other reasons involved in some cases, e.g., Russia and many countries in Central Europe were under strong German technological influence when the decision was made, and these countries would hardly let linguistic considerations outweigh the advantage of buying or copying reliably proven designs. (They did not do so in much simpler cases, e.g., the Russian Morse code is quite unsuited to Russian letter frequencies.) Nevertheless, some historical research might be justified on this point; but better still, some reasonably objective tests using modern methods might be used to measure the noise resistance of various languages, and the test noise would not have to be limited to the formal noise introduced by the distortion of a telephone channel.

Of course, a higher efficiency must automatically result in a lower noise resistance; on the other hand, it is possible to increase the redundancy of a code so ineptly that both its efficiency and noise resistance are lowered. A fair measure of the "quality" of a language from the point of view of transmitting information would therefore be the product of information density and noise resistance; both could be measured with respect to some reference language to evade the difficulties of absolute measurements. This parameter would presumably remain roughly constant if information density and noise resistance are traded "fairly," and a decrease would signify that one of them is sacrificed without fair compensation by the other.

A quantitative comparison of the complexity of the grammars of various languages also appears possible. The number of branches, i.e., the number of forks times the number of their individual branches, in a MORON-type program is indicative of the complexity of the grammar. The count would have to be made in programs based on representative samples of the grammar, although it would not be necessary to make the grammar complete, i.e., capable of producing all possible syntactic structures of the language. As a simple example (which does not, however, meet the requirement just stated), consider the simple program constructing two-word sentences of the type *They sing. He knows.* The flow chart of such a program is given in Fig. 6.2 on p. 221. A similar program in Danish would have no forks at all, since Danish has no special ending for the 3rd person singular in the present tense, and therefore it needs no check criterion or any of its implementations for this case; it would simply combine any pronoun with the infinitive of any verb. On the other hand, Latin would need a separate branch for each person, and each of these branches would again branch out for the check morphemes of the different conjugation types, which would more than offset the absence of pronouns.

This example of two-word sentences in the present tense was chosen only for its simplicity, and it would, of course, be quite insufficient to characterize the complexity of the entire grammar. For example, Danish has a simpler present tense conjugation than English, but its grammar is more complicated in other respects, e.g., its nouns have two genders which are not assigned on the basis of biological sex. Nevertheless, the principle of counting the total number of branches in more sophisticated MORON-type programs could be used to obtain a quantitative comparison of the complexity of the grammars of various languages.

7.2. Computer Science

The applications of the theory outlined in this book involve computer science only in association with computational linguistics, artificial intelligence, and machine translation, and these topics are discussed elsewhere (Chapter 6, Sec. 7.3 and Sec. 7.4, respectively).

There is, however, at least one application that does not come under any of these three headings, namely, economic programming of error diagnostics.

The storage capacity of a computer, i.e., the number of its memory locations, is necessarily limited, and part of that capacity is used up by the software. The software consists of programs that come with the computer, in particular, the compilers, housekeeping programs (for recording users and their processing times, for accounting, billing, etc.), and debugging programs for fault finding.

A compiler not only translates the source language, such as Snobol or Fortran, into machine language, but it also has a diagnostic routine which checks the submitted program for source language errors, and when it has worked through the entire program, the compiler will list the reasons why it could not understand certain lines (statements) of the program, e.g.,

LINE	ERROR
47	RIGHT PARENTHESIS MISSING
92	ILLEGAL MIXING OF MODES
117	VARIABLE PRD2 NOT DEFINED
192	TRANSFER TO NON-EXISTENT STATEMENT
212	LOG IS NOT A FORTRAN FUNCTION
279	LOOP ENDED BY NON-EXECUTABLE STATEMENT
309	FORMAT STATEMENT MISSING

The listing of errors, or "diagnostics," uses up further storage space. Detailed diagnostics can require several hundreds of such messages. Although, like newspaper headlines, they often omit check morphemes like *the, is, this is, are,* etc. in order to economize on storage space, the diagnostics are stored as sentences *en bloc*, and therefore they waste considerable storage capacity that could be made available to the user of the computer. In minicomputers, where the compiler often uses up a significant fraction of the total storage capacity, the diagnostics are sometimes kept short by listing only a number, e.g., ERROR 45; the user then looks up a table of errors, where under 45 he will find, for example, "Same number used for two statements."

However, a much simpler and far more effective way to save on the storage needed for the diagnostics is to make the computer construct the message rather than to select it from the memory where it is stored *en bloc*. The computer then stores only the required words in a lexicon and constructs the sentences in a natural language by the method described in Sec. 6.10, in particular, on. pp. 262 and 266-267. Although the sentence-constructing subroutine needs additional storage space, the storage of many sentences *en bloc* is reduced to the storage of a comparatively small lexicon of words, since many words, such as *statement, variable, missing, by, to, not,* as well as verbs and nouns with different

endings keep recurring in the diagnostics. The diagnostics, in turn, use
only very few syntactic structures differing by more than omitted parts
of speech. This may result in a substantial net saving of storage capacity.

Professor F. Huber of the University of Colorado Electrical Engineering Department has investigated this point by processing concordances
of the diagnostics and by other means; he found that the method will result in substantial savings of storage space when the number of diagnostics is large. As this book goes to press, he is about to finish writing
a routine that will construct some 400 diagnostic statements (400 are
needed, but the routine could, of course, produce thousands more). This
sentence-constructing subroutine is steered by the diagnostic routine of
a Fortran compiler on the same principle as the subroutine ENG in Sec.
6.10 produced sentences like *She is very heavy for a woman* when controled by the main program which compares the weight of someone's wife
to the average weight of the American adult woman. The commands of the
compiler simply switch in the required fork branches, and the check morphemes are added automatically by the designated branch.

When this program is finished, Prof. Huber intends to write similar
programs that will construct the diagnostics in either English or German
(or both) when steered by *the same commands* of the diagnostic routine
of the compiler. Where the two languages have the same criterions for
choosing the branches of a fork, such as plurals or third persons of verbs,
this presents no difficulty, since the corresponding fork will simply have
the same name in the two sentence-constructing subroutines, and they
will implement the corresponding check morphemes in English and German, respectively, when called by the steering program. But there are
also check criterions in one language which are absent from the other.
For example, German has no continuous tenses, and English has no rules
of gender concord (as far as computer diagnostics are concerned, English has no gender at all — everything is neuter). Thus, in the two sentences

RIGHT PARENTHESIS IS MISSING
RECHTE KLAMMER FEHLT

there is no correspondence in English to the German check morpheme *-e*
of *rechte*, which implements the gender concord with the feminine noun
Klammer, and there is no correspondence in German to the English continuous tense (there is no such tense as "ist fehlend" in German).

However, this is easily overcome by introducing "dummy forks" at
the points where a check criterion is absent from one language, corresponding to a "real" fork in the subroutine of the language that has such
a criterion. A dummy fork, for the moment, is one whose branches all

lead to the same point. Where English asks the test question "Right now or in general?" and implements it by the continuous or general tense, respectively, German has no such check criterion; it would therefore have a dummy fork switching in the general (the only) German tense regardless of the value signaled by the steering program. In practice, there would not even be any need for a "dummy fork;" the German subroutine would simply ignore all instructions concerning a continuous tense. Similarly, the fork in the German subroutine implementing the gender concord morpheme in *rechte* would be controlled (most easily) by a gender code with which *Klammer* is stored in the German lexicon; there would be no such code in the English lexicon. Or, if the gender fork were set by the steering program, rather than automatically by the subroutine itself, the command setting this fork would be ignored by the English subroutine. "Dummy forks" would therefore occur only in the arguments of subroutines; the subroutine would ignore them, whereas the subroutine in the other language(s) would use the corresponding argument to set a genuine fork.

Such subroutines producing the diagnostics (and perhaps the output of other parts of the software) in any desired natural language are probably more than mere curiosities. Economy of storage is, of course, achieved by a single sentence constructing subroutine, whether in English or in another language. However, the English diagnostics of an American or British made computer present a bigger problem to foreign users than the English expressions used in many other fields such as aviation, radio amateur traffic or sports. There is, for example, not a Czech boy over ten who does not know the words *foul, goal, out, center half, power play* or *body check*; but he can use them without understanding their general meaning, in fact, most Czech sports commentators do not seem to realize that *body check* are two words, since they inflect it as though *check* were the Czech diminuitive suffix *-ček*, diminishing the (non-existent) noun *bodyk*. (That is, *body check* is treated as if it meant *a little bodyk*, where no one has the faintest idea what a big bodyk, or any bodyk, might be.) Similarly, radio amateurs communicate in a code derived from English (RX = receiver, TX = transmitter, OM = old man, BF = bloody fool), and they often do so with little or no knowledge of English.*

But computer diagnostics are not that simple. They are not standardized, and to understand 400 different sentences of the type FILE CAN-

---

* I was once asked to interpret between an American and a Czech who knew practically no English, but as soon as they found out that they were both radio amateurs, they had no further need of me; they communicated by *dah-dit-dah-dah-dit*-ing at each other.

NOT BE ACCESSED (with dictionaries giving all the wrong meanings of *file* and *access*) the user must either know English fairly well or forego at least some of the advantages of error diagnostics. Error diagnostics in the language of the country are therfore not a luxury.

Foreign language subroutines for error diagnostics conserve the saving of storage space achieved by constructing rather than selecting the required messages. But they also have other advantages. They can not only be written in any desired language, but it is also open to the programmer to express tne diagnostic in any way he finds convenient; the diagnostic does not have to be a literal translation of the original message. Moreover, once such a program has been written for some natural language, it need not be controled only by the diagnostic routine of the compiler; it is available (possibly after enlarging the lexicon and the syntax) to any other steering program for expressing its output in that natural language.

7.3. Artificial Intelligence

The vast majority of computers now in use are being programmed to perform mechanistic chores, using only their speed, memory and reliability as an advantage over an army of mindless, but obedient slaves who could do the same thing at greater expense, in a longer time, less reliably, and requiring more space. The program giving orders what to do is still written by an intelligent human being.

But this is not going to remain so for very long. A better way to organize such an army is to put a hierarchy of intelligent officers in command. At each level they decide how best to accomplish a task assigned by their superiors, subdivide it into partial tasks to be accomplished by their subordinates, and order them to accomplish it. The general at the top of the hierarchy may still be a human being, but the job of the other officers can be performed by "intelligent" programs, and it can be performed much better than the commander could ever hope to do it; the entire organization will far outstrip the commander not only in speed, memory and reliability, but also in intelligence.

For intelligence, as defined by most dictionaries, is the capability of adapting one's actions to unforeseen circumstances. This capability is either acquired by learning from experience, or achieved by logical inference, and programs can be written to do both. They can therefore adapt to unforeseen circumstances, and they are thus intelligent; they are, in fact, quite often more intelligent than the man who wrote them.

This may seem like a paradox, but there is really nothing surprising about such a statement. Man has designed machines that surpass him in speed, force, nimbleness, and many other properties; intelligence is just another such property. The reader might object that this argument is flawed, since man used his intelligence for designing machines with these properties; but to use his intelligence for machines with higher intelligence might be something like pulling oneself up by one's own bootstraps. Not so. The bootstrap stunt is impossible because the center of gravity of a system cannot be changed by internal forces (a consequence of the constant moment theorem, which follows from Newton's Second Law of Motion). But there is no natural law forbidding the self-regeneration of intelligence.

There is, however, no need to become entangled in philosophical arguments, for the fact is that a wide variety of intelligent programs has already been written. There are programs to play checkers and other games, programs to prove mathematical theorems, programs to balance assembly lines, programs to write programs, programs to teach other programs, programs to stop mobile automatons from bumping into walls or falling downstairs and to make them find an electrical outlet to charge their batteries when they are "hungry," and many others. These are not mechanistic programs like MORON, which produces only grammatical gibberish by slavishly following the rules of English grammar. They can learn from experience, and they make sophisticated decisions. To give an example, Dr Arthur Samuel, of IBM, has been perfecting a program to play checkers since 1947. The program makes its own decisions by evaluating its overall position in the game. It also learns from champions' games, and from experience by playing against other computers. It is an excellent checker player which beat many outstanding human checker players; most important, however, it beats its own programmer.*

It is generally agreed that artificial intelligence may reach a level comparable to natural intelligence within the next one or two decades. And Language is just as closely intertwined with artificial intelligence as it is with natural intelligence and thinking. In a sense, computer languages and compilers with their diagnostic routines are forerunners of "intelligent" programs, although there is very little intelligence associated with them. A compiler, in the analogy of officers commanding subordinates according to commands received from their superiors, is just such an officer. To make a computer print the number stored at a memory location called X is a complicated operation involving several commands in machine language and a series of electrical signals to the line printer. In Basic, the command given by the superior (the programmer) is

* See, e.g., J.R. Slagle, *Artificial Intelligence*, McGraw-Hill, New York, 1971. However, Artificial Intelligence is now developing very rapidly, and the interested reader should follow the latest literature as it is published.

PRINT X; the compiler, or intermediate officer in command, will then issue the required instructions. This involves little intelligence, because there are few "unforeseen" circumstances. If, for example, the programmer misprinted his instruction as PRIND X, the compiler would cause the computer to print ILLEGAL STATEMENT (or in some time-sharing systems, WHAT?). However, it would be possible to write a compiler which interprets all words differing by only one letter from PRINT as PRINT, and to print the message I ASSUME YOU MEAN "PRINT;" IF NOT, STOP ME.

There are, of course, never any truly unforeseen circumstances to which intelligence adapts; they are unforeseen as special cases, but they are foreseen within a class of circumstances defined by a general rule. Thus, a "slavish" compiler would have to be told all the 125 acceptable misprints of the word PRINT to produce the above reaction, whereas an "intelligent" compiler would be programmed to decide for itself whether the word differed by more than one letter from a legal instruction and was therefore acceptable. The presence or absence of intelligence is therefore a difference in quantitative degree, not a difference in a sharply defined qualitative criterion. The fact that a compiler, in its current form, refuses to accept illegal statements and signals this to the operator, is itself a feature of intelligence, if only a very primitive one.

The relation of *natural* Language to artificial intelligence is twofold: the use of Language for instructing a computer, and the use of Language as a computer output. Although both functions can be described by the common concept "communicating with a computer," they are, in fact, very different, since the former involves computerized analysis, and the latter computerized synthesis, of a natural language.

It is quite evidently much easier to synthesize language than to analyze it, at least when this is done by computer. (When done by humans, it seems to be the other way round — traditional or analytical grammar preceded generative grammars by centuries, and many people, in particular, children, learn to understand a language before they can speak it properly.) The synthesis of meaningful sentences can be accomplished, for example, by appropriately switching the forks in a MORON-type program, as has been shown in Sec. 6.10, and discussed from another aspect in Sec. 7.2. The grammatical rules are already incorporated in such a program (running as a subprogram), and the problem of deciding how to switch the forks, that is, of knowing what to say, is essentially a problem of artificial intelligence rather than one of linguistics. In the sample program described in Sec. 6.10, for example, the program never made any linguistic decisions; it computed values such as the deviation of the weight of a man from the average weight of the adult American male, and if it found the deviation to be minus 50.2 pounds, it would switch the forks of the subroutine in such a way as to construct the sentence *He is very light for a man*. The main program could equally well produce its output in another code, for example, in Cherokee, or in the usual digital code used in computer print-outs, which would simply print the number −50.2 in the column labeled (say) "deviation." On the other hand, the same subroutine constructing English sentences can be called by various main programs, whether "stupid" or "intelligent," and it will always produce grammatical sentences; to what degree they are meaningful is entirely determined by the calling program (or human), not at all by the subroutine.

Analysis of a message coded in a natural language is incomparably more difficult. The ultimate reason for this is that natural languages are ambiguous codes; the same event may be coded by different messages (of the same language), and the same message may correspond to different events, as has often been noted in the preceding pages. It has also been noted that coding events in a natural language almost always means a loss of information. It is easy to "coarsen" a message when coding; it is far more difficult to restore the missing information in decoding a message, and quite often this is impossible. There is no way of establishing the exact weight of the subject of the message *He is very light for a man*.

Similarly, it is easy to separate the grammar and the meaning in synthesizing sentences; it has already shown how this can be done by a main program and a subroutine individually. But in analyzing a message, the two cannot be easily separated, as is evident from the sentences

    HE IS VERY LIGHT FOR A MAN
    HE IS VERY LIGHT FOR A START
    HE IS VERY LIGHT FOR A VERY GOOD REASON
    HE IS VERY LIGHT FOR ALL I KNOW
    HE IS VERY LIGHT FOR THE TIME BEING
    HE IS VERY LIGHT FOR SUCH SKIS
    HE IS VERY LIGHT FOR A MAN TO CARRY

in which *for* is always a preposition followed by a noun or a noun clause, not a conjunction as in *He is very light, for he eats little*. Obviously, such messages cannot be decoded by processing the grammar and the meaning separately, e.g., by first analyzing the syntactic structure, and then looking up the vocabulary in the hope of identifying the coded event; at least this is not possible in English, which relies heavily on semantic decoding owing to its flimsy system of check morphemes.

In these sentences, as in most others, grammar (the rules of the code) and meaning (the coded event) are closely intertwined for decoding. *Start, reason* or *the time being* have no weight, and this is information that the computer must store in order to decode the messages correctly. Skis do have weight, but they do not have masculine gender, and this again is knowledge that must be stored in the computer if it is to recognize that *He is very light for a man* and *He is very light for such skis* do not code the same type of event. Once again, "knowledge" boils down to the capability of assigning reasonable probabilities to certain events. This is easy enough when the number of events is limited; the real problem is how to organize this knowledge when the coded events are large in number and dissimilar in character.

Many systems for analyzing sentences in natural languages have been developed, but they either analyze only formally (by parsing, for example), or they use a limited vocabulary and a limited set of grammatical structures. Parsing (ascertaining the part of speech of the individual words of a sentence) is obviously useless by itself for decoding the above sentences, since they all have the same syntactic structure (for plus noun or noun clause).

Yet the problem is not hopeless (it cannot be, for the human brain solves it very quickly). In the above examples, the formal ambiguities are caused by the many functions of the preposition *for*. These ambiguities are resolved by semantic decoding, i.e., by examining the probabilities of the several events coded by an ambiguous message. In the above cases, this rules out all but one use of *for* in each message. In *He is very light for a man*, the *for* is of the type *for a member of his set*; in *He is very light for such skis*, the *for* is of the type *for the use of*; etc. A program can distinguish these meanings if its lexicon is semantically coded as in Sec. 6.9 (reference is made to the principle, not to the specific and very simple codes used there). For a structure such as

[subject] *is* [adjective] *for* [noun phrase]

the program can decide whether the *for* means *for a member of the subject's set* by checking whether the subject and the noun governed by *for* belong to a common set, and if so, whether the elements of this set have the property described by the adjective. The sentence *He is very light for a man* would pass this test, since *he* and *man* refer to elements of the set of male persons, and each element of this set has the property of weight (even the primitive semantic code described in Sec. 6.9 would do the job in this case). The sentence *He is very light for such skis* would not pass the test, since the gender discord between *he* and *skis* signals that the two do not belong to the same set; *He is very light for a good reason* would not pass the test because the elements of the (intersecting) set have no weight; etc.

A combination of grammatical and semantic codes in a lexicon to which the program is sent to look up words it has encountered can therefore be used to resolve ambiguities in identifying an event coded by the sentence. However, for reasons given in Sec. 6.9, semantic coding will eventually run into difficulties when the semantic ties become too distant. The above method for identifying the use of the preposition *for* would work for the sentence *He is very light for a man*, but not in all contexts. It would fail to identify the correct event in the sentence

> *He is only a little boy and he can be carried to a doctor; he is very light for a man.*

The usual method of semantic decoding, which consists of comparing the probabilities of the two events (whether the boy is a very light man, or whether he is very light for a man to carry), cannot be immediately used, since the events must first be identified before their probabilities can be compared.

The method of semantic coding as used (for a very small universe) in Sec. 6.9 can therefore be used only to some extent, but it will work in many cases, especially when combined with grammatical characteristics (such as the gender discord between *he* and *skis*). Eventually, however, learning routines will have to be used rather than active programming.

On the other hand, the error-detecting characteristics of natural languages, in particular, check morphemes, can be a powerful aid for identifying the syntactic structure of a sentence submitted to a computer. Moreover, the search for the syntactic structure can be simplified and speeded up by comparison with the rules of a choice-and-check grammar as used in MORON-type programs – provided the language has an abundance of check morphemes, and this, unfortunately, excludes English. The fact that it is possible to identify the structure of a sentence syntactically, without referring to a lexicon, is perhaps best illustrated by Lewis Carroll's nonsense poem

> *'Twas brillig and the slithy toves*
> *did gimble and gyre in the wabe*

where, given only the "anchor points" *'twas, and, the, in, did*, there is no difficulty in identifying *brillig* and *slithy* as adjectives, *toves, wabe* as nouns, and *gimble, gyre* as verbs. This identification can be made on the basis of the position of these nonsense words with respect to the genuine English words in the sentence. Unfortunately, this is so only because the syntax of the poem is very simple. In more complex syn-

tactic structures, this cannot be done, in English, without reference
to a lexicon; in fact, it may not be possible to recognize the syntactic
structure even then in English. Consider, for example, the following
syntactic labyrinth:

> *Bonham ordered a platter of six superburgers which when*
> *Grant declined he ate all of as they drank.*

(This has not been concocted by the author, but by James Jones,
who used it in *Go to the Widow-Maker* without commas, as above, and
preceded by the subordinate clause *When they first came in, ...*) The
syntax of this sentence could be identified only by a highly intelligent
program, and to identify the coded event, it would need not only semantic information, but also knowledge of probabilities of various events.
(How else would it know whether Grant was declining superburgers or
Latin nouns, or whether he declined from the peak of his glory?)

Yet in other languages, the check system will identify the syntactic
structure without looking up the words in a lexicon (except for "staple"
words like the article, relative pronouns, conjunctions, etc.). Even in
German, a weakly inflecting language, this is much easier than in English:

> *Bonham hatte eine Platte von Superburgern bestellt, die,*
> *wenn Grant ablehnte, er alle aufass während sie tranken.*

A heavily inflecting language, such as Latin, will identify the syntax, in particular, the ties between various words, even more clearly.
The English relative pronoun *which* excludes animate nouns, but leaves
open number, case, gender for the noun to which it refers, if, indeed, it
refers to a noun, and not to a clause. The German relative pronoun *die*
reduces these possibilities to a feminine noun in the nominative or accusative singular, or to any noun in the accusative or nominative plural.
The Latin relative pronoun *quos* reduces the possibilities to a masculine
noun in the accusative plural; if we coin the 20th century Latin word
superburgerus, the sentence becomes

> *Bonhamus imperavit patellam sex superburgerorum quos,*
> *cum Grantus eos recusavit, ille omnes edit dum bibebant.*

The more redundant the check system of the language, the easier it
becomes to analyze the sentence. In addition to the check criterions
posed by Latin in the above sentence, Czech would implement the word
drank with a check morpheme indicating that the subject is 3rd person
plural, masculine, animate; this pinpoints the drinkers as Bonham and
Grant, whereas in English, German and Latin, the drinking could have
been done, for all the poor computer knows, by the six superburgers.

At first sight this might seem like asking the computer to make a large number of complicated decisions based on many comparisons and inferences. However, the process can be simplified and automated by the following rule:

Every legal syntactic structure represents a single and continuous path through the flow chart of a choice and check program such as a (suitably expanded) MORON-type program. Each check morpheme identifies one or more branches of a fork, and therefore segments of possible paths. The segments forming one continuous path are sequential (contiguous) in the flow chart and identified by contiguous flags. If more than one path can be formed by segments with contiguous flags, the sentence is syntactically ambiguous.

This rule will be explained in more detail in connection with machine translation, where it finds an immediate application.

7.4. Machine Translation

Whatever successes have been achieved by machine translation (and they have not been earth-shaking), are, for the most part, based on word-for-word translation systems. The few translation machines now in operation (not in research or development) translate from Russian into English; the programs of these machines essentially look at each word and its morphological form in the Russian sentence, look up the word in a dictionary, and then translate the word and morphological form into its English equivalent. Naturally, the translations are not very smooth, and both the Russian original and the English translation must be edited by a human editor. The quality of such translations is usually described as poor to mediocre. On the other hand, considering the comparatively primitive method of word-by-word translation, the translations are surprisingly good.

Attempts have been made to computerize translation on a higher level, i.e., on the syntactic and semantic levels, but they have not resulted in translations substantially better than the word-by-word method.*
Many linguists and computer scientists involved in these projects have therefore become pessimistic about machine translation, and have indicated a need to discover more about the structure of Language in general before a new start on the problems of machine translation can be made.

The author has had no practical experience in machine translation, and this should be kept in mind when reading the following proposal. However, it appears plausible that the error-correcting code model of

---

* H. Borko (ed.), *Automated Language Processing*, Wiley, New York, 1967.
R. Gunzenhäuser, *Nicht-numerische Informationsverarbeitung*, Springer Verlag, Wien-New York, 1968.

Language might open up new possibilities for translating on the syntactical level. The proposal amounts to translating the syntax first, and substituting the specific words afterwards (except for certain "staple" words such as conjunctions, relative pronouns, etc., which must be recognized in the syntax translation stage). This idea is not new; but the method of its automatic implementation probably is.

The main program of this system would have two "aids;" an English MORON-type program, and a Russian MORON-type program. To keep them apart, we will call them John and Ivan, respectively. Both programs should contain all syntactic structures likely to be encountered in the text. John works as a subroutine for the main program, but Ivan is only a skeleton program consisting of flags and conditional transfers. It needs no lexicon or check implementations; it only identifies the syntax.

The main program, apart from recognizing "staple" words, would first look at the morphological forms of the Russian words, that is, at their endings containing the check morphemes, without considering their meaning. The check morphemes, when viewed "backwards" as identifiers of the check criterion which they implement, are highly ambiguous. For example, the ending -и can indicate the nominative plural of masculine or feminine nouns, or the genitive singular of a feminine or neuter noun, or the dative singular of a feminine or neuter noun, or the infinitive of a verb, or the past tense plural of a verb, etc. Analogous statements hold for other endings. (The situation in Latin is similar, if less complicated, e.g., the ending -ae may correspond to several cases of a noun or adjective.) These ambiguities are, of course, resolved by the syntactic structure of the sentence, but the combination of possibilities (including the inapplicable ones) leads to very large numbers, of which only one (as a rule) results in a grammatical sentence. A program based on searching through such vast numbers of possibilities until it finds a grammatical one would probably be prohibitively involved to write, and very slow in execution as well.

This is where the program Ivan comes in. Imagine that every time the main program finds a check morpheme, all the branches adding this morpheme in the flow chart of Ivan light up. Thus, many branches of Ivan would light up when the program finds the ending -и at the end of a word. However, after the program has thus examined every word of the Russian sentence, there will (as a rule) be only a single "lit" path on the flow chart of Ivan from the beginning to the end of the program, and this uniquely determines the syntactic structure of the sentence. (Branches will be "lit" not only by check morphemes, but also by the staple words such as conjunctions and prepositions.) The other "lit" branches would not form a continuous path through the program from beginning to end, but only partial paths corresponding (at best) to phrases that do not fit into the structure of the given sentence.

The "lighting" of the paths on the flow chart is, of course, only used here as a convenient form of explaining the system. A program based on this idea would not light anything; it would check which sequence of hoisted flags on the flow chart of Ivan corresponds to a grammatical structure, that is, which of the flags are sequential. (For an example, see p. 240: the flags W(10), W(13), W(14) are sequential; W(9), W(10), W(11) are not.) To keep Ivan down to a reasonable size, a number of simplifications could be introduced, for example, main clauses and subordinate clauses could be analyzed separately, thus essentially using the flow chart of Ivan twice over for one sentence, and therefore drastically simplifying it. But let us just keep to the basic ideas.

The main program would now "translate" the identified Russian syntactic structure into the equivalent English syntactic structure by switching the forks of the subroutine John at all points determining the syntax (not the vocabulary) in the same manner as explained in Secs. 6.10 and 7.2. This step is the translation on the syntactical level and should result in a smoother translation than the word-by-word method. Where the word-by-word method would produce *of the leg of the table* or *of the paw of my poor dog*, the syntactical method will produce *of the table leg* and *of my poor dog's paw* (by a rule to be discussed below). Moreover, John will, by its automated implementations, correctly produce an English word which is not listed in the dictionary opposite the Russian word occurring in the sentence, as we shall see in a moment.

After the syntax of the English sentence has thus been mapped by setting the forks of John, the actual words are looked up in a Russian-English dictionary. Since the part of speech and other grammatical characteristics are already known from the run through Ivan (actually, from Ivan's flags), the look-up would be much faster than the usual alphabetic look-up. For example, the word рвач ordinarily necessitates access to the dictionary determined by the four letters of this word plus the blank following it (to exclude words which merely start with these four letters). But if the program already knows, from Ivan's flags, that the unknown word is a masculine noun, it needs access only to the first two letters, for Russian has no other masculine noun starting with these two letters; this assumes that the dictionary is ordered first by grammatical characteristics, and then alphabetically within each group.

But more important than the access times, the program John will produce words that cannot be found in the dictionary by a word-by-word translation. If the dictionary were slavishly followed word by word, this would result in such ungrammatical English phrases as *to depend from*

something, to contradict to somebody, to be angry on somebody, etc.
The program John will insert its own prepositions in such cases (see
Secs. 6.6 and 6.7). The Russian preposition is needed only for identification of the syntax, and even if it should be needed for its meaning,
John will overrule it with its own preposition, since there is no fork
between *depend* and *on* (for example). Even when there is a fork between
verb and preposition (*to fight — against, over, about,* or transitive), the
choice in such a program is only among grammatical structures, for
John, being a MORON-type program, can produce only grammatical sentences; this is guaranteed by the conditional transfers and flags of the
program. It is incapable of producing sentences like *I of nothing did not
see* or *He stronger of us*, which are word for word translations of Russian sentences meaning *I did not see anything* and *He is stronger than
we are.*

The final step would be the resolution of ambiguities. Syntactic ambiguities are rather rare in Russian owing to its great redundancy in
check morphemes; in any case, Ivan will give a warning of a syntactic
ambiguity, because it corresponds to more than one path through the program (contiguous flags will connect into more than one continuous path).
Particular homonyms can be resolved by semantic coding, as discussed
for the homonym *face/person* on p. 261. A more frequent, and more formi-
dable, problem is the implementation of English check criterions that
Russian does not have, that is, the setting of forks in John which do
not correspond to any forks in Ivan. This includes such criterions as
"recently or long ago?" for implementation by perfect or past, "at the
time or in general?" for implementation by the continuous or general
tense, but above all, "definite or indefinite?" for implementation by the
definite or indefinite (or no) article. This, however, is a problem common to all translation systems, human translators not excluded. Human
translators solve it by semantic decoding, i.e., by examining the event
coded by the sentence, and perhaps programs to do the same will eventually be written, but this is not directly relevant to the issue of syntactic translation now under discussion.

Let us now consider an example, the Russian sentence

Языковые ассоциации и количественные оценки системы
речи могут быть существенно различными для говорящего
и слушающего.

(If you do not understand Russian, so much the better; neither does
a computer.)

The program will look at the ending of the first word, which is -ые.
This is the ending of an adjective in the nominative or accusative plu-

ral for any of the three genders; therefore, six branches of the flow chart of Ivan will "light up," one for each gender in the nominative plural and accusative plural branches. Only one of these will eventually be found applicable, since the others will not "connect" into a continuous path.

The next word ends in -ии, the ending of a noun in the genitive singular, dative singular, nominative plural, or accusative plural if the noun is feminine and ends (in the nominative) in -ия; or the genitive singular or dative singular or prepositional singular of a neuter noun ending in -ие. If this had been the first word of the sentence, all these branches of Ivan would have lit up. However, the adjective that preceded this word has a gender concord flag which forbids all cases that would lead to adjective-noun gender discord; hence only two of these branches will light up, the nominative and accusative plural. These will connect to two of the previously lit branches; the other branches of the adjective that were lit after looking at the first word (adjective 1) lead nowhere.

The next word is a "staple" word, и (one of the basic words recognized by the program). This is recognized as the English word *and*.

The next two words are again adjective and noun, and as before, the only paths that will connect are the nominative and accusative plural branches.

The next two words have noun endings; these endings are again ambiguous, but the only case that will connect a path is the genitive singular for both.

We now have only two paths leading continuously from the beginning of Ivan to this point of the sentence, and one of the two paths is now "killed" by the next word, могут, which has the ending of a verb in the third person plural, present tense. The third person plural resolves the ambiguity of nominative or accusative plural: Only the nominative branches will connect to this verb. (Because of the flexible word order in Russian, it is possible to put the object in front of the verb; however, in that case the "staple" word *they* or another subject would have appeared before the verb.)

In the remainder of the sentence, this single path may branch out again into several paths, but all but one of these will again be "killed" by some check implementation which does not provide a contiguous flag.

Since the main program needs Ivan only to find a series of contiguous flags forming a continuous path through the flow chart, it is obvious that Ivan is only a skeleton program: It consists only of forks, flags and conditional transfers (the staple words are represented by flags, too). It has no lexicon, and it poses check criterions, but does not implement them. Its output is a string of contiguous flags, representing the syntactic structure of the Russian sentence. When the program has thus determined the syntactic structure of the entire Russian sentence, it will "translate" it into the equivalent English syntactic structure by throwing the forks in the subroutine John, leaving only the actual words optional. This necessitates a Russian-English "syntactic dictionary" indicating such equivalences, and it is here that the cramped style of word-by-word translations would — one hopes — disappear. Many transformations, some of which will be discussed below, can simply be incorporated in the syntactic dictionary at this point; in particular, the word order can be changed, for example, the direct object, which often appears in Russian *before* the verb, can be "moved" behind the English verb. No actual moving is, of course, involved; the two structures simply correspond to each other in the syntactic dictionary. (This would be particularly important for German-English machine translation, since German word order differs more strongly from English word order than Russian word order does; there are no inversion rules and no separable verb prefixes in Russian.)

In the present case, the syntactic structure of the Russian sentence as revealed by the program Ivan is

Adjective 1 + noun 1 + AND + adjective 2 + noun 2 + noun 3 (gen. sing.) + noun 4 (gen. sing.) + verb + BE + adverb + adjective 3 (complement of BE) + preposition + adjective 4 (pres. participle) + AND + adjective 5 (pres. part.) + [missing noun to be restored].

The last word corresponds to a lit branch which bypasses a noun, i.e., a noun whose insertion is optional, because it can be restored. This would occur in English rather rarely in cases like *the accused* or *the affluent*, but is very frequent in French, German, Latin and Russian, as discussed in more detail in Sec. 5.5.

The syntactic dictionary would not have to contain all possible structures of both languages; in the great majority of cases, a fork in Ivan would correspond to a fork in John, and the switching of one would cause the switching of the other; the syntactic dictionary would therefore really be a dictionary of exceptions to this rule. We will consider such exceptions or special tricks for the above structure in a moment; however, if we merely switch corresponding forks, the above Russian structure is also an acceptable English structure: If we arbitrarily insert words into the program John with its syntactic forks determined by this structure, it might produce an English sentence like this:

The white crows and the green chimpanzees of the zoo of Rawalpindi want to be extremely attractive for the arriving and departing [visitor].

The articles and other English check morphemes are supplied by
John in the same way as by Moron; the above articles, including the absence of an article before *Rawalpindi*, would result from leaving the
"definite-indefinite" fork permanently in the "definite" position.

The above sentence is only an example showing the syntactic structure of the sentence. The actual translation differs merely in the words
to be substituted in that structure. These words are now looked up by the
program in the Russian-English dictionary. The program now knows more
than the parts of speech; it also knows genders, cases, etc., which will
not only speed the dictionary look-up as discussed before, but may also
be helpful in resolving possible ambiguities. In this case the dictionary
look-up will result in the translation

> THE/0 LINGUISTIC ASSOCIATIONS AND THE/0 QUANTITATIVE
> ESTIMATES OF THE/A SYSTEM OF THE/A LANGUAGE/SPEECH
> CAN/MAY BE SUBSTANTIALLY DIFFERENT FOR THE/A SPEAK-
> ING AND THE/A HEARING [PERSON].

The 0 denotes absence of an article; the noun *person* could be restored from the semantic codes given with *to speak* and *to hear* (but,
as we shall see in a moment, this noun is not needed).

There are two types of ambiguities to be resolved: the Russian homonyms resulting in the English *language/speech* and *can/may*, and the
English check criterion definite-indefinite with its article implementations, which Russian does not have. The two meanings of the above
homonyms are very similar, and they are therefore both difficult to resolve and not extremely critical. Strictly speaking these words are not
genuine homonyms of the type *lock/castle* or *calf(animal)/calf (part of
leg)*, but merely Russian words with inexact English equivalents, a point
to which we shall return presently. Since this is a problem which is not
peculiar to *syntactic* translation, let us dispose of it quickly: We choose
language instead of *speech* (at random, for example), and *may* instead of
can (with the justification that if ability or know-how were involved rather than eventuality, and the distinction were important, then the Russian author would have chosen another verb, уметь). The choice of
definite-indefinite for the article implementation is very difficult; it can
occasionally present problems even to a human translator, and a sophisticated program would be needed to make the decision. However, we can
make a sweeping decision governed by expedience rather than semantics:
The definite article is (statistically) much more frequent than the indefinite article, so that if we leave John's fork "definite-indefinite" permanently in the "definite" position, the choice will be more often right than
wrong, and it will never be ungrammatical (John will not allow *the Rawal-*

pindi, if *Rawalpindi* is coded as a proper name, see Sec. 6.7). Also, the definite fork is easier to program, since the definite article has only one form, whereas the indefinite article has three (*a* or *an* in the singular, absent in the plural).

When the ambiguities are thus (or otherwise) resolved, the translation becomes

> THE LINGUISTIC ASSOCIATIONS AND THE QUANTITATIVE ESTIMATES OF THE SYSTEM OF THE LANGUAGE MAY BE SUBSTANTIALLY DIFFERENT FOR THE SPEAKING AND THE HEARING [PERSON].

This is, of course, no better than a word-by-word translation; nor can it be, for switching Ivan's and John's forks in unison must ultimately result in what is essentially a word-by-word translation (the only difference is that John guarantees a grammatical English result).

However, we can now examine some rules that can be incorporated in the "syntactic dictionary," the program that determines the equivalent setting of Ivan's and John's forks when this differs from a one-to-one correspondence. The phrase *of the system of the language* is an unusual one in English, which mostly uses adjectivals where Russian has two successive genitives. The occurrence of such structures is sufficiently frequent to justify a rule. This rule is the following:

Whenever Ivan's flags indicate the structure

> NOUN 1 (genitive) + NOUN 2 (genitive),

set John's forks to produce the following structure:

(a) if Noun 2 is inanimate, make it an adjectival attributed to Noun 1;

(b) if Noun 2 is animate, proceed as in (a), but make the adjectival a Saxon genitive.

The rule can also be generalized by

(c) use rule (b) also for animate nouns qualified by an adjective, possessive adjective, ordinal numeral, or any of these.

The rule accomplishes the following:

Word by word	Syntactic
of the system of the language	*of the language system*
of the leg of the table	*of the table leg*
of the hat of the driver	*of the driver's hat*
of the paw of my small dog	*of my small dog's paw*
of the wish of the third old man	*of the third old man's wish*
of the chemistry of the professor	*of the professor's chemistry*
of the professor of the chemistry	*of the chemistry professor*

The rule results not only in a smoother translation, but also in one less article dilemma (*professor of the chemistry* is a grammatical possibility, but hardly a very likely one). Even if it should backfire on occasions, it appears to be useful (I have not been able to think up such a counterexample, which does not mean there is none). But most important, the rule is a syntactic one, which requires no transformations of an English sentence; it is simply entered into the "semantic dictionary" by easily programmed statements, and the sentence containing *of the system of the language* is never produced or even processed.

Second, the Russian structure consisting of a present participle followed by a missing noun (a noun to be restored) is also sufficiently frequent to justify a rule:

If a present participle is followed by a missing noun to be restored (indicated by a flag bypassing an optional noun in Ivan), add *-er* instead of *-ing* to the corresponding English verb; look up the result among English nouns; if it is there, use it.

This rule may be morphological rather than syntactical, but that is only a question of nomenclature; it can be programmed in the syntactical dictionary just as if it were purely syntactical, for all it does is to set John's forks accordingly.

This rule will replace *hearing person* and *speaking person* by *hearer* and *speaker*; it will not, however, produce the words *arriver* and *departer* in the sentence about the Rawalpindi zoo on p. 288. (That sentence, incidentally, would be improved by the other syntactic rule: *of the zoo of Rawalpindi* would be replaced by *of the Rawalpindi zoo*.)

If, then, the above two rules were incorporated in the syntactic dictionary, none of the preceding translations would be produced or even processed; the program would directly produce the following translation:

THE LINGUISTIC ASSOCIATIONS AND THE QUANTITATIVE ESTI-
MATES OF THE LANGUAGE SYSTEM MAY BE SUBSTANTIALLY
DIFFERENT FOR THE SPEAKER AND THE HEARER.

The above two rules were given as examples in connection with the unsatisfactory phrases *of the system of the language* and *speaking and hearing* [*person*]. But evidently such rules can be thought up by the dozen, and more important, they can be programmed by simple statements in the syntactic dictionary without disturbing the other parts of the program (such as Ivan, John, the search routine and the look-up routine); the system could therefore be syntactically improved in operation with a minimum down time.

It is believed that such a translation system on the syntactic level would be superior to one that translates word by word and patches up

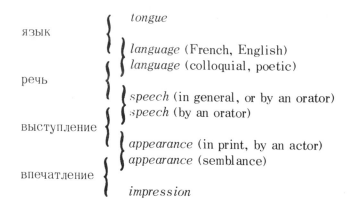

Fig. 7.1. "Staggered" correspondences between
Russian and English nouns.

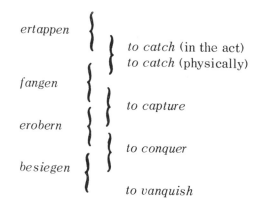

Fig. 7.2. "Staggered" correspondences between
German and English verbs.

the unsatisfactory English translation afterwards. However, there remain the numerous and enormous problems that are not problems of syntax, but of vocabulary. For example, the prepositions of one language rarely correspond uniquely to those of another. When the preposition is a check morpheme determined by grammatical rules (such as *on* in *depend on*), the change is easily accomplished, as we have seen. But when the preposition is optional, this can lead to great difficulties. The Russian preposition *y* is similar to the German *bei* and the French *chez*, but has no exact equivalent in English, where it may be *at, near, with, for*, and sometimes it requires idiomatic translations (у нас = *chez nous* = *bei uns* = *in our country, among our people, in America, where I come from, back home,* etc.).

Similar difficulties are met with nouns, adjectives and verbs. In the above sample sentence we met a Russian word which looked like a honym, *language/speech*. In reality, this is merely a typical case where a Russian noun does not cover the same range of concepts as its English colleagues; the words in a Russian-English dictionary generally do not, as it were, stand opposite each other in a one-to-one correspondence, but they are staggered as shown in the chain in Fig. 7.1, which includes *language/speech* as part of this chain of nouns. The same is true of other parts of speech and other languages, as shown in Fig. 7.2 for the correspondence, or failure of a unique correspondence, between German and English verbs. These chains are symbolic, for in reality, a word in one language may be translated, in different contexts, by many words of another language, not just two as indicated in Figs. 7.1 and 7.2.

No suggestion is offered here what to do about this ugly problem. The structure of Language as an error-detecting code is a syntactical feature; it can also be applied to questions of morphology, but hardly to the semantics of vocabulary.

Nevertheless, there seems little doubt that Moron-type programs can be used to achieve syntactic translation by searching for a continuous path through the flow chart in the source language and accordingly switching the forks of the Moron-type program in the object language. To what an extent this represents an improvement over word-for-word translations is difficult to predict without experimental evidence.

7.5. Psycholinguistics

The close relation between thinking and Language has long been recognized, if little understood, by both linguists and psychologists. If we knew how the brain constructs sentences, it would be far easier to write linguistic programs by copying its procedures. But the processing of information by the brain, whether linguistic or other information, is one of the frontiers of science. We do not even yet know how the brain recognizes patterns — how, for example, it recognizes a square as a square regardless of its size or orientation. Machines have been built to recognize typewritten ZIP codes, but they cannot recognize squares; and the machines that can recognize squares cannot read ZIP codes.

Knowledge of linguistic processing in the human brain is evidently even less advanced than the knowledge concerning pattern recognition. As yet, research is limited to very indirect tests and a mass of contro-

versial circumstantial evidence. Moreover, this evidence is very prone
to misinterpretation. For example, a recent work on psycholinguistics
points out that in spite of the long and tedious hours spent by children
in rote practice of arithmetic operations, an adult who can multiply a
pair of three-digit numbers is rare; yet adults can easily produce complicated strings of sentences with subtle and intricate interrelations.
This is no doubt true; yet the conclusion that human thinking is better
adapted to language than to arithmetic operations is not justified on
that basis, regardless of whether it is true or not. People are in constant contact with Language throughout their lives; they get nowhere
near as much practice with numbers (or they would not have to learn
arithmetic operations by rote). On the other hand, the card player who
remembers which of 52 cards in a deck are no longer held by his part-
ners, and repeats this feat in game after game, is taxing his memory
with an unsystematic set of objects to a far greater extent than if he
were multiplying two three-digit numbers. Perhaps the most convincing
illustration that this type of storage is merely a matter of practice is
the ease with which all Russians manage to remember three names for
every person (*Ivan Sergeyevich Kovalov*), of which they use the first
two on occasions which roughly correspond to those when one precedes
the surname by *Mr.* in English. This is a feat which most non-Russians
find almost impossible, yet Russians perform it with the greatest ease,
because they have had plenty of practice since childhood. Thus, whilst
it may be quite true that the human brain can more easily memorize items
interrelated by a consistent system than items stored "one by one," the
fact that people are better speakers than arithmeticians lends no support
to such a conclusion.

No one knows precisely how the brain constructs grammatical sentences. The fact that these sentences can be regarded as messages of
an error-detecting code does not necessarily mean that the brain constructs them on that basis. Yet there is some evidence, though it is admittedly flimsy, that in some cases, especially for complex sentences
that the speaker has never used before, the brain may use a method rest-
ing on such a basis. This is not at all to say that the mechanism is the
same as, or even reminiscent of, that used in the computer programs
based on error-detecting codes, for these programs lack (as yet) a feature that is obviously very significant in the brain – learning. Also,
simple sentences like *Let's go home* are very likely learned, stored and
used *en bloc*, without any construction from individual words. Others,
such as *let's go away, let's go to the game*, may be formed by analogy
and substitution, again not involving much original, "creative" construction. Yet it is hard to believe that long, complex sentences could be con-

structed in this way. In more complex structures, the mechanism of choosing the information morpheme strings and supplementing them by check morphemes (which is also the ultimate basis of the computer programs discussed in Chapter 6) might possibly play a part. It does seem that the brain often handles strings of information morphemes (words and roots of words) in a different way than check morphemes. This suggestion is based on three features that may be observed in the speech of those who are learning a language and have not yet learned it, that is, in the speech of children and foreigners:

1) They learn (strings of) information morphemes much more quickly than the rules for inserting the check morphemes,

2) on beginning to learn these rules, they assume a simplicity and consistency of the check system which it does not, in fact, have,

3) having mastered the check system in one language, they will incorrectly apply it to the information system of another. (The first two features are common to children and foreigners, the third applies to foreigners only.)

When a child begins to talk, it will produce ungrammatical sentences consisting of non-redundant information morphemes, with the check morphemes omitted, e.g., *Annie want milk, that my coat, see tractor, Daddy bring me ball* (or *Daddy bring ball* or *Daddy ball*). There have been many investigations of children's speech,* and they all confirm this fact.

A foreigner just beginning to learn a language and forced to speak in it will produce sentences of this kind also.

From ungrammatical sentences lacking check morphemes it is but a small step to ungrammatical sentences using the wrong check morphemes. Thus, children and foreigners will produce such sentences as *I eated* or *She teached*. True, a child will say *I went* rather than *I goed*, and *I came* rather than *I comed*, but this, as pointed out by Deese,** is merely a consequence of the high frequency of the words *go, come*, giving the child frequent occasion to hear the correct forms. In irregular verbs of smaller frequency, such as *abide, weave, slide*, the wrong past tense is sometimes used even by native adults, and in many cases (*dream, learn*) the regular form is now considered grammatical.

There are other cases of using a wrong check morpheme (*fishes, aircrafts*), but in English this is not particular evident, because English does not have as many check morphemes as other languages, as we have often seen before. In the Slavic languages, such mistakes are much more common. The past tense of verbs exhibits gender concord, so that *I was*

*E.g., G.A. Miller and F. Smith (eds.), *The Genesis of Language*, MIT Press, Cambridge, Mass., 1966; T.R. Dixon, D.L. Horton (eds.), *Verbal Behavior and General Behavior,* Prentice-Hall, Englewood Cliffs, NJ, 1968.
**J. Deese, *Psycholinguistics*, Allyn & Bacon, Boston, 1970.

shows whether the speaker is a man or a woman. It is quite common for little Czech and Russian boys, if they learn the language from their mothers and sisters, to speak as if they were women; this does not happen when the boy has plenty of male company, or ceases as soon as he has it. The difference between the possessive adjective meaning "belonging to the subject of the sentence" and the possessive adjectives of the English type causes the sentences *I took my ball* and *He took my ball* to have a different possessive adjective in each case. This is not learned by Slavic children until they are well into school age, and some adults never learn to use the possessive adjectives correctly. Presumably Roman children had similar difficulties with *suus* and *eius*, although this difference occurs only in the third person. Yet the possessive adjectives, in particular, the word *my*, are among the first words a child learns to use.*

But the above examples (many more could be given) are only a transition between the first and second features mentioned above. The use of wrong check morphemes due to the false assumption that the check system is simple and consistent occurs in much more sophisticated structures which a child begins to use only much later; foreigners, of course, make such mistaken assumptions soon after they have begun to learn the language. For example, the negation of a property described by an adjective is often accomplished, in English, by prefixes such as *un-* or *in-*, but this is a mere tendency; the false assumption that it is a consistent rule will make children and foreigners ask for the meaning of *couth* and *ruly* in the mistaken belief that they are opposites of *uncouth* and *unruly*. Analogous inconsistencies of seemingly opposite adjectives also occur in other languages. The German *unwirsch* and the Czech *nevrlý* both mean *brusque* or *ill-tempered*. One would therefore suppose that *wirsch* and *vrlý* mean *amiable, mild, well-tempered*, but they do not; there is no such word in either language.

In the mistaken belief that the word *not* will negate an English verb, students of English will produce such sentences as

> *You can come if you want to, but you must not come if you do not want to,*

---

*A side remark, which has little to do with the point under discussion: The words *my*, *mine* are among the first grasped and used by a child, coming shortly after *mummy*, and this is one of many indications that property rights appear to be biologically inherent, untaught and natural; the word *my* is one of the human analogies of a dog urinating on landmarks to stake out "his" territory. Socialism and other collectivisms run counter to this trait of human nature. Historical experience has shown that collectivisms and statisms of all kinds are not motivated by the desire to abolish property rights, but on the contrary, by a lust for power that merely seeks to transfer them.

where *must not* is intended to mean *need not*. The negation rule would have worked with the verb *to have to*, and it works in any language in which *must* is not subject to inconsistent peculiarities (e.g., *Sie können kommen, wenn Sie wollen, aber sie müssen nicht kommen, wenn Sie nicht wollen*). But in English, a *not* following *must* does not deny the *must* (as it denies *can, may, ought, will, should*, etc.); it denies the subsequent verb, and the whole structure indicates the compulsion *(must)* of *not* doing something, which results in a prohibition. This is a very peculiar inconsistency, and a major stumbling block for students of English: *I have to go* means the same as *I must go*, yet *I do not have to go* does not mean the same as *I must not go*. The stumbling block is again the mistaken assumption that negation is accomplished on the same basis for all verbs (even if the formal implementation differs for auxiliary and other verbs). Nor is this the only difficulty of *must*. *He had to go* is not the same thing as *He must have gone*, at least not in British English, where the first denotes compulsion and the second the result of an inference. In American English, the two are becoming interchangeable, and many British viewers of the first transmission of men on the moon *must have been* startled by the first sentence of President Nixon's telephone call to the astronauts: "This *has to be* the most historic telephone call ever made by an American president."

Nor is English the only language to use negatives and opposites inconsistently. In the Slavic languages, two negatives do not necessarily cancel each other, and often double negatives (equivalent to a single negative in English) are obligatory. The English *I will not ever want anything from anybody anywhere* is rendered in the Slavic languages as "I will not never want nothing from nobody nowhere." The point is not whether such a use of multiple negatives is logical, but rather whether it is consistent. It is not, for in other cases two negatives can cancel each other. The Russian structure *cannot* + *not* + verb has two negatives which cancel each other; the phrase "We cannot not conclude" (Мы не можем не заключать) means *We cannot but conclude* or *We are forced to conclude*.

The use of prepositions is another feature where English is very inconsistent. If something is dependent *on*, why should it be independent *of*? Similarly, *on* and *off* are known to be opposites, and this will lead the student of English to believe that if shoes are put on, they should also be put off; and if they are taken off, they should also be taken on.

The same mistaken assumption that the system of a language is consistent leads both children and foreigners to the invention of words that the language "should" have, such as *onliness, allbody, eachbody, unhungry, uncle-in-law, to bejoy*, etc. The same is true in other languages,

for example, those that have diminuitives often include some that are
not derived from the "big" concept; the Czech word *hlouček* means a
small gathering of people, and judging from the diminuitive ending *ček*
and the analogy with other words, a Czech child will sometimes conclude that a large crowd is *hlouk* or *hluk*, but the former does not exist,
and the latter has a totally different meaning. In the case of foreigners,
the invention of words may be merely an attempt at a translation, e.g.,
unhungry may be a translation of the German word *satt*, which has no
exact equivalent in English. But in the case of children inventing words
in their native language, this is obviously due to the false assumption
of consistency.

Perhaps the most striking demonstration of separate processing for
information and check morphemes is the mixture of, say, English information morphemes with the check system of another language, when
English is incorrectly spoken by a foreigner. A German will say *I am
here since yesterday*, because the present tense would be used in German, or he may even use the German word order *I am since yesterday
here* (*Ich bin seit gestern hier*). A Frenchman will say *I love the nature,*
inserting the definite article just like in *J'aime la nature*. Slavs will
leave out articles, or quite frequently they will insert them where they
do not belong in an effort to overcompensate. Gender is often assigned
in accordance with the native language of the speaker: Regardless of
the sex of a cat, a Frenchman will refer to it as "he," and a German,
Czech or Russian as "she." A Hungarian will often refer to a woman
as "he," because he is not used to the concept of gender at all.

Quite similarly, an American or Englishman will often use English
check features in foreign languages. Typically, in German, he will use
ich war and *ich bin gewesen* by the rules of *I was* and *I have been*. This
is not actually wrong, since it makes little difference in German whether
one uses past or perfect; it is simply a wasted check feature. Similarly,
he will often say *ma main, meine Hand,* моя рука, where he should say
la main, die Hand, рука. In both English and German, conditional and
temporal clauses require the present tense rather than the future; Eng-
lishmen and Germans therefore say literally "until you hear from me"
in Slavic languages, where Slavic grammars require (literally) "until
you will hear from me," (a construction which, conversely, is used
incorrectly by Slavs in English).

All of these examples suggest that the human brain may handle check
morphemes of a language differently from the information morphemes.
It is, however, only a tentative suggestion based on admittedly flimsy
evidence. Besides, analogies between natural processes and their man-
made imitations are usually very limited. A bird, for example, has a

capability of acceleration and an energetic efficiency that is totally unmatched by the most modern jet plane. Comparisons between thinking and computer processing are, as yet, equally ludicrous: The cells of the brain acting as memory locations appear to be "wired" to each other by a fantastic amount of interconnections, perhaps as many as 60,000 links from each cell to other cells. As shown by recent experiments with brain tissue taken from mice embryos, these interconnections organize themselves into the required patterns in test tubes containing growth-sustaining solutions; the software, as it were, builds its own hardware. These are feats that cannot be matched simply by increasing storage capacities and reducing access times; there is a qualitative difference here that makes analogies between thinking and computer processing necessarily limited — as yet.

As yet. The maxim that "there are some things the human brain can do that a computer will never be able to do" is based on no more than a comfortable hope. All available evidence points strongly to the contrary. The day will surely come when the artificial intelligence of computers will match and surpass the intelligence of the men who built them; a day, in the author's opinion, not to be feared, but to be looked forward to.

The arrival of that day is inseparably bound up with our better understanding of the structure of Language.

Index